Visual Impairment

Access to Education
for Children and Young People

Edited by

Heather Mason

and

Stephen McCall

with

Christine Arter
Mike McLinden
Juliet Stone

D1513652

David Fulton Publishers

London

David Fulton Publishers Ltd
Ormond House, 26–27 Boswell Street, London WC1N 3JD

First published in Great Britain by David Fulton Publishers 1997

Note: The right of Heather Mason and Stephen McCall to be identified as the editors of this work has been asserted by them in accordance with the Copyright, Designs and Patents Act 1988.

British Library Cataloguing in Publication Data
A catalogue record for this book is available from the British Library

ISBN 1–85346–412–0

Typeset by FSH Print and Production, London
Printed in Great Britain by the Cromwell Press Limited, Melksham

Contents

This text is dedicated to Elizabeth Kate Chapman OBE
in recognition of her contribution to the education of children
and young people with a visual impairment

Foreword

This book embodies the positive philosophy that children with a visual impairment are entitled to access to the full national curriculum during their school years.

In the UK, education placements for pupils and students with special needs range across a continuum from special schools and colleges, with day or residential attendance, to specialist units or individual integration into mainstream provision. Placement results from inter-disciplinary assessment and consultation and requires parental agreement. Lack of sight and measurably impaired vision constitute special needs in educational terms. The writers who have contributed to this major text are teachers and lecturers from both the specialist and mainstream areas of provision and have considerable first-hand experience in teaching pupils and students with a visual impairment.

There is also a substantial input to this book from the academic staff of the University of Birmingham, UK, which has gained a considerable reputation both nationally and internationally through research and specialist teacher training in the field of visual impairment. These writers have also contributed chapters on specific topics and have shaped sections of the text into a complete publication which reflects recent and relevant professional practice and continuing research.

A historical perspective which outlines the growth and clarifies the structure of the present educational continuum, will be of interest both to those who wish to retain, and those who wish to change it. However, for teachers, whether their work is in classes of pupils with little or no sight or in supporting individual pupils in local mainstream schools, the challenge of curriculum access for their pupils (despite sight difficulties) remains crucial to their work. Effective teaching strategies and the provision of appropriately adapted learning materials are essential but their pupils may well need to acquire skills additional to the standard curriculum such as mastering braille, and developing independent mobility. In planning the extent to which such skills are needed, and in developing appropriate materials and strategies throughout the curriculum, the teacher will be dependent upon an appreciation of the pupil's needs through observation, assessment and a knowledge of the effect that visual loss or impairment in its different forms can have on a pupil's capacity for learning. The encouragement of study skills and the provision of a positive learning environment can also be conducive to overcoming difficulties in specific curricular areas, especially those which have a high visual demand. Familiarity with relevant assessment procedures in visual, educational and psychological aspects of the pupil's functioning enable the teacher to work with other professionals and to interpret test results in a meaningful way. Such knowledge is central to the teacher competencies discussed in this text and in the sections of the book detailing specific curricular areas.

Educational technology has transformed the access to most curriculum areas, speeding communication in tactile to print codes and vice versa, presenting flexible and highly defined screen images, visual stimulation materials and individual self-monitoring programmes within the taught curriculum. All these approaches to curriculum delivery are considered in the text in relation to the needs of learners with sight problems or lack of vision.

Further education and training for students who are visually impaired provides its own curricular challenges in preparing students for employment opportunities, higher education courses and continuing personal development. Issues relating to this educational stage are examined by professionals involved in such work.

There is an increasing need for the development of individually based educational programmes for those children and young people who have a visual impairment and severe multiple disabilities. Their needs are incorporated into this text. Professionals in educational, social, psychological and medical disciplines whose practice involves children and young people with visual impairment will find this book informative. It will also serve as essential reading for students undertaking relevant training courses. Finally, and hopefully, it may be interesting for parents whose sons or daughters are visually impaired to share through reading, the aspirations of those entrusted with the education of these young people.

Elizabeth K. Chapman OBE

Acknowledgements

The editors and authors would like to acknowledge the assistance of the following in giving advice and comments and permission to reproduce photographs: Nick Bacon, Heather Jones, Jan McCall, RNIB Condover Hall School and RNIB Rushton Hall.

In addition the book would not have been possible without the generous cooperation of colleagues, pupils and students in the many schools, colleges and services.

Our special thanks to Lin Walsh for her patience and understanding and contribution to the process of editing and formatting the text.

Finally, our thanks must go to our families who have been very patient during the last 18 months.

Contributors

Stuart Aitken

Dr Stuart Aitken is a Research Fellow with the CALL Centre University of Edinburgh and Principal Officer (Research & Practice) with Sense Scotland. The joint posts reflect a long-standing interest in integrating the implications and methodologies drawn from theory and research into application and delivery within everyday settings of classroom, home, community house or elsewhere.

Christine Arter

Christine Arter a lecturer in special education at the University of Birmingham has had extensive experience in both mainstream and at George Auden School for visually impaired children in Birmingham. She is currently Honorary Secretary of VIEW and is the VIEW representative on the RNIB Executive Council and is a trained OFSTED Inspector.

Angela Beech

Angela Beach is a specialist PE teacher at St. Vincent's School for partially sighted children in Liverpool. She is the Secretary to the RNIB/VIEW (Association for the Education and Welfare of the Visually Handicapped) PE curriculum group and an a member of British Blind Sport Association.

David Bennett

David Bennett BSc (Hons), MC Optom. trained at City University, and at Moorfields Hospital, London. He currently works in private practice and at Queens Medical Centre, Nottingham. His specialist interests include working and assessing children with a visual impairment, contact lenses and the diagnosis and treatment of glaucoma.

Anthony Best

Anthony Best PhD is Headteacher of RNIB Condover Hall School, Shrewsbury. Prior to this appointment he worked at the University of Birmingham carrying out teacher training and research in the field of visual impairment. He has worked extensively overseas and has contributed to several publications on the education of children with visual impairments. His special interests are in multi-handicap, deafblindness and staff development.

Ann Bond

Ann Bond qualified as a medical practitioner, and worked in general practice until her eyesight deteriorated. She took up counselling, and worked with people in a variety of settings, including some with visual impairments. She is a trained medical psychotherapist in the NHS, with a special interest in patients with severe physical illness. Ann obtained the Diploma in Working with the Dying and Bereaved: A Psychoanalytically Informed Experiential Approach and was awarded the Fay Goldie Memorial Prize for her achievement on this course. She was registered blind in April 1996.

Nick Bozic

Nick Bozic is currently employed as an LEA Educational Psychologist. Prior to this he was a Research Fellow at the University of Birmingham's Research Centre for the Education of the Visually Handicapped (RCEVH). He has a special interest in the role of educational technology in special education, has written several papers in this area and co-edited the book *Learning through Interaction: Technology and Children with Multiple Disabilities.*

Miranda Kate Brookes

Miranda Brookes teaches children with visual impairments in Leicester and is a member of ADVISE (Art and Design Visual Impairment Special Education). Her MEd research concerns the role of aesthetic experience in the teaching and learning of young people with visual impairments, *throughout* the curriculum and relates to her work as a teacher, a lecturer and as an artist. She has exhibited widely in the UK and abroad for 20 years and has contributed to a range of publications.

Colin Brookes

Colin Brookes is a Senior Lecturer in Education at De Montfort University where he teaches on various education and art education programmes at graduate and postgraduate levels. He initially taught in schools, having obtained specialist subject and teaching qualifications in art and design.

Marianna Buultjens

Marianna Buultjens is co-ordinator of the Scottish Sensory Centre at Moray House, Institute of Education, Edinburgh. Since 1984 she has been the main tutor on the Diploma Course for Teachers of Visually Impaired Children and has carried out research on a variety of topics including assessing functional vision of young people with MDVI. She has taught in mainstream and special schools and currently works half day a week with the peripatetic service in Edinburgh to keep in close contact with children, families and schools.

Sue Clamp

Sue Clamp is Deputy Headteacher of St Vincent's School, Liverpool. She has extensive experience of teaching Mathematics to pupils who are blind.

Rory Cobb

Rory Cobb is RNIB Regional Education Officer for the Midlands and South West providing curriculum support. He has worked in the field since 1982 as a history teacher at RNIB New College, Worcester and later as RNIB Outreach Adviser, specialising in curriculum information and advice to mainstream schools with visually impaired pupils. He is chairman of the RNIB/VIEW Curriculum Group network and is particularly involved in issues concerning access to GCSE and other public examinations.

Pat Everest

Pat Everest, a teacher at George Auden School for pupils with a visual impairment since 1985 has considerable experience of working in mainstream schools as a PE teacher.

Carol Gray

Carol Gray graduated in German and French and has worked in a variety of secondary school settings, including in specialist education for pupils with a visual impairment and is a qualified teacher of the visually impaired. She now works as a lecturer in the School of Education at the University of Birmingham, as PGCE tutor for Modern Foreign Languages and organises a Professional Option course for PGCE students in Special Educational Needs. A central focus of her work is that of equality of opportunity, with particular reference to appropriate access to language learning.

Helen Hendrickson

Helen Hendrickson is a Speech and Language Therapist and is employed by Premier Health NHS Trust (Staffordshire). In addition, she is the Royal College of Speech and Language Therapy Regional Advisor for Sensory Impairments and holds a specialist caseload in this area. She has written a number of publications on the topic of augmentative and alternative communication for people with a visual impairment and additional difficulties.

David Hussey

David Hussey is Headteacher of RNIB Rushton Hall School, Kettering. Previously, he worked as a teacher at RNIB Condover Hall School.

Mary Kingsley

Mary Kingsley, Headteacher at the Royal London Society for the Blind's Dorton House School has had wide experience in the field of visual disability which includes working as a service teacher in a specialist college for pupils with a visual impairment and as a head of an LEA Service for Visual Disabilities. Mary is also a qualified teacher of pupils who are deaf.

Rita Kirkwood

Rita Kirkwood is Headteacher of RNIB Sunshine House School Northwood and has worked in special education since 1982, after a number of years as a mainstream science teacher. She has also contributed to the training courses for teachers of the visually impaired and is a registered inspector for OFSTED, taking part regularly in inspections of special schools throughout the country.

Christopher Lewis

Christopher Lewis is Headteacher of Priestley Smith School for pupils with visual impairment, Birmingham. Christopher is a registered OFSTED inspector and has been involved in the inspection of many special schools.

Jeanette Lomas

Jeanette Lomas is Deputy Head at Exhall Grange Special School, Coventry for pupils with visual and/or physical disabilities. Having worked in the field of visual impairment since 1979 Jeanette's experience has been in all areas of the continuum of provision for the education of pupils with a visual disability.

Kay Malin

Kay Malin is a teacher of PE and Art and Design Technology at George Auden School for pupils with a visual impairment since 1987 and has wide experience in mainstream education.

Heather Mason

Heather Mason is Senior Lecturer at the University of Birmingham. Previously she worked both in mainstream education and at Priestley Smith School, Birmingham. She has worked extensively overseas and is an OFSTED inspector. Her PhD thesis developed a new assessment tool for blind pupils, the STIP (Speed of Tactile Information Processing).

Stephen McCall

Stephen McCall is a Lecturer in Education (Visual Impairment) at the University of Birmingham, School of Education. Previously, he taught at St Vincent's School, Liverpool and was a peripatetic teacher for seven years. He has undertaken teaching and consultancy work in Eastern Europe, Africa and the USA. He has directed funded research into literacy for touch readers and among his publications is the Birmingham Braille Course.

Mike McLinden

Mike McLinden is a Lecturer at the University of Birmingham with special responsibility for Multiple Disabilities and Visual Impairment. He has worked with a range of pupils with special educational needs including EBD, MLD and visual impairment. Mike worked as Research Fellow at the University of Birmingham on the 'Moon as a Route to Literacy Project' and helped in the development of a variety of teaching resources for Moon.

Brian McManus

Brian McManus, a teacher of PE at St Vincent's School for visually impaired pupils since 1986 has wide experience in mainstream schools.

Steve Minett

Steve Minett Head of Science at RNIB New College, Worcester works with visually impaired students teaching physics to GCSE and Advanced Level. He has a PhD in Special Education from the University of Birmingham which reflects his particular interest in the role of practical work in science education and its value in encouraging motivation and self-confidence in students with a visual impairment.

Heather Murdoch

Heather Murdoch is a Lecturer in Special Education at the University of Birmingham and is joint Co-ordinator for programmes in the education of children with multi-sensory impairment (deafblindness). Previously she taught pupils with MSI across the age range, as a class teacher and then in an advisory role. Her research interests include the development of children with MSI, functional sensory assessment, repetitive motor behaviours and appropriate preparation for staff working with pupils with MSI.

Dorothy Spragg

Dorothy Spragg is Deputy Head of the Sensory Support Service in Coventry, and provides support for students on the Distance Education Course at the University of Birmingham. She has worked extensively over the past 17 years in supporting visually impaired children. She has also worked for RNIB as a senior lecturer in further education.

Juliet Stone

Juliet is a member of the team of tutors for the courses for teachers of children and young people with visual impairments. She is an OFSTED inspector, a trained mobility specialist and has worked extensively abroad. Formerly, she was Senior Advisory Teacher in Gloucestershire with responsibility for pupils with visual impairments. Her publications include *Mobility for Special Needs*.

Jane Sutcliffe

Jane Sutcliffe is Head of Business and Enterprise Division at Queen Alexandra College. She has extensive experience in mainstream and special further education colleges.

Hugh S. Taylor

Hugh Taylor is Head of Shawgrove School and the Support Service for visually impaired children in Manchester. After working at RNC Hereford he moved to the Institute of Special Education in Melbourne, training teachers of children who are visually impaired. His research interests include visual functioning in pre-school and multiply impaired children.

Michael Tobin

Michael Tobin is the Director of the Research Centre for the Education of the Visually Handicapped at the University of Birmingham. His research areas include the educational and psychological development of blind and partially sighted children, and with methods of assessing their achievements; he has been concerned with the structure of braille and with the teaching and learning of braille and other tactile codes

Introduction

Heather Mason and Stephen McCall

The purpose of this text is to examine the elements that ensure access to the full curriculum for children and young people with a visual impairment. It takes into account the wide range of provision in which children with a visual impairment receive their education and draws upon the expertise of professionals from a variety of backgrounds.

A central theme of the book is educational entitlement and a major focus is access to subjects in the National Curriculum for England and Wales. We suspect, however, that many of the principles of access to the curriculum which are covered in this book are applicable the world over. Attention is also given to the special curriculum that is specific to children and young people with a visual impairment.

It is anticipated that the text, either in part or in its entirety, will be of interest and practical use to:

- specialist teachers and support staff working with children with visual impairment across the whole spectrum of educational settings;
- students of children with a visual impairment;
- practitioners/professionals and lay persons with an interest in children with visual impairment, such as educational psychologists, speech and language therapists, ophthalmologists, optometrists and governors of schools;
- parents of children with a visual impairment.

The chapters are arranged within nine sections to make it easier for readers to navigate their way through the book and to identify quickly the information they are seeking. At the beginning of each section there is a short introduction which summarises the main topics. Authors have been invited to bear in mind the needs of readers for practical advice which is underpinned by sound theory.

Throughout the text, the editors have faced the dilemma of finding appropriate and consistent terminology to describe the children and young people who are the subject of this book. The generic term **visual impairment** is used to describe the continuum of sight loss. Where a distinction is necessary, the term **blind** is used to describe children who rely predominantly on tactile methods in their learning while the term **low vision** is used with reference to children who are taught mainly through methods which rely on sight. We have adopted the practice of referring to 'the child' or 'young person with a visual impairment' rather than 'the visually impaired child' in order to acknowledge the fact that the child should be the emphasis rather than the disability. We have maintained this usage even though in some instances it leads to cumbersome expression.

The decision to embark on developing this text was prompted by a number of factors. The business of education is change, and in recent years the education of children with a visual impairment in the United Kingdom has been subject to major upheavals. Services for children in areas of low incidence of disability are particularly vulnerable in times of volatile change and unless the educational needs of children are clearly defined they may not be met. We are aware of several major issues relating to access and entitlement which shaped our thinking:

- the increasing numbers of children and young people with a visual impairment who are being educated in mainstream settings;
- the rapid of expansion of local education authority (LEA) advisory services and non-teaching support staff;
- the impact of recent legislation such as the 1993 Education Act and the ensuing Code of Practice;
- the changing population in many of the special schools for children with a visual impairment;
- the increasing number of pupils who have multiple disabilities in addition to their visual impairment;
- the fact that the National Curriculum Orders are beginning to settle down into a form where the issues of entitlement and access to the full curriculum as they apply to pupils with a visual impairment could be understood.

We felt that existing books addressed some but not all of these issues. Many of the best texts had a North American focus and we thought that the time was right for a book which had a clear British perspective. The move away from a 'deficit' view of disability towards a philosophy which acknowledges differences in the development of all children and young people has informed our editing of the text, as has our commitment to the notion that all children and young people with a visual impairment have an entitlement to a 'special curriculum' which embraces:

- orientation and mobility;
- specialised communication skills;
- visual perceptual skills;
- self-help, social and independent living skills;
- study skills incorporating the use of specialised information technology (IT);
- training in the use of low vision devices (LVDs).

The views expressed in this book display our commitment to the concept that there is a need for an array of educational provision to meet the diverse needs of children with visual impairments and that parents and children should have a choice of special and inclusive provision.

The book endorses our commitment to a defined set of competencies for those teachers who work directly with children and young people with a visual impairment or who advise other teachers and parents about the needs of this group (see Chapter 44) and we believe that this level of competence can only fully develop through mandatory one-year full-time equivalent training programmes for teachers of the visually impaired.

EDUCATION, PROVISION AND CONTEMPORARY ISSUES

Chapter 1
Historical Perspectives

Stephen McCall

Introduction

This chapter will provide a brief historical account of the development of educational services for children and young people with a visual impairment in the United Kingdom. An attempt will be made to identify the key events, personalities and influences which have shaped the current provision and practice described in this book.

The beginnings

The first school for blind children in Europe was established in Paris in 1784 by Valentin Hauy, but it is clear that in various parts of Europe a small number of blind children received formal education before this date, sometimes in local schools alongside children who were fully sighted. In later life a handful of these children went on to achieve national and international prominence in various cultural and academic fields.

   One of these exceptional individuals was the English academic Nicholas Saunderson who was born in 1682 and lost his sight in infancy through smallpox. He was educated in a school in Penistone in Yorkshire and excelled in classics and later in mathematics. He subsequently attended Cambridge University, where he was appointed to a professorship in mathematics and led a distinguished career until his death in 1739 (Ritchie 1930). Other examples include the distinguished Scottish clergyman and schoolmaster Thomas Blacklock who, although blind from infancy, was educated at a grammar school. He wrote poetry and was a friend of the poet Robert Burns.

   Lowenfeld (1974) pinpoints the emergence at the beginning of the eighteenth century of these 'self-emancipators' as one of the factors which prompted an interest in the education of people who were blind. However these examples mask the grim existence of poverty and ignorance which was the fate of most people who were blind in the Europe of the eighteenth and early nineteenth century.

Special schools and local board schools

During the turmoil surrounding the French Revolution, Hauy's school temporarily foundered and he continued his work in Berlin and St Petersburg where he helped start new schools for the blind. The next two decades saw schools established in other major cities throughout Europe.

The first school for the blind in the United Kingdom was opened in Liverpool in 1791 and it was followed by schools in Edinburgh, Bristol and London and other major cities. British schools were pioneered by philanthropic voluntary bodies or religious organisations and were often linked to workshops and homes for blind adults called 'asylums'. Initially the schools were primarily concerned with teaching vocational skills, for example the charter for the Liverpool school mentions that the blind would be instructed in 'Music or the Mechanical Arts and so be rendered comfortable in themselves and useful to society' (Best 1992).

Although schools for the blind were well established in Britain by the 1860s, they were independent institutions catering for only a proportion of the blind children who needed education. According to Hurt (1988), the campaign to secure elementary education for all children who were blind began in 1869. Elizabeth Gilbert, the blind daughter of the Bishop of Chichester, organised a petition calling for the inclusion of children who were blind into the imminent national legislation for universal elementary education.

Universal elementary education was introduced in Britain in 1870 but while there was no obligation on local school boards to include in their provision children who were blind, significant numbers of blind children were admitted to local schools. Alexander Barnhill, in the preface to his 1875 book *A New Era in the Education of Blind Children, or Teaching the Blind in Ordinary School* claimed that 'There are 50 blind children now being taught in this manner in Scotland and only 102 being taught in institutions for the blind' (Barnhill 1875).

The visiting societies which had been set up in many cities in the 1830s and 1840s to seek out adult blind people and to teach them to read had discovered blind children who were receiving no education. Barnhill's Glasgow was no exception, 'even within our own city where an excellent asylum existed, a considerable number of such children were met with growing up without education – the parents either unable or unwilling to have them admitted as inmates to the institution.'

Barnhill argued for the education of blind children in the ordinary school on the basis that this was the only way of securing education for all blind children:

Much difficulty or expense has usually stood in the way of the admission of blind children into institutions and many have been entirely neglected. In these circumstances the pleas of educating blind children in the ordinary school must be acknowledged to be of the strongest character.

Sufficient indication already appears that the country will not tolerate the education of 50% in institutions and leave the remainder to grow up uncared for.

When Barnhill advocated free education in local schools for blind children but he was not arguing for a closure of special schools but rather acknowledging that the education of all blind children could only be achieved by use of the local mainstream schools.

The Royal Commission on the Blind and Deaf and Dumb which reported in 1889 noted that in addition to the work in Glasgow, school boards in London, Bradford, Cardiff and Sunderland had also undertaken the instruction of children who were blind:

> In most cases the children follow the ordinary timetable with their seeing companions and associate with them both in school-time and play-time.
>
> In London the blind children usually attend the ordinary schools, but also on special days they receive special instruction at centres of which there are 18. In 1888 the total number of blind children was 132.

The commissioners were generally in favour of the education of blind children with the seeing:

> The free intercourse with the seeing gives courage and self reliance to the blind and a healthy stimulus to which enables them to compete more successfully with the seeing in after life than those who have been brought up altogether in blind institutions.

In the wake of the Commission, the Elementary Education Act (Blind and Deaf Children) was introduced in 1893. This laid an obligation on local boards to provide for the education of blind children from the ages of 5 to 16 years, a major achievement at a time when the minimum school leaving age for children was ten years.

Contrary to what might have been expected, around the end of the century the practice of educating blind children in mainstream schools seems to have declined and the special schools were left to cope with the demand on their own. A number of factors seem to have been responsible for this change. One may be that the 1893 Act contained a clause for a new procedure by which schools had to be certified as 'suitable' for teaching the blind and, clearly, special schools would have been more likely to meet the requirements for certification than local board schools. Moreover in the Education Act of 1902 the smaller education boards were subsumed by the larger local education authorities, and most of these new education authorities appeared to wish to meet their obligation to blind children by paying for them to attend the established voluntary schools for the blind.

The special schools for the blind consolidated their position and the move to educate blind children in local schools lost its momentum for another 70 years. It evidently did not die out entirely however, because a survey by the College of Teachers of the Blind and the National Institute for the Blind (1936) reported that 'It is interesting to note that the present practice in Glasgow, as described by one of our Scottish witnesses is for blind children to attend one of three centres in schools for the sighted'.

At the beginning of the new century, the numbers of children in the special schools for the blind increased, although these schools were somewhat selective in their approach.

Wilson, in his preface to the fourth edition (Wilson 1907) of *Information with Regard to Institutions, Societies and Classes for the Blind in England and Wales*, stated that:

> The following may be considered as general rules affecting all pupils seeking admission at any school for the blind.
>
> They must be entirely, or for all practical purposes, blind, not deficient in intellect or physical power, of good health, not subject to fits, not suffering from cutaneous disease or other disorder likely to be prejudicial to the fellow scholars, and must either have been vaccinated, or have had the smallpox.
>
> In conclusion, I may add that it is extremely difficult to give any recommendation as to what is best to be done with the sick, weakly, and otherwise 'defective' blind who are ineligible for admission to the schools for the blind.

By 1907 residential schooling had become the norm for blind children and a list of over 33 residential schools catering for 826 males and 639 was catalogued by Wilson.

In this year also, the College of Teachers of the Blind (CTB) was established which examined teachers in schools for the blind and awarded diplomas to those who met its requirements. Attainment of the CTB Diploma within three years of the commencement of work in a school for the blind became mandatory under government regulations for teachers.

Schools for the partially sighted

Around the turn of the century the educational needs of children with low vision were beginning to be recognised as different from those of children who were blind. The classification for blindness had been so vague that children with partial sight could as easily have ended up in schools for the blind as in their local schools.

A young ophthalmologist, N. Bishop Harman, was made responsible in 1902 for the ophthalmological service to schools for the blind in London (Hathaway 1964). Harman had found that many children in London schools for the blind had sufficient vision to benefit from sighted methods of instruction and on his recommendation, children with high myopia and other forms of partial sight loss were tentatively introduced to sighted methods of instruction in London schools for the blind.

The first class for children with partial vision was established in 1908 at an elementary school for sighted children in the London borough of Camberwell. Initially reading and writing were prohibited and teaching and learning was conducted orally. Practice gradually changed to allow work through large handwritten type on chalkboards (Figure 1.1).

Other classes were established in mainstream schools in London and around the country but while some special classes survived, by 1930 most of the provision for 'partially blind' children was provided in separate special day schools.

In 1931 the National Board of Education set up a committee under the leadership of

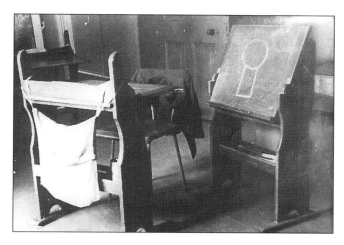

Figure 1.1   A'Harman' desk from one of the first classes for children with partial sight

Crowther to enquire into the education of 'partially blind children'. Among the recommendations were that 'partially sighted' was a more appropriate term for these children and that they should not normally be sent to schools for the blind.

The committee's medical representatives also recommended a relaxation of restrictions on reading and writing and physical training that had been practised up to that time in the name of 'sight saving', an erroneous belief that residual vision would be exhausted through use and needed to be preserved by restricting its application. Sadly the Crowther Report made little impact upon the education of children who were partially sighted and the numbers of places in day classes remained limited until the advent of the 1945 Education Act (Department of Education and Science (DES) 1972).

A range of provision

By the 1930s a variety of educational provision was available across the age range. The National Institute for the Blind had set up 'Sunshine Homes for Blind Babies' around the country in 1918, 1923, and 1924 (College of Teachers of the Blind/National Institute for the Blind (CTB/NIB) 1936). These homes, which catered for 'children ... who cannot be adequately cared for in their own homes' offered residential education for some pre-school children 'from earliest infancy'. Pre-school children not in Sunshine Homes often received visits from welfare workers called 'home teachers for the blind', a role which had evolved from the visiting reading teachers of the previous century.

'Elementary' education for children who were blind remained compulsory between the ages of five to 16. Most children attended one of the special schools for the blind until the age of 16 and then transferred to a training centre for the blind where they received vocational instruction in skills such as basket making, bedding, brushes, boot repairing, weaving or piano tuning.

At the age of 11 or 12, some of the most able blind children were selected for 'secondary' education which was provided at Worcester College for the Blind, Chorleywood College for Girls with Little or No Sight, or The Royal Normal College for the Blind. These centres prepared their students for public examinations which could lead to University or careers in the professions.

Even in the 1930s, it was recognised that educational provision for the 1062 boys and 921 girls of school age who were identified as having a visual impairment was in need of reorganisation. The majority of the 34 special schools had small numbers of children (sometimes as few as 20) and could not offer breadth in curriculum or sufficiently homogeneous teaching groups.

The CTB and the National Institute for the Blind (CTB/NIB 1936) recommended a national reorganisation which would involve fewer and larger schools which would all be residential. They also proposed regional residential nurseries for under fives and considered reorganising schools for the blind along the lines of the new system proposed for mainstream schools whereby all children would leave elementary school at the age of eleven to attend separate senior (secondary) schools. The Second World War disrupted plans for development and many of the special schools in the cities were temporarily relocated in rural areas for the duration.

The years which followed the Second World War were marked by a consolidation of special school provision. The 1944 Education Act redefined categories of 'handicap' and included for the first time the category of the 'partially sighted' which it defined as 'pupils who by reason of defective vision cannot follow the ordinary curriculum without detriment to their sight or to their educational development, but can be educated by special methods involving the use of sight'.

Between 1945 and 1947 four boarding schools which previously accommodated both blind and partially sighted pupils were redesignated as schools for the partially sighted only. In the late 1940s some of the schools for the blind in the north of England were reorganised into primary and secondary schools and children changed schools at the age of eleven.

The late 1940s and early 1950s saw an unexpected increase in the numbers of children who were educationally blind. These children, often born prematurely, developed in early infancy a condition known then as 'retrolental fibroplasia' (RLF) which led to severe visual impairment and sometimes associated additional disabilities. At first the causes were little understood but an association was made with the ways in which the administration of oxygen to premature babies was regulated. As a result of improvements in the oxygen treatment of premature babies the condition was largely overcome, but the legacy was a bulge in the numbers of blind children in residential schools in the 1950s and 1960s.

Schools for children with additional disabilities

A major gap in the provision was the lack of suitable places for blind children with additional learning disabilities. In the 1930s educational provision was limited to Court Grange School at Abbotskerswell in South Devon, a small residential school established in 1931 by the National Institute for the Blind for 34 children described as 'retarded' who had a fair chance of 'reclamation' (CTB/NIB 1936).

However, in the 1930s, and for many years afterwards, the children who were most severely disabled were regarded as ineducable. The Ellen Terry Homes for Blind Mentally Defective Children accommodated 30 children 'whose condition was such that they could not benefit by education' (CTB/NIB 1936). Blind children with major epilepsy were also excluded from schools for the blind and unknown numbers of children who were visually impaired and who had additional severe disabilities remained outside the education system until after the Education (Handicapped Children) Act (DES 1970).

In response to growing concern about these children, a school established by the National Institute for the Blind in 1947 at Condover Hall, a 16th century House in rural Shropshire. The first headteacher, Stanley 'Oscar' Myers, became a pivotal figure in the development of the education of blind and partially sighted children with additional disabilities. The school originally catered for 60 children aged 7–16, but in 1959, in response to the growing demand, the RNIB opened Rushton Hall School in Northamptonshire for children in the 7–11 age range who were educationally blind and who had additional disabilities, and Condover became a secondary school for children in this group who were aged 12–17. In the same year 'Pathways', a unit for children who were deafblind, was established at Condover (Myers 1975).

Teacher preparation

The College of Teachers of the Blind (CTB) remained the driving force in the development of teaching methodology, and up until the 1950s was solely responsible for the professional training of all teachers of the blind. Most teachers who worked in special schools had previously taught in mainstream schools and were required to achieve the mandatory CTB qualification while working full-time in their new posts.

The first training course in an institute of higher education for teachers of children with visual impairments was set up at the University of Birmingham in the mid 1950s. The first group of six students were admitted to a one-year full-time course leading to a diploma. The course, first under the leadership of Myfanwy Williams, and subsequently of Elizabeth Chapman OBE, flourished and by the 1980s it had subsumed the national role of the CTB in teacher training, offering both full-time and distance education courses up to degree level for teachers from throughout the United Kingdom and around the world.

In 1970 the Research Centre for the Education of the Visually Handicapped (RCEVH) was established at the University of Birmingham under Dr Michael Tobin. Among its early work was research into the simplification of the braille code and a longitudinal study of children with visual impairment.

The growth of integration

By 1970 the education of children with visual impairments again became a focus for national review. The sharp reduction in the numbers of children who were educationally blind, which was experienced after the group of children with RLF passed through the school system, led to calls for a reorganisation of provision. Anxieties also began to surface about the narrowness of the educational choice available to parents of children with visual impairments.

The debate about the integration of children with visual impairments into mainstream schools was rekindled as evidence began to emerge from small-scale experiments which involved the integration of children from residential schools for the blind into local mainstream secondary schools. In 1961 St Vincent's, a Catholic all-age residential school in Liverpool for children who were blind and partially sighted, began sending some of their most able older children to the nearby mainstream Catholic grammar schools for lessons. The children were supported by an experienced teacher from St Vincent's who advised class teachers at the grammar schools about the needs of the children and helped the children with their homework when they returned to St Vincent's each evening. A similar experiment at Tapton Mount School in Sheffield was begun in 1969 when four children based at the school received their secondary education at the local secondary comprehensive school.

The results suggested that, with the right level of support, some children who were educationally blind could succeed academically in mainstream schools. However, at the time, expertise in educating children with visual impairments was found almost exclusively in special schools and local education authorities (LEAs) had few local alternatives to offer.

In 1968 Margaret Thatcher, who was then the Secretary of State for Education and Science, commissioned an enquiry into the education of the visually handicapped chaired by Professor M. D. Vernon. At the time educational provision comprised 18 schools designated for the blind, 19 schools designated for the partially sighted, two schools which were authorised to take both partially sighted and blind and 8 mainstream schools which contained classes for the partially sighted.

The Report of the enquiry was published in 1972 (DES 1972) and a number of recommendations were made regarding the future development of services. It was proposed that a national plan be drawn up for the 'Distribution, organisation and management of special schools and other educational services for the visually handicapped'. Other recommendations included the establishment of regional multidisciplinary assessment teams for pre-school children and a recognition that these children should not normally board away from home. Instead it proposed that pre-school children should be supported by a visiting or 'peripatetic' teacher employed by the LEA who would visit children at home, advising their parents and supporting the children's integration into local pre-school nurseries.

This recommendation was prompted in part by the success of an experimental service which had recently been set up in the Midlands. Although in the 1950s the heads and senior staff of each of the seven Sunshine House Nursery Schools were making home visits to families on request, this service was available only to the few children associated with the nursery schools. In response to anxieties expressed in the 1960s by the heads of special schools about developmental delay among children entering special schools, the principal of Lickey Grange School was given permission by his employers, the Birmingham Royal Institution for the Blind, to set up a pilot scheme to provide a free visiting service for pre-school children living within a 50 mile radius of Birmingham. The first specialist peripatetic teacher specifically for pre-school children and their families was a former head of a Sunshine House School, Heather Jones, who took up her new post in January 1970.

Although the uptake for the service from LEAs was slow, many children were referred through personal contacts, and requests for support came not only from parents, nurseries and playgroups but also from teachers in local schools who had children with a visual impairment in their classes. Paediatricians and developmental psychologists in the newly developing assessment centres and child development units of hospitals also called on the service, and soon requests for support or advice began to be received from all over the United Kingdom. In 1971 The Royal National Institute for the Blind agreed to take over the advisory service and appointed two more experienced teachers of the visually impaired. The team grew steadily to meet the increasing national demand.

While the Vernon Report had stopped short of commending integration it suggested that 'further experiments be carried out ... with the education of visually handicapped children in ordinary schools, either in ordinary or special classes'. At the same time as the RNIB was expanding its advisory service, a few local authorities began to appoint advisory teachers of their own. Manchester and Cleveland were among the first LEAs to set up services supporting children with visual impairments in mainstream schools. Most of the early 'peris' recruited by the LEAs were qualified teachers from special schools for the visually impaired. These teachers gradually built up the levels of local support available to parents and their children. The focus of these services was initially upon supporting pre-school children and on providing teaching support for partially sighted children in mainstream schools. The services expanded rapidly and in some authorities, teams of peripatetic teachers began to offer teaching and advisory support across the whole age and ability range of children with visual impairments.

The Warnock Report (DES 1978) provided the results of a government enquiry into the education of children with special needs and reinforced the trend towards the education of children with special educational needs in mainstream schools. The subsequent 1981 Education Act (DES 1981) specified that children with 'special educational needs should normally receive their education in the local mainstream school provided that this was compatible with the efficient use of resources'.

This further accelerated the growth in the number of LEA advisory services for children with visual impairments in the 1980s. Children with partial sight were now most commonly educated in mainstream schools and this began to have an impact upon the intake of special schools for the partially sighted. During the late 1970s and early 1980s schools for the partially sighted experienced rapidly falling rolls and many had to close.

The few that did survive began also to offer services to children who were educationally blind and, in effect, the distinction between schools designated for the blind and those designated for the partially sighted disappeared, as the surviving special schools embraced the full range of visual impairment and a wider range of ability.

The growth of visiting or 'peripatetic' teaching services continued and by the beginning of the 1990s virtually all the local education authorities in Britain had established services of their own. As these services worked in mainstream schools, a fuller picture began to emerge of the population of children with a visual impairment. Figures for the size of the population were continually revised. By the 1990s, reports were suggesting that the true figure was in the region of 19,500 children, of whom two-thirds were estimated to have an additional disability (see Chapters 2 and 32).

Although special schools for the visually impaired cater for only a small proportion of these 19,500 children, the decline in the population of some of these schools seems to have levelled off. A growing consensus is emerging among educators about the need for an array of services in each region, to offer to parents a choice of different types of educational provision for children with a visual impairment. The current and future challenges are reviewed in the next chapter, but the achievements and failures of the past deserve to be recorded and marked.

Chapter 2

Educational Provision

Rita Kirkwood and Stephen McCall

Introduction

This chapter gives a brief overview of the current range of educational provision in the United Kingdom for children and young people with a visual impairment, and attempts to identify some future trends. It is intended for the reader who is unfamiliar with the field and provides a background for other chapters in the book.

The population

The precise number of children with a visual impairment in Britain is difficult to quantify. The lack of a commonly agreed definition of visual impairment (see Chapter 6) makes the results of any survey open to question, and the problem is further compounded by the lack of a uniform system of identification. In England the Department for Education and Employment no longer collects information on individual children and the information on children in Scotland is held by social services departments who compile their data from registration records held by local Societies for the Blind. It is only in Wales that statistics are held centrally by government (Clunies-Ross, Franklin 1996a). Estimates in the last decade have varied from 10,000 children 'with visual impairments' in the 3–19 age range (RNIB 1992) to 22,000 children 'with a seeing difficulty' in the 0–15 years age range (Bone and Meltzer 1989). The most recent estimate is based on returns collected by the Royal National Institute for the Blind (RNIB) in 1995 from education services for the visually impaired in local education authorities (LEAs). These returns suggest that there are between 19,000 and 20,000 children up to the age of 16 in England, Scotland and Wales who have a visual impairment. This figure was obtained by extrapolating data returned by 106 LEAs and is based on a sample of 76% of the total population of this age group (Clunies-Ross and Franklin 1996a). Over 6,000 (34.5%) of these children were identified as having 'severe and multiple disabilities' in addition to visual impairment. This compares with the findings of the 1992 survey which estimated that 56% of children with a visual impairment have another permanent illness or disability (see Chapter 32).

In addition to the school-aged children identified in the RNIB study, LEAs reported almost 1400 pupils aged 16 to 19 with a visual impairment, of whom over 40% were reported as having multiple disabilities in addition to their visual disability. However since LEAs now fund only a proportion of students in further education, this figure is known to be an underestimate.

The latest figures suggest that visual impairment affects 2.11 children in every 1000 up to the age of 16, and it is therefore considered a 'low incidence' disability. The low incidence of visual impairment in children has some significant implications for their education. For example it means that:

- visual impairment does not have a high profile in the national debate about educational planning;
- the small numbers of children in any given area poses problems for those planning provision at local level and consequently teaching expertise and specialist educational resources are spread thinly in some areas.

The current range of educational provision

Educational provision for the children and young people with visual impairment currently comprises a wide range of services including:

- informal family support groups;
- mainstream playgroups or nurseries (kindergartens);
- specialist nurseries;
- mainstream schools supported by the visiting LEA peripatetic/advisory service;
- units or resource bases attached to mainstream schools;
- special schools for children with visual impairments;
- other special schools, e.g. schools for children with severe learning difficulties, schools for children with physical disabilities;
- mainstream colleges of further education;
- specialist colleges of further education.

The choice of educational options available to children with visual impairments and their families depends, to some extent, on where the family resides. There are wide variations in the amount and quality of support available across the United Kingdom, and although the needs of the child should be the starting point in decisions about placement and provision, these decisions are also inevitably affected by local financial considerations and judgements about the efficient use of resources.

Support for the under-fives

Most LEAs are able to offer support and advice to parents with young children from qualified specialist teachers of the visually impaired. Their involvement takes a variety of forms and often includes the planning and delivery of developmental teaching programmes and liaison with other services (see Chapters 40 and 41). These visiting or 'peripatetic' teachers can often visit families as soon as a diagnosis of visual impairment has been made and they will usually accept referrals from medical, educational and social services and sometimes directly from parents themselves.

Most pre-school provision tends to be local and is often offered on a part-time basis at a local LEA nursery or in a playgroup. In both cases the peripatetic teacher will liaise with the staff over the placement and progress of the child, offering training and advice to the staff as necessary. A number of the special schools for children with visual impairment offer nursery provision and have outreach services which support local families with young children. This support may include providing information, assessment, advice and training, and opportunities to meet other parents.

Where the child has complex needs, there may be a case for specialised support. This may take the form of a nursery within the child's town which has been resourced for children with special needs, a specialist regional assessment centre or possibly a special school with a residential facility. For example there are two Sunshine House Schools run by the RNIB which cater for children from the age of 2 to 11 years, on a day or residential basis.

The effect on the pre-school education of children with visual impairments of the proposals for the expansion of the number of nursery school places has yet to be seen, but if early intervention is to be effective then any new system of funding will need to take account of the high cost of providing appropriate placement for some children.

Local mainstream schools

The pattern of integration is similar in England, Scotland and Wales, and overall 59% of primary aged children and 46% of secondary aged children with visual impairments attend mainstream schools (Clunies-Ross and Franklin 1996b). An increasing proportion of the estimated 839 children who use braille are in mainstream schools, and there is some evidence to suggest that there may now be as many braille users in mainstream schools as there are in special schools for children with a visual impairment.

Success in the mainstream setting depends not only on the level and effectiveness of the support available, but on the personality and wishes of the pupil and their family and the attitude of the staff at the school. Where placement in the local school is the preferred option, the level of support for each child with a visual disability will be determined by a formal system of assessment defined in the Code of Practice of the Department for Education (DfE 1994) relating to the education of children with special educational needs which ensued from the 1993 Education Act (DfE 1993). Children with severe visual impairment will usually become the subject of a Statement of Special Educational Needs which will define the support to which they are legally entitled.

Tobin (1990) expressed some concern about the difficulties of providing the additional curriculum subjects such as mobility and braille instruction for children in local mainstream schools who are educationally blind (i.e. who learn predominantly through touch). However, it is generally recognised that most children with low vision who do not have additional disabilities will receive their education in mainstream schools and will be supported by a visiting specialist teacher.

The advisory or 'peripatetic' teaching services for the visually impaired differ in their structure and in their roles (see Chapter 40) and these variations can affect the amount or quality of support children receive. LEA advisory teachers often have a far heavier caseload than their counterparts in other countries, for example a teacher–child ratio of 1:10 is normal in the USA, Sweden and Australia, whereas between 1:40 and 1:60 is not uncommon for advisory teachers of the visually impaired in the UK (RNIB 1990). A number of local authorities have reorganised and streamlined their support services in the last few years, often combining the service for the visually impaired with the service for the hearing-impaired, and occasionally with the service for children with physical or learning disabilities. Economic pressures on local government and the recent creation of new small unitary authorities have led to the reduction or division of services in some areas.

Schools with a resource base

Some children who need a greater level of support than can be provided within the local school may attend a mainstream school within daily travelling distance which has a specialist resource centre for children with visual impairment. The availability of such resource bases within mainstream schools varies across the country, and this type of provision serves more pupils in Wales than in England or Scotland, and is more common in secondary schools than primary schools (Table 2.1).

Table 2.1 Percentages of children with a visual impairment in mainstream schools with a specialist resource centre (Clunies-Ross and Franklin 1996b)

	Age, years	
	5–10+	11–16
England	4%	7%
Wales	8%	19%
Scotland	6%	7%

Although it may involve additional costs for transporting children, LEAs have adopted this system partly because it allows scarce and expensive teaching resources to be concentrated in a cost-effective way. Children usually receive most of their lessons in the mainstream classroom but will use the base for collecting, storing, or producing materials and for receiving additional special instruction. The children have the support of a specialist teacher or a support assistant in the classroom at times when it is judged to be appropriate (see Chapter 41). The resource base provides the materials and supplies the equipment that the child needs in each lesson. Many children who are educationally blind and who attend mainstream schools receive this type of provision. A few LEA special schools for children with physical disabilities or severe learning difficulties have resource bases for children with a visual impairment and additional disabilities.

An essential prerequisite to the success of resource bases in either mainstream or special schools is the full acceptance and support of the host school and the integration of the base into the school.

Special schools for children with visual impairments

The proportion of pupils who attend special schools which are designated for children with visual impairments varies from one area to the next, but it constitutes only a small proportion of the total population of children with visual impairments (see Table 2.2).

Table 2.2   Percentage of children with a visual impairment in special schools for the visually impaired (Clunies-Ross and Franklin 1996)

	Age, years	
	5–10+	11–16
England	7%	12%
Wales	2%	4%
Scotland	13%	25%

There are currently 23 special schools designated for children with visual impairments: 18 in England, five in Scotland and none in Wales. Some regions have a wide range of special schools to choose from; others have none. In the absence of national planning (see Chapter 1) schools have evolved largely independently of each other and are not formally coordinated into a national or regional network. Nevertheless, the schools can be categorised into two broad groups.

First, there are Non-maintained (independent) schools, which have a regional or national intake and normally offer both day and residential facilities. Some residential schools close at weekends, others close during traditional school holidays and a few offer 52 week per year provision. These schools are usually run by charitable trusts such as the Royal National Institute for the Blind, the Catholic Blind Institute and the Royal London Society for the Blind. The schools take a variety of forms: some offer provision for the whole age and ability range of children with visual impairments while others provide exclusively for the education of children with visual impairments and additional disabilities (see Chapter 42). They rely for most of their income on the fees they charge to the LEAs of the children who attend the school.

Secondly, there are LEA special schools. These are generally day schools with a local intake (usually within an hour's travelling time). Currently only one LEA school has residential facilities and a regional intake.

Although there is a lobby for the complete abolition of special schools (Dessent 1987) there is a continuing demand, both from LEAs and parents, for special school placements. A number of special schools for children with visual impairments have closed over recent years, but those that have survived continue to meet this demand and many are evolving to develop additional or alternative services. This evolution may take the form of increasing the age or ability range of the intake or narrowing it towards greater specialisation. All the special schools now cater both for children who are educationally blind and for children with low vision.

The population of special schools for children and young people with visual impairment has generally shifted significantly in the last 20 years and there has been a marked increase in the proportion of children in these schools with complex needs and additional learning, physical and behavioural difficulties. In many of these schools the changes in the population have necessitated the retraining or redeploying of teaching staff, and/or the appointment of new staff with appropriate expertise.

Teachers in special schools for children with visual impairments are required to obtain the mandatory qualification as a teacher of the visually impaired within three years of appointment. There is currently discussion at government level about the future of the mandatory requirement for teachers of children with sensory impairment, but there are strong representations from those working in the field to retain it (see Chapter 44).

Other special schools

Up to 29% of school-aged pupils with visual impairment are placed in special schools which are not designated schools for the visually impaired. These are most often schools for children with moderate or severe learning difficulties (SLD) or schools for children with physical disabilities. Table 2.3 provides a national breakdown of the figures:

Table 2.3 Educational placement of pupils with VI in non-designated special schools (Clunies-Ross and Franklin 1996)

	Age, years	
	5–10+	11–16
England	29%	33%
Wales	31%	31%
Scotland	18%	16%

Teachers in these schools are not required to have a mandatory qualification and many schools have no specialist teachers of the visually impaired among their staff (see Chapter 32). It is estimated that on average about 20% of pupils in schools for children with SLD have a significant visual impairment, and that 90% of pupils who are visually impaired and who have multiple disabilities are in schools which are not specifically designed for them (Griffiths and Best 1996).

Post-school provision

On leaving school, an increasing number of students with visual impairment are following courses at their local college of further education (see Chapter 12). The Tomlinson Report (Further Education Funding Council (FEFC) 1996), a major government enquiry into provision for students with special needs in further education (FE), endorses the principle of greater inclusivity and the proportion of students with visual impairments in local colleges is likely to increase as the recommendations of the Report are implemented. In England there are currently six specialist colleges for students with visual impairments who are over the age of 16, and each offers a range of courses in vocational preparation and training and rehabilitation. In recent years the colleges have undergone dramatic change and, in addition to younger students, most now cater for significant numbers of adults with a visual impairment. Funding for students in the FE sector is derived from a number of agencies but most commonly from the Further Education Funding Council.

Standards in education for children with a visual impairment

The range of schools where children with a visual impairment receive their education are subject to inspection by the Office for Standards in Education (Ofsted) and are judged on the quality of education they provide as measured by the attainment and progress of pupils in areas of the National Curriculum, the social, cultural, moral and spiritual development they provide for their pupils and the efficiency of the school.

Current regulations require all schools to be inspected on a four-yearly cycle, which becomes a six-yearly cycle after the first round of inspections. Reports of the inspections are in the public domain and available on the Internet. Summaries of the reports, including the main findings and key issues for action, are sent to all parents with children at the school, and school governors are responsible for drawing up an action plan to address the key issues identified in the report. Schools that are deemed to be failing to provide an adequate education for their pupils may be subject to closure.

LEA advisory and peripatetic services are not included in this system, although there is support from the LEAs themselves for inclusion of these services into the system of inspection (see Chapter 44).

Future provision

According to Boucher (1996), the factors that will influence policy and provision in the future for special educational needs include: the statutory entitlement to a broad and balanced curriculum, the introduction of small unitary authorities, competition between schools, rising class sizes in mainstream schools; increased financial independence for state schools, and the reduction in the role of the LEA. 'All are having, or will have, an impact on the strategic planning, provision and funding for special educational needs' (Boucher 1996).

Services for children with low incidence disabilities are particularly vulnerable at a time of radical educational change. Some professionals within the field of visual impairment feel that in this uncertain climate there is a need for a thorough review of the organisation and funding of educational services for children and young people to ensure that the range and quality of provision is maintained.

As has been seen in the previous chapter, attempts to establish a coherent organisational framework for education in this field have been largely unsuccessful in the past. In the absence of a national strategy, existing provision will continue to be rationalised as market forces and competition dictate. While competition might be a useful mechanism for ensuring the improvement of services in other fields of education, in low incidence disabilities its benefits are doubtful. The duplication of provision and resources for low incidence disabilities over and above that needed to ensure choice, can be viewed as wasteful, particularly in a context where there is a national imbalance in the availability and quality of services.

Some form of national planning seems necessary for the coordination of services to ensure consistency of choice and quality at national, regional and local levels. Best (1996) proposes an 'array' or a coordinated network of interlocking and interdependent services funded on a regional basis. Any major reorganisation of services along these lines will involve a major process of consultation within the field, and the beginnings of this process are under way.

BLINDNESS AND LOW VISION

This section is concerned with the medical and psychological consequences of sight loss in children and shows how the information which is gained from assessment can help to inform the processes which give children access and entitlement to the curriculum.

Chapter 3 discusses the general effects of sight loss on the development of children and the author follows the progress of a child with a visual impairment through infancy to adolescence. Chapter 4 provides the basic information about the anatomy and physiology of the eye and the process of seeing which a class teacher might require when talking to parents and medical professionals or when reading reports on children.

Chapter 5 examines the most common causes of visual impairment in children and explores the main educational implications of each condition. Chapter 6 explains the different ways in which the various aspects of vision can be measured. It defines the role of the teacher in assessing the functional vision of the child and shows how this information can be crucial to ensuring the child's access to the curriculum.

The chapter on low vision devices (LVDs) is written by an optometrist with a special interest in the education of children with a visual impairment. He describes the ways in which LVDs might be used by pupils, within the school curriculum and for leisure activities, and provides an excellent practical guide to the advantages and disadvantages of different types of devices.

The final chapter in the section examines the issues surrounding the various psychological assessment procedures available to professionals working with children and young people who are blind or have low vision and how the resulting information can help answer questions of entitlement and access.

Chapter 3

The Effects of a Visual Loss

Mary Kingsley

Introduction

In this chapter the development of a child who is fully sighted is compared and contrasted with that of a child who is visually impaired. The effects of a visual loss in four developmental areas, social and emotional, language, cognitive, and mobility and orientation, are considered. The impact of the combination of those effects upon the functioning and learning potential of the individual is discussed.

Social and emotional development

Sam's mother Ms Morgan spent a long time looking into his eyes. She began to worry that something was wrong. Ms Morgan said to her mother that she was worried that Sam couldn't see properly. Her mother said 'No don't be silly of course he's all right'. But after that Granny began to look a little more closely and a couple of weeks later said to Grandad 'I'm a bit bothered about the little 'un. I'm not sure he's seeing right'.

Meanwhile Ms Morgan reckoned her Mum must be right – Mothers were always right.

Ms Morgan's partner, David Evans, had also noticed that his son didn't seem to smile at him when he smiled, Mr Evans thought 'Oh well I've never been good with kids and even my own son doesn't respond to me'.

Ms Morgan went along to the clinic for Sam's six-week check. She had put him back in his pram and was walking out of the door when she said to the health visitor: 'Do you think he can see properly?' The locum Health Visitor busy with the paperwork and running late said 'Umm I'm sure he's OK.'

Eventually some weeks later Ms Morgan bursts into tears in her GP's surgery and expresses her fears and worries. Then the referral to the district hospital and subsequently the regional hospital concurs, and the diagnosis is made.

What are the feelings of all those people in that scenario? Guilt, which is not being addressed at the moment by anyone, anger which is going to explode in many different ways, along with a whole range of other emotions.

Granny's OK, she'd mentioned it to Grandad. He'd done nothing; she'd done her bit, she was in the clear and any way she didn't like that David Evans, why couldn't he marry her daughter and make an honest woman of her! However Ms Morgan is left with the guilt and the difficulty. Perhaps she shouldn't have been on that holiday, gone to that exercise class, drunk that wine.

Mr Evans, when he heard the news about his son's visual disability, thought 'Oh he's never going to play for England now. What's the point of trying to do anything with Sam?'

Scenarios similar to that described above are repeated in many families who have a child with a disability. At this point the family will need help to realise that the situation is not entirely bleak. With correct support and teaching, Sam will be able to develop the skills he needs to realise his full potential and become an independent, well-balanced and socially adept adult.

Support for the family may come from a variety of different sources. They can be helped by professionals, friends and other parents who have a child with a visual impairment. They may receive visits from social worker for the visually impaired attached to the local authority social services department, or from the local education authority's advisory teacher for children with a visual impairment. Among other professionals who may be involved are the paramedical staff from the local child development centre.

The parents will normally undergo a period of grieving for the 'normal' child they have lost. These grieving stages will include denial, anger and ultimately acceptance; although for some parents acceptance may take many years to achieve. This 'grieving' is a process that is common for parents of children with any type of disability. The parent's feelings will affect their relationship with each other and with the child and this in turn will influence the child's emotional and social development.

Other factors will also affect the early parent–child relationship such as the degree to which the parent understands the effects of the visual impairment. Elstner (1983), when considering abnormalities in the verbal communication of visually impaired children, says:

> Let us also consider the perspective of the sighted people in the blind baby's environment. They unconsciously expect the culturally predetermined reactions and behaviour pattern of sighted babies which would act as the trigger for their affectionate responses towards the child. They therefore misinterpret the blind baby's expressionless face as reflecting rejection or lack of interest. As Wills (1978) formulates it, the child and the world around him communicate 'on different wavelengths'.

As Sam became older, he went to the local playgroup but he was often ignored by the other children. Little children play in parallel for a time, doing the same activity as each other but not cooperating. They learn to cooperate partly by observing each other play and making eye contact. Sam with his visual disability is not able to see clearly what Rosita and Ferdinand are doing and so does not get invited 'to join in'. This cooperation must be skilfully stage-managed by an adult in charge who understands Sam's needs.

When Sam and his friends play together it usually involves turn-taking with a toy. Sam doesn't understand that the toy continues to exists when it has left his grasp so he needs a continual verbal commentary to enable him to make sense of what is happening and to learn to take turns.

As children become older they need the skills to initiate and sustain social relationships. If their body language does not conform with that of their peers they may find socialising difficult. Consider the way that Sam, who is now a teenager, still raises his hand when answering a question in class. At the beginning of his school career he will have been told to put his hand straight up in the air – imagine the keen infant class raising their hands. However the pupil with a severe visual impairment may not be aware that with increasing age and sophistication the signal gets smaller – think of the casual raised finger from the college student.

The very fine nuances of body language which are observed and integrated into their behaviour by children with sight, contrast dramatically with the sometimes gauche body language of a child with a visual impairment. Some teenagers with a visual impairment find it difficult to lose the inappropriate mannerisms or 'blindisms' developed in childhood. 'Hand flapping', which is normal and somewhat appealing in an excited two year old looks alarmingly out of place in a fourteen year old like Sam. Inappropriate body language of this kind can give the initial impression that Sam has severe learning difficulties rather than a visual impairment. Other socially inappropriate mannerisms can include eye poking and rocking. Those who work with Sam will need skills in diminishing those behaviours. As with all behaviour modification, positive reinforcement of good behaviours is more appropriate than negative comments. When Sam was eye poking as a small child it would have been better if his parent or carer had given him a stimulating toy to play with, rather than constantly shouting 'Don't do that!'

From this rather bleak discourse on the effects of visual loss on social skills emerges the importance of informed advice which will enable the parent, carer or professional to understand the child's needs and intervene in an appropriate way at the right time.

Language development

Although research on the development of language in children who are visually impaired is by no means conclusive (see Chapter 33), there is some evidence of differences in the language development of these children, in the areas of:

- the acquisition of the sound system or phonology
- the syntactic use of words.

Lewis (1987) suggests that visual impairment has little noticeable impact upon the development of pre-language and Illingworth (1972) suggests that:

> The normal blind child just like the sighted, begins to vocalise at eight weeks, squeals with pleasure and 'talks' when spoken to at twelve weeks, says syllables 'ba /ka /da' at 28 weeks, may say one word with meaning and imitate sounds at 48 weeks, and may have two or three meaningful words in his vocabulary by one year of age. After this stage, the severely visually impaired child's language slows down while the various developmental steps tend to be delayed. For example, the normal child may frequently repeat his first words without understanding them fully; so does the blind child but for longer periods.

Elstner (1983) suggests the reason for this delay in children who are blind stems from their inability to observe the joint and simultaneous nature of visual and auditory events. Consequently, these children miss valuable stimuli for speaking, and lose many communicative opportunities.

This is the reason, according to Fraiberg (1974) that blind children rarely initiate any 'vocal dialogues' themselves, even under favourable environmental conditions. The blind infant learns at an early age 'to distinguish voices, but they come from the unknown and return to the unknown, thus blind infants remain dependent on the initiatives of the people around them' (Rogow 1972).

In much early dialogue, the two conversational partners need a common object about which to communicate and talk. This **reference object** and the two conversational partners constitute the **reference triangle** (Trevarthen 1974). Typically, one conversational partner will follow the other's line of gaze, and make reference to the object, 'Oh, isn't that a pretty bird' (and then extending the conversation), 'look at his lovely wings'. This communication triangle is much more difficult to establish if one of the partners cannot see and has only sound clues to work on. When the young baby with a visual impairment suddenly 'stills' to listen, the more mature conversational partner has to notice that momentary stilling and then make a calculated guess as to which of the many background noises the infant is paying attention.

Visual impairment has an effect on the acquisition of concepts and meaning. Elstner (1983) comments that infants who are visually impaired tend to use language in a different way from infants who are fully sighted. An infant who is fully sighted will use language not only for communicative purposes, but also for the acquisition of concepts, whereas a child with a visual impairment, having achieved the use of language, uses it primarily for communicative purposes, and not for the acquisition of concepts. This may be the explanation for the finding (Mills 1983) that blind children remain at the stage of echolalia (repeating the same sounds over and over) for a prolonged period, and tend towards **verbalism** (the use of words which are not rooted in first-hand experience).

Children with a visual impairment appear to be able to acquire the formal structure, or the 'syntax' of language, with relative ease. However, the absence of the visual stimulus seems to be responsible for the high incidence of articulatory mistakes among young blind children, for example substitution of /l/ or /r/ for /w/.

It is helpful if parents, carers and teachers can listen carefully to a child's developing language, ensure that the child can articulate the correct sounds, and then encourage the child to articulate the sound correctly perhaps through word games, songs and rhymes.

Cognitive development

Lowenfeld (1948) stated that blindness imposed three serious limitations on the satisfactory development of cognitive functioning:

- in the range and variety of the child's experiences
- in the ability to move about
- in the interaction with the environment.

Jan *et al.* (1977) suggest that some problems of cognitive deficit may be due to information deprivation, based on the fact that other senses cannot process information as efficiently as vision can. For example when children who are fully sighted do jigsaw puzzles, they can look at an individual piece and determine which way up the piece goes and decide the approximate area in which the piece fits. The brain is able to process the colours, shapes and shading on the piece almost simultaneously to determine its location. There is no other sense that can provide so much information so quickly.

However, there is no firm evidence that these limitations necessarily restrict potential. Lewis (1987) considers the intelligence of children who are blind and discusses the conflicting evidence as presented by Kolk (1977) and Tillman (1967, 1973). Kolk reviewed a number of studies concerned with the intelligence of blind children and concluded that 'in general average IQ scores do not differ significantly' for blind and sighted children. Tillman however argues that there are significant differences. Using the Verbal Scale of the WISC (the Wechsler Intelligence Scale for Children), Tillman reported an average IQ of 92 for 110 blind children aged 7–13, compared with 96.5 for a matched group of sighted children. Tillman (1967) analysed results from individual test items and found that the sighted children were superior to the blind children on comprehension and tasks which required children to spot similarities. There were no differences between the blind children and sighted children on information, arithmetic and vocabulary scales. Others have reported that blind children may actually be superior to sighted children on digit span tasks. The explanation proposed by Tillman for the apparent differences is that blind children fail to integrate all the various facts they learn, so that each item of information is more likely to be kept within a separate frame of reference from every other item. Children who are blind are not disadvantaged on items which require information, like those in the arithmetic and vocabulary scales, but they are disadvantaged on items such as comprehension or judging of similarities, which require the child to relate different items of information. It is as though all the educational experiences of the blind child are kept in separate compartments. If this is correct, then it may be concluded that, as in perception, vision provides the child with the opportunity to make links between different experiences, links which assist the child in making the most effective use of their experiences.

Motor development, mobility and orientation

The terms **mobility** and **orientation** have specific meanings for people who are visually impaired and for the professionals who work with this client group. While early training in mobility and orientation is usually provided by visiting teachers of the visually impaired, advanced skills to enable people with a visual impairment to travel safely and independently around their neighbourhood using long cane techniques is usually given by qualified rehabilitation officers.

Tooze (1981) makes the following distinction between orientation and mobility:

> Orientation is the ability to understand the relationship that objects have to one another – the creation of a mental pattern of the environment. Mobility training involves the acquisition of the set of skills and techniques which enable a visually handicapped person to travel more easily through his environment.

The development of skills in orientation and mobility is inextricably linked to the early development of movement. Jan *et al.* (1977) suggest that:

> Severely visually impaired children with intact nervous systems who have not been given adequate opportunities to learn motor skills are often delayed in their development. They are frequently hypotonic, poorly co-ordinated, walk on an insecure base and their feet are extremely rotated.

Best (1992) suggests that children who are visually impaired cannot easily monitor their movement and so may have difficulty understanding what happens when they move or stretch a limb, bend at the waist or roll over. If they are not able to see other people clearly they will have fewer terms of reference, and may not realise what 'sitting up straight' means or how to 'march like a soldier'.

Without clear vision children may experience difficulty in creating a mental map of their surroundings. Without appropriate intervention, they may not know in which direction to go or how to find their way round obstacles to get to their goal. Uncertainties about their surroundings may lead to a lack of confidence in exploring the environment. Lack of effective vision may also remove an important source of motivation for a child in as much as they may not be able to see the attractive objects, which would encourage them to attempt to crawl across a room or to reach out. Reaching to sound is more complex than visually directed reaching and usually occurs in all children at a later stage of development. Children with a visual impairment therefore typically show delays in motor development. This has been quantified by Reynell (1978), who established a delay beginning at about 6–8 months and continuing throughout the pre-school days. At the age of 5, the children in Reynell's sample were, on average, 12 months behind children who were fully sighted. In order to develop as confident and independent travellers, children who are visually impaired will need skilled intervention from a very early age to promote motor development and coordinated and purposeful movement, and, as they develop, a carefully structured programme to teach them the techniques of travel (see Chapter 17).

Summary

In this chapter the effects of severe visual impairment have been considered.

The effects of a visual loss are wide ranging and impinge on every area of the child's development. Some of the strategies for minimising the potentially adverse effects of visual impairment have been briefly explored, and additional information on these strategies will be found elsewhere in this book.

Chapter 4

Anatomy and Physiology of the Eye

Heather Mason

Introduction

This chapter attempts to give the reader a basic understanding of the anatomy of the eye and the processes involved in vision. It is intended mainly as a reference section.

Structure of the eye

It is useful if parents, teachers and other professionals have some understanding of the anatomy of the eye (Figure 4.1) because it can help them to grasp the causes and implications of the child's visual impairment.

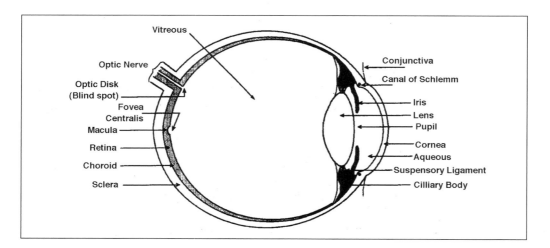

Figure 4.1   The human eye

The visible part of the eye is globular in shape and is protected by the eye lids. The conjuctiva, which has many blood vessels, is a transparent film which covers the inner surface of the eyelids and the front of the eyeball up to the cornea. It prevents any foreign bodies in the eye such as an eyelash or contact lens, from slipping around the back of the eye. Together with the lacrimal gland which produces tears, it contributes to keeping the cornea moist. Tears have an important function as a lubricant and help to prevent the eye from 'drying out'. Excess tears drain out through the small holes in the eyelids and flow into the nose. The eyelashes (on the outer eyelids) are similar to cat's whiskers in that they react quickly to external stimuli causing the eye to blink rapidly and avoid injury.

The tough wall or 'white' of the eye is called the sclera. It is opaque and protects the more delicate parts of the eye. At the front of the eye, continuous with the sclera, is the cornea, the circular window of the eye. It has no blood vessels and is transparent and bends the light into the eye. Although it is thinner than the crystalline lens within the eye, the cornea is the strongest converging lens. Together with the lens, the cornea focuses the optical image onto the retina at the back of the eye. The cornea, which contains many nerve fibres, is the most sensitive part of the human body and severe pain can result from even minor irritations. It can become opaque if it is damaged in any way or becomes infected.

The crystalline lens, like the cornea, is transparent when healthy. It is biconvex in shape and is made up of water and proteins. It does not contain any nerve or blood vessels and is elastic in structure. However, this elasticity diminishes with age resulting in the problems that most people have with reading small print during middle age (presbyopia).

The lens divides the eye into two segments: the part of the eye in the front of the lens is known as the anterior chamber and is filled with a clear watery fluid, the aqueous, which is continually produced by the ciliary body. The aqueous provides the lens with essential nutrients, helps to remove waste products and regulates the ocular pressure and shape of the eye. Excess aqueous is drained away by the trabeculum – a network of filtration canals in the angle of the anterior chamber.

In addition to producing the aqueous, the ciliary body contains three types of cilary muscles which help to focus the lens, maintaining a clear image on the retina.

The area behind the lens which is lined by the retina is sometimes known as the 'great' or posterior chamber of the eye. It is filled with vitreous, a jelly-like transparent substance which fills four-fifths of the eye. Like the aqueous, the vitreous does not contain any blood vessels or nerve fibres and is mainly (99%) water. The remaining one per cent consists of collagen and hyaluronic acid which gives the vitreous the consistency needed to maintain the of shape to the eye. If for any reason the transparency of the vitreous is reduced, through infection for example, visual acuity is affected.

Light passes through the crystalline lens and the vitreous and reaches the innermost layer of the eye, the retina. The retina is made up of several layers containing two main types of cells, each of which have a role in responding to the visual stimuli by a photochemical reaction. The resulting information passes along the optic nerve to the brain. The most sensitive part of the retina is called the macula, the fovea being the central part of the latter. The fovea consists of rocket-shaped cells called 'cones' which are sensitive to minute detail and colour, and so are responsible for the most acute vision. Cigar-shaped cells called 'rods' are most numerous in the peripheral part of the retina, and are more sparsely distributed in the central area. These cells are particularly sensitive to movement and are extremely light sensitive, and so operate best in reduced illumination.

Between the retina and the sclera is the choroid, the main circulatory layer of the eye through which blood is carried to nourish the various parts of the eye (especially the optic nerve head).

In front of the lens is the iris, the round coloured part of the eye containing muscular tissue which can contract or expand, and in doing so control the amount of light passing through the pupil, the centre of the iris, onto the retina. The ciliary body lies between the iris and the choroid and these three structures make up the uveal tract.

How the eyes 'see'

The eye has two very distinct visual abilities:
- central vision
- field or peripheral vision

and different parts of the retina are responsible for their functioning.

Central vision

When the eye looks at an object this is viewed along the visual axis. At one end will be the object whilst at the other end is the retina or to be more precise, the macula.

The macula is a small part of the retina approximately 5.5 mm diameter at its widest part. The central part of the macula, the fovea, is responsible for the most acute vision and is made up entirely of cones. These photo-receptive cells function best in high illumination and allow the eye to discriminate fine detail and colour and are therefore essential for many of the fine motor and visual tasks carried out by children in and out of the classroom. It is this type of vision which is essential, for instance, for reading, and damage to the macula has significant implications for learning.

Field or peripheral vision

The remaining visual field of the macula is made up of photo-receptor cells called rods. The rods have increased sensitivity in low levels of illumination and are necessary for providing visual information about what is in the periphery of our vision beyond the shape image that is perceived by the fovea. For example, when concentrating on reading the words in the centre of this line, you are aware of the words at the ends of the line which are out of focus. Similarly, there is an awareness of words above and below the line depending upon the size of print. The peripheral retina collects hazy images of the surroundings and these become clearer as they approach the macula.

Partial or full loss of vision (tunnel vision) in this area has serious educational implications. For example, the pupil will have considerable difficulty in finding their way around in low levels of illumination (night blindness). These implications are discussed more fully in the chapter on eye conditions.

Each eye has a visual field and with both eyes open their fields overlap, giving binocular

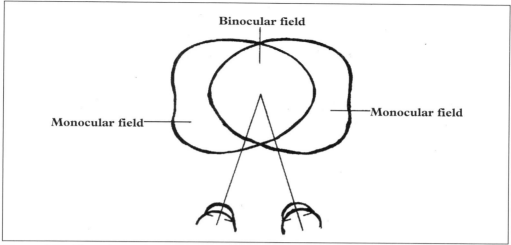

Figure 4.2   Binocular and monocular fields

vision in this area (Figure 4.2). This is necessary for perception of depth and sense of position in space and perspective.

Normal sight

1. Distance vision

Parallel rays of light enter the eye through the pupil. The light is refracted ('bent') as it passes through the cornea and the crystalline lens onto the macula. During this process the ciliary muscle is relaxed (Figure 4.3).

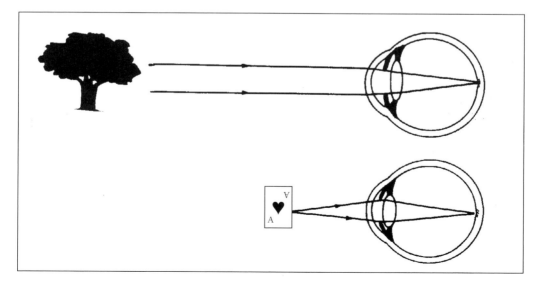

Figure 4.3   The eye focusing for distant and near vision

2. Near vision

To view near objects in focus, the cilary muscle contracts as the light passes through the lens. This increases the strength of the lens, allowing the light to focus onto the macula. Unfortunately, as part of the ageing process, the lens hardens and does not respond in the same way to the cilary muscle, resulting in the need for reading spectacles!

Visual pathways

This is a term given to the nervous pathways which connect the back of the eye to the visual cortex, the specialised area of the brain which interprets the inverted images seen on the retinae. How this happens is quite complicated.

The visual field of each eye is divided up into a nasal and temporal side. The visual pathway (Figure 4.4) on each side is made up of the:

• optic nerve consisting of fibres from both the nasal and temporal fields;

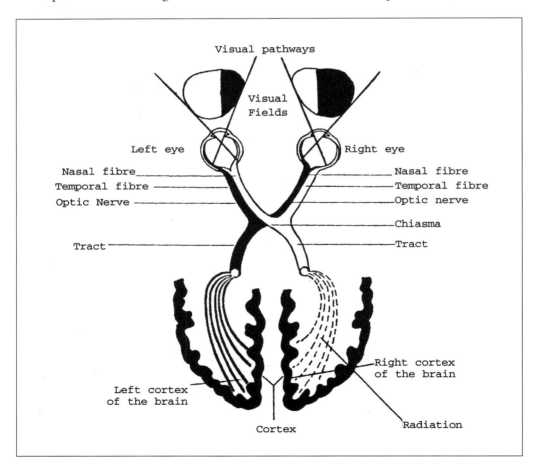

Figure 4.4   Visual pathways

- the chiasma where the optic nerves from each eye meet; the nasal fibres from each retina cross over to the other side and the temporal fibres stay on the same side and form the
- optic tract, and
- optic radiations, which spread into the
- occipital cortex.

The right cortex receives information from both the left halves of the visual fields whilst the left visual cortex receives information from right halves of the fields. As Figure 4.4 shows, the optic nerve fibres from the temporal halves of the visual fields go to the cortex of the same side but those from the nasal fields cross over at the chiasma and go to the cortex of the opposite side.

There are in fact, two major visual nerve pathways to the visual cortex of the brain, one via the lateral geniculate nucleus (LGN) and the other via the superior colliculus.

Analysis of the visual information, for example that relating to colour, is begun in the primary visual cortex, the visual information starts to be analysed, for example information relating to colour. Some of this information is then sent backwards to the superior colliculus. However, it can be seen from Figure 4.5 that information to the superior colliculus may be received directly from either the retina or via the LGN.

The visual pathways from the retina to the LGN are known as peripheral visual pathways whilst those which go to the visual cortex are known as central visual pathways. A visual impairment can originate in either or both of these pathways. Those who are interested in this aspect and would like more detail are recommended to read the accounts by Hyvärinen (1995a, b).

Some common misunderstandings about vision

These misunderstandings relate to some of the most common statements made by teachers and others coming into contact with a child or young person who has a visual impairment for the first time.

Why isn't the child wearing glasses if their vision is so poor?

Spectacles do not always help to correct or improve a visual impairment. Those eye conditions affecting the retina, optic nerve and other parts of the eye cannot be helped by spectacles. Refractive errors such as long and short sight (hypermetropia and myopia) can usually be assisted by wearing a corrective lens, that is spectacles or contact lenses, but because these children are visually impaired, their sight will not be corrected to the standard of normal vision. Some pupils who are photophobic may require tinted spectacles while other may wear special filters.

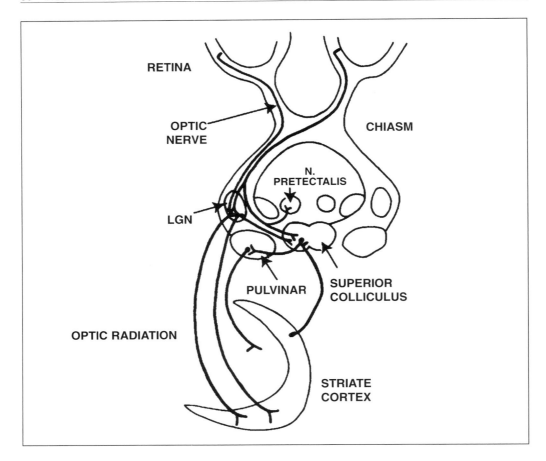

Figure 4.5 Adapted, with permission from Hyvärinen (1995b)

Will the very close working distance harm the eyes?

Holding a book close to the eyes will not harm vision or cause shortsightedness (myopia). For some pupils, it may be the only way of getting the print into focus. Bringing print closer to the eyes is also a way of enlarging the print, this is known as relative-distance magnification. If the distance between the object, for example printed material, and the eye is halved, the retinal image doubles in size. If the distance is increased by one-quarter or one-eighth then the retinal image size increases four or eight times. This relationship is shown in the Table 4.1.

Table 4.1 Relative-distance magnification.

Original distance	New distance	Magnification
40 cm	20 cm	2×
40 cm	10 cm	4×
40 cm	5 cm	8×

Is it wise to limit the visual activities of the child; can existing sight be lost through use?

Sight cannot be conserved, so always encourage the use of vision but do be aware of visual fatigue and recognise the signs that the pupil is tired.

Some children seem to prefer different lighting levels – why is this?

Lower levels of light will not harm the eyes. As a result of some eye conditions, for example albinism, a child may require a lower level of lighting to feel more comfortable. Other children will benefit from much brighter light, perhaps in the form of an individual lamp, often known as task lighting.

Does the loss of vision in one eye reduce vision by 50%?

While there is loss of vision on the affected side and general loss of depth perception, it is not a loss of half the visual system. Obviously there are implications for classroom management, for example seating arrangements, for the child with monocular vision. Children with normal vision in the remaining eye are not usually registered as visually impaired.

If a pupil is registered blind, does this mean they have no sight at all?

Less than 10% of the population registered as 'blind' are totally blind. Many have useful residual vision, or are aware of the differences between light and darkness. Some children who are registered blind can cope with print – perhaps enlarged or by using a low vision device – for some of their activities and use braille for others.

Are the other senses of a child with a visual impairment better than those of the other pupils?

Having a visual impairment does not mean that other senses are highly developed, for example hearing or the sense of touch. Greater emphasis may be placed on teaching strategies to enable these to be developed more fully. For instance, listening skills are a very important part of the curriculum for these pupils (see Chapter 15).

If the child wears glasses all the time, will this stop the muscles in the eyes from working properly?

The wearing of spectacles or contact lenses does not make the eyes 'lazy'. Not wearing them means that the child is missing out on vital visual information. Check with the optometrist if in any doubt.

Chapter 5

Common Eye Defects and their Educational Implications

Heather Mason

.

This chapter describes some of the more common visual impairments the teacher is likely to meet either in a mainstream setting or a special school for the visually impaired. Most eye conditions in children relate to refraction difficulties which can usually be fully corrected. Severe visual impairment is relatively rare in children (see Chapter 2).

For each impairment described, specific advice relating to classroom management is offered which can be used when drawing up Individual Education Plans as part of the requirements of the Code of Practice (DfE 1994). In some instances, the specialist resources the child will need to overcome the impairment will be indicated. A knowledge of the resources required will clearly be essential to those concerned with the financial management of services.

A severe visual impairment cannot be considered in isolation from the emotional, social and psychological impact it has upon the individual and the family as a whole. Eye defects must be considered within the whole context of visual functioning and its impact upon the processes of learning.

What causes a visual impairment?

Many of the conditions and syndromes which result in visual impairment are genetically determined and can be passed to the child through either one or both parents who may not always be aware that they are carriers. In some societies, it is common for first cousins or other close 'blood' relatives to marry and this increases the chances of eye conditions and any other impairment being passed on. Thus it is important that genetic counselling is available to those who are at risk so that they can plan from an informed standpoint.

Conditions can arise during the development of the foetus, some having no obvious explanation while others result from infections such as rubella. During the process of birth there is always the possibility of trauma, and for premature births, where the birth weight is less than 1300 grams and where high levels of oxygen are required to sustain life, a condition known as 'retinopathy of prematurity' sometimes occurs. A condition known as 'cortical visual impairment' results from a range of neurological disorders which can damage the visual pathways before and after they are fully formed (Jan 1993)

Childhood illnesses, viral infections, brain tumours or injuries such as those sustained in road accidents are possible causes of visual impairment in childhood. Sustained treatments with drugs such as some types of steroids may also have a temporary or permanent effect on the visual system.

In some hot countries eye diseases such as trachoma (which is the world's most common cause of visual impairment) are spread by insects. Unhygienic conditions compounded by generally poor primary health care and diet deficiencies account for the majority of the world's severe visual impairments (Dobree and Boulter 1982). In some developing countries, common childhood illnesses like measles are the major causes of blindness in children. In these countries only a relatively small proportion of cases of blindness result from genetically determined conditions, retinopathy of prematurity or visual pathway damage (Baird and Moore 1993).

The transmission of infections from animals is not confined to tropical countries. Publicity is regularly given to the dangers of blinding diseases such as toxoplasmosis which can be passed through the mother to the unborn foetus by cats, and toxocaria which children can contract through contaminated dog faeces.

Types of visual impairment

There are several ways of classifying visual impairment. This section begins with a description of errors of refraction and, for ease of reference, the remainder are listed alphabetically. The list is no means exhaustive and space prohibits the description of some of the lesser known eye conditions.

Errors of refraction

For most children with straightforward refractive errors, their vision will be corrected to normal. Problems will usually only arise if spectacles or contact lenses are not worn for the purpose for which they have been prescribed. Children and young people are considered as visually impaired only when their best corrected vision falls significantly outside the normal ranges for near or distance visual acuity.

It is essential that teachers in all areas of the curriculum are aware of when the child should wear glasses; advice should be sought from the optometrist if in any doubt. This information could be written into the Individual Education Plan (IEP) along with other information relating to access to the curriculum.

Myopia (shortsightedness)

In normal vision, parallel rays of light coming from a distance should focus on the retina at the fovea – the central point of the macula. If the eye is too long from back to front, as it is in the condition known as 'myopia', then the rays of light are focused between the lens and the macula, and this results in blurred distance vision. Spectacles or contact lenses containing concave lenses (minus lenses) can be used to correct this. Near vision is always good provided that the object is brought closer to the eyeball.

In most cases of myopia the lengthening of the eyeball is only moderate and becomes static with skeletal growth and correction should be possible to 6/6. However, in a small proportion of myopes the eyeball continues to grow. This condition is known as 'progressive myopia' or 'high myopia' and normal visual acuity cannot be achieved through the use of spectacles or contact lenses. The stretching of the retina caused by the abnormal growth can affect the efficiency of the macula and may result in holes or rents in the peripheral or central retina. Since there is a risk of a 'detached' retina, advice must always be obtained from an ophthalmologist before the child participates in activities such judo or any other 'contact' sports, or in aspects of other games such as diving in swimming, or heading a football.

Educational implications of myopia
- The wearing of prescribed spectacles or contact lenses will be essential for most tasks; children may need some encouragement to wear them.
- For near tasks, the child may find it easier to work without spectacles and bring work close up to the face (see Chapter 7).
- There may be problems with distance vision, for instance seeing the blackboard.
- The use of a desk lid which can be raised or a book stand will encourage good posture when reading and writing. This specialist equipment may be obtainable from the support services for the visually impaired or the school may need to purchase it.
- All printed materials including diagrams and maps must have good contrast and clear print of an appropriate size; this can be determined by the optometrist.

Hypermetropia (longsightedness)
In this condition the eyeball is too short and the rays of light focus behind the retina resulting in blurred and in extreme cases non-effective vision. Simple hypermetropia can be corrected to normal vision with convex lenses (plus lenses) so that the light rays are focused onto the fovea. Problems usually occur only when it is associated with other visual conditions such as cataracts. In these cases, although spectacles will be prescribed, visual acuity will be reduced. This condition may be associated with a squint.

Educational implications of hypermetropia
- There is loss of accommodation (the ability to focus) when objects are brought close to the face.
- Long periods of reading or other close tasks should be avoided as they cause discomfort; the child may complain of visual fatigue and eye strain (headaches, fluctuating vision).
- Some pupils may have been prescribed low vision devices such as a hand-held

magnifier, a telescope or a closed circuit television (CCTV); it is essential to provide training and encourage children to use them (see Chapter 7).

Astigmatism

The main cause of astigmatism is the variation of the refractive power of the cornea or lens due to irregularities in its curvature. This results in a distorted image on the macula. It can be simple to rectify with a cylindrical correction built into the lens of the spectacles, but difficulties can arise when it is associated with myopia and hypermetropia. When it is associated with another visual impairment, correction can be difficult and it can result in reduced visual acuity.

Educational implications of astigmatism

The points to note are similar for hypermetropia, with the addition of the following.
- Young children may confuse letters and numbers.
- Visual fatigue may be a problem after long periods of close visual work, or at the end of a day or a week.

Other visual impairments in the classroom

Achromatopsia or cone dystrophy

This is a hereditary condition which affects more males than females. The underdevelopment of cones in the macula results in total colour blindness and reduced distance visual acuity. As a result of the loss of cone function, the rods are not inhibited in daylight and are severely over-exposed. Children and young people with this condition are therefore highly photophobic and have nystagmus. The educational implications are the same for the next condition, albinism.

Albinism

This is an inherited condition, affecting all racial groups, associated with lack of pigment or the inability of the body to produce melanin. Children with albinism may have white hair, fair skin or may have no outward sign of the condition.

In the severe form of albinism, known as 'oculocutaneous' albinism, the macula is underdeveloped and another visual condition known as 'nystagmus', a rhythmic oscillation of the eyes, may be present (see section below). In addition, the very pale skin of children with albinism burns quickly and severely in strong sunlight, especially when exposed to higher levels of ultraviolet light than normal, such as light reflected off snow or the sea. Children with this form of the condition usually have a high degree of visual impairment and rarely achieve more than 6/36 on the Snellen test, but will benefit from using some type of low vision aid or CCTV (see Chapter 7).

Educational implications of albinism and cone dystrophy

- Photophobia will be a major problem.
  - Pupils should be encouraged to wear tinted spectacles with proper absorptive filter lenses, plus an eyeshade/baseball cap when outside in sunshine.
  - Natural lighting in classrooms will have to be carefully controlled, for example venetian blinds will be needed to cut out direct sunlight. This may have major financial implications for mainstream schools and colleges.
- Any form of 'glare', for example light coming in through dirty windows reflected off glossy surfaces, will be uncomfortable, and pupils may need to work in an area of the classroom where there are lower levels of illumination.
- A book stand or desk lid which can be raised should be provided, as the pupil may prefer a very close working distance.
- Pupils and students will benefit from the use of prescribed low vision aids.

Aniridia

Aniridia is a congenital and usually inherited condition in which the iris has partially or completely failed to develop. What appears to be a black iris is, in fact, an enlarged pupil. Aniridia affects both eyes and is usually associated with other visual impairments such as nystagmus, photophobia, displaced lens and occasionally cataracts (cloudiness of the lens). Glaucoma (increased ocular pressure) is often present and pupils may experience discomfort and pain in the eye as a result.

Educational implications of aniridia

- These and similar to those associated with albinism.
- Visual fatigue, headaches or general discomfort in the eyes following periods of intense close work may occur.
- A good contrast is needed between the print and the paper.
- Pupils and students will benefit from the use of prescribed low vision aids.
- If nystagmus is present, look at the recommendations for that condition.

Cataracts

A cataract, an opaqueness of the lens of the eye, is one of the major causes of visual impairment in both the young and the old. People with a cataract liken the experience to looking through a very dirty car windscreen The cloudiness of the lens prevents the passage of some of the rays of light onto the retina. While there are several types of cataracts, most of those present in children are congenital cataracts (that is, present at birth), while in old people, they are part of the normal ageing process. Although some children may have had the affected lens removed very early in life, making the eye aphakic (lacking a lens), they will still experience severe visual problems.

It is essential that the teacher requests guidance from the ophthalmologist or optometrist, as visual acuity depends upon the position, size and depth of the cataract. Children with cataracts in the periphery of the lens need increased levels of illumination, while children with central opacities have better vision in low lighting. Cataracts which are untreated may result in a squint. There may be marked variations between the functional vision of children with cataracts who are recorded as having the same visual acuities.

Cataracts are associated with other conditions such as Down's syndrome, and are commonly present in babies whose prenatal development has been affected by rubella. Cataracts may also result from environmental circumstances, for example Australian aborigines, both young and old, are at risk of cataracts caused by high levels of ultraviolet light from the sun (Mason and Gale 1997).

Educational implications of cataracts

Make sure that:
- glare of any kind (such as that caused by direct sunlight or light reflected off shiny paper) is avoided;
- the light source is behind the child;
- good contrast is provided between print and paper;
- the appropriate print size is determined;
- low vision aids for close and distance work are provided, with appropriate training in their use;
- a book stand is available if a close working distance is preferred; it will prevent posture problems.

Be aware that:
- some cataracts cause reduced vision in dark and dimly lit areas, while others produce sensitivity to bright light and reduced colour perception;
- the wearing of spectacles will usually improve central vision, but reduce the field of vision, affecting safe movement in the environment.

Coloboma

This inherited condition is often characterised by a keyhole-shaped pupil, but the deformity may appear in other parts of the eye. Decreased visual acuity may be accompanied by nystagmus, squint and photophobia. It is not unusual for cataracts to be present. Some children with colobomas may also have microphthalmia (small eyes). Depending on where the gap appears, there may be a reduction of the field of vision in the lower part of the eye. It may associated with other conditions, for example CHARGE syndrome (Coloboma, Heart defect, Cloacal Atresia, Retardation, Genitourinary defects, Ear anomalies) (see Good 1993, for further information).

Educational implications of coloboma

- range of associated visual conditions has implications for:
  - seating arrangements
  - the management of lighting conditions in and outdoors to avoid direct sunlight or glare.

Glaucoma

In cases of glaucoma there is an increase in the intra-ocular pressure which can affect the blood supply to the optic nerve head. There are different types of glaucoma: it can be a disease in its own right or may be associated with other conditions, such as aniridia. One type of glaucoma found in children is buphthalmos ('ox eye') and is distinguished by an enlarged eye or eyes. It is a serious condition, and if not treated may damage the lens, retina or optic nerve. Other types of glaucoma are characterised by reduced fields of vision and visual difficulty in areas which are dark or dimly lit.

Educational implications of glaucoma

- These are similar to those of aniridia.
- The eye drops which may be used to maintain the correct ocular pressure also dilate the pupil, making the eye photophobic.
- It is essential that the eye drops are administered at the correct time; a point to remember when organising school trips.
- The appearance of the buphthalmic eye/s may be abnormal, so the child may be subjected to insensitive comments.

Hemianopia

Hemianopia is an absence of visual field, often in the right or left half of each retina. As the cause of the condition lies in the visual pathways, the macula is usually unimpaired and there may be some central direct vision. Pupils may adopt an unusual head posture in order to make the best use of their visual processes. Figure 5.1 illustrates the restricted visual fields of a pupil with hemianopia.

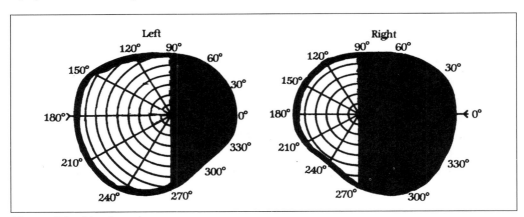

Figure 5.1   Hemianopia

Educational implications of hemianopia.

- Tracking and scanning skills may be difficult, especially with left hemianopia (i.e. where the left half of the field of vision of each eye is defective), and this will have implications for reading.

- Placement in the classroom is very important so that the pupil can take in as wide a field of vision as possible.
- The young child may require a programme of visual perceptual training.

Keratoconus

Keratoconus is a condition of the cornea, usually affecting both eyes, in which they becomes 'cone' shaped resulting in a distortion of the visual field and gradual loss of distance visual acuity. In severe and untreated cases, scarring can occur or the cornea can rupture and a corneal graft may be necessary. Keratoconus is thought to be inherited and may be associated with a range of other conditions, such as retinitis pigmentosa, aniridia, Marfan's and Down's syndrome. In some areas of the world, for instance Australia, there has been an increase in incidence, attributed to intolerance to wattle (acacia) pollen and the subsequent 'rubbing of eyes'.

Educational implications of keratoconus
See Myopia and Astigmatism.

Macular degeneration

This is a description of a group of conditions, for instance Stargardt's dystrophy, which affect the fovea and macula. The latter are concerned with seeing minute detail, thus there is a reduction of near vision and reduced distance vision. Scotomas (visual field defects) develop and magnification is needed to see around them. Colour perception and contrast sensitivity may also be affected. Unfortunately many of these conditions are progressive, leading to severe visual impairment.

Educational implications of macular degeneration
The child will benefit from:
- the use of a prescribed hand held low vision aid and/or CCTV;
- good illumination for all tasks;
- a line marker when reading;
- textbooks and worksheets with good print–paper contrast;
- using thick, dark lined paper and black fibre-tip pens for recording their work;
- a programme of visual perceptual training;
- training in eccentric viewing techniques if they adopt an unusual head position for reading.

Try to avoid:
- glare of any type;
- textbooks and other books with print across the illustrations.

Nystagmus

This is a rhythmic involuntary repetitive movement which usually affects both eyes. Nystagmus can occur on its own, but is more likely to be present with other visual impairments, such as albinism, aniridia, congenital cataract. Children with nystagmus have considerable problems (which may increase with stress of any kind), especially in fixation skills, as there is no mechanism for them to hold their eyes still in any position. Some pupils may be helped by being trained to identify the 'null point' – the eye position or direction of gaze in which the movement is most reduced.

Educational implications of nystagmus
The child will benefit from:
  • line markers for reading;
  • reading and writing materials with good bold print, contrast and few distractions.
Remember that:
  • close visual tasks for extended periods of time can lead to visual fatigue;
  • many children turn or tilt or nod their head to obtain the best focus; do not criticise or correct this.

Optic atrophy (OA)
'Optic atrophy' is a generic term which describes the degeneration of the optic nerve. The optic nerve transmits messages from the retina to the visual cortex of the brain. OA can affect a range of visual processes, including visual acuity, field of vision and contrast sensitivity, and can result in loss of vision in the central or peripheral fields and difficulties in adapting to reduced illumination. It can occur on its own or may be linked to other conditions and may be progressive or non-progressive.

Educational implications of optic atrophy
These are similar to those of macular degeneration.
  • Lighting conditions which are glare-free, with perhaps an individual source of light (such as an Anglepoise lamp) are important.
  • Low vision aids are usually prescribed, for instance a hand-held illuminated magnifier or a CCTV or, in some cases, a telescopic lens fitted to spectacles.

Optic nerve hypoplasia (ONH)
Hypoplasia means 'underdeveloped'. In ONH the optic nerve head, called the 'optic disc', appears smaller than usual. This is an emerging major cause of low vision in young children and is seen in premature infants (Good 1993). ONH has educational implications similar to those of optic atrophy.

Retinitis pigmentosa (RP)
RP is a name given to a group of progressive conditions which affect the retina, especially the peripheral area which contains the rods, that is the cells sensitive to vision in dim light. It results in 'tunnel vision' and night blindness. RP is far more common in boys and may be associated with a range of syndromes such as Usher's syndrome (RP plus deafness), Leber's amaurosis and Laurence–Moon–Biedl syndrome. Many of those with RP are

photophobic and may have to wear tinted glasses. The progression of the visual condition varies, but it can be very rapid during adolescence and the young person may become unable to learn by sighted methods. A careful check has to be kept on the person's vision and any suspected changes reported. Professional counselling may be needed for pupil and family.

Educational implications of retinitis pigmentosa

- Due to the contracting visual field there will be difficulties in:
  - the scanning and tracking skills needed for reading;
  - gross motor skills and general mobility, the pupil may appear to become increasingly clumsy;
  - adapting from bright to dull light (the pupil will function as 'blind' in dark areas or at night).
- Some children may be helped by:
  - the use of yellow acetate over print to improve contrast;
  - CCTV and field expander low vision aid;
  - good contrast print materials;
  - a well lit and glare-free working environment;
  - dark lined paper and black fibre pens;
  - use of the smallest print possible, so that the remaining field of vision receives the maximum amount of information (see Figure 5.2).
- As RP is usually progressive, the special curriculum should include:
  - touch-typing;
  - mobility training (especially at night);
  - braille, if total loss is a prognosis.

Figure 5.2   The benefits of small print for those with RP

Retinopathy of prematurity (RoP)

Formerly known as 'retrolental fibroplasia' this condition occurs in some premature babies of very low birth weight who have received oxygen therapy. Although the processes are unclear, damage to the developing retinae ensues. The severest cases result in blindness, visual acuity is often very poor and there are often associated difficulties, for instance myopia, glaucoma, retinal detachment or nystagmus. There may be associated learning difficulties.

Educational implications of retinopathy of prematurity
Educational implications are similar to those of macular degeneration plus:
- pupils with RoP may need extra help in developing
  - orientation and mobility skills
  - fine and gross motor skills
  - visual perceptual skills.

Squint
The term 'squint' is synonymous with 'strabismus', 'lazy eye', 'cast' or 'wall eye'. While there are different types of squint, the most common type to be found in a child is a manifest squint. This is an obvious deviation of one eye, inwards, outwards, upwards, downwards or a combination of these movements. The squint may be present all the time or intermittently, such as, only without glasses, at a certain distance or when the child is tired. Manifest squints can occur at any time and age, but many are congenital and treatment usually takes place before the child starts school. The peak age for the onset of squint is between 1 and 4 years.

An uncorrected squint will impair and prevent binocular vision, reducing the field and depth of vision, and if a squint occurs with another visual condition, such as cataracts, then a careful assessment of the child's visual functioning should be made, as the squint adds a serious difficulty to an existing problem.

Any child with monocular vision will be at a disadvantage in games or other activities which rely upon rapid eye–motor coordination. Close supervision is needed in practical lesson such as chemistry or food technology.

Educational implications of squint
- For young children the unaffected eye may be occluded (patched) resulting in severely reduced visual acuity and possible teasing.
- Double vision may occur when the eye is not patched.
- Attention should be paid to seating in the classroom to maximise use of the 'good' eye.

Additional syndromes and conditions

Cortical visual impairment (CVI)

CVI can be described as temporary or permanent visual loss caused by a disturbance of the posterior visual pathways and/or occipital lobes (Jan 1993). These disturbances may result from many causes (some of which are unknown) which include increased levels of oxygen given to the pre-term baby, congenital brain malformations, head injuries (including non-accidental injuries), failure of the shunt (the draining valve) in hydrocephalus. The retinae of these children appear normal and it is often the visual behaviour of the children which helps in the diagnosis (Jan 1993). For example, such children may:

- not appear to be blind, but may have a very short visual span;
- see very little and their visual skills may vary from minute to minute;
- see lines and shapes but not recognise them;
- discriminate colourful objects, especially yellow and red, more easily than black and white ones;
- turn their heads to look at objects, as peripheral vision may be better than central vision;
- gaze at lights including the sun (very dangerous!);
- be photophobic;
- have a 'blind sight', a level of subconscious vision which enables them to move around without bumping into objects;
- have good navigational skills;
- have associated neurological problems, for instance motor disabilities;
- look at objects at a very close distance;
- only see stationary objects;
- have jerky, abnormal eye movements (not nystagmus);
- be low functioning and uncooperative.

Some degree of visual recovery is thought to be possible so this information is vital to those working with such children. Expert intervention is needed. A good starting point is *Vision for Doing* by Aitken and Buultjens, (1992) and Hyvärinen (1995b).

Down's syndrome

A high proportion of pupils with Down's syndrome have visual problems including cataracts, nystagmus, refractive errors and strabismus (squints).

Marfan's syndrome

Marfan's syndrome is an inherited condition, characterised by abnormally long and slender fingers, toes and other bones, congenital heart problems, general muscular underdevelopment, and eye defects such as subluxated lens (dislocated lens) and clefts of the iris resulting in general blurring or even double vision. In addition, distance acuity and focusing on near tasks will be poor.

Retinoblastoma

This a malignant tumour of the retina. In many cases, the eye is enucleated (removed) but in cases where it is not, vision is often damaged as a result of the radiation treatment.

Rubella (German measles)

The effects of rubella depend upon the timing of the exposure of the foetus to the virus, the first three months being the most dangerous time. Exposure can affect the development of the eyes, ears, heart and lungs. Visual defects take the form of cataracts, corneal opacities, glaucoma, and microphthalmia (underdeveloped eyes). Many of these children are very sensitive to light, and surgery for cataracts is often unsuccessful due to viral infections present in the eye.

Usher's syndrome

This is a dual sensory impairment which is progressive in nature. A major cause of deafness amongst adults, this condition is distressing as it is associated with retinitis pigmentosa (see above) which can also lead to blindness. As the syndrome appears in three different forms, medical advice must be sought. Young people with this condition need careful and expert counselling and guidance.

Chapter 6

Assessment of Vision

Heather Mason

Introduction

In this chapter the differences between visual acuity and functional vision are explained and the ways in which the vision of a child can be assessed are examined. The reader is also alerted to some of the more obvious indications of visual impairment.

The majority of severe visual problems are picked up at birth or within the first few months. In some cases they will be identified at the maternity hospital or by the health visitor, in other cases it will be the parents who first notice their baby's visual difficulties. Once it is suspected that a child may have a visual impairment, the paediatrician or family doctor will refer the child to an ophthalmologist. Some difficulties may not be brought to light until the child reaches school, where they are revealed either through routine medical screening or as a result of indications in behaviour or academic attainment which alert teachers to a possible visual difficulty. Jose (1983) and Mason (1995) list some of the indications of a visual impairment which may be observed within the classroom.

1. Appearance of the eyes
Normal eyes are clear and straight and should move together and fix steadily. Symptoms of abnormalities may include:
- inflamed, cloudy, bloodshot or weeping eyes;
- eyelids which are drooping, swollen or encrusted;
- frequent sties;
- squint of any kind (eyes appear crossed at any time, one eye turned inwards or outwards, eyes don't seem straight especially when the child is tired);
- unusual eye movements including a rapid involuntary movement of both eyes either in a horizontal or vertical direction, sometimes called 'dancing' or 'wobbly' eyes (the medical term is 'nystagmus');
- blinking, rubbing and screwing up of the eyes and obvious discomfort in bright light, eyes feeling 'dusty';
- cloudy appearance of the corneas.

2. Other indications of a visual impairment

Observations of the child's general behaviour can provide evidence which might suggest a visual impairment:

- movement of head rather than eyes while reading;
- an unusually short or long working distance;
- poor posture at the desk, sitting awkwardly or in a bent or twisted position;
- an unusual sideways gaze when concentrating on a visual task;
- frowning or facial grimaces;
- complaints of dizziness, headaches or general eye discomfort;
- clumsy movements, bumping into objects at the side or at the feet, moving down steps cautiously;
- fear of heights;
- stumbling over or bumping into objects;
- poor balance;
- reluctance to join in playground activities;
- not answering to questions or commands unless addressed by name (often mistaken for 'rude' or uncooperative behaviour);
- turning head to use one eye only or covering one eye;
- tensing the body when reading or viewing a distant object.

3. Signs in school work

While many children with no visual impairment display some of the following symptoms, it is possible that singly or in combination these observations may indicate impaired or fluctuating vision:

- inconsistent quality or variations in the amount of work completed;
- unusual fatigue during or after completing a visual task;
- deterioration in reading after a lengthy period;
- poor attention or concentration span, especially when activities are being demonstrated across the room;
- fumbling over fine hand–eye coordination activities;
- wanting to be very close to a TV or computer monitor;
- errors in reading and writing, especially reversals and omissions;
- difficulties in reading long words;
- confusion in reading certain letters, such as 'cl' for 'd', 'm' for 'n';
- writing and spacing letters and words in an unusual manner;
- tiny, slanting writing with little awareness of lines;
- partly formed letters or letters drawn in the wrong sequence;
- problems with reading back own handwriting;
- difficulty in copying correctly from the blackboard or even from a textbook or other sources;
- an increasing gap between comprehension and reading rate, and accuracy scores on a standardised test such as the Neale Analysis of Reading Ability;

- very slow reading rates, using a finger to keep place and to guide the eyes;
- consistently losing the place when reading;
- difficulty in searching for information on a page, for instance when using a dictionary or interpreting a graph;
- restlessness and lack of interest in activities requiring prolonged close work;
- difficulties in reading poor quality worksheets or in processing information which is not presented in a linear manner;
- written work which does not reflect oral ability.

Regardless of the age of the child, it is essential that any suspicions of visual impairment are fully investigated.

Assessment of visual acuity

This section looks at the different ways in which vision can be assessed. There are two main types of assessment, one which measures the amount of vision children have and another which assesses functional vision, that is how well children use the amount of vision they have.

Visual acuity can be described as:
- the ability to discriminate high contrast fine detail at a distance;
- the power of the eye to distinguish form;
- the sharpness and clarity of vision;

A full assessment of vision would normally include:

1. a distance vision test;
2. a near vision test;
3. a field of vision test to indicate if the field is full or restricted;
4. a colour vision test to check whether colours can be recognised and named;
5. a contrast sensitivity test to see how contrast affects how the child uses their vision;
6. an assessment of visual functioning, i.e. how the child uses their vision for specific purposes.

In the first three tests above, each eye is usually tested independently and then both eyes are tested together. Binocular visual acuity is normally slightly better than monocular vision and a lesser value can be an indication of a problem. Near and distance vision will normally be tested with and without any visual aids such as spectacles which the child may have.

Lea Hyvärinen, well known for her developmental work in devising appropriate visual acuity measurements for children, is of the opinion that when testing children, it is better to start with near vision testing since this enables the child to learn the testing procedures and symbols.

One of the problems facing the ophthalmologist during clinical assessment of a small child is that many of the testing procedures assume that the child is able to cooperate verbally. A picture of the child's vision can, however, be built up in three ways:

- objective vision tests which involve some triggering and recording of reflexes in which the child does not participate actively, such as reactions of the pupil of the eye to light, electrical responses from the cerebral cortex;
- subjective vision tests which require active and specific responses from the child, for instance, matching, comparing;
- behavioural observation of specific or non-specific behaviour such as performance in tasks within the school or home. This usually involves the cooperation of a wide range of people including parents, teachers and carers for example and is not necessarily medically orientated.

Objective tests

Without relying on participation from the child, the ophthalmologist can draw conclusions about the child's vision from the following.

- The appearance of the eyes and the back of the eye.
- The position and movement of the eyes, such as the presence of nystagmus or squint or abnormal head posture or gaze.
- Blinking reflexes.
- Changes in the shape or size of the pupil when a light is shone in the eye.
- The child's reaction to OKN (optokinetic nystagmus) procedures. Jerky movements of the eye (nystagmus) can be produced by rotating vertical stripes or random dots on a drum in front of the eye.
- The response to electrophysiological investigations in which the transmission of visual information from photoreceptors in the visual cortex triggers off measurable electrical responses. There are two main methods of investigation:
  - ERG (electroretinogram), which is the examination of the electrical changes produced within in the retina;
  - VEP (visually evoked potential), which involves measuring the electrical responses of the visual cortex of the brain to various light sources.

It can be seen that these tests require highly skilled interpretation and that they yield information about the basic prerequisites of vision. They can provide information about the functioning of the visual reflexes or of the visual cortex, but they cannot provide information about how the brain is interpreting the information which has been received.

Subjective vision tests

These are assessments of vision which require children to use their hearing, motor, speech and language skills to understand and to respond to instructions. They may be inappropriate for children with severe additional cognitive or physical disabilities. They are usually administered by medical personnel but they may also be employed by trained teachers of the visually impaired.

For tests of this kind, it is useful (and sometimes essential) to have two people involved. This allows one person to record the information while the other presents the test to the child. It may also be useful to use a video to record responses as this provides valuable baseline information for future comparisons.

In all these procedures the tester must be thoroughly familiar with every aspect of the test and the conditions required for administering it.

Tests of distance vision used with children

The Snellen Test

The most common method of measuring distance vision is by means of the Snellen test chart which consists of letters or numbers or pictures arranged in rows of different sizes (Figure 6.1).

Each row of letters on the chart can be recognised at a certain distance by people with normal vision, for instance, at 60, 36, 24, 18, 12, 9 or 6 metres. Children stand 6 metres away from the chart and if they can read down the chart as far as the row of the 6-metre letters, then their visual acuity is 6/6 (pronounced 'six-six') or 'normal'. If they can read only as far as the 24-metre letters, then their visual acuity is 6/24 ('six-twenty four').

The top figure always represents the distance from the chart, and the bottom figure, the distance at which the normal eye can see the letters. In other words, if the distance vision is 6/24, letters which can be read by the normal eye at 24 metres can only be read at 6 metres by the child. The figure is not a fraction of normal sight, and it is not uncommon to have considerable differences in distance vision of the two eyes, such as 6/6 and 6/24.

If children are unable to read the 60 metres line (the top letter on the chart) at 6m, then their vision is less than 6/60 and the test is carried out at a shorter distance. If the child can read the top letter from 3 metres away from the chart then a figure of 3/60 is recorded but if the child can only read the top letter from 1 metre away, then the visual acuity is 1/60. Where the vision is less than this, it was sometimes the practice to estimate the child's ability to count fingers (CF) at varying distances between 15 centimetres and 1 metre. If the child is unable to do this then vision may be recorded as PL, LP or LPO, which are variations on 'Perception of light only'.

Definitions

Terminology is difficult to avoid when talking about visual acuity and the same terms may be interpreted differently from one country to another. However, the definitions of the World Health Organization (WHO) are now widely accepted.

Table 6.1   Classification of visual acuity

Visual acuity	WHO classification
6/6 to 6/18	Normal vision
<6/18 to ≥3/60	Low vision
(Worse than 6/18 but better than or equal to 3/60)	
<3/60	Blind

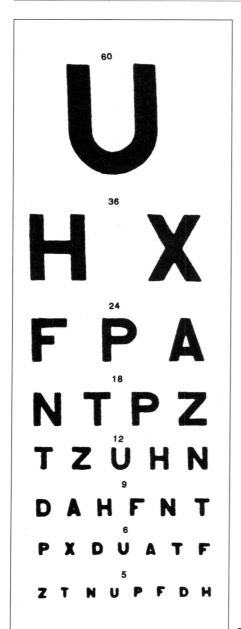

Figure 6.1 A Snellen chart.

The STYCAR Test

The Sheridan Test for Young Children and Retardates (STYCAR) consists of a series of assessments which reveal information about a child's:

- approximate visual acuity
- field of vision
- perception of shape.

Three sub-tests are used in order to gather information: the miniature toy test, the ball test and the letter test. The miniature toy test consists of two sets of 2-inch high cars, aeroplanes, dolls, chairs, knives, forks and spoons; two sets of $3^1/_4$-inch high knives, forks and spoons; and one 5-inch high doll. These are presented to the child at set distances starting with 3 metres. The child's ability to match and identify the items is recorded.

The Sheridan ball test is used to ascertain approximations of children's visual acuity and field of vision and it can be applied in two different ways; by rolling each ball or by attaching it to a rod. In the rolling balls test, different sized white balls are rolled on a black surface between two people. The visual behaviour of the child, who sits at a predetermined distance from the activity, is observed. The child can be included in the 'game' by being encouraged to collect the ball and put it in a bucket. In the other ball test, one of the testers stands behind a dark screen and moves white balls (attached to a rod) from various positions at the side to the centre of the screen. Another variation is for the tester to stand behind the child and move the balls forward in various directions. In each case, the observer is watching at what point in the visual field the child notices the balls. It is suggested that this test can be used with children with a mental age of 6–8 months and beyond.

The Sheridan letter test consists of white plastic symmetrical letters of the alphabet (e.g A, O, H) which have to be matched by the child to letters on cards. The child is not required to identify the letter by name, only to identify its shape by pointing.

The BUST (Perception of Form/Visual Acuity) tests

These are Swedish tests of form perception and visual acuity, and can be used with children whose mental age is between 18 months and 7 years. There are three sub-tests (or series) consisting of pictures of objects or shapes on playing cards. The first series comprises nine pictures of differing sizes of a cup, a flower, a wheel and a clock; while the second consists of pictures of spectacles, scissors, a spoon and a fork. Actual objects are also used alongside these cards. The final series has a similar number of cards (again in differing sizes) depicting a ring, a square, an apple and a house. There are a variety of ways in which the cards and objects can be used, and the idea is to make the matching activities into a game. The tasks within the game can be increased in difficulty, for instance the child can be asked to choose between smaller pictures which are quite similar (scissors/spectacles; wheel/clock). Skilled observers can obtain a useful visual measurement using these materials.

Kay Picture Test

This consists of a series of cards depicting shapes of familiar objects, for example, train, bird, boot or fish, in varying sizes representing equivalents from 60 metres to 6 metres on the Snellen chart.

Sonksen–Silver Acuity System (SSAS)

The SSAS has been designed to assess visual acuity in children as young as two-and-a-half years. It uses a linear display of letters (O, X, H, T, U and V) in a flip-over booklet. The child has to match the letters to a key card. The test is usually administered at 3 metres or

6 metres. The smallest display of five letters which can be identified by children gives an indication of their visual acuity, either monocularly or binocularly. It is a quick test and has been used extensively with excellent results with younger children (Salt *et al.* 1995).

Tests of near vision used with children

Near vision acuity is the vision used for tasks such as reading, writing and other types of close work. Testing near vision usually consists of reading print of different sizes. Each print size is given an N number, the larger the N number, the larger the print. N5 is the smallest type size; some children who are visually impaired will use print as large as N60. The size of print is recorded with the distance in centimetres at which it is read, for example 'N5 at 25 cm' (see Figure 6.2).

Just as in distance acuity measurement, there are a number of ways in which near visual acuity of young children can be assessed. Examples would include the Reduced Kay Pictures test, the BUST-LH and the McClure Reading Test Types, which are graded both for size and reading age.

This assessment is crucial as it enables the optometrist to advise about the size of print needed by the young person in schoolwork and also the type of low vision aid (see Chapter 7) which may be appropriate.

Testing fields of vision

The size of field of vision represents the area that a person can see from all parts of the eye when looking straight ahead. Some conditions, for example retinitis pigmentosa, can result in severely reduced fields of vision (such as tunnel vision), or others may cause 'scotomas' – areas of the retina where there is reduced sensitivity and functioning. Having a scotoma has been compared to looking at a jigsaw with a piece of the puzzle missing. The field of vision can be mapped out so that it can be compared with normal vision (for example, see Figure 6.3).

Tests of colour perception

The most common loss of colour vision is in the red/green part of the spectrum and is usually inherited, with more males (9%) being affected than females (1%). According to Hyvärinen and Lindstedt (1981), the practical clinical significance of this type of 'uncomplicated colour vision deficiency' in a healthy child is not very great. However other kinds of losses, which may include blue/yellow deficiency, may provide important clues in the diagnosis of a visual impairment. Teachers will need to appreciate the nature of any colour loss to make the necessary curriculum adaptations for the child. A knowledge of the type of colour deficiency will be important in devising suitable materials for training the child's residual vision.

N5
Here is a dog and here is a ball.
The dog has fun with the ball.

N6
Here is a girl and here is a cat
The girl can play with the cat and a toy

N8
Here is a boy and here is a big dog.
They have fun with the ball.

N10
Here is a pig and here is a tree.
I can see the pig and the big tree.

N12
Here is a girl and here is a shop
It is a sweet shop and a toy shop.

N14
Here is a man and here is a cat.
The cat has fun with a toy

N18
The boy and his sister go on holiday. They go

N24
The brother and sister walked

N36
On the way they

N48
They go out in a

Figure 6.2 Example of N Print Test

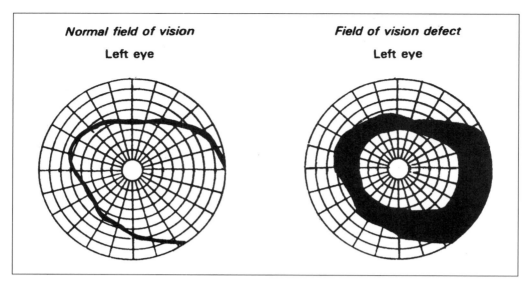

Figure 6.3 Fields of vision

There are several tests used for testing colour vision but the one most likely to be recognised by teachers is the Ishihara Test, which consists of pseudo-isochromatic or confusion plates. These plates intermingle a number or symbol in a background of coloured dots. The normal eye can see the symbol or number, but children who have a loss of colour vision loss will be unable to see the numbers or will interpret them wrongly. This test will not detect blue-yellow defects.

Another type of test requires the subject to match a range of colours (hues and saturations) or to put them in 'hue order'. Two examples of these are the Farnsworth-Munsell 100 Hue Test, which is suitable to use with children as young as six, and the City University Colour Vision Test. None of these three tests are considered entirely reliable for children with severe visual impairments.

A more recent test, the PV-16 Quantitative Vision Test (Hyvärinen 1995b) can be used with very young children as well as with older children and adults. It is similar in many respects to the Farnsworth test but has some unique diagnostic aspects.

Contrast sensitivity

It has been found that some people who appear to have normal visual acuity when assessed using the traditional Snellen chart experience a noticeable loss of functional vision in particular circumstances. These people typically have poor responses to medium or low frequencies in a contrast sensitivity test. In practical terms this means that they will be unable to read easily unless it is a very dark print on a white background in good illumination. Reduced contrast sensitivity can also have a negative effect upon mobility and orientation especially in poor lighting conditions. As Hyvärinen (1995b) points out, for many everyday functions, the ability to appreciate contrast is important. In communication for instance, facial features and expressions are usually at low contrast. Because visual communication between parent and child during the early months of life is so important, Hyvärinen suggests that the visual sphere in which the infant can respond to low contrast facial information should be evaluated continually. One way of doing this is to use the 'Hiding Heidi' Low Contrast Face Test designed by Hyvärinen.

Behavioural observations to determine visual functioning

It may be possible to obtain some idea of the pupil's visual acuity by using the methods described, but it then becomes important to find out how well the child makes use of vision in the performance of daily tasks. This use of vision is known as 'visual functioning'. Two pupils with no obvious learning or additional difficulties, but with exactly the same type of eye condition and recorded visual acuity (for instance, 3/60), may function in quite different ways. The first child may be eager to use their vision and display good mobility and orientation skills; the other may perform like a child who has no vision at all.

Keeffe (1995) lists factors which can affect how well a person can see and recognise objects:

- whether objects are familiar or strange
- distance of objects
- size of objects
- detail or simplicity of objects
- amount of light on the object
- contrast against the background
- colour of the object
- whether objects are still or moving
- how easy the object is to find
- position of the object
- time available for looking.

It is very important to be aware of the possible range of visual functioning within groups of children with additional difficulties. According to Barraga (1983), visual functioning is primarily developmental: the more visual experiences the child has, the more the pathways to the brain are stimulated, and the greater the accumulation of a variety of visual images and memories. It is crucial to have a clear understanding of the present level of visual functioning of a child with a visual impairment and to be aware that it can be improved with training.

This assessment of functional vision is usually made by the qualified advisor/peripatetic teacher of the visually impaired. The teacher will collect information from a range of people regarding the visual functioning of the children and from the children themselves. To assist in assessing the child's visual skills the teacher might employ commercially available procedures such as the *Look and Think* procedure (Chapman *et al.* 1989), or

Vision for Doing (Aitken and Buultjens 1992) if the child has additional difficulties.

The teacher will conduct a thorough investigation into the child's strengths and weaknesses in the way they use their vision and note the child's:

- preferred lighting and position in class and for certain activities, for example, watching TV, observing teacher demonstrations, using a computer;
- access to blackboard information;
- mobility in familiar and unfamiliar places, and ability to adapt to changing lighting conditions;
- preferred print sizes and contrast;
- ability to cope in practical activities, such as science;
- ability to cope in other areas of the curriculum, such as sporting activities – does the pupil take a full and active part in all team and individual events?
- speed of working – the amount of unfinished work is a useful indicator;
- personal organisational skills, for instance, is the child continually losing things?
- ability and willingness to use any prescribed LVAs, such as CCTV, hand magnifier.

Other observations may include:

- level of independence
- social integration in and out of the classroom.

In addition, the child should be observed and assessed in a range of 'visual' perceptual skills which might include:

- locating and fixating on an object long enough to recognise it;
- tracking moving objects, scanning with the eyes, and moving the gaze from one object to another;
- discriminating objects, for example recognising an object from the outline shape;
- identifying patterns, for instance recognising symmetrical and non symmetrical patterns or matching identical features such as numbers and letters;
- hand–eye coordination, for instance completing a tracing activity such as a maze;
- identifying facial expressions and body gestures.

The observations and resulting profile should take account of the child's social, cognitive and intellectual development. It should also contain information about the child's working environment, recommendations about adaptations which are needed, and any training in special curricular areas, such as mobility and orientation or keyboard skills, which will facilitate access to the mainstream curriculum. The report will also suggest specific activities which will help to improve any visual perceptual skills found to be underdeveloped. It will also follow up the suggestions made by the ophthalmologist regarding the use of low vision aids. If this information is to be written into a Statement of Special Educational Needs, in England and Wales, then it must either be written by a qualified teacher of the visually impaired or in consultation with one. (See Part 2 Section 7 (5) of the 1994 Regulations, Department for Education (DfE) 1994.)

Summary

Measurement of a child's vision tells only part of the story about how a child 'sees'. How the child uses their vision in and out of the classroom is the critical factor in educational performance. Two children with the same visual condition and eye condition may function quite differently. Good classroom practice will harness all the information available to ensure access to the curriculum and will acknowledge that with training, visual perceptual skills can be improved.

Chapter 7

Low Vision Devices for Children and Young People with a Visual Impairment

David Bennett

Introduction

The plethora of low vision devices (LVDs) provides low vision practitioners with a wide range of options for assisting the child with a visual impairment. There should be no circumstance under which the child with low vision is unable to be helped with a form of low vision device appropriate to the child's educational needs.

A visual welfare team, including an optometrist, a teacher of the visually impaired, a rehabilitation officer and the child's parents will need to consult together and with the child to provide the most suitable forms of devices for the child's individual requirements. The importance of assessment by a suitably qualified optometrist cannot be stressed too highly, as an accurate spectacle prescription is the first stage in a low vision consultation. The optometrist, who has a high degree of knowledge about the particular disease processes involved, can perform the refractive examination and assess and advise on the low vision problems presented.

For many children, a low vision device can be an extremely versatile item. In other cases, devices may be of limited or specific help, and there is no standard approach or uniform solution since each child has different visual needs.

The use of reading stands

Many optical devices require close and critical working distances, which are more easily facilitated by the use of a reading stand. Reading stands of many designs are available for use with low vision devices (Figure 7.1). The stand should have an adjustment for varying its height and angle and include a supporting shelf on which to place reading material. Some stands incorporate a clip at the top of the stand which will hold loose papers in place.

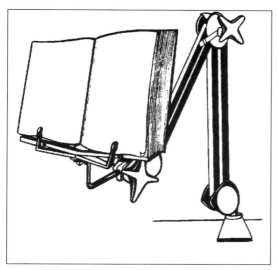

Figure 7.1

LVDs: three key elements

The importance of light

The most effective LVD is light. Light is the first LVD that should be considered, questioned and assessed during a low vision consultation. If the ambient light levels are low and there is insufficient light available, an Anglepoise lamp with a moving omni-directional head should be used, preferably a lamp with a low wattage (Figure 7.2). The low wattage is essential for comfortable use as the heat produced is minimal in comparison with that from a standard incandescent bulb.

Figure 7.2

Spectacle prescription

The second and next most effective low vision device is an accurate spectacle prescription that has been correctly fitted. Between 10 and 15% of children with a visual impairment may be assisted by spectacles and often this is all that may be required.

The use of magnification

The third element to be required is a type of external magnification. This magnification can be obtained by:

- increasing the size of the object (size magnification)
- decreasing the working distance to the object (relative distance magnification)
- increasing the visual angle (relative angular magnification), usually done by a multi-lens system such as a telescope.

It is often the case that all three basic techniques are used simultaneously. If this is the case then the resulting magnification will be the product of the magnification supplied by the various methods. In the following example, the child with a visual impairment wishes to watch television and requires 2× magnification to do so. There are three possible options:

- supplying the child with a television set which has a larger tube diameter of 50 centimetres (cm) instead of the present 25 cm;
- reducing the distance at which the child sits from the habitual 6 metres (m) to a distance of 3 m
- supplying the child with a telescope giving 2× magnification;

If all three are supplied together then the total magnification achieved is not 6× but 8× (that is $2 \times 2 \times 2$).

Myopia

Children with a visual impairment caused by high levels of myopia can often be seen removing their spectacles in order to view close objects. This should come as no surprise to the teacher. The level of myopia in dioptres (D) is the reciprocal of the focal length of the myopic eye (that is, 1 metre divided by the focal length). Children with myopia who are observed removing their distance spectacles should not be discouraged from so doing as this will enable them to achieve a level of magnification consistent with their uncorrected myopia. For example, if the child is a myope of −10.00 D, the uncorrected eye has a focusing point at 1/10 m (10 cm), giving an effective magnification of 2.5×. Similarly, a myope of −12.00 D will have a close working distance of 1/12 m (8 cm) from the eye and will have an effective inbuilt magnification of 3×.

Magnification devices

Now let us look at the devices available to the child with a visual impairment. These can broadly be classified into three categories:

1. *Basic low technology magnifiers*
   hand magnifiers
   stand magnifiers

flat bed magnifiers
line magnifiers
2. *Mid-range technology magnifiers*
spectacle mounted devices
telescopic devices
3. *High technology magnifiers*
closed circuit television (CCTV) and electronic magnification.

Basic low technology magnifiers

The hand magnifier

This is the simplest and most widely used form of LVD (Figure 7.3). Great care is needed here as the magnification quoted on the magnifier may not be the one that has actually been prescribed for the child. The reason for this is that manufacturers use different formulae for calculating the magnification for their devices. In the United Kingdom we use the formula:

Magnification (M) = F/4

where F is the dioptric power of the magnifier.
Throughout the rest of Europe and in other countries the formula:

M = F/4 + 1

is used.

To avoid confusion it is always best to state the dioptric power that is required. Most manufacturers now state the dioptric power of the magnifier on the packaging or in their published catalogue and magnification levels can therefore easily be calculated.

Within the hand magnifier group, powers range from +4.00 D (1×) to +24.00 D (6×). Above these powers the magnifiers are occasionally referred to as 'loupes' and the range can extend to +64.00 D (16×). The usual design of the hand magnifier is a simple plano-convex or bi-convex lens surrounded by a ring of plastic and supported by a plastic handle. Hand magnifiers must be used at a distance from the eye which is close to the magnifier's focal length. For example, if the magnifier is specified as +12.00 D (3×), then it should be held at a distance of 8 cm from the eye. If the child is wearing reading spectacles then they must be taught to maintain a constant distance from the eye to the magnifier and to bring the print in from behind until focus is achieved.

Figure 7.3

The stand magnifier

Stand magnifiers, like their hand-held equivalents, are readily available. The intricacies of the optics of modern stand magnifiers need not be discussed here, however, one particular question is frequently asked: 'should the child with a visual impairment wear their distance or reading glasses with the magnifier?' The answer to this is simple. As a rule of thumb, if a +4.00 D lens is placed over the magnifier and the image through the combined system remains in focus then the child must use the reading spectacles. If the image is blurred then the habitual distance correction should be used.

Stand magnifiers are available from 8.00 D (2×) to 80.00 D (20×) in illuminated and non-illuminated forms (Figures 7.4 and 7.5). In the higher powers, they usually contain an illuminated lamp giving even illumination across the reading surface. At such high levels of magnification a large amount of light is required, and devices may be powered by mains electricity, battery, or a combination of both. It is normally advised that mains power is used as batteries run out at an alarming rate.

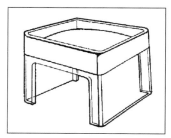

Figure 7.4

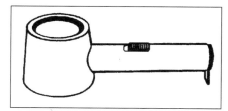

Figure 7.5

A simple stand magnifier is often the first device to be offered to a child with a visual impairment. If the child's acuity is reasonable, then a 20.00 D magnifier is often suitable. When small children are presented with a stand magnifier such as a Coil Horseshoe magnifier, they often place it correctly on the page, have a quick look through then push it away to one side to check that the object is still there! It is at this stage that intervention by way of effective training is needed, with adequate demonstration.

The flat bed magnifier

Also called a brightfield magnifier, the flat bed magnifier is of a fixed focus paperweight type (Figure 7.6). It is has a hemispheric plano-convex design and is used with the plane portion of the magnifier placed in contact with the working plane or reading material. Flat bed magnifiers are available in a variety of diameters from 20 mm to 90 mm and have quoted magnifications of between 1.75× and 2.00×, although recent aspheric lens technology has pushed the magnification up slightly to 2.2×. If a child uses the flat field magnifier between 4 and 5 mm from the work surface, it is usually a sign that a higher magnification is required or that the child's spectacle prescription needs to be checked and updated.

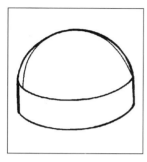

Figure 7.6

Flat bed magnifiers may be mounted in plastic rings which protect the lens surface from damage. They can be used with reading spectacles if appropriate. The main advantage of flat bed magnifiers is their light gathering properties. In this respect, a diffuse light source such as daylight or artificial room light is preferable, since a direct light source from a spotlight tends to cause troublesome glare from surface reflection and hence decreases visual performance. The second advantage is the lack of optical distortion and this will both benefit and maintain binocular potential. Disadvantages are that the field of view is relatively small and the devices are heavier than the equivalent hand or stand magnifier.

The line magnifier

Utilising the same principle as the flat field magnifier, line magnifiers are made in a plano-cylindrical form from optically moulded plastic (Figure 7.7). They lie on the working plane parallel to the reading material and have magnification factors of between 6.00 D (1.5×) and 8.00 D (2×). Some types of line magnifiers have an in-built centimetre or millimetre scale or line and most have a finger grip at one end for easy manoeuvrability.

Figure 7.7

Mid-range technology magnifiers

Spectacle-mounted devices

A spectacle prescription is commonly the most useful LVD that a child with a visual impairment will use. In its simplest form, this device comprises convex or positive lenses mounted in a spectacle frame. The device will give the user the maximum field of vision for a given magnification, with the minimum weight and if made in appropriate form, acceptable thickness. When the magnification levels are high, then base-in prisms are incorporated into the prescription to aid the user's convergence ability. An example of this type of LVD is the Coil Hyperocular range, whose magnification runs from between 4× (+16.00 D) to 12× (+48.00 D).

A distance prescription can be incorporated into a bifocal version of this magnifier. The bifocal lens is screwed into a mounting ring on the front surface of the spectacles, enabling interchange between different magnifications. The Keeler LVA 12 is an example of this bifocal arrangement and magnifications can be varied from 2× (+8.00 D) to 9× (+36.00 D). All lenses are available in plastic and so are light and comfortable to wear.

The 'clip-over' type of device is a simplified version (Figure 7.8). Optically moulded pieces of plastic, again incorporating base-in prisms, are attached by a plastic clip to the front of the spectacles and are available in monocular and binocular forms. The clip-over may be flipped up out of the line of sight so that the distance prescription of the spectacles can be used. Magnifications range from 2× (+8.00 D) to 4× (+16.00 D) binocularly and up to 5× (+20.00 D) monocularly.

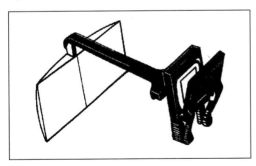

Figure 7.8

Telescopic devices

The simplest and most practical method of improving distance acuity in children with a visual impairment is to reduce the distance between the eye and the object of regard. By halving the working distance, the retinal image size is automatically doubled, yet image quality is unimpaired. Problems arise if the working distance from the eye to the object of regard is fixed. In this instance, telescopic LVDs are the method by which distance vision is improved. Telescopes are designed as fixed focus or variable focus and can be independent from, or attached to spectacles. There are two basic types of telescope:

- the Galilean
- the Keplerian, or astronomical telescope.

Both these devices use positive (convex) objective lenses, the objective being the lens positioned closest to the object, but differ in the power of the eye lens; the Galilean type uses a negative eye lens (concave) and the Keplerian type a high positive type eye lens (convex). The spectacle mounted types are normally Galilean and used for reading, the hand-held types may be of either design and are commonly used for distance viewing. All telescopic devices are specified in the format A × B, where A is the magnification of the system and B the diameter in millimetres of the objective lens.

Variable focus telescopes

These devices have a variable length between the objective lens and the eye lens, giving the telescope a large focal range. The lenses are contained within a protective metal housing preventing damage from atmospheric dust. By rotating the metal housing the telescope will focus from distance to near. Good examples of variable focus telescopes include the Eschenbach range of short-focus monoculars and the Keeler 8× monocular. The Keeler device is especially useful as it is enclosed in a rubber armoured coat further protecting it from damage in the classroom (Figure 7.9).

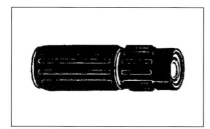

Figure 7.9

Ranges imported from Japan have excellent optics, anti-reflection lenses and magnifications between 2.75× and 10×. Most telescopes of this type are hand-held but those with lower powers can, with the aid of a clip mount, be attached to a pair of spectacles. If the child with a visual impairment has similar acuity in both eyes, then the telescopes can be mounted binocularly into a spectacle frame, also incorporating the child's prescription.

Fixed focus telescopes

These devices lack the variable focus element of the telescopes described above and hence can only be used in conjunction with the child's distance prescription. They are primarily used for distance viewing only. A typical example of this device is the inconspicuous 'finger ring' telescope (Figure 7.10).

Fixed focus near telescopes may also be mounted onto a spectacle lens incorporating the child's prescription. Carl Zeiss and Eschenbach produce comprehensive ranges. Fixed focus distance telescopes are also made in binocular form, as in the theatre-type binocular, and as such are able to incorporate a pupillary distance adjustment.

Figure 7.10

High technology magnifiers

Closed circuit television (CCTV)

CCTVs tend to be used today for children with more severe visual impairment who require a higher degree of magnification than can be obtained from an optical type of device. CCTVs comprise a television camera mounted above an X-Y moveable table and connected to a video display monitor (Figure 7.11). In most cases the camera is fixed, pointing down towards the platform, requiring the object to be placed underneath the camera lens. The platform has no height adjustment and therefore magnification can only be obtained electronically or by the use of a zoom camera. Magnifications range between 2× and 100×. It is important to use a good quality monitor where flicker frequencies are greater than 50 Hertz (Hz) because this has the effect of eliminating the mains flicker which has been found to reduce acuity in low vision cases. Modern systems are made with a flicker frequency of above 60 Hz.

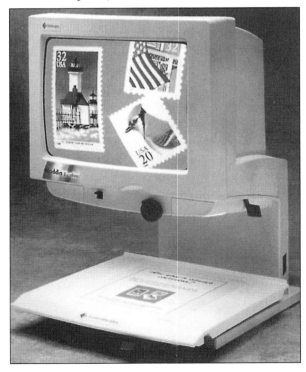

Figure 7.11

CCTVs are available in either monochrome or colour versions. The use of colour CCTVs for children with a macular dysfunction is questionable as black and white systems will often give better results. The two options available with monochrome CCTVs are displaying black print on a white background or using a negative system to provide white on a black background. It is has been found that using the white on black arrangement is more comfortable and gives better acuity for those suffering from retinitis pigmentosa.

A great advantage of the CCTV system is the ability to vary the illumination and contrast of the image produced. A child with a visual impairment will often prefer a higher contrast than exists on the original document. Experience has shown that children with degenerative macular conditions and those involving loss of transparency of the optical media, require considerably more illumination and contrast than would normally be expected.

More complex CCTV systems may provide additional features. They may be linked to a typewriter or interfaced with a computer. A distance camera may also be incorporated so that the blackboard as well as reading material may be viewed. In this case, the CCTV will have a split screen so that the distance material may be seen on one side and reading material on the other. It is also possible to 'shutter' parts of the screen so that a typoscopic arrangement can be obtained, that is, where only one line of print is showing. In the black on white mode the shutter parts are black and in the white on black mode they appear white. Facilities are also available for underlining text.

There are, of course, many problems associated with CCTV systems as compared with their simple optical counterparts. They are significantly more expensive and lack portability. The latter problem has been addressed in more recent years with the introduction of a hand-held computer mouse type of camera linked to a conventional television set (Figure 7.12). Its range of magnification is variable, depending on the size of the screen but with larger, modern 'flat' screens, magnifications of up to 25× can be achieved. All hand-held portable systems are currently available only in black and white; however, colour systems will become available in the near future.

Figure 7.12

The use of CCTV in combination with other devices

Other LVDs may be used in conjunction with the CCTV. For example, a simple line magnifier with a mount on either side of the screen can be an effective way of increasing the magnification from a display unit. Alternatively, a hand magnifier may be mounted on a flexible arm, similar to an Anglepoise lamp so that it can be pushed in front of the screen and back out of the way as simply as possible. Another way of improving CCTV magnification is to interface it with a computer system, for which special software is required.

Filter lenses

In the first part of this chapter, emphasis was placed on the use of light when dealing with children with a visual impairment. In general, increased illumination is essential for accurate, swift and comfortable reading. However, in some medical conditions light actually impairs vision and reduces acuity. Children with cone dysfunctions, achromatopsia, albinism, unoperated cataracts and corneal scarring are all prone to reduced vision under high illumination, and decreasing the unfocused, scattered light reaching the retina can be extremely helpful. The typoscope, a black shield which covers the reading page except for the horizontal split aperture to expose one line of print, can reduce light scatter by decreasing the amount of reflected light on the white page. With distance viewing, specialist sunglasses are of great benefit. However, off-the-shelf sunglasses are not advised. Practical experience has shown that proprietary tints are not dark enough to be of benefit to the child with a visual impairment and, in the case of photochromic lenses, the range of change is less than that which is desired. For many, the darker the lens that is prescribed, the more comfortable the vision.

Sunglass lenses have recently been developed specifically for use by those with a visual impairment, namely the 'NOIR' range and a series of filter lenses, known as CPF lenses, are available from Corning. There is no question that the use of these filters provides many people with a great source of comfort. Those with the pathological conditions mentioned above have found their visual acuity to be improved by as much a whole line on a Snellen chart when wearing these lenses.

Prescribing low vision devices

Psychological factors need to be taken into account when prescribing for children with a visual impairment. There is little point in prescribing an array of low vision devices if the child refuses to use them. Placing pressure upon a child to use a particular device may result in their rebelling and a refusal to acknowledge the help that the device may provide. It is important for parents to share in the burden of this psychological process of acceptance, and communication links between the parents and the child's visual welfare team must be maintained to maximise the child's potential for further visual development. Adolescence still remains a stumbling block in low vision rehabilitation. Children who happily use LVDs at the age of 12 often refuse to use them during their teenage years. The choice of devices prescribed at any particular low vision assessment must give due deference to cosmesis and the environment in which it is to be used. Acceptance of complex optical devices is often difficult and a relaxed attitude to their prescribing and use will often help. Insistence on use in any particular situation is likely to find the child refusing to use the device at all.

Conclusion

Children with a visual impairment may be assisted by a variety of devices and should be encouraged to use them at home, at school and at play. Children often reject low vision devices at their first assessment but rather than give up, the visual welfare team should aim to encourage the child at each assessment to experiment with various devices of suitable magnification. Encouragement and correct training with these devices will lead to a gradual acceptance by the child. Training in the use of both optical and non-optical low vision devices must be given to the child in order that they may use the device to its fullest effect. Routine assessment and follow-up should be advised every 6–12 months and sooner if the child, teacher or parent so wishes. More information on training with low vision devices can be found in a recent video entitled *Low Vision Aids – Effective Management of Children With a Visual Impairment*, produced by the University of Birmingham.

Chapter 8
Assessment Procedures

Michael Tobin

Introduction

This chapter concerns the assessment of abilities that are relevant to the progress of children with visual impairments during the course of their school years. The remit here is the description and evaluation of procedures that can be used by teachers and educational psychologists for determining children's needs and abilities in the school setting.

The organisation of the chapter, moving from the general to the particular, reflects the author's belief that there is a set of factors applicable to all assessments and which the teacher and psychologist must therefore take into account and that will then guide them in their selection of procedures for identifying needs and abilities. Before these universals are discussed an even more general point must be made.

The performance recorded on a single occasion on a test administered by someone hitherto unknown to the child may grossly underestimate the child's true ability. The imperfection of the test may be exacerbated by the child's nervousness, by the tester's unfamiliarity with the nuances of non-verbal signals, and by the more general problem of establishing the kind of rapport that facilitates the highest level of achievement, and it is the latter that must be the primary goal of the assessor.

General classificatory factors

Because of their influence upon the choice of measurement tools and upon the nature of the relationship between the assessor and the client, it is essential that information be obtained about the learner's age, the age of onset of the visual impairment, the extent of any residual sight that he or she may possess, and the presence of any other disabling conditions.

Chronological age gives clues, not always entirely reliable of course, as to the likely extent of the learner's knowledge base and of the kind of language that will be appropriate. For example, in attempting to measure the reading skills of a six-year-old one would use a different test from the one to be used with a 15-year-old. But it is not only the content of the test that might differ for the older learner in terms of complexity; one would also have to be prepared to discuss the purpose of the testing, to explain whether or not feedback could or could not be given, and to justify the need for applying time limits. With the younger child, there is usually an unquestioning acceptance of the authority of the assessor, but with older learners the notions of empowerment and autonomy have to be recognised if the necessary cooperative environment is to be established.

The age of onset of the impairment, and its duration, can also have a bearing upon the 'what' and 'how' to test. The totally and congenitally blind four-year-old whose sensorimotor development is being assessed with the Reynell–Zinkin Scales (Reynell 1979) may still be having difficulties in sorting beads into two sizes (big and small) and then putting them into corresponding big and small beakers, a task which could be done by many two-year-old normally sighted children and by many three-year-old partially sighted children. A 15-year-old and newly blinded learner may be experiencing considerable difficulties in mastering the intricacies of Standard English Braille, and will therefore have to be assessed very differently from a congenitally blind age-peer. In each case, the choice of test and the manner of presenting it will entail careful consideration, involving decisions as to whether or not the strict rubric of the test manual can be followed.

Most children registered as blind have some potentially useful residual vision, and it is incumbent upon assessors to understand what that vision is and for what purposes and under what lighting conditions it can be used. It is insufficient to rely solely upon the objectively measured visual acuities recorded in medical files. Such information will not unequivocally determine the ideal size, colour, and contrast levels in print-based teaching materials for any given child. The assessor working in the classroom may have to adopt a trial and error approach, using practice items from printed tests to ascertain whether they are within the visual capacity of the young person. Essentially, the assessor will have to devise informal observational methods for measuring the appropriate various visual competencies, but with younger children, a more formal checklist, such as the *Look and Think* procedures (Chapman *et al.* 1989), will produce useful information about perceptual and cognitive skills, and will be helpful in deciding whether commercially published achievement tests would be usable for assessing other skills.

As will be discussed below, most children with visual impairments have other disabilities. This makes it essential that the assessor should know of the existence of these conditions, and should be able not only to select appropriate procedures for measuring them and their effects but should also recognise the need for input from a multi-disciplinary team. No single individual is likely to be expert enough in all the related disciplines to carry out a comprehensive assessment without such support.

What these classificatory factors serve to demonstrate is the heterogeneity of the 'target' population, since they introduce sources of differentiation over and above those we have to be aware of when assessing children with normal vision. Failure to take them into account may render useless the results of the testing or, at the very least, lead to an underestimation of abilities or a misconstruing of needs.

Specialised procedures for pre-school children

The Reynell–Zinkin *Developmental Scales for Young Visually Handicapped Children* (Reynell 1979) cover the age range 0–5 years and assess six conceptually different, but overlapping, areas of functioning, namely: social adaptation, sensorimotor understanding, exploration of the environment, response to sound and verbal comprehension, vocalisation and expressive language (structure), and expressive language (vocabulary and content). The user-manual makes the point that the 'examiner should understand that in using these procedures he is carrying out an assessment rather than administering a test' (Reynell 1979). This implies that the assessor may be scoring the items either by presenting particular tasks directly, or observing the child in her familiar environment, or seeking information from care-givers, and that it will often be necessary to use alternative materials and equipment to determine whether a skill has generalised to a variety of situations.

The scales focus attention upon important skills and developmental progression, and thus enable users to compare children with their age-peers, including those with normal sight, those with partial sight, and those who are blind. They bring out, too, some of the problems encountered by children who are visually impaired as they seek to understand and gain some control over their physical and social 'worlds'.

The *Oregon Project for Visually Impaired and Blind Pre-school Children* (Brown *et al.* 1986) deals with many of the same competencies, and is designed as both an assessment and a teaching programme. Its origins lie in the Portage Project; that is, its rationale and materials are based upon the practice of specialists visiting children's homes, where they work with the parents in setting up goals and exercises for the children. The set of nearly 700 items covers such areas of development as cognition, language, self-help, socialisation, and fine and gross motor skill.

The Reynell–Zinkin and the Oregon Project procedures are especially useful for members of visiting teacher services, nursery teachers, and other professional workers whose work with children is done in the everyday settings of homes, schools, or day nurseries.

Specialised procedures for school-aged children

The *Look and Think Checklist* (Chapman *et al.* 1989) is a means for teachers to assess perceptual and some cognitive skills in children aged 5–11 years. It is intended for administration in the classroom setting, and is described as 'an instrument for the orderly and structured observation of a child's present level of functioning in specified visual skills' (Chapman *et al.* 1989). It contains 18 sub-scales concerned with discriminating among and visually identifying, three- and two-dimensional objects, with assessing hand–eye coordination skills, and with preliminary screening of colour differentiation abilities. It is not a test of visual acuity, of visual fields, or of any physiological aspects of visual functioning. Its rationale is that effective looking depends also upon adequate experience, a willingness to use whatever residual vision there is, and the use of language and other cognitive skills to help direct attention and interpretation. It is claimed that many young, severely visually disabled children have not had adequate opportunities and incentives to use what little vision they have, and the Checklist is a collection of methods to help teachers discover what a child can do, in the classroom rather than the 'ophthalmic' clinic, with a view then to devising exercises (regarded as games by the learner) that will encourage the use of scanning, searching, discriminating, matching, and other perceptual and cognitive skills.

No perceptual quotients or age-related scores are obtainable from the *Look and Think Checklist*. It is, therefore, a criterion-referenced instrument, and the authors see it as a tool for assessment and teaching.

The measurement of intelligence is now based upon the notion that intelligence is multi-faceted. There are different kinds of intelligence which therefore must be measured with different instruments. The *Williams Intelligence Test for Children with Defective Vision* (Williams 1956) represents the older conceptualisation, in which a global intelligence quotient was the numerical product of the test. In fact, the Williams Test, which is the only British test standardised for the population of children who are visually impaired, contains items that can be grouped into larger categories, such as short-term memory, vocabulary, verbal fluency, reasoning, spatial imagery, and the retrieval and application of knowledge. However, separate scores for these distinct abilities cannot be derived from the Williams Test.

When teachers wish to obtain information about a child's abilities in terms of these different mental processes, they recommended to ask an educational psychologist to administer some of the sub-scales of the *British Ability Scales* (BAS; Elliott *et al.* 1983). Among the 23 sub-scales of the BAS, there are some that can be readily used with blind children. For example, the test items in the similarities, recall of digits, and the word definitions sub-scales are all presented orally and require oral responses. For children who are partially sighted, these same sub-scales are also appropriate, and for some of these children useful information can be gleaned from their performances on the BAS speed of information processing, matrices, and block design sub-scales.

The BAS speed of information processing sub-scale consists of items (each occupying a whole page) which require the child to scan lines, first of circles, enclosing varying numbers of small squares and then for older subjects, numbers increasing in length from single-digit to five-digit numbers. In each line, the circle with most squares or the largest value number has to be selected. This task is relatively easy, and what is of interest is the speed of mental functioning. They do, also, 'require certain basic perceptual skills' and although the test was designed for children who are fully sighted, it can, in the writer's opinion, be informative about the difficulties likely to be experienced by learners who are partially sighted on tasks that involve visual exploration of text, of pictures, and of the kinds of diagrams and tables found in science, mathematics, geography, and similar subject matter. A high score will be especially informative but a low score may be as much the product of the learner's impaired vision as of his mental processing speed. For a child going into mainstream schooling, a high score on this test will be a good predictor of ability to cope with the visually presented materials that are characteristic of current methods of teaching. A low score will alert teachers to the need to seek alternative methods of achieving the same objectives.

As will be discussed below when looking at ways of assessing reading skills, reduced speed of processing is one of the educationally handicapping consequences of blindness and low vision, and should be taken into account by teachers, psychologists, and institutions designing examination papers. To complement the print version of the BAS sub-scale, Hull and Mason (1993) have devised and standardised a tactile speed of information processing test. It is easy and quick to administer, and consists of tactile shapes and, for the older subjects, brailled numbers. As yet, no public data are available on the test's predictive power in relation to school achievement, but even without that supportive back-up its users can observe how successfully and efficiently a learner deals with the scanning, processing, and interpreting of the tactile patterns of the test. Of immediate practical significance to teachers is the finding that the brailled numbers take about three times as long to be processed as their counterparts in the BAS print version (Hull and Mason, 1993).

As reading is the bedrock upon which access to the curriculum rests, its assessment must be given especial attention so that appropriate programmes of teaching and remediation can be prepared. In distinguishing between teaching and remediation, the writer's intention is to bring out the importance of regarding the teaching of reading as an activity that should be maintained throughout the whole course of schooling and not merely confined to the primary school years. This is particularly necessary for braille, where the teaching of 'higher order' reading skills should continue after basic mastery of the complexities of the fully contracted code has been acquired. The monitoring of progress in braille cannot be done at all effectively unless the teacher-assessor is herself a competent sighted or touch reader, and thus able to make valid inferences as to the probable causation of any errors made by a young reader. Mistakes may be due to failure in detecting the presence of one of the dots in the braille cell, to inversion and reversal problems, to upper and lower cell mis-readings, or to uncertainty about the meaning of contractions. The diagnostic value of a test must therefore be evaluated, and in this respect there is still much to be said for long-established instruments such as the *Tooze Braille Speed Test* (Tooze 1962) and the *Lorimer Braille Recognition Test* (Lorimer 1962) which are available from VIEW (formerly the Association for the Education and Welfare of the Visually Handicapped).

Both of these tests enable users to pinpoint what Lorimer has described as unique 'braille factors' in the reading process. However, they are word-recognition tests, rather than tests of continuous prose reading. For the latter purpose, the braille version of the *Neale Analysis of Reading Ability* is recommended, since it simultaneously measures accuracy, speed, and comprehension, with the tester's manual making possible the calculation of reading ages and centile rankings when comparisons with population characteristics are required. By tape-recording the child's oral reading, the assessor can re-hear and analyse the performance to diagnose faults and so facilitate the drawing up of a remedial programme. What the Neale test demonstrates, by the availability of print norms, is that tactile reading systems are associated with dramatically reduced reading speeds. This phenomenon has implications across the whole range of the curriculum, for learners, teachers, and the regulators of public examinations. More time for studying texts and for completing examinations is needed, braille-writing machines have to be provided, and some learning, especially at the recording and revision stages, will have to be assisted by the use of audio-tape recorders.

Although the difficulty of slow processing of information is not as great for the student who is partially sighted, it is nevertheless a major problem, and in using printed tests, such as the Neale, the assessor must be prepared for results on the speed sub-scale that are markedly inferior to the student's achievements in terms of accuracy and comprehension of reading. Except for very young readers, the use of word-recognition tests is not recommended as these are likely to hide the low vision reader's difficulties when confronted with 'real' reading, i.e. long passages of continuous prose.

As a quickly administered test of vocabulary, the *British Picture Vocabulary Scale* (BPVS; Dunn *et al.* 1982) can be informative in other ways, as it allows close observation of the use of residual vision by learners who are partially sighted. Each page of the BPVS has four line drawings, and the child chooses the drawing that best represents the word spoken by the tester. During the assessment session, there is the opportunity to note how close to the page the children have to bring their eyes, whether they scan left to right and up and down in a systematic manner, and whether altering the intensity and position of the source of any artificial light makes the task easier. It was not designed as a means of assessing functional vision but the experienced teacher will be alert to clues of this kind that are relevant to functioning in the classroom. In so far as the BPVS measures receptive vocabulary, it also reveals something of the child's prior learning opportunities at home and in school. What is essential is that scores on this test must be evaluated in relation to performance on other, non-visually based tests so that the effects of the visual impairment can be estimated.

Visually impaired learners with other disabilities

The RNIB survey (Walker *et al.* 1992) and other investigations have shown that the majority of children who are visually impaired have other physical, sensory, and cognitive impairments. Some of the procedures already described, such as the Reynell–Zinkin and Oregon Project, do address this issue. In so far as these instruments are primarily concerned with developmental factors operative in the first five or six years of the child's life, they are rather less relevant when it is a matter of assessing the skills and the progress of school-aged learners, especially during the adolescent period. Some older children are so massively delayed in development that it is almost inevitable that assessors will be focusing upon competencies normally attained in early infancy. In these circumstances, many of the test items in the Reynell–Zinkin and Oregon procedures will still be appropriate.

A system that is age-independent and that does more than its title suggests is *Vision for Doing* (Aitken and Buultjens 1992). It has the great merit that assessment and remediation are treated as one. While the emphasis is indeed upon methods of assessing the functional vision of learners who have multiple disabilities, it is concerned too with how learners can be helped to develop and use that vision for enlarging their understanding of the objects, events, and other phenomena of their physical and social environments. The authors describe their principal aim as to 'help staff who are not specialists in visual impairment'. It achieves that objective certainly; its value to the specialist teacher is just as great.

One other instrument that is based upon the belief that assessment and teaching must go hand in hand is *The Next Step on the Ladder* (Simon 1986). It is the outcome of investigations and practices developed over many years in the Deaf/Blind Unit at Lea Hospital in Bromsgrove, under the leadership of Gerry Simon, and while again much emphasis is given to the use of any remaining sight the child may have, its overall orientation is towards equipping the learner to function more independently in the setting of home and school.

An instrument that has been constructed with the needs of older subjects in mind is the *Profile of Adaptive Skills* (Stockley and Richardson 1991). It is described as a rating scale for measuring the personal and social skills of older adolescents and young adults with moderate to severe learning difficulties. One of its unique characteristics is that the 'profile' that emerges from the recording of the client's achievements can be informative for the students themselves, their instructors and their employers, and can then be used by other people who have responsibilities for their care and further development. As it is designed to be administered repeatedly, it can reveal how skills, abilities, and independence are progressing. Its genesis in a college of further education for visually impaired young people tells us much about its validity and its practicality.

Conclusion

The justification for using formal test procedures for assessing the abilities and needs of children with severe visual impairments is that such tests are likely to incorporate the hard-won knowledge and experience of fellow professionals. They allow us to observe, in a structured and well rehearsed manner, a range of variables that are known to impinge upon the student's capacity to cope with the problems of everyday learning and the demands of the school curriculum. If they are based upon theoretical and empirical evidence that has stood the test of time, they enable the tester to obtain, in a relatively short period, the kind of information that the experienced teacher or educational psychologist would otherwise acquire throughout the course of a prolonged series of observations in the classroom, the playground, or elsewhere. They are, therefore, efficient. They can, of course, also help to test hypotheses based upon more informal observations. Their validity is in a sense put to the final test by the extent to which they accord with the judgements of the experienced teacher. What they can also do is alert one to unsuspected strengths, areas of weaknesses, and needs.

While the specialist tests, that have been devised for, and standardised on representative samples of learners with visual disabilities, should be used whenever possible, there is also much to be said for using carefully selected tests standardised for learners who are fully sighted, especially those instruments that can be administered orally and that call for oral responses. As the author has argued elsewhere, the child who is blind 'is, after all, first and foremost a child, following the same biologically determined developmental course as sighted children, and having the same general educational and social goals as his fully sighted peers' (Tobin 1994). Since the justification for any kind of educational assessment is that it should assist children, parents, teachers and others in their efforts to enable the children to realise their potential, and make schooling and vocational choices rational and attainable, then any kind of ethically defensible tests which generate information and which the assessor is qualified to administer should be used, provided that due care in administration and interpretation is exercised.

THE CHILD AND THE YOUNG PERSON WITH A VISUAL IMPAIRMENT

This section reviews the possible effects of a visual impairment on the development of a child or young person, and suggests strategies whereby parents, teachers and others can help to promote progress.

The early years of a child's life set the patterns for future development. In Chapter 9 the social and emotional development of pre-school children with a visual impairment is considered along with their acquisition of motor, visual and tactual skills, their use of language and their development of independence. Chapter 10 describes the issues which affect the success and achievements of the child at school. The considerations that enable children with a severe visual impairment to access the curriculum and participate fully in the social life of the school are described.

The period of adolescence can be a turbulent time for any young person, and the particular challenges which face young people with a visual impairment who are confronting this landmark in their lives are explored in Chapter 11. The physical, cognitive, social and emotional changes of adolescence are considered and their impact on education is assessed. Chapters 12 and 13 are concerned with the transition of young people with visual impairments from school to further education, training, employment or unemployment. The choices that face young people and the vocational guidance they require to make informed decisions about career paths are outlined.

During this period of change and transition many young people with visual impairments will welcome the opportunity to discuss their feelings and experiences and some may need professional counselling. Chapter 14 is written by an experienced counsellor, Dr Ann Bond, who herself has a visual impairment. Ann illustrates her arguments with examples concerning young people she has counselled who have had difficulties coming to terms with their visual impairment, and she discusses strategies which can help young people move forward.

Chapter 9
The Pre-school Child

Juliet Stone

Introduction

It is now fully accepted that the most crucial period of a person's life is the early years, when the basis of all future development and progress is laid down. Although generalisations can be made about paths of development, each child's progress will be unique. In this chapter the effects of a visual impairment on early development are discussed and strategies are suggested which may be utilised by parents, carers and professionals to overcome possible delay. The particular aspects of social/emotional, motor, visual, tactual and language development will be discussed as will general issues such as encouraging initial moves to independence.

Research into development

Researchers into the early development of young children with visual impairments have been divided in their opinions as to how a visual impairment may affect development. On the evidence of his longitudinal research, Tobin (1972a) stated that there is likely to be an overall delay in their development which is usually overcome by adolescence, while others, including Fraiberg (1977), suggested that children with visual impairments make detours from the developmental path followed by children who are fully sighted. Yet another view (Norris *et al.* 1957) was that with appropriate early intervention, children with visual impairments would achieve the same developmental milestones at the same time as children who are fully sighted.

Emotional and social development

There are factors which may interfere with the natural development of the early bonding between the baby with a visual impairment and its parents. One of these is the lack of eye contact. Body play must replace eye play to communicate the maternal-concern and love which facilitates the development of the self-concept. More than the usual amount of time needs to be spent cuddling, holding, fondling and moving the baby who has a visual impairment, and soothing, comforting sounds and words from parents help establish emotional bonds between themselves and the child. Parents may need help in understanding the individual and perhaps unique responses of their child to them. A baby with a visual impairment may not make the excited movements of anticipation that parents expect as they approach their child. They will need to understand that the reason their baby becomes still and quiet as they approach is because s/he is concentrating on listening for them. The baby may make minuscule movements of fingers and toes as a response to their voices which parents can easily miss.

Some babies will need to stay in hospital immediately after birth and this is particularly true of babies born prematurely. Unless great care is taken by all the professionals concerned, this separation may affect the parent–baby bonding.

When the diagnosis of a visual impairment is given, some parents may feel guilty at being in some way responsible for the child's disability and may then go through a period of rejecting the child. Parents may experience feelings of trauma as they face up to the reactions of others, such as family and friends, and this may be more of a problem if the child has a disfiguring eye condition. Even when the parents have accepted the child's problem, they may experience feelings of distress and anxiety about how they are going to cope with, and manage the child. They may feel anxious about the child's eye condition and its implications for the future.

All of these difficulties are understandable, but they may make it more difficult for the parents to establish close bonding with the child. The need of the child with a visual impairment to achieve the first level of affective development, that is, human attachment, must be recognised. If the child does not experience close human interaction, their personal security in relating to others and eventually to the world is reduced.

In the first few months the baby will grow responsive to its parents and show feelings of pleasure and comfort. The child will learn to make an association between the human voice and tactual intimacy so that, once the association has been made, the human voice from a distance begins to unite the child with the world. Parents and siblings provide the basic social-emotional setting for the development of positive affective behaviour. Close, loving relationships enable the toddler to gain a sense of inner control and to begin to cope with the strong feelings which can be experienced at that age.

Motor development

A lack of sight or a severe visual impairment can seriously affect the motor development of a child. This can be considered as a secondary implication of a disability. A visual impairment does not directly lead to uncoordinated movement, but it may retard the child's movement in two ways. First, the absence of clear vision will greatly decrease the motivation to move. The first purposeful movements of children who are fully sighted are often seen when they wriggle to grab something they see which is just out of reach. This initial effort strengthens the muscles they need to carry out the movement in a more coordinated fashion. For babies who have a visual impairment, this visual motivation is reduced or absent. Secondly, without clear vision a child may be fearful to move, because they feel unsafe and uncertain in their surroundings and need the security of staying still.

The effect of both these factors can be reduced. In the first few months, control of the body, exploratory and purposeful movement can be encouraged and a feeling of security developed. The daily activities of bathing and dressing and the use of massage can help babies begin to understand their own physical separateness from the world. Infants without sight frequently dislike lying prone, and there is nothing to attract them to achieve and prolong the raised position whereby babies who are sighted learn to support their head and shoulders. With help, a child can learn to lift the head, control head movements early and achieve other motor skills in sequence (Jan *et al.* 1977).

An accurate body image is essential for the development of later coordination, posture and mobility (Cratty and Sams 1968). For the child with a severe visual impairment, an understanding of the body, its parts, and how these relate to each other will have to be taught systematically. Too often, the teaching stops once the young child can identify the main body parts, such as hands and feet and it is assumed that the child can learn incidentally from then on. This may not happen and children should be taught to identify and name body parts such as knuckles, ankles and hips. The child will need to understand terms such as 'knee high', 'waist level', 'shoulders down' which are often used to encourage good posture and mobility. Bathing can be a good opportunity for the baby or young child to learn about the body. Splashing in the water, being surrounded by it and feeling mother trickling it down the back, all help the infant to become aware of him/herself as an individual, separate from the environment.

To a child who is blind, the world is no more interesting when sitting upright than when lying down, so s/he is not necessarily enthusiastic about sitting up because lying on the floor is more comfortable. Children who can see quickly learn to balance themselves when sitting up. Parents can assist their children who are visually impaired to acquire this skill by propping them safely on a settee and bouncing them while holding their wrists, then their fingertips, until they are ready to be bounced astride the parent's knee or ankle.

Once children who are blind are able sit unsupported they may become 'stuck' at this stage and remain so for several months. It is a time when babies who can see may demonstrate rocking and flapping movements, but for them, this will be a transitory stage. These actions are soon lost as the baby becomes increasingly busy and active in learning the movements preparatory to walking. For children who are blind it is often a time when the motor development slows down and compensatory movements may develop and/or become reinforced. They may put their natural energy, which would otherwise have found purposeful outlets, into rocking, poking or flapping, all of which can affect their learning and social acceptability. The horizons of children who can see are dramatically widened once they can sit but children who are visually impaired may remain almost as limited as they were before, because the only additional information they gain is through incidental body contact with the floor and other objects in the environment. Crawling, a stage often missed by children with severe visual impairments, can be encouraged through the use of attractive sounds, smells and if appropriate, brightly coloured toys. The advice of a physiotherapist who can demonstrate ways of encouraging movement can be very helpful. Cratty (1971) indicated ways of encouraging a child to become mobile. These can be incorporated into the physiotherapist's programme during visits to the child's home, where parents can help the child towards mobility in a known environment. The child's musical box, the mother's voice or the enticement of things the child likes to eat, may be used as lures to encourage forward movement in ways appropriate to the child's development. Cratty suggested that mobility skills in children who are blind usually precede the development of language and that children become more interested in touching and holding objects once they can crawl, walk barefoot and feel the walls and the floor.

Having been encouraged to stand supported and to jump, bounce and make stepping movements on the parent's knee, the child will next learn to do this on the floor. When they are able to stand holding onto furniture, children can be shown how to pull themselves up by it and learn to move sideways and get safely down. Once they are able to move in an upright position or on the floor, some of the opportunities that children who are fully sighted have at this stage become available to them. Some blind babies begin to walk alone at the same age as babies who can see while others take longer, needing to keep in touch with walls or furniture before gaining confidence to walk alone. The arrangement of rooms needs to be kept unchanged, at least when the children first begin to move. Children with visual impairments have to rely on things being where they anticipate them to be, otherwise the spatial map that is being built up loses consistency and they may become confused and discouraged. A child who is blind can learn to manage stairs safely, given the opportunity, from an early age. Climbing and later walking up, first with help and then alone, is relatively easy, but coming down needs closer supervision.

Once the child is walking confidently, running can be encouraged. Obviously, a child who is visually impaired is going to need a deep feeling of security and specific support to attempt this. Even when their hands are held by an adult either side, the young child may be timid about moving around, but this should be encouraged.

Children need to test the limits of their physical strength and stamina. They usually spend much of their time testing, extending and enjoying their physical capabilities, and ways of giving the visually impaired child the same feeling of exhilaration in movement must be found. A safe open space, with no obstacles can be provided where the children feel secure enough to run freely. Instead of holding hands, adults can run, holding a hoop behind them which the children hold can hold onto. Trampolining is marvellous for developing body awareness and co-ordination and for using the child's natural energy. Balancing, jumping, swinging and climbing, using push and pull toys are also helpful, but in all these the safety factors must be considered and parents, carers and pre-school staff will need advice on how to make them safe and secure for the children with visual impairments. As well as encouraging the development of motor skills, parents can provide opportunities for their children to become aware of auditory or tactile clues which will help in orientation.

Children who are blind may learn to produce sharp sound effects by clicking their tongues or uttering short, high-pitched sounds. As they click their fingers, tap objects or clap, the children will experiment with echo-location, thereby increasing their receptive and interpretative abilities. As a result, they may feel encouraged to explore new territory.

A small, high-walled yard offers freedom for independent, active play once a child has a developed awareness of reflected sound. Both Fichtner (1979) and Tooze (1981) describe games and activities that can be fun and helpful, and those working with young children should refer to these for further ideas and suggestions. Permitting the child who is blind to encounter the same bumps, bruises, falls and other natural consequences of independent action that all children experience, is difficult for some parents (Barraga 1976). The natural inclination is to protect such 'helpless' children from a seemingly hostile world, but to do so may engender in them feelings of inadequacy and incompetence and make them needlessly dependent. The potential in young people for independent travel at a later stage is directly proportional to the extent of the early learning experiences they were given by parents and carers and the encouragement they received to reach out and be independent in movement.

The development of the use of vision

It is critically important that from infancy children are encouraged to make the most efficient use of any visual capacity they may have (Barraga 1976). Attention to visual stimulation at near distance in the first two or three years can enhance the child's visual development to the maximum, which in turn will help stimulate and accelerate psychomotor and cognitive development. Children with small amounts of residual vision may be not, at first, be able to make sense of the distorted and confused visual images but even when acuity is poor, the brain can receive visual impressions and learn to interpret them accurately. Learning to interpret visual information takes time, and adults must allow the child sufficient opportunity to respond to the visual images presented. Objects need to be presented from different angles and the baby should be encouraged to reach for and take them as the carers name them.

Depending on the type and severity of the impairment, the child may have difficulty developing visual skills such as fixation, tracking, focus, accommodation and convergence. When very little light can enter the eye or reach the nerve centres in the retina, muscular control may be slow to develop and assistance, guidance and even training may be necessary to allow the child to use vision as skilfully as possible. As more and more visual stimulation occurs, the child will naturally begin to use vision with greater efficiency. The brain is able to combine the visual images with auditory and other sensory information, so that the child can use vision as a contributing sense in the development of cognitive skills.

Parents are often the first to notice when a little one seems aware of light, for example when curtains are opened on a bright day or a light is switched on in a darkening room. The baby may turn to, or away from the window or screw up the eyes and this may indicate awareness of light. Even minimal light awareness can help children orientate themselves in space.

Light plays an important part in arousing visual interest and the beam of a small torch (covered, if necessary, by a film of thin tissue) encourages the baby to attend and can help the child to learn to hold the eyes steady and locate a specific object. Bright and sparkling materials will gain attention, and shiny baubles, sparkling tinsel and prismatic foil provide visually fascinating lures. Such lures can be brought close to the child, then moved slowly away to encourage fixation and to encourage the child to learn to move the eyes to follow objects. Objects should be turned, introduced from the sides, from above and from the front so that the child learns to recognise an object from various viewpoints. A commentary should be provided so that words begin to be associated with the visual images received.

The environment and the materials that the children often use can be adapted to help them see more. For example contrast helps to make objects easier to see and a red plate on a white feeding tray or a yellow one on a dark surface provide clues to their position. Chocolate drinks can be presented in a yellow cup, milk in a red one and cereal can be seen more easily when in a dark coloured bowl.

Once the child is visually interested in, and has some knowledge of objects, pictorial representations of the objects can be introduced. Initially the pictures should be of familiar objects such as a banana, a key and a comb, which can be presented alongside the pictures. Pictures in many early books are clear and simple in shape and show an object in its usual colour against a contrasting background. Once the child enjoys looking at pictures and can identify them successfully, smaller but still simple pictures of the same objects may be introduced.

There are few materials and toys made especially to help the child with a visual impairment, but suitable choices include slow-moving toys which flash or sparkle, wind-up toys which realign themselves after contacting an object in their path, pop-up toys, bubble blowing outfits, balloons, small brightly coloured sweets and tiny cake decorations. The toy catalogue available from the RNIB contains some useful suggestions.

The sense of touch

It is sometimes thought that children with visual impairments will naturally make the most of their sense of touch. Unfortunately this is not usually so. Far from reaching out to the world, children are likely to withdraw their hands from any strange tactile sensations and will need encouragement to use their hands. One vital developmental step is for the children to be able to place their hands together at the midline (Fraiberg 1977). An object held in one hand without the involvement of the other cannot be explored tactually and children cannot learn the shape and form of an object unless one hand holds it and the other is used to explore the shape and texture. Without the motivation of clear sight babies may not be attracted to 'play' with their hands, but lap games, such as 'pat a cake' can develop the ability to use them together. Parents, carers and others should be careful not to place an object suddenly in the child's hands. This may well lead to a withdrawal and an aversion to the use of the hands and it is much better for the adult to place his or her hand over the child's hand, guide it to the object and gently encourage the child to take hold of it.

Language development

Most parents naturally talk to their babies, but those with a child who has a visual impairment need to understand how crucial their language is. Long before the baby is ready to talk, parents can name the objects that the child meets, such as bottle, cup, and shoe and describe simple movements such as 'up' and 'down'. Commentaries on the baby's experiences ('We're going into the kitchen, can you hear the washing machine?') will help the child gradually to make sense of what is happening in the environment. Some parents initially may find it difficult to provide this commentary but most soon get into the habit of it. Parents and carers can encourage children's own communication by responding to their vocal sounds, being pleased when they attempt words, and sharing the enjoyment of 'talking' with them.

The question of background noise in the home is one that may need handling tactfully. Many parents, understanding the isolation of their babies, surround them with noise from television, radio or tape recorder. This can prevent the babies from listening to and developing an understanding of the natural environmental sounds around them. Short periods of exposure to nursery rhymes on tape, or television programmes containing songs and jingles can be enjoyed by the baby and give parents a respite.

As the baby begins to talk, parents may need to be reminded to allow sufficient time for the child to respond to their questions and conversations and not provide the answer themselves too quickly. Questions that invite responses: 'Who's that?' 'What's that noise?' will encourage the child towards meaningful speech. Although the child will enjoy repeating words and sentences that are heard, it is important that the development of language is related to the child's own experience and relates to objects which the child has explored.

The development of independence skills

Tooze (1981) suggests that a dependent child makes a dependent adult. A balance must be found between giving sufficient help to the child who is visually impaired and firm encouragement towards doing things independently. Feeding is a good example of where finding this balance can be difficult. Obviously it is an area in which a child with a visual impairment may take a considerable time to achieve competence and will need specific teaching in some of the skills involved. Parents are often anxious to ensure their children eat sufficient amounts and can be tempted to continue feeding them long after the stage when the children should be attempting this for themselves. Although parents may feel that the children will find it easier to feed themselves and make less mess when they get older, there is a possibility that they will lose the motivation to do so.

Toilet training

Toilet training is another area that can give rise to additional problems for the child who is visually impaired, who may be fearful of the potty or of transferring to using the toilet. Sensitive handling of the child (and a lot of patience) should bring success. These are often the problems of child management that parents are most worried or concerned about, and professionals working with the families must be empathic to this.

Learning self-help skills

The RNIB booklet *Guidelines for Teachers and Parents of Visually Handicapped Children with Additional Handicaps* includes some helpful advice on achieving toilet training and other self-help skills such as dressing and undressing, and managing personal hygiene. The following points should be remembered.

- The child should be encouraged to start learning these skills as soon as possible.
- It can take longer for the child to learn, practise and perform these skills. Extra time must be 'budgeted' into the daily routine, so that the child can learn to do things independently, for example cleaning teeth, putting on their coats, fetching shoes etc.
- Specific teaching of these skills will be necessary. The principles of task analysis which include breaking down the skill into the sub-skills involved and teaching these separately are useful. (For some useful examples, see Best 1986.)
- Adaptations of utensils and clothes can help, for instance a special feeding plate, an appliquéed motif on clothes.
- As far as is possible and appropriate in the family situation, an established routine should be followed. The child who does not see well may miss the clues that help to anticipate events.

Behaviour difficulties

Some young children with a visual impairment show behaviours that cause concern to their parents and those who work with them. Common examples of these behaviours are flicking fingers in front of the face, twirling on the spot, eye-poking and rocking. These behaviours are often transitory and children will stop doing them after a few weeks. If they continue and it becomes difficult to absorb the children in other activities, then help should be sought. Distraction is the best policy, although some older children will respond to a discussion about the situation. One little girl, Gina, constantly played with her false eye. Fortunately, Gina was very interested in her appearance and her mother explained that without her eye Gina did not look very pretty. Gentle reminders on this theme helped to stop the behaviour. Getting cross about it would have had the opposite effect. Gina could easily have learnt to use the behaviour as a weapon against her mother.

An environment which is lacking in stimulation can exacerbate these behaviours, but overstimulation can have the same effect and make the child retreat from a world which is found to be too demanding. Some of these behaviours are not only socially unacceptable, but can be harmful (for instance eye poking) and it is important to discover what causes them. This involves very careful observation of the child and noting exactly what is happening before the behaviour starts. One blind child had frequent episodes when he became very distressed at his play school. It took some while for the staff to realise that it was the central heating boiler coming on that was upsetting him. The noise was so much part of their environment that they did not notice it.

Obsessive behaviour is also common with some young children with visual impairments and the obsessions can include almost anything, such as stairs, doorhandles, washing machines, a particular item of clothing. Children can be extremely hyperactive and distractible, though the child with a severe impairment is more likely to become withdrawn and passive, sometimes to the extent of being unable to relate to care-givers, rejecting being held and cuddled. There are many useful books and leaflets which deal more fully with the management of behaviour, and these should be referred to by teachers who wish to gain more insight into this subject.

Problem solving

Overcoming challenges and mastering skills is as important for children with visual impairments as for any other child. One of the ways in which this can be encouraged is through developing, from a very early age, problem solving strategies. These can be started by involving the child with every activity: 'What's that noise?' 'So where could we be?' 'How does this work?' 'What will happen when you push this?' Children will need to be encouraged to take risks and to get used to the occasional scratch or bruise.

Assessment and training packages

There are a number of developmental checklists designed to help parents and professionals assess the pre-school child, and some include reference to the particular areas relevant to children with a visual impairment, for example, the use of functional vision and mobility. Perhaps the most widely used of these is the Portage material. Devised in America, it consists of detailed checklists of skills in major areas of development (such as motor, language, socialisation) along with activity cards which give ideas for helping a child move on to the next step. Although the sequences and activities were not devised specifically for children with visual impairment, the materials have been used successfully with children with a visual impairment.

A number of packages have now been published which are specifically designed for use with children who are blind. Probably the most well established material is the Oregon Project which comprises a manual, skills inventory, and teaching activities.

As has been stated earlier in this chapter, each child's progress will be unique. The value of these packages is more to do with helping him/her progress to the next appropriate developmental stage, rather than comparing the individual child with others.

Pre-school placement

There is a wide variety of educational provision for the pre-school child, although the range differs between localities. Many children integrate very successfully into ordinary nursery or play schools, whereas other children will feel more comfortable with staff who are used to working with children who have disabilities, perhaps in an opportunity play group. In areas of large populations, there may well be a special school for children with visual impairments which has a nursery group which would offer a very specialised placement.

Clearly, when contemplating placing children into a non-specialist setting, several factors need to be taken into consideration, the main ones being the attitude of the staff and the physical environment. Preparations for the placement must be made carefully and in-service training should be provided for the staff. Advice from a specialist teacher of children with a visual impairment concerning organisation, management and appropriate educational programmes, is also important and it is also helpful if the preparations include discussions with parents of the other children.

Conclusion

The first few years of children's lives should be exciting and fulfilling, for them and for those involved with them. With information, advice and a good deal of common sense, parents, carers and teachers can help this to be equally true for children with limited or no sight and lay the basis for progress and achievement once they reach school.

Chapter 10

The Primary School Child

Christine Arter

Introduction

It is difficult to generalise about the impact of visual impairment on a child's development. The needs of each child will vary and factors such as personality, age of onset of impairment, degree of visual loss, the presence or absence of additional disabilities and cognitive ability will make each child unique. The aim of this chapter is to provide some general, practical advice that may be useful to teachers with little experience of teaching children with a significant visual impairment. More detailed advice about many of the issues which are introduced here can be found in other chapters.

Children enter school bringing with them a variety of experience and abilities; each child will be at a different stage of development and each child will have different strengths and unique areas of weakness.

Children starting school

In most cases, children with a severe visual impairment will have been identified long before they begin school. Usually a qualified teacher of the visually impaired would have visited the child and the parents at home and would have worked with the child from an early age, assessing the child and advising parents on how best to help their child and may have been involved in advising parents about the choice of school for their child (see Chapters 39 and 40).

It is important that the school is receptive to the child, and that the placement has the full support of the headteacher and staff. However, it is not enough that the school is willing to accept the child – teachers and care assistants need training and advice from a qualified teacher of the visually impaired – before the child enters the school. As staff work with the child they will learn a great deal about the child's abilities and visual difficulties and will develop ideas and techniques about how best they can present materials to the child. It is important that staff continue to receive training and that expertise and knowledge is disseminated to all the staff within the school, not just to those teachers working closely with the child. In this way all the school staff can adopt a consistent approach when teaching the child.

Before the child enters the school, the teacher of the visually impaired will normally provide the school with full details of the child's vision, having completed a visual assessment of the child outlining the general implications for learning. This will provide the class teacher with a baseline, and will enable the teacher to develop an Individual Education Programme (IEP).

In some cases the child's visual difficulties may not become apparent until after the child enters school. At this stage the school SENCO (special educational needs coordinator) would start to implement the Code of Practice (DfE 1994). At stage 3 of the Code, the child would be referred to the qualified teacher of the visually impaired for advice and a full visual assessment. (For a full discussion on visual assessment, see Chapter 6.)

It is enormously helpful if links with parents are established before the child joins the school. Parents are usually encouraged to visit the school before the child starts. This enables parents and teachers to establish a good relationship and teachers can work towards allaying any fears or anxieties that parents might have. Opportunities for the child to make several visits to the school with parents, before actually starting, may help to reassure the child. Throughout the child's school career effective home–school links allow parents to work closely with teachers to help their child to sustain progress.

The school environment

It is essential that the classroom environment itself is carefully assessed. For example the control of lighting is an important consideration. Good, diffused lighting is necessary, but glare needs to be avoided, especially for those pupils with sensitivity to bright light (photophobia). It may be advantageous if the light source comes from behind the child, or from the side, and some children will require additional task lighting when completing close work. Effective blinds are necessary to control direct sunlight from outside, and the teacher should try to avoid speaking to the class when standing in front of a window, since the child with a visual impairment may find the glare from the window uncomfortable or even painful. If blackboards are used some consideration should be given to the light source. Light from an adjacent window may make it impossible for the child with a visual impairment to see the board, and wherever possible the use of the blackboard should be avoided (Best 1992). It is better to present work on a clearly written worksheet and in this way the task is made easier for the child, thus avoiding unnecessary fatigue. If a blackboard is used, it is imperative that the handwriting is clear and the colour of the chalk used should be considered, so that the colour used is one that the child can most clearly see. The board should be washed clean to give a good, dark contrast and the child may prefer to be placed near to the blackboard, in a position that suits them, enabling them to make best use of their residual vision. For example if the child has no useful vision in the right eye it makes no sense to allow the child to sit to the far left of the board.

The work surface should also be considered. A good, clear colour contrast with a matt surface is preferable, thus avoiding problems with reflected glare. If the work surface is unsuitable a dark, coloured sheet of sugar paper placed on top of the table sometimes proves helpful. A flat work table may prove difficult if the child has to bend to peer closely at work, resulting in poor posture and fatigue. An adjustable work surface could be provided, thus enabling the child to work in a more comfortable position. Sometimes a book stand proves useful, and a raised magnet board can also be employed (Figure 10.1).

Figure 10.1

Shiny gloss painted walls and highly polished floor surfaces may cause uncomfortable glare. Walls may be painted with a matt paint to overcome problems of associated glare, but floor coverings are costly to replace with a more satisfactory alternative. Doors, handles and light switches can be difficult for the low vision child to locate unless they have a clear, bold colour contrast. Brightly coloured tape may be used to highlight door furniture and light switches.

Wall displays need special consideration since a good colour contrast is required. Mounting work on a bright, luminous background may make it easier for the child to locate the display, and clear, dark print on labels is essential. It is important that work is displayed at the child's height, not too high up where it cannot be seen or touched. Tactile displays should be available for the child who is blind, with braille labels at the correct height, enabling the child to feel and read them.

For a more detailed discussion of issues related to the learning environment refer to Chapter 21.

It is important to allow the child to explore the layout of the classroom. The teacher may need to guide the child around the room, explaining the layout. Any possible areas of danger should be discussed with the pupil. It is advisable that the arrangement of furniture and location of storage areas remain constant. The children should be taught where things are stored, so that they can find things for themselves and thus achieve some degree of independence. Expectations should be the same for the child with a visual impairment as for any other child (Chapman and Stone 1988, Best 1992). The child will also need guidance to find their way around the school as a whole. It is essential for the child to be able to find those areas of the building that are important, such as the cloakroom, the toilets and the school hall for example. In an ideal situation a mobility officer would be able to work with the child when first starting school, to teach the child the layout of the school and start to develop good mobility skills. Unfortunately this is not always possible and this early training may become the responsibility of the teacher.

A mobility programme in the early stages of schooling may help the child to develop good body image and spatial awareness, and as the child grows older the mobility officer will encourage the child to develop self-help skills. It is important for the teacher and the mobility officer to collaborate and work closely together. Parents can also be involved in helping their child to develop skills. For example some visually impaired children often find difficulty in dressing and undressing and also in fastening shoes. When parents are made aware of these problems they are usually willing to work on these skills at home, and may purchase clothes that are easy for the child to fasten.

In order to be like the other children, the child with a visual impairment should be expected to conform to school rules and it is essential for the teacher to carefully explain the school rules and routines to the child. This may be a harder task for children with a visual impairment since they are unable to learn by watching and copying their peers.

Adapting the curriculum

The aims of education for the child with a visual impairment should be the same as those for any other child, with full entitlement to a broad and balanced curriculum and access to the full mainstream curriculum (DfE 1994). To achieve these aims some modifications and adaptations to the mainstream curriculum may be necessary.

Chapman and Stone (1988) suggest that children with visual impairments may have had less exposure to incidental learning than their fully sighted peers. For example they may not be aware of the print in books as their mother reads to them. The child with a visual impairment may not be able to see print on advertisement hoardings or titles on the television (Arter and Mason, 1994).

Most young children will have developed an understanding of many concepts well before they start school. For example they will have seen tables of different heights, shapes and construction and are able to recognise what a table is, and what it is used for. This concept may not be so readily understood by the child with little or no sight. By watching parents pour milk from a carton into cups or a jug, a child will start to develop some idea of the conservation of volume. This information may not be learnt incidentally by the child with a visual impairment and may need to be taught systematically.

Parents or a qualified teacher of the visually impaired may have worked with the child to try to compensate for any lack of incidental learning, but this will not be true in all cases. The child may have been overprotected and not allowed to learn by exploration. The teacher should be aware of a possible lack of incidental learning and will need to try to overcome this problem with a carefully structured programme, with lots of concrete examples and 'hands on' experience. For example in mathematics when teaching computation, practical examples will be necessary. Real money could be provided, and lots of experience filling containers of different sizes will be required to help the child to gain some understanding of volume.

Discussion about the different activities which form part of the school day, may help the child to develop concepts and understanding. It is important that any new words that are introduced are carefully explained. Directive questions can be used to help the child to understand and may also help the teacher establish whether the child has fully grasped a concept (Chapman and Stone 1988). Scott (1982) describes gaps in the child's understanding as 'unexpected black holes'. The child may actually misunderstand a concept. For example a blind child was observed when playing with a lorry. He started to make the noise made by a lorry when it reverses, and told the teacher that his lorry was reversing, while he continued to push the lorry forward. This simple example serves to demonstrate that the child had clearly not understood the concept of reversing, although he spoke about it with apparent understanding and confidence. All of the time, and in all subject areas, the teacher should be aware that concepts may not be fully grasped.

A hands-on approach, enabling the child to actually handle materials is essential (Chapman and Stone 1988, Barraga 1986). For example a visit to a museum can often be arranged so that children have the opportunity to touch and feel artefacts. A visit to an environmental studies centre or a natural history museum may provide the child with the chance to feel the size and shape of the more common birds and animals that the child with full sight is able to see in books, gardens, the countryside or a zoo. The child with a visual impairment would be able, for example, to feel the soft fur and the long ears of a rabbit, or the wings, large face and eyes of an owl. By using tactual exploration, the children's understanding of the world about them will be increased.

This hands-on approach is important for areas of the curriculum such as history and geography. (For a full discussion of the different areas of the curriculum see the section on The Mainstream Curriculum.)

In curriculum areas such as science, the child with a visual impairment will benefit from being close to the teacher to observe any practical demonstrations. It is essential for the teacher to clearly explain what is going on and wherever possible to allow the child to handle any apparatus and materials being used. It may be necessary for the teacher to repeat the practical demonstration in a one to one situation. Demonstrations using a closed circuit television (CCTV) may prove helpful (Figure 10.2) and an illuminated magnifier or a microscope may be useful when examining small creatures or plants. Children should also be

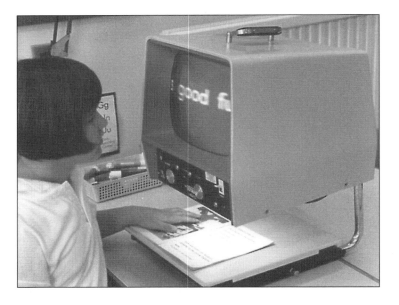

Figure 10.2

encouraged to use all of their available senses. For example in science they may use their listening skills to listen for the buzzer when an electrical circuit is complete.

The use of print

As the child grows older and starts to read further difficulties may need to be addressed.

For the child with low vision it is imperative that the quality of the print materials used should be carefully considered. Assessment should reveal the optimum print size for the child. Work may need to be enlarged to allow the pupil to read the print clearly. However,

Figure 10.3

enlargement is not always a panacea because it does not always make it easier for the child to see. For example it would make the task of reading harder for the child who has tunnel vision. Furthermore large sheets of A3 paper become somewhat unwieldy for the child and difficult to use, and many children are sensitive to the fact that their reading material is different and larger than other children's books or worksheets.

Some children with low vision may find a CCTV or a low vision aid (LVA) useful (Figure 10.3). The ophthalmologist may prescribe an LVA and will usually give the child advice on how to use it. It is often helpful for the teacher to talk to the ophthalmologist, to gain advice on how to help the child use their LVA effectively. Children will need some training to help them utilise such tools efficiently. For example they need to be taught how to keep their LVA clean, and how to look after it. The use of the CCTV may be difficult for some children, particularly if they have problems with coordination. (For a further discussion of low vision aids, refer to Chapter 7.)

Some thought should be given to the presentation of work (Mason 1995). Written work should be presented using clear, dark print, with the background providing a good, clear contrast. Some children find a particular use of colour to be helpful; however black print on a white background is usually advantageous. Some consideration should be given to the space between letters, words and lines of print. A cluttered page may well cause confusion and therefore it is important that work is clearly set out, without too much information crowded on to the page (Davies 1989).

If commercially produced schemes are used, it is suggested that these are selected carefully. Clearly presented materials should be chosen, avoiding wherever possible those materials where the words are printed on top of a coloured background or picture. Many current schemes adopt this format and are highly attractive to the child who is fully sighted; however, this approach may cause severe problems for the child with a visual impairment, because it does not provide a clear colour contrast. Some books use different decorative and attractive fonts, these may also result in confusion for the pupil with a visual impairment. Choice of commercially produced schemes is often quite limited when the needs of the child with a visual impairment are taken into account.

As the child gets older and makes progress, the print size in books often becomes smaller and so each situation will need to be reassessed. It may be necessary for the child to be encouraged to adopt new techniques, for example the child may benefit from using an LVA. Advice should then be sought from the optometrist.

For older pupils the amount of reading required will increase, and the English National Curriculum Key Stage 2 (DfE 1995) demands that children learn to use the library and develop higher reading skills such as skimming texts and searching for information in books. These activities are not easy for pupils who are is visually impaired. Throughout their school life they are going to need longer to complete tasks. To find a page in their reading book they may peer closely at the number, when they have located it on the page. Children who are fully sighted can usually flick through a book, glancing at pictures, headings, page numbers and possibly the first sentence to find their place very quickly. This is often not the case for children with a visual impairment. When writing, each time they look away from the text to write, they then have to go through the same laborious process of finding their place again. This slower rate of working is well documented (Best 1992, Chapman and Stone 1988, Mason 1995).

When reading, children with a visual impairment may perhaps see only part of a word at a time. They are often unable to scan a whole word, or allow their eyes to look on ahead and skim along the line of print as a sighted reader does. Children may be helped by using a line marker or a typoscope (a cut out window made from stiff card), so that they view only one line of print at a time. Reading is a much slower process for the child with a visual impairment and may remain so. Since reading is so hard and tiring for many children with a visual impairment, it may well never become a pleasurable activity for them. This may have an important impact on the child's reading ability. Children become proficient readers by reading, and thus practising the skill.

It may be possible to reduce the amount of material the child has to read by using a tape recorder to tape work. For example, comprehension questions could be recorded on tape to eliminate yet another reading task.

Handwriting skills

Handwriting may be a difficult activity for children with a visual impairment. Often their handwriting is untidy, despite their best efforts, because they are not able see what they have written. Their hand–eye coordination may well be poor, making pencil control particularly difficult (Arter *et al.* 1996). They will need to work on hand–eye co-ordination tasks to help them improve. Presenting the same type of activity over and over again places great demands on the child and the teacher, who will require inventive ability to produce interesting and stimulating examples of the same type of activity. It is essential for teachers to use their skill to encourage and inspire the child and make him or her feel that progress is being made, when in fact the improvement is limited and slow.

With letter formation exercises the child may need to be shown how to hold the pencil, and how to form the letter correctly. It is preferable that the child avoids developing bad habits of incorrect letter formation. The use of the CCTV for individual demonstrations of letter formation is often helpful. The kinaesthetic approach is also useful, whereby the child makes large movements to establish the correct letter formation, for example by tracing the letter in the air. The child will need repeated practice and may find it difficult to keep the writing in a straight line. Dark lined paper, available from the Partially Sighted Society (address at the end of the chapter), can be a very useful aid. The child may find it advantageous to use a thick, black felt pen or a black biro, instead of a pencil, in order to see more clearly what is being written. It is recommended that the child's views be sought about what is best for them. Good quality biros and pens are essential because biros will easily smudge, and the tip of the felt tip pen soon wears down making writing illegible. Since the children are often unable to clearly see what they are writing, they will probably write slowly and again will need longer to complete a task.

Often children find it extremely difficult to read their own written work because it is untidy, and it may well be advantageous for them to learn to touch type. It is important that the child is encouraged to learn to touch type at an early stage. This will eventually remove the sheer physical effort involved in the handwriting process, and will be very useful for all children in this technological age. As the child grows into adolescence and adulthood, handwriting will remain an important skill for signing cheques and forms for example, and notes may need to be taken when advanced technology is not readily available.

Although it has been clearly stated that it usually takes longer for pupils with a visual impairment to complete their work, it is imperative that the teacher ensures that the child has a longer period of time to complete a task, otherwise they may feel frustrated at never experiencing the satisfaction of actually finishing a piece of work. Realistic goals should be set which allow the child to achieve success.

In the same way that it has been suggested that the tape recorder may be used to lessen the amount that the child is expected to read, the tape recorder could be used to record the child's answers. Children also enjoy telling stories on to a tape rather than laboriously writing them out. However, this usually takes practice before the child is able to record stories clearly and well.

With greater use of taped material and increased dependence on verbal explanations and descriptions, listening skills will need to be trained to achieve the high levels required by older pupils. (See Chapter 15 for a full discussion of listening skills.)

Training in the use of residual vision

Children may require a programme to train them to use their residual vision to maximum effect. For example they may need to be taught to scan systematically, to discriminate and to look for details. Often children with a visual impairment find it difficult to distinguish facial expressions and body posture. The *Look and Think* programme (Chapman *et al.* 1989) is particularly useful in assessing children's use of residual vision and in suggesting follow-up programmes to train them to use their residual vision to maximum effect.

The needs of the blind child using braille

For many children who are educationally blind, reading braille can be a slow process, since the tactile reader can only 'read' one braille cell at a time, and is unable to scan a line of print. The child learning to read using braille must rely on tactual abilities and auditory skills. The child with full sight, who has poor auditory skills may rely more heavily on visual skills such as visual sequencing and visual memory, to learn to read. The child who is blind must concentrate on using auditory skills when learning to read, even though these may be an area of particular weakness.

Spelling is a more difficult task for the child who is blind, and who must learn to read and write words using word signs, contractions and abbreviations, and yet must also learn the full spelling of a word for typing to produce a print copy. The obvious disadvantages to the child of a lack of incidental learning when attempting to spell and to read have already been stated.

It is important for the child who learns by touch to be trained from an early age, to interpret tactile pictures and diagrams. For the young child tactile pictures that accompany braille text will add to interest levels and will also provide early experience in the development of tactual skills. Material presented in a tactile format will be of increasing importance as the child grows. For example, mathematics and geography in the secondary school curriculum, will make increasing demands on the pupil's ability to interpret tactile information such as graphs, tables and diagrams. Tactile materials need to be carefully prepared to ensure that the child is able to fully comprehend the material. (For a full discussion of the preparation of tactile materials, refer to Chapter 18.)

Although the child who is blind will rely solely on braille or typing to communicate, it is felt to be important for the child to learn to sign their own name (Arter *et al.* 1996). The primary age child will enjoy signing cards made at school for parents and friends. Such an approach can be used as an incentive to help practise this important but difficult skill.

The problem of fatigue

Many children with a visual impairment put extra effort into achieving a good standard and this often results in fatigue, tension and stress. It may be necessary to allow time for the pupil to relax tense muscles. For example children may feel especially tense after a mobility lesson, when they have started learning a new and demanding skill. Subjects like art and craft, drama and PE may be particularly helpful in providing the opportunity to relieve tension. The use of learning games may also alleviate stress.

The child with a visual impairment, like all children, needs a great deal of positive support. However it must be remembered that some children will be unable to see a smile or a nod. The teacher should address the child directly, saying the child's name, and then giving praise, assistance and encouragement.

A summary of special considerations

The child with a visual impairment may need:
- realistic targets, allowing a longer amount of time to complete work;
- practical demonstrations to be repeated;
- visits and hands on experience;
- discussion to ensure understanding of the language used and the concept being taught;

- training in the use of listening skills;
- training to use touch typing;
- mobility training;
- training to develop full use of residual vision;
- training in the effective use of LVAs (including the CCTV).

All of these needs have to be accommodated in an already crowded timetable. Many teachers complain that they are unable to cover all aspects of the National Curriculum and yet for the teacher of the pupil with a visual impairment extra time must be found to fit in these additional activities.

Social/emotional issues

The child may come to school from an over-protective home environment, where there has been little opportunity to mix with other children and therefore to develop good social skills (Zell Sacks *et al*. 1992). School, whether a special school or an integrated setting, may be far from home. Children may arrive at school in a taxi and then be whisked off home again, with no chance to chat to friends on the way home or to stay for after school activities. Some teachers work hard to ensure that pupils do have the opportunity to attend after school activities.

The child may have experienced interrupted schooling because of hospital appointments and treatment. This will affect academic progress and the opportunity to develop sustained friendship patterns. This may be especially true for the child with additional disabilities.

The child's eye condition may make the child look different. Other children may stare out of curiosity and because they want to understand the difference, or they may make fun of the child. To overcome such problems the child's visual problems could be described and explained to the rest of the group. Special equipment could be demonstrated, allowing pupils to use the equipment themselves and thus to appreciate some of the associated difficulties. The other children should be encouraged to help and support the child with a visual impairment, however, it is important for them to be discouraged from over-protecting the child.

Within the classroom the child with a visual impairment may sit apart from other children surrounded by the bulky enlarged texts or braille books and equipment. Desks will often need to be situated at the side of the room by a power point, so that a CCTV or a tape recorder can be used (Figure 10.4). This may be a particular problem for the student with additional disabilities who uses a wheelchair. A support assistant may work closely with the child. All of these factors may make it difficult for the child to freely socialise with his or her classmates.

Children can be encouraged to work in groups. This may take special skill on the part of the teacher or support assistant, as the extent of timely adult intervention should be at a minimum. The child with a visual impairment could be placed in a group situation where there is something to offer others in the group. Group recording of work can also

Figure 10.4

be used to lighten the load of the child with a visual impairment, where writing is an onerous task. This is true integration or inclusion, where the child with a visual impairment works in close association with peers.

In the playground, misunderstandings may arise because the child with a visual impairment cannot see the facial expressions or body language of the peers. The child with a visual impairment cannot see that someone has bumped into him or her by accident and may then complain of being pushed or bullied. The child may bump into other children because she or he can't see them, or because she or he has have poor motor coordination. Children may reply by hitting out first and asking questions later. The pupil with a visual impairment may not be invited to join in competitive team games either in playtimes or PE lessons. Peers may feel that the child with a visual impairment is always favoured. For example the pupil with a visual impairment may always sit at the front, or is always allowed to touch examples or artefacts first, and this may lead to resentment and bullying.

Scott (1982) suggests that the child with a visual impairment in an integrated setting, may feel isolated and alone. There may be no other pupil who will understand the problems and experiences of being visually impaired and with whom he or she can talk freely and share confidences. If the child with a visual impairment does have problems in mixing with peers, and in making and sustaining friendships, the child may develop a poor self-image (Lawrence 1987), and this may result in a complete lack of confidence. Such problems are not easily solved; however the skilled teacher should continually seek to encourage the child to develop good social skills and positive relationships with peers.

Conclusion

It is essential for the teacher to encourage pupils to overcome their difficulties and thus enable them to fulfil their potential and adapt to a rapidly changing world. Teachers should be constantly vigilant to ensure that they set high standards for their pupils, without lowering levels of expectation. The teacher's aim should be that pupils become independent learners, taking a full and active role in all spheres of life.

Useful address

The Partially Sighted Society, Queen's Road, Doncaster DN1 2NX; Tel: 01302 323132.

Chapter 11
The Adolescent

Rita Kirkwood

Introduction

Adolescence is a time of turbulence and change characterised by those events, biological, psychological and social, that mark the transition from childhood to adulthood. It is a period in life when individuals begin to adapt and adjust their behaviour and thinking to the new set of challenges and opportunities which they will face as adults. This transition becomes more difficult for young people if the significant adults in their lives fail to allow them the degree of independence of which they are capable, or conversely if adults remove the boundaries of control so quickly that young people are left uncertain and floundering. Parents and the professionals who work with young people are faced with achieving this balance in a society where the role of adolescents is rapidly changing.

The effects of a visual disability

One crucial aspect of adolescence is the development of a positive sense of identity and self-esteem. This is sometimes difficult for young people who, in addition to the normal quota of self-doubt and uncertainty, have a visual impairment. The process of establishing an identity is determined to a great extent by the way we relate to, and are influenced by, those around us. Adolescents who are fully sighted learn a great deal of what is expected of them by observation of the behaviour of others, and a lack of sight can make the process of adolescence more difficult than it might otherwise be. It is important not to underestimate the impact that a visual disability can have on the development of autonomy and independence, but it is also unwise to generalise about its effects. Judy Taylor, blind from the age of eight, said that she felt certain 'that the years of adolescence were made neither more nor less difficult by [her] disability' Taylor (1989).

The effects of visual impairment on adolescents may vary according to the extent of their loss of sight and the age at which onset of the condition occurs. Magee and Milligan (1995) assert that it is the consequences of the loss, rather than the loss itself, that causes the anxiety and grief felt by many late-blinded people. Adolescents who are losing their sight need to come to terms with the fact that as adults they will be denied experiences, such as having a driving licence, which they may have taken for granted that they would one day enjoy.

Physical development in adolescence

Let us examine more closely the areas of development involved in adolescence, starting with the physical changes of puberty and the particular challenges these may bring to a young person who has a visual disability.

While there may be clues in the family history, no one knows for sure when their body is going to start changing. To adolescents who are fully sighted the physical changes of adolescence such as growth of breasts and body hair in girls, or facial hair in boys, are obvious. By looking in the mirror they can observe the changes in their own bodies and they are able to compare themselves with their friends who are also undergoing change. This brings a measure of reassurance, even though they may not initially be comfortable about how they look. A young person who cannot see, often has to rely on a spoken description for an understanding of these changes, and touching taboos in our society will limit their opportunities to explore body changes in others.

If they are not to be disadvantaged in relation to their peer group, young people with a visual impairment need relevant and clear information about the changes in puberty. This information should be given before puberty starts and the approach in the classroom should encourage questions and invite open and frank discussion. As puberty starts between the ages of 10 and 15 for most young people, the process of learning should begin in the primary school.

The strong emphasis placed on physical attractiveness in our society means that a young person with a visual impairment has to address the vexed question of his or her appearance. The changes in body chemistry that accompany puberty often bring with them additional concerns about greasy hair and spots, and the adolescent with a visual impairment will need clear advice about grooming and personal hygiene. Deeper anxieties may revolve around the physical deformity which accompanies some visual disabilities. Facial deformities in particular may cause great concern to young persons, particularly at the time in their lives when they have become most aware of their appearance and have a desire to conform with prevalent standards of attractiveness. Sensitive counselling at this time is important if they are to overcome these anxieties and grow in self-esteem (see Chapter 14).

Cognitive development in adolescence

As the egocentricity that is in evidence at the beginning of adolescence diminishes, so the ability to think in an abstract way increases and the young person progresses in their development of analytical and deductive skills. In Piagetian terms, intellectual development in adolescence is characterised by the move from the concrete to the formal operations stage. Cunningham (1993) challenges this view by suggesting that only about 50% of adults appear to reach this stage in intellectual development. It is thought that the change from the concrete to the formal operations stage is to a large extent dependent on real-life experiences and the amount of practice people have in using analytical and deductive skills. This finding has important implications in education, and explains the modern emphasis on problem solving and the 'hands-on' approach to the curriculum for children.

Teachers working with students who have a visual impairment will try to encourage them to work independently and to derive their own solutions to problems in all areas of the curriculum (see Chapter 19). It is an important part of this process that students are allowed to make mistakes, short of those which involve unnecessary health and safety risks. The level of support offered to each student by classroom assistants should be carefully directed by the class teacher, to ensure that the additional presence of an adult does not reduce the student's opportunities for learning independently and through interaction with classmates.

In addition to the opportunities for experiential learning, an adolescent with a visual impairment will need opportunities to access the knowledge that is derived from the incidental learning experiences which form the background of a sighted person's cognitive development. Teachers and parents need to ensure that the gaps in the adolescent's general knowledge are identified and filled, or the young person may suffer embarrassment because of basic misconceptions. The information required may be as fundamental as explanations of which way up a bird flies, or why people cannot see round corners, or whether eyelids are transparent.

Social and emotional development in adolescence

It is possible to define three interdependent strands in the social and emotional development of young people: personality, relationships and moral reasoning. It is important that adolescents develop as far as possible the ability to make informed decisions for themselves, to develop a positive sense of identity and to establish peer relationships in order to progress to independent adulthood.

For adolescents with a visual impairment, there are a number of factors that may affect the ease with which these aims are achieved. A major factor is often the lack of eye contact, which makes communication more difficult and which can hinder the development of friendships. This can largely be compensated for by training in social skills which equips them, for example, to participate confidently in meetings, to approach people they do not know in social situations and to accept or refuse help graciously when it is offered by a well-meaning member of the public.

The lack of visual cues sometimes makes it difficult for a person with a visual impairment to judge when to stop talking in a conversation or when the person they are talking to wishes to move away. However, there are compensatory perceptual skills that can be learnt, such as interpreting sound cues in the voice of the person who is speaking. Hull (1990) describes these cues as the 'unintended nuances of the voice'. The ability to deploy social skills varies from person to person. The quiet, more introverted person with a visual impairment may need encouragement to make the effort to overcome their natural shyness in social situations. The young person who is outgoing and sociable may have already developed these skills and will simply need to refine them through practice.

Independence skills can promote the development of a healthy self-image. When considering the curriculum for young people with a visual impairment, there is often a conflict between the requirements of the National Curriculum and the need for additional lessons in areas such as mobility and self-help skills (see Chapter 17), braille or information technology (IT). Pupils in their teenage years should be consulted about timetable priorities, and given every opportunity to develop as much control over their own learning as they are capable of managing. A person entering adolescence needs to be encouraged to assume responsibility in decisions about their life, and indeed there is a legal requirement that the views of pupils with special educational needs should be taken into account throughout the transition years of 14 to 16.

Some of the consequences of their visual impairment may be difficult for young people to accept. They may not, for example, wish to be seen carrying a bulky brailler around the school or they may not wish to be seen using a low vision aid or a white cane. Pupils with high levels of self-esteem will generally find it easier to be different from their peers than those with less confidence. The school may need to develop a strategy for addressing this delicate issue.

Erikson, quoted in Bee (1985), described the main focus of adolescence as being the acquisition of a sense of identity while fending off a sense of confusion, and he noted the areas of sexuality and future occupation as particular sources of conflict. The resolution of conflicts in these areas will take time and may involve a period of indecision, but a successful outcome is important in helping individuals to establish an integrated identity. Persons emerging from adolescence who have not learnt to face the challenges posed by these conflicts may be dogged by low self-esteem and a lack of direction as adults.

During these turbulent years most young people need to experiment in order to establish an identity apart from their parents. Increasingly, perhaps, these experiments can cause lasting harm. Many children experiment with drugs, drinking and smoking while still at school and continue these habits into adult life. With the reduced job opportunities for people who have a disability, the drug culture may come to be seen by some young persons as providing a sense of identity that they feel is otherwise unattainable. However, underlying difficulties which are resolved this way may well re-emerge at a later date.

Without legitimate opportunities to exercise control and make decisions for themselves, young persons with a visual impairment may choose an unhealthy and ultimately unsatisfying way of expressing their personalities. Young people with disabilities usually benefit from an environment in which constructive criticism and positive feedback are key elements. They need to feel valued and appreciated, but also need to have a measure by which to gauge their own performance and behaviour and opportunities to show initiative, take responsibility and make decisions about their own learning.

Transition plans

The role of the school in the transition of 16 year old pupils who are the subject of a statement of special educational needs, is clearly defined in the Code of Practice (DfE 1994). A transition plan has to form part of the first annual review after these pupils reach the age of 14 and it has to be reviewed annually thereafter. It forms the basis of planning for the young person's transition to adult life. The plan is drawn up following a review meeting convened by the local education authority (LEA), to which parents, the headteacher, relevant staff, and other providers (such as social services and the careers service) are invited. The transition plan looks at ways of encouraging and facilitating the involvement of young people in planning for their own futures and identifies the support and resources that may be required to implement the plan. The Code of Practice states that 'the views of young people themselves should be sought and recorded wherever possible in an assessment, reassessment or review during the years of transition'. This procedure formalises the role of the school in preparing pupils with disabilities for this transition to adulthood (see Chapter 12).

The framework for transition planning described by the Code of Practice places emphasis on the acquisition of independent living skills and the growth in personal autonomy. The use of records of achievement can be another effective method of helping young people recognise and value their own progress and can encourage them to take on responsibilities which will help them acquire the skills they will need in the future.

Aspects of the curriculum

Adolescents who have a visual impairment are entitled to the same range of educational opportunities as their peers. This includes access to the full range of the National Curriculum subjects as well as any extracurricular activities offered by the school. There should be no discrimination because of the student's lack of sight and the challenge for the teacher is to devise ways that access can be achieved.

There are many ways in which pupils who are blind are able to join in practical lessons, and often simple adaptations to equipment or the adoption of alternative teaching techniques, such as cooperative working in small groups is all that is required. The wish to stay behind after school to participate in extra-curricular activities may conflict with local authority transport arrangements, but schools should try to resolve these difficulties in the interests of the development of the pupils and their social integration outside the classroom.

For adolescents with visual impairments who receive their education in mainstream schools, the opportunity to mix with other people of the same age with similar disabilities can often be beneficial. Some support services and special schools arrange activity weekends and summer camps for students with a visual impairment and these can provide valuable opportunities for young people to share experiences and identify common concerns.

The timing of the introduction to braille for adolescents with a deteriorating eye condition can sometimes be a particularly difficult decision. It is accepted by most teachers that it is important to make the best use of residual vision and to encourage its full use for as long as possible. A comment from one adult who went blind during adolescence was that instead of being taught braille, he wished he had been put in front of the television to absorb as much with his deteriorating vision as possible before that door closed for ever. While it is now commonly held that it is better to wait until the young person chooses to learn braille of their own volition, the pressures of public examinations and the need in secondary schools for an efficient means of access to the written word, often make this waiting approach a difficult one to adhere to (see Chapter 16).

Conclusion

As we have seen, adolescence is a time when young people begin to assess the implications of their visual impairment for their future lives. There are some weighty issues that they need to grapple with, for example some will be aware of an hereditary aspect of their visual condition which may affect the sight of any children born to them in the future. In some of these issues the role of teaching staff is not to offer advice or opinion but to provide relevant information when the pupil feels the need for it. In this instance the school would rely on outside help and arrange genetic counselling from an ophthalmologist. Professionals and parents don't have all the solutions to the challenges of adolescence, but they can help the young person to find their way through this turbulent and exciting period.

Chapter 12
Transition to Adulthood

Sue Wright

Introduction

Transition from childhood to adulthood can take many years. The smoothness of the passage depends upon both the characteristics of the individual and the environment into which he or she is being received. For young people with a visual impairment, negotiating the complex, confusing and occasionally hostile forces of the adult world can be particularly frustrating. It is no easy task, and one which young people and their personal and professional mentors must recognise and take seriously, beginning preparation sooner rather than later.

The aim of transition in its simplest terms is to reach adulthood but this means rather more than achieving physical maturation. Transition is a social process, defined by the Office for Economic Cooperation and Development/Centre for Education and Research Innovation (OECD/CERI) (1986) as comprising four main areas:

- personal autonomy and independence from parental control;
- economic self-sufficiency, usually through employment;
- new relationships and roles within and beyond the family;
- participation in community life as citizens with legal rights, responsibilities and access to resources.

In this chapter the particular effects of the visual impairment on the transition process will be considered. It should not be forgotten, however, that the experience of transition is also influenced by the unique social, economic, ethnic and gender characteristics of the individual, all of which 'customise' the process, and neither should visual impairment be regarded as a set of personal deficits which must be corrected before some unchallenged notion of normality is achieved. These are important issues which must of necessity be debated elsewhere. Corbett and Barton (1992) may prove a useful starting point.

Personal autonomy and independence from parental control

For professional practitioners working with young people with a visual impairment, there has traditionally been an emphasis on developing the skills considered necessary to participate fully in adult life, away from parental (or professional) control. Social communication skills are considered central to this process.

According to Stockley (1994) assessment and observation suggest that social communication skills are delayed and immature in some young people with a visual impairment. While she denies that visual impairment itself is responsible for poor socialisation, she adds that it cannot it be assumed that these young people 'will maturate automatically and develop the confidence and self-esteem required to communicate on equal terms'.

Some young people with a visual impairment will have experienced their childhood in a protected or sheltered or segregated environment in which activities and influences, by default or deliberation, might have been limited.

As the Further Education Unit (FEU 1992) claimed with respect to young people with severe physical disabilities:

> many... had missed ordinary formative experiences in their early lives, for example, being allowed to make mistakes and learn from them, being allowed to exercise choice, being expected to accept responsibility and being involved in making decisions which affected their own lives and the lives of others.

The recent impetus to develop advocacy and self-advocacy skills reflects concerns about the effects of these restricting experiences. An increasing number of people with disabilities are asserting their right to protect and act on behalf of their own rights and interests with persuasion or force.

The core components of the advocacy process have been described by Clare (1990) as:
- being able to express thoughts and feelings, with assertiveness if necessary;
- being able to make choices and decisions;
- having clear knowledge and information about rights;
- being able to make changes.

The drive for self-advocacy and self-determination is often a painful one. Inevitably an increase in control by one group in society leads to a decrease in control by another. Parents and professionals may well feel threatened, devalued and pushed aside. They may feel offended by the new view of the world which casts them as, at best, over-protective but well-meaning and, at worst, oppressors with a vested interest in maintaining dependency. The sometimes strident accusations of emerging radical groups should not deflect from the general belief that young people with visual impairment can and should be empowered to make their own choices in life, even if this is not always in the interests of parents and service providers.

The role of parents, educators and other professionals is to encourage, as mentors, the development of those skills which underpin advocacy and self-determination within a framework of knowledge, skills and values.

Information gathering is vital to the process of exercising choice; yet information is often presented in a visual medium or distilled through a third party. Searching for a job is an example. As opportunities narrow for all young people, the ability for young people with a visual impairment to compete in the employment market is threatened. Access to current, unbiased information becomes more difficult, and there is a danger of narrow, unimaginative and uncritical advice being the only information available. (See Chapter 13 for a fuller discussion.) Mike Oliver (FEU 1992) describes the following scenario: 'Some blind people, on taking A-Levels at a well-known grammar school, report that they were then exhorted to decide whether they wished to be a lawyer, a physiotherapist or an audio-typist.'

Without alternative sources of information and insight, students who are visually impaired may have difficulty resisting such pressure and choosing their own paths.

Personal autonomy requires the maximisation of learning opportunities and the full achievement of educational potential. In what has been described as the 'jungle' of post-16 qualifications, young people with a visual impairment need to be able to keep abreast of curriculum developments and to distinguish between the different learning routes; for example, appreciating which of BTEC National, GCE A-levels or GNVQ is most appropriate for their needs and aspirations.

They should also, as individuals, be able to distinguish which styles of learning best suit them. Learning methods have evolved beyond the didactic approach which characterised the educational experience of previous generations. Modern students are expected to take more control over their learning and to exercise more choice in their approach to tasks and their responses to them. The acquisition of relevant study skills is therefore of greater importance (see Chapter 19). The appropriate use of access technology will be a particularly significant factor for students who are visually impaired. Demanding suitably adapted hardware and adaptive software, ensuring equal access to limited computer resources, and keeping up to date with innovations can be essential for a student's success. It is important that the significance of such support is understood by everyone to whom a young person goes for advice, not simply the teacher with responsibility for information technology.

Young people with a visual impairment may have to rely heavily on other partners in the transition process. Having developed the skills which have been considered central to adequate preparation for adulthood, they have to negotiate the professional systems and deal with the personnel who can ease or block their route.

McGinty and Fish (1992) listed as many as 35 categories of professionals who can be involved in the transition process. Armstrong and Davies (1995) suggest that young people may be confused by a fragmentation of responsibilities between different agencies, including schools, local education authorities (LEAs), social service departments, career advisers and training bodies. In my own experience, professional colleagues and parents can also be confused by the complex and changing array of personnel, policies and procedures which impact upon the students and which may vary from one locality to another.

Within education, an attempt at clarifying goals and coordinating provision is embodied in the 'Transition Plan'. This is described in the Code of Practice on the

Identification and Assessment of Special Education Needs (DfE, 1994) as

> a document which sets out the arrangements which an authority considers appropriate for a young person during the period when he or she is aged 14 to 19 years, including arrangements for special educational provision and for any other necessary provision, for suitable employment and accommodation and for leisure activities, and which will facilitate transition from childhood to adulthood.

When it works well, transition planning significantly improves the coordination of services and enhances continuity, for example between school and college. However, it only applies to young people with a Statement of Need (that is, statemented students); practice around the United Kingdom is variable, and not all students with a visual impairment are being statemented.

Transition planning, nonetheless, imposes cooperative practices upon the professionals involved, demands rigour in the recording of evidence and recommendations, and – not least – encourages young people themselves to participate more fully in the decision-making process regarding their transition.

Wood and Trickey (1996) suggest that the promotion of self-advocacy is inherent in the Code of Practice which emphasises the importance of personal, social and independent living skills in the pursuit of personal autonomy and self-advocacy. But, as Wood and Trickey point out, a common curriculum framework to meet these needs has not yet been devised.

New relationships and roles within and beyond the family

The family is often the most stable, the most committed and the most significant element in the child's development. At the time of transition, however, the family's role can easily become marginalised, as professionals focus on the emergent adult, and young people begin to choose their own way.

Wertheimer's study (1988) remarked on the relatively low level of parental involvement in the educational process of young adults, compared with their involvement in earlier years. This lack of involvement results in lost opportunities on both sides. Parents are less likely to be knowledgeable about the educational processes, the options open and the support services available to their children, and educators are deprived of the unique insights and skills parents have concerning their offspring.

The OECD/CERI study (1986) points to four aspects of parents' involvement in transition which require attention:

- a greater awareness by professionals of parental needs and potential contributions during the transition process;
- the recognition of the parental role in fostering independence and developing their child's adult status;

- the need for closer cooperation in overcoming some of the inherent conflicts of interest highlighted by self-advocacy work and the development of autonomy;
- an extension of the role of parents in improving services, both while young people are dependent upon family support, and afterwards.

The SKILL (National Bureau for Students with Disabilities) Report (SKILL 1993) supports this view, emphasising both the 'expert' knowledge of parents about the needs of their offspring, and their crucial and central role in assisting them towards independent economic and social life. SKILL suggest the promotion of parent groups to harness these contributions, and voluntary organisations such as LOOK and the National Blind Children's Society go some way towards providing such a network of information and mutual support for parents of young people with a visual impairment.

For many families, the transition of young people towards adulthood can be a testing time. The transition years can be characterised by clashes of personality, priorities and principles as young people develop their individuality and move closer to the norms and values of their peer group. The search for an individual identity separate from the family is common to all young people, but for those with a visual impairment there may be added and special dimensions to the process.

Nixon (1991) quoted one parent's perspective:

> With all the uncertainties of the future at least (my child) has the closeness of our family as a constant ... but we are concerned about how she will do, how she will handle her life. The future is a question mark, a big blank.

Some young people with a visual impairment will not have a family that is not so close or so constant; a dysfunctional family may not be in a position to care or be concerned about the future. For others, the family may be too heavy an anchor, offering an over-protective environment, which fosters dependence and isolation, reinforced by social and administrative structures which make self-reliance and autonomy difficult.

Social networks for young people with a visual impairment may be limited (Chapman 1978), restricting their initiation into a youth culture with its own rapidly changing fashion, music and social activities. Initial acceptance into a social group can often, for young people, be based upon superficial criteria of clothing, haircut and less definable 'style'. Missing the visual cues offered by independent social interaction or media images, youngsters who are visually impaired must rely on 'interpreters' – family or residential workers – to guide them. Autonomous choices are harder, and integration of the individual into wider social networks may therefore be less successful.

There is still considerable prejudice and misunderstanding about sexuality and disability which can result in the discouragement or denial of the sexual needs of people with visual impairment. Opportunities for young people to make friends, explore relationships and satisfy sexual needs may, deliberately or otherwise, be thwarted by close surveillance by their parents or carers. Literally or metaphorically, moving away can be very difficult to achieve.

While living independently away from the family home may be a goal for most young people, those with a visual impairment may have to compromise on housing. Burchard *et al.* (1991) found that 'sheltered' accommodation, that is, supervised apartments offered opportunities for both personal independence and community integration. Tenants with disabilities reported the same degree of lifestyle satisfaction and personal well-being as family-based peers.

When choosing accommodation, geographical location and access to transport may be a constraining feature for young people with visual impairments, since most are denied the independence afforded to car drivers. A sound foundation in mobility skills is essential to ensure successful transition to independent accommodation.

Economic self-sufficiency, usually through employment

Historically, people with a visual impairment have not been expected to be economically self-sufficient. As Finkelstein (1991) notes: 'In the formative years following the industrial revolution, the modern concept of disability became associated with expectations of a life of dependency upon charity and beggary.'

As social welfare organisations developed and social security systems became more sophisticated, the requirement and the motivation to earn a living reduced. An extremely hostile employment environment often viewed people with disabilities as unproductive, uncompetitive and burdensome. Yet for most adults, work or employment is a funda-mental component of life which confers status, economic security and opens up social networks. Young people with visual impairments have as much right to access the rewards of the workplace as their peer group and personal and professional mentors need to support that aim.

Chapter 13 of this text delves more deeply into the role of the education and careers services in preparing young people for employment. The emphasis on career awareness and job search skills is an essential element of the education of all young people in transition. Students with a visual impairment demand additional support in information gathering, decision-making and self-advocacy to ensure equal access to the labour market. Specific strategies need to be devised to overcome some of the barriers presented by the employment world. The latter can include (Clare 1990)

- lack of information and support for employers;
- lack of legislative intervention, such as the enforcement of quota systems;
- the state of the labour market;
- a benefits system which creates financial risks for those attempting work and penalises those who might wish to work part-time.

Sowers and Powers (1991) quote very practical examples of potential difficulties encountered in the workplace: using the bathroom, getting into and around employment sites, eating and drinking while at work, and communicating with co-workers.

For young people in educational settings where work experience schemes are available, such difficulties can be identified during work placements, and appropriate programmes devised. Close partnership between teachers, mobility officers and employers will enhance the likelihood of successful placement.

The opportunity to consult with older people with a visual impairment about their experiences in the workplace is another means of identifying and overcoming potential difficulties. At its most refined, a mentoring system, where employees who are visually impaired work closely with aspiring applicants, serves not only to prepare the way to employment, but also to reassure and raise the young person's confidence.

As young people with visual impairment approach adulthood, they must learn the intricacies of a benefits system which may have been managed entirely by their families or other carers until that time. They must learn what to claim, how to claim, how to budget and how to maintain their entitlement. The present benefits framework is inextricably linked to training or employment. Attendance at a training course can result in a cut or withdrawal of benefit. Part-time employment (an increasingly common feature of the current labour market, and one with attractions to some young people with disabilities) can lead to the 'benefits trap': a situation where there is no incentive to earn because claimants are better off financially on benefit. Application for benefit can be a lengthy and cumbersome process. The application form for Disability Living Allowance (DLA), for example, takes several hours for a student to complete, even with professional help. While all students have to contend with council tax exemption forms and student loan applications, students with visual impairments may also have to negotiate the immensely complex DLA form, and/or applications for student fund support.

In addition to understanding issues relating to benefit and pay, young people with visual impairments who wish to access further education must be aware of the funding mechanisms which support study and training. Since the 1992 Further and Higher Education Act, statutory funding for young people has moved from local authorities to the Further Education Funding Councils (FEFCs), one for England and one for Wales. FEFCs are charged with ensuring a continuum of funding for students in transition who have disabilities. They must also ensure that 'public funds are used cost effectively' (Vaughan Huxley 1993).

Students wishing to access specialist day or residential provision in independent or 'non-sector' colleges are faced with a funding council which may be reluctant to fund this relatively more expensive form of provision. FEFCs currently require students to attend an interview at a 'sector' or mainstream college and will consider a specialist setting only if the sector college cannot meet their needs. This can be a time-consuming and demoralising process, which emphasises dis-ability rather than ability. Students may require tenacity and assertiveness to achieve their own preferences in spite of the view that for some students with disabilities, 'therapy, care and even the residential experience itself are an important and integral part of teaching and learning' (Griffiths 1994).

The deficit view of disability which appears to be inherent in some of the current funding mechanisms for students with visual impairment, contrasts sharply with current thinking regarding their entitlement to appropriate education and training. The Tomlinson Report (FEFC 1996) describes this thinking:

We want to avoid a viewpoint which locates the difficulty or deficit with the student, and focus instead on the capacity of the educational institution to understand and respond to the individual learner's requirement. This should not focus on the disability itself but on what it means for the way that person can learn, or be helped to learn, even more effectively.

This is an important concept for all involved in the transition process: governors, managers, teachers, parents, careers officers, social workers. It also places considerable responsibility on the student, to identify and articulate his or her own individual learning style and to match that with what Tomlinson describes as 'an appropriate educational environment' (FEFC 1996).

Economic self-sufficiency will rely ultimately upon an appropriate educational placement and this requires prudent matching of individual needs, skills and aspirations with appropriate education and training programmes.

Participation in community life

The late 1970s and 1980s saw the emergence of new thinking with regard to the rights of people with disabilities. The Warnock Report (Department of Education and Science 1978) and the Education Act (1981) sought to promote greater inclusion in society via the formal education process. Further education, in particular, was expected to equip young people with disabilities with the skills to take on new roles in the community, as part of greater autonomy and independence.

Reports by the OECD/CERI (1988) and the King's Fund Centre (1986) supported change in this area; yet we do not well prepare our young people with disabilities for citizenship. There is relatively little in the way of formal curricula in this area in schools and colleges, and it could be argued that there is a laissez-faire reliance on media forces and informal social networks to educate for adult status. While in the United Kingdom citizenship is conferred at the age of 18, with formal voting status, little is done to explore the opportunities and responsibilities such status brings.

The Tomlinson Committee (FEFC 1996) recommends the development of a pre-foundation award called 'Skills for Adult Life', made up of the following units:
- employability (preparation for working life);
- understanding roles in the family, including parenting skills and relationships;
- understanding the local community, including travel, leisure pursuits and voluntary work;
- understanding the society in which we live, including the laws and the individual benefits and allowances.

Were such a recommendation to be implemented, we could be more confident about easing the transition to adulthood of young people with visual impairment.

Chapter 13

Careers and Vocational Education

Sue Wright

Introduction

In industrial societies 'work' or paid employment, is a fundamental component of the lives of most individuals. It confers status upon them and helps them to establish economic security, social networks and a stake in the general prosperity and development of the nation. Its converse, unemployment or non-employment, brings with it financial, social and psychological difficulties.

Most young people view the acquisition of work as a major goal. It allows them to live independently of their parents, control their own lives and take responsibility for their own futures.

In recent decades, however, this critical part of the transition process from childhood to adulthood has been made more uncertain by the growth of youth employment and by the development of new structures and programmes which, in effect, delay economic and social maturation. For young people with a disability, such as those with a visual impairment, negotiating these barriers and structures can be extremely difficult. They will need planned, systematic and expert support to improve their chances of employment.

Working definitions

Career development has been described as a constant process of formulating work values and a vocational identity (Bagley 1983). Havighurst (1964) postulates six stages of career development.

1. Identification with a worker, occurring during early childhood. The child acquires the concept of work, which becomes part of his/her self-orientation during this early stage.
2. Acquiring the basic habits of industry, occurring in early adolescence. The child learns how to get a 'job' or piece of work done, how to stay on task, how to put work ahead of leisure activities.
3. Acquiring identity as a worker in an occupational structure. The individual prepares for an occupation or job through pre-employment training at school or college, initial work experiences, and part-time jobs. The link between payment for work and economic independence is realised during this period.

4. At 25+, becoming a productive person, moving up and gaining responsibility in an organisation.

5. At middle age, reaching the peak of a career, paying more attention to the civic responsibilities associated with their occupation, and providing guidance to young people in stages 3 and 4.

6. Later in life, withdrawal from the workforce.

Such a model can provide a framework for the identification of intervention strategies appropriate to people who are visually impaired. While disability may bring different kinds of life experiences, the process of career development remains the same.

The formal education years provide the first setting for intervention. **Careers education** has been defined (Careers Service 1995) as 'a means of developing individuals' knowledge and understanding of themselves, and opportunities in education, training and employment, and of developing the skills necessary to make informed decisions'.

Careers guidance provides 'a means of helping individuals to apply relevant knowledge, understanding and skills to their own particular circumstances when choices have to be made' (Careers Service 1995).

In practice careers education and careers guidance are closely interwoven and are concerned with a range of activities aimed at helping young people make the transition towards educational and vocational success. These have been categorized by the CEC (1988) as follows:

- Information: providing clients with objectives and factual data.
- Assessment: making a diagnostic judgment about the client's suitability for particular options.
- Advice: making suggestions based on the helper's own knowledge and experience.
- Counselling: helping clients explore their own thoughts and feelings about their present situation, about the options open to them, and about the consequences of each option.
- Careers education: providing a programme of planned experiences, designed to develop in clients the skills, concepts and knowledge that will help them to make objective career choices and transitions.
- Placement: helping clients to achieve entry to a particular job or course.

From these activities it is hoped that individuals will acquire a range of competencies, including the abilities to:

- assess their own personal qualities, skills, needs, interests, attitudes and values;
- seek and sort information about opportunities in education, training and work;
- match personal information with information about opportunities;
- select and use an appropriate decision-making strategy to choose between opportunities;
- use an action-planning process to achieve their goals;
- use self-presentation skills in a selection process;
- cope with the transition from one work environment to another (NCET 1996).

Working with students who are visually impaired

In what sense are young people with visual impairments particularly equipped to acquire these competencies? Are there barriers to acquiring skills and knowledge in this area which are peculiar to their disability, and if so, how can they be overcome?

Access to information about job opportunities which appears in newspapers, on noticeboards or at Jobcentres, for example, may well be restricted for young people with little or no sight. Their casual acquaintance with job roles may be limited. Even in families where youngsters are normally involved in family work-related activities, young people who are visually impaired may be excluded. Opportunities to meet adults who are visually impaired and who can act as role models or mentors for employment can be rare. Opportunities for direct experience of the world of work, through part-time jobs or work experience, may similarly be restricted.

Self-presentation skills may be underdeveloped in some young people with visual impairment. In highly competitive selection processes, employers may regard 'inappropriate' posture, gait and other non-verbal mannerisms (see Lombana 1980) as distracting and discouraging. Patterns of behaviour which are tolerated in the segregated settings within which many children who are visually impaired grow up may not be acceptable in the mainstream workplace, particularly when a growing emphasis is placed on marketing concepts surrounding presentation skills and customer care.

The selection processes for employment may include psychometric or other psychological tests which are neither designed nor standardized for applicants who are visually impaired. Smith *et al.* (1991) cite one individual with a visual impairment:

> I failed the psychometric tests because of the speed factor. The tests themselves were not too difficult. I got a very high success rate in what I managed to get through, I was told, but I just did not manage to get through enough because of the size of print.

These examples suggest that there are special considerations to be taken into account when preparing young people who are visually impaired for the world of work. However, opportunities for young people do not present themselves in a social vacuum (see Armstrong and Davies 1995). The problem may lie with the 'receiving society'; in this instance the labour market. Corbett and Barton (1992) remind us of 'a failure to address the nature of the society into which integration is being advocated'. They describe such a society as 'unequal, offensive and divisive'.

However, the aim of the author is to review what can be done to support the career development of learners who are visually impaired in the current social climate. At this stage it may be helpful to examine the roles of the key participants in this critical operation.

Working with students in schools and colleges

In the United Kingdom careers education and guidance for young people is the responsibility of schools and colleges, and of the Careers Service. The National Curriculum Council (NCC) Circular Number 6 (1990) identified the area as one of its cross-curricular themes. It is not an additional subject but should be taught through the subjects of the National Curriculum and through other timetabled provision, and promoted through the wider aspects of school life. The NCC's document (1990) outlines ways in which this can be achieved. Two other documents consolidate guidance on careers education issues: *Looking Forward* (SCAA 1995) issued by the School Curriculum and Assessment Authority (SCAA), and a paper issued jointly by both the Employment Department and Department for Education (1994) entitled *Better Choices: Working Together to Improve Careers Education and Guidance – The Principles*. This latter paper (produced immediately before the formal amalgamation of the two government departments) urges a closer partnership between training and enterprise councils (TECs), local education authorities (LEAs), schools and colleges and the Careers Service.

Quality control of careers education in schools is managed primarily through the Office for Standards in Education (Ofsted). Its *Guidance on the Inspection of Special Schools* (1995) requires schools to provide documentation to show how careers education is coordinated, how it draws on pupils' experiences within subjects and how it is enhanced by links with employers and training providers. With respect to careers guidance, Ofsted inspectors are required to measure how effectively the school draws on the expertise of outside agencies (particularly the Careers Service) to provide impartial and well-informed advice, and how the school then relates this advice to pupils' needs. Careers education and guidance is expected to be 'objective and even-handed ... [and] ... free from gender or other stereotyping'. Ofsted inspectors also assess 'whether those involved in providing careers education and guidance have access to appropriate professional development to prepare and assist them in their work'.

Working with the Careers Service

The Careers Service is the major partner of schools and colleges in the delivery of careers education and guidance. New arrangements for its operation came into force on 1 April 1993. These implemented the Trade Union Reform and Employment Rights Act 1993 (TURER) through which the duty to provide Careers Services was transferred from local education authorities to the Secretary of State for Employment. TURER gave the Secretary of State powers to make whatever local arrangements seemed most appropriate in each area. Following a process of competitive tendering, contracts have subsequently been awarded to a variety of consortia, involving personnel originally employed by local authorities and new players from industry and associated bodies such as TECs.

A major aim of TURER is 'to encourage innovation and flexibility in service delivery and more business-like approaches to management and quality, thereby improving the efficiency and effectiveness of the Careers Service' (Watson *et al.* 1995).

Apart from a brief acknowledgement of the principle of equal opportunities, there is little in the documentation which relates specifically to young people with disabilities. Careers Service guidance does, however, specify that people with disabilities are part of the client group 'until they are settled in their learning intention' (Careers Service 1995). This suggests that schools and colleges are entitled to access the service on behalf of people with disabilities, even after the statutory school-leaving age. In practice, the availability of the resources to match the entitlement varies according to local arrangements and priorities.

Walker *et al.* (1992), in an RNIB survey, asked parents whether their children aged 11 and over (and considered able to work in the future) had seen a careers adviser. Overall, nearly 50% of the children had not, 25% had, and in the other cases the parents did not know whether their children had seen a careers adviser. Most of the parents who did not know had children who were attending special schools. Only 5% of parents with children in ordinary schools did not know.

Professionals working in formal educational settings with young people who are visually impaired, need to work in partnership with colleagues in allied services to access the resources and expertise for careers education and guidance. Within schools and colleges it is important that governors and senior managers understand legal requirements and prioritise resources to meet them.

Other agencies

There are some non-governmental contacts and agencies which will support educational professionals in the job-search task. The Royal National Institute for the Blind has an Employment Network. There are also local networks of employers (such as Employers' Disability Forums) with an interest in disability issues. Consortia of schools and employers may have formed a 'compact' relationship to enhance motivation and encourage school achievement; it is important that students who are visually impaired are represented in such activities.

A working curriculum

The first step in devising a curriculum framework within which careers education and guidance can be delivered is to establish free and open discussion, resulting in a clear written policy which:

1. recognises legislative and inspection imperatives;
2. highlights the importance of this area for visually impaired pupils and students;
3. Clarifies the rights and responsibilities of all those concerned in this area.

Developing such a policy requires the involvement of governors, coordinators and teachers. A working group, with a set timetable, could address the task. Parental and employer representation should be encouraged. The group would need to collect relevant information, agree aims and objectives, decide on content and determine methods of delivery. It would then fall on the coordinator to write the policy. Monitoring the success of the policy and ensuring that it meets learning needs will require both internal staff development and the involvement of external partners, such as parents, employers and other community members.

Delivery of a careers education and guidance programme can begin at the primary stage. Etheridge (1978), Woal (1974) and Bauman (1971) describe programmes in the United States which introduce children who are visually impaired to work options and work routines and encourage visiting workers in the elementary school classroom. The aim is to increase awareness of occupational roles early in life and encourage an interest in the world of work. Play, especially role play, can be another successful means of exploring this area. The involvement of parents can be useful; they can share their work experiences with the class while fostering an appreciation of their own child's work capabilities.

In the middle school years, experience in real work settings around school (the office, the grounds) can be introduced, so that pupils can begin to explore various types of employment (indoor/outdoor, in a team/alone, busy environment/quiet environment). Such opportunities allow for an early development of work-related skills such as getting to the right place at the right time, organising and adapting the work environment and selecting the appropriate aids and equipment for the task.

Lombana (1980) suggests four factors which can affect whether a person with a disability will succeed in a given job:

1. the ability to meet the physical demands, to accomplish tasks efficiently;
2. not being a hazard to themselves;
3. not jeopardising the safety of others;
4. not aggravating the disability.

At secondary school level, vocational experience can be extended beyond school to placements in the community. Clayton (1977) describes such a programme at the Maryland School for the Blind in the USA. Lawrence (1973) details an intensive five-week residential work experience programme, designed to enhance achievement in students who are visually impaired by making heavy demands upon them, and by heightening their self-awareness and self-esteem. At this stage specific skills training can be introduced, together with supportive training in orientation and route-learning and independent travel skills. Work experience can also provide the motivation that is the starting point for vocational development (Wilson, 1974).

In the later years of secondary school, from age 13 onwards, and particularly in Year 11 prior to school leaving, more systematic approaches to job searching can begin. While individual teachers will continue to address general issues of employment and the labour market within their own curriculum area, it is at this stage that a specialist member of staff (personal tutor, careers teacher, employment officer) can focus on the individual student's needs, aspirations and opportunities.

For many young people who are visually impaired, further education and training will be the next step. However, this should not obviate the need for specific job-search training at this stage. Not only is an early start in the process, with regular reinforcement, likely to improve students' knowledge of the task ahead, but the skills developed are flexible and can be accredited as part of formal coursework in the general curriculum. To restrict job-search training to the few who are actively seeking work in Year 11 is both divisive and wasteful of a key motivational opportunity.

A careful matching process can then take place between individual students and opportunities. Travis (1993) describes her role in this process at Queen Alexandra College. Two particular initiatives are worth noting. She spends time with small groups of students, visiting Jobcentres to familiarise the students with the layout, personnel and procedures and with the special facilities available for people who are unable to read the cards on display. Learning to negotiate the bureaucracy of the Employment and other government Services is of itself an indispensable life skill for many adults who are visually impaired. Training should begin before the point of urgent need.

The second initiative is the mock interview process, where students respond to real job advertisements through a simulated process which requires them to submit application forms and CVs and attend formal job interviews. The interviews are conducted by real employers who are unknown to the students in formal, unfamiliar settings, and the interview is videotaped for subsequent discussion and feedback. Careful audio-description of the video is given to those with little or no sight. This daunting process is usually the first opportunity for students to critically examine their performance. It provides a realistic appraisal of their strengths and weaknesses and a clear indicator of future training needs.

Students who are visually impaired need to develop the social and behavioural skills expected by employers and employment organizations. Stockley (1994) suggests that these skills may be underdeveloped in young people who are visually impaired:

> ... it cannot be said that visual impairment on its own is responsible for poor socialisation, but neither can it be assumed that visually impaired children will mature automatically and develop the confidence and self-esteem required to communicate on equal terms.

Sowers and Powers (1991) describe employment barriers encountered at work by students who are visually impaired, such as: 'using the bathroom, getting into and around employment sites, eating and drinking while at work, and communication with co-workers'.

Professionals working with students in this area need above all to know the abilities of individual students, in order to avoid the unnecessary or inappropriate intervention which Cockburn (1987) describes as 'a patronising slur on young people's qualities'.

Working with information technology

Information Technology (IT) is an invaluable tool in the job-search task, and indeed in careers education and guidance generally. According to the National Council for Educational Technology (NCET 1996):

> IT is centrally placed to the acquisition and development of career-related competencies. Using a range of devices from mobile telephones to computers, the handling and processing of information can be made easier, quicker, more sophisticated and more productive'.

Many learners who are visually impaired are already familiar with technological aids and can apply their skills to searching for a job. Referring to students with disabilities, the NCET (1996) report continues:

> Using IT to provide individualised learning support, particularly through the use of specially written software, not only enhances students' development of life skills, but increases their motivation and satisfaction ... IT not only enables access, it also helps to support them in areas such as communication and presentation or their work. This can have a great impact on their careers work.

Software programs have been developed which can
• help students assess themselves and suggest new ideas;
• provide information about opportunities;
• help students decide between alternatives;
• teach students how to write an application or look for a job.

Most programs written for use in careers education and guidance fulfil one or more of these functions. For example, MICRODOORS is mainly concerned with helping students learn about occupations and training requirements. COIC CAREER-BUILDER assesses interests, skills and work values. Computer simulations are particularly valuable and can allow the student to experience decision making in a particular job-role, such as a supermarket manager or a secretary. The *Careers Software Review* of the NCET, first published in 1990 and regularly updated since, lists over 70 programs that can be used in careers education and guidance.

The information technology skills acquired by students who are visually impaired can be demonstrated to good effect in the production of their individual National Record of Achievement (NRA). Launched in 1991, the NRA was designed to help individuals plan their future development in education, employment and training. Smartly bound in a glossy cover, it reviews and records achievements at school, including formal qualifications, interests and extracurricular activities. In many respects this has advantages for students in residential provision, who can reflect in their NRA the greater breadth of activity and achievement that their participation in the 24-hour curriculum often affords.

Dearing (1996) claims that 80% of schools use the NRA with Year 11 students, and, in supporting its value as a transitional record for employers and education providers, advocates its introduction at age 13 rather than 16 years. It is certainly a useful means of recording and reviewing achievement, and allows the student the opportunity to shape its production in both content and style. This involvement of students in the planning process is an integral part of their entitlement to the careers education and guidance curriculum. (See too *Guidelines for Maintaining the Educational Entitlement of Pupils who are Visually Impaired*; North West Support Services for the Visually Impaired, 1994.)

Working with families

In advice to parents on the importance of play (RNIB 1995b) the RNIB urges: 'Your help is vital to ensure that your daughter or son *does* explore and get to know a world that is clearly not visible'. The relevance of such advice is not confined to the early years. Families continue to be interpreters of the visual world, for much of their lives, to children and young people who are visually impaired. Their role is not only as conveyors of information, for example describing the jobs of people met on the way to school, but also as transmitters of values such as punctuality which permeate the world of work. Clarke (1980), researching the influences on education and vocational choice, concludes that professional guidance services are often much less influential than the informal day-to-day influences of parents, other relatives and friends.

Family members are role models for young people. In their descriptions of their own working lives and in their observations about other employees, they can have a strong impact on the way their children perceive working adults and the expectations they may have of their own future.

Increasingly documents such as the *Parents' Charter* (1994a), the *Code of Practice on the Identification and Assessment of Special Educational Needs* (1994), and the *Careers Service Guidelines* (Careers Service 1995) have strengthened the legal rights of parents or guardians to participate in key decision-making areas relating to their child. Unless parents understand the benefits of employment for their child, they may not support their child's efforts to secure it. In the hostile employment environment of a recession, where redundancy may be a common feature of family or community life, it is easy to develop low expectations. The role of professionals is to provide families with information about employment, the contributions it can make to their child's life, and to advise parents realistically about employment prospects for their child. They should do this while valuing the unique perspective that families can bring to the individual needs and aspirations of their offspring, and the insight they may have into the local labour market. This latter point is particularly applicable to students in residential provision, where the staff may be unaware of the 'occupational realities' (Armstrong and Davies 1995) in the student's home area.

Conclusion

Careers education and guidance must be an integral part of the curriculum for any young person. For students who are visually impaired it deserves particular prominence because their transition from school to work is often a more complex process.

To neglect the area of careers education and guidance would be not only discriminatory, but a denial of the right of a person with a visual impairment to be included in society through participation in the labour market.

Chapter 14
Counselling

Ann Bond

Introduction

In this Chapter I shall discuss the emotional impact of vision loss and coping with, and adapting to the ensuing changes, and I shall explore the question of whether there are added and specific difficulties for the adolescent. During these discussions I shall look at the ways of supporting persons with a visual impairment, their family, and those involved with them professionally.

Several years ago I developed an eye condition which caused serious deterioration of my sight, as a result of which I am now registered as partially sighted. This necessitated a change of direction from my medical career in general practice to my current work as a clinical assistant in psychotherapy in the National Health Service. During this time I have been privileged to undertake counselling work with young people and adults with visual impairment. It is through these professional relationships and my own experience that I have been asked to contribute to this book. For reasons of confidentiality, personal details have been changed to protect the identity of clients. This chapter is dedicated to those who have helped me to develop insight into the world of the person with a visual impairment.

The emotional impact of vision loss

In his book *Blindness: What It Does, and How to Live With It* (Carroll 1961), Carroll writes of his work with young people returning from the Second World War who had received injuries resulting in severe damage to their eyesight.

Carroll talks of four major effects of the loss of sight on a person. The first is the loss of a sense of independence. This is extremely painful, particularly for young adults who often feel they have only recently acquired a sense of being less dependent on the family. They describe feeling like a young child again, one who needs a great deal of help. The second effect is the loss of 'social adequacy', as Carroll describes it. This can affect the visually impaired person in many circumstances, such as at social events, eating in a restaurant, or meeting a new crowd of people. Carroll also refers to a loss of obscurity. Many young people have described to me their feelings of discomfort that they cannot now merge into the background, for example because they are using a white cane or have a guide dog. The other effect, which to my mind is probably the most important, is the lowering of self-esteem. Carroll describes how this can lead to other losses, such as loss of a job or a relationship. He emphasises the need to mourn the loss of sight, in order to be able to adapt to the visual impairment.

Some of these changes can be tackled through practical help, such as mobility training, low vision aids, braille and modern technology. When I attended for rehabilitation, this practical approach was offered and was extremely useful to me. However, there seemed to be something missing. Everybody appeared very cheerful and most of the time this appearance was maintained. My inner experience was very different, and yet as nobody asked me how I felt (and I felt exquisitely vulnerable), I thought that I must be different and so I acted in the same cheerful manner. This was not useful.

Klein (1976), in her paper 'Mourning and its relationship to manic depressive states' describes very clearly the importance of mourning. Most work describing mourning refers to the loss of an emotionally important person. But it has come to be recognised that one can experience grief over the loss of an emotionally important part of oneself. Most people relate to the experience of grieving. The usual first effect of loss is shock denial. We all defend ourselves against emotional pain, and denial is one way of doing this. It prevents us being overwhelmed by the experience until we feel ready to start to think about it.

> A young woman, A., came to see me. She was distressed because the professionals working with her felt that she needed to begin to learn braille and start mobility training. A. felt that this was not so, and that she could still see adequately. Her eyesight was, in fact, deteriorating rapidly. I saw A. on two occasions at monthly intervals, and in the sessions she was able to discuss her feelings regarding her eyesight. She was frightened at the prospect of not being able to do all she would like to do, which included a career in art. She expressed feelings of anger and disappointment and sadness but she recognised that crossing a road on her own was dangerous. I understand that shortly after this she started mobility lessons, and was able to talk to her teachers about her difficulties in the classroom.
>
> Miss B. was very distressed after being registered blind, but if she expressed any emotion to those around her, several responses were offered. She was asked 'Have you thought of anti-depressant tablets?' Another response was 'I think I would rather be deaf.' Yet another was 'I know somebody worse off than you, but she still smiles.'

Of course, most people who are going through a traumatic experience are aware of others' dilemmas, and feel guilty because they are not coping. But, at this stage, such responses from others can increase one's sense of isolation and hopelessness. The most helpful response to somebody in this situation is to listen and acknowledge the distress.

It is not helpful to make assumptions about the reaction to loss. The grieving process is unique to each individual.

Breaking bad news

It is always a difficult task to convey bad news, and there are some people who are able to assimilate it more quickly than others. The way bad news is given can make a difference.

It often needs to be said more than once, and support should be given both then and subsequently.

Our own life events have a very powerful way of deepening our understanding about loss and grief. For a doctor, an excellent way of learning is to be a patient, although I do not think this should be mandatory in our training! I would like to illustrate this with my own experience. Some years ago I was referred to an ophthalmologist, following a severe deterioration in my eyesight. I felt anxious and frightened, and yet hopeful that something could be done to stop the problem. I was seen in a large room with little privacy, as several doctors were seeing patients in this room. The doctor was brusque and rude to me, and it felt as though all he could see in front of him were two eyes stuck on a piece of wood. I felt angry, and wanted to say something about this but I felt too vulnerable. His assistant then carried out some tests on me in the same rough manner, not explaining what he was about to do, and being irritated with me if I moved my head. I experienced a great deal of discomfort, and felt angry and misused. When I came out, I met the consultant in the corridor, talking to a colleague. He turned to me, and told me that it had been nice meeting me, but there was nothing they could do to help. I went out feeling stunned, angry and let down. I told the family about what he had said, and it was just words, and I shut out my thoughts.

A short while later, as the condition was getting worse, I was sent to see another eminent doctor. I remember sitting in the waiting room, dreading my name being called, and feeling very irritated with a mother and her daughter, who was about 20, who were laughing and joking. I felt very isolated and frightened. The doctor greeted me by my name, and asked me to tell him the problem. There was privacy, only one doctor to each room, and no interruptions. He listened carefully to what I said, and seemed interested in me as a person. My anxiety became less, and I started to feel less fearful. His assistant carried out the same tests as the ones in the previous hospital, but he explained what he was about to do, and warned me when he thought it might be uncomfortable. I felt his concern and care, and was able to cooperate quite easily while he was carrying out these tests. In fact, the discomfort was minimal. The consultant then spent time explaining the results and what possible treatments were available. However, he also told me that the prognosis was poor, and that I would need to think of adapting my life and work.

When I came out of the room I was crying, and I felt some relief from this. I did not feel hostile. The mother in the waiting room looked at me and said, 'It's awful isn't it?' I no longer felt isolated, and she talked about her daughter who was losing her sight very rapidly. I think we comforted each other. I felt that this doctor had helped me to face my problem, and my grieving had begun.

Visual impairment and the young person

I have not worked with young children, but I would like to give some examples of the inner worlds of the adolescent with a visual impairment, as they have been described to me.

M. is a person in mid-adolescence, who described to me an experience at a skating rink. 'M' was one of a group of visually impaired children who were learning to skate. They moved with great trepidation onto the ice, holding hands and clinging on to the side of the rink. After a while, M. let go and took a few steps, only to fall. M. described the feelings of panic and helplessness at not having anything to hold on to, and not knowing where the side was. This is how M. often felt in everyday life. It seemed to help to talk about this, and for M. to feel that someone was trying to understand the inner experience. We were then able to do some thinking about the current concerns in M.s life, and M. was able to look at possible ways forward.

Most of the young people with a visual impairment with whom I have spoken have been between the ages of 16 and 18, at a time when they are about to make attempts to move into the adult world. As we all can remember from our own adolescence, this can be a time of confusion and turmoil. It usually begins around the age of 11 or 12, and often this stage of life is not completed until the mid-20s. Several of the young people I have worked with have had eyesight problems for a long time, but their vision is deteriorating at this stage of their development, and they are having to face the prospect of both becoming blind and moving into adulthood. One could view adolescence as the giving up of childhood, and this in itself can cause emotional upheaval. For a young person whose sight is deteriorating, moving into a more independent state is hampered by the fact that they feel less independent, due to the losses I have described.

D. was a young man who had always had some problems with his eyesight, but at the age of 17 his condition worsened dramatically and he was told he would be registered blind. He spent time expressing his anger and frustration, as he was about to start taking driving lessons, enjoyed playing cricket, and was looking forward to going to college. He was bewildered as he felt his independence had been taken away from him, and in fact he felt quite childlike again, which was frightening to him. It was important for me to acknowledge these feelings. At this stage, I do not think it is helpful to give reassurances, like 'Never mind, you can play a different sort of cricket, with a larger ball which makes a sound.' He needed acknowledgement of his disappointment that a sport which he had very much enjoyed was no longer available to him. It helped him to understand his feelings of regression and dependency. I understand that after a period of adjustment on a practical level, he was able to fulfil his ambition to go to college.

All young people worry about their physical appearance. This is the time when they experiment with clothes and hairstyles. Young people with visual impairment have talked to me about their disappointment and frustration regarding such matters. Sometimes well meaning parents or friends will buy clothes for them without any consultation and without taking into account the fact that the wearer often regards choice of clothing as an expression of their own personality.

It is an important learning experience for an adolescent to make mistakes. There is often a fine line between protecting adolescents and allowing them enough freedom, and in the case of a young person with visual impairment this can prove even more difficult to achieve.

F. was a 16-year-old girl whom the staff suggested I saw, as she appeared anxious and worried about leaving school. She talked to me of her parents, who were very important to her and very caring. However, if F. wanted to do some cooking, mother's response was that she would have such a mess to clear up. F. had not been allowed to do any ironing, because her mother feared that she would burn herself and mother would be quicker at it anyway. Her mother had transmitted her anxiety to F. over her ability to function independently without harming herself, to the extent that F. believed she would never manage to cope on her own.

Of course, sometimes the young person with a visual impairment needs to think about safety. For example S., who was 13 years old, was very angry with her parents as they would not allow her to visit her friends on her own after dark. She was also expected to be home at a certain time if she had been out with friends. S. felt that her parents were punishing her for being blind, and it was important for her to be aware that most parents would put up this rule for a 13-year-old, visually impaired or not. It is important to emphasise that adolescents with visual impairments will have the same anxieties as adolescents who are fully sighted, and not every difficulty can be attributed to sight loss. However, the nature of the visual loss will, to some extent, determine its effect on the individual. The effect of a sudden unexpected loss of eyesight from an accident or a physical cause such as cerebral tumour or haemorrhage can be devastating. Several children who have had tumours have spoken to me with great insight about their illness and the possibility of dying. Often this subject is avoided by those around them for fear of distressing them. In my work with patients with severe life-threatening illness, I am continually being reminded by young people that they have a great capacity to face their situation. They often try to protect their parents from distress. However, in my experience, both child and parents can find relief and comfort if they have the opportunity to share their thoughts and feelings. Not everybody wishes to see a professional therapist, but this option should at least be available and offered.

Earlier in this chapter, I spoke of the effect of the loss of self-esteem. As human beings, we all struggle with this aspect of ourselves, but when there are major changes in our lives, the struggle may be more difficult. There is no doubt that attitudes in society have a major effect on the life of a person with a visual impairment, and these need to be continually addressed. However, it would be easy to put all of the difficulties into the external world, whereas our inner world also plays a part in our relationships with others. I would like to illustrate this.

Shortly after severe deterioration of my vision (at that time I had been registered blind), I went on a family holiday abroad. One afternoon, I decided to stay in our log cabin by a lake while the rest of the family went out. I felt secure in the fact that I had been taught enough about independence from the practical help I had. I felt pleased with myself that I was not nervous about staying on my own. As the afternoon progressed, I became aware of depressive feelings, and realised that regaining my independence was not the whole answer to overcoming my problems, but that my inner security had taken a battering. I came to see that I could exist and survive, but that in order to feel that my life was rich, I needed to look at my inner resources. What I had to look at was whether I still felt that I could love and be loved now that I was visually impaired. The question that had to be asked was 'How did I view myself?' It took some time to struggle with this, but this is part of the work of mourning.

Conclusion

I have given a picture of some of the emotional needs of people with visual impairment. A supportive network is required in order to meet these needs. There should be a range of support available. These should include counselling and psychotherapy. There is a range of psychotherapies: behavioural, family therapy, and supportive psychotherapy. Therapy can be individual or in a group setting. Brief work is often useful, particularly with crisis intervention, but there is, I feel, a place for longer-term work. The type of therapy chosen should be offered only after a skilled assessment has taken place, and when distress is recognised, early intervention is essential.

The most valuable thing that can be offered is the experience of being listened to and taken seriously.

THE SPECIAL CURRICULUM

In the introduction to this book the editors note their strong commitment to the notion that children and young children with visual impairment should have access to an additional special curriculum. This section is concerned with some of the key elements of this curriculum.

Listening skills feature in the National Curriculum Orders (English) for all pupils. For the child with a visual impairment, listening skills take on a particular significance and the reasons for this are discussed in some detail in the first chapter of this section. The author also examines the ways in which specialist technology can be used to facilitate access to the curriculum through listening, for example by the use of variable speed tape recorders.

Reading and writing are based upon braille for most children who are blind. Chapter 16 introduces the reader to the braille code and considers issues relating to the introduction of literacy through touch. The chapter discusses the production of braille and the technology which can help children to access the curriculum. Recent developments in the use an alternative tactile code for children who are unable to benefit from braille are explored, and issues surrounding choice of communication methods and the mechanics of reading through touch are addressed.

The final chapter in this section examines two intertwined areas of the special curriculum: mobility and self-help skills. There is international concern that many young people are with visual impairment leave school as competent scholars but lack basic skills in mobility and independence. This final chapter offers practical advice about the development of the skills which are essential to the social and vocational future of the student.

Chapter 15
Listening Skills

Christine Arter

Introduction

It was a commonly held misconception that people who are blind automatically develop a better sense of hearing to compensate for their sight loss. However teachers of children with a visual impairment are aware that listening skills do not develop naturally but need to be taught through systematic programmes of instruction (Bischoff 1979, Mangold 1982). Indeed Harley *et al.* (1979) fear that young children with a visual impairment who have not been encouraged to interact with their surroundings may have a tendency to withdraw into themselves and make little attempt to listen to or comprehend the sounds within their environment.

The purpose of this chapter is to examine the development of listening skills in children and young people and to examine their applications in learning.

The importance of listening skills

Children are expected to be able to sit, listen and comprehend when they enter school but teachers know from experience that some children find this a difficult task. The development of listening skills is an important element in the education of all children.

Writers generally agree that vision is the coordinating sense and it is estimated that 80% of the information received by people who are fully sighted comes through the visual channel (Best 1992). Many children with a severe visual impairment rely predominantly on information they receive through their sense of hearing. They are expected to comprehend and assimilate information about their environment through sound and language and need to develop effective listening skills for a variety of applications.

An obvious area where listening skills are important is in orientation and mobility (see Chapter 17). Best (1992), for example, describes the use of 'sound shadows' which enable the blind listener to detect a solid object which interrupts the source of a sound. He provides the illustration of a closed classroom door, which affects and alters the quality of the sound received from within the room. Stone (1995) suggests that a basic aim of mobility training programmes is to teach children to use their hearing to travel efficiently and safely. For instance in order to know when it is safe to cross a road, the child needs to be able to interpret the sound of oncoming traffic and the audible signals at pedestrian crossings.

As the child with a severe visual impairment progresses through school, listening to material recorded on tape provides an efficient alternative medium to print and braille for some study purposes. Children with very low vision often find it difficult to process print text quickly, and Harley *et al*. (1979) suggest that the average braille reader reads two or three times more slowly than the average print reader, achieving speeds of around 100 words per minute (wpm) compared to the 250 wpm of the print reader (Aldrich and Parkin 1989, Mangold 1982). It is generally held to be more difficult for readers with a visual impairment to skim read text or to scan text to find specific information and relocating one's place in the text can also take more time.

Highly developed listening skills can also help students to take full advantage of the opportunities for access to computers, electronic reading devices and talking calculators that synthesised speech provides (see Chapter 20). In public examinations some students with a visual impairment will use an amanuensis and it is essential that they are able to listen and concentrate for extended periods and work quickly to deadlines.

Listening skills also feature prominently in leisure activities. Music and talking books are among the most popular leisure pursuits among people with a visual impairment from all age groups, and Salt (1986) even suggests that by listening to music the child with a visual impairment will develop the 'mind's ear' which will extend their imagination through sound.

The listening environment

There is constant background noise in many homes, where the radio, television, compact disc player and the computer game often compete for attention. Many children and adults become oblivious to the high levels of noise in their environment. Some children will need to be trained to listen selectively, to distinguish important sound information from superfluous background noises and to develop what Mangold (1982) describes as an 'auditory focus field'. It is often possible to adapt the school environment to cut down unwanted background sounds, for example carpeted areas and curtains can effectively reduce echoing sound (Best 1992). Quiet rooms or quiet areas can be designated for listening activities and these can be particularly valuable in an open-plan situation. Effective and calm classroom management can help to avoid the situation where the teacher has to speak in an increasingly loud voice to be heard above the continuously rising noise in the classroom.

Most children are able to watch the teacher's facial expressions and interpret her body language as she speaks, and often a child will refrain from a particular action when the teacher directs a glance at them, or shakes her head. The child with a visual impairment may miss these visual clues and have to rely only on what they hear. The teacher should therefore speak clearly, using a varied tone and volume (Best 1992). When addressing a child with a visual impairment, it is also good practice to begin with the child's name, otherwise the child may not know to whom the teacher is talking.

Mangold (1982) draws attention to 'auditory closure': the ability of the listener to complete the missing parts of words or sentences that are not heard in their entirety. The fully sighted listener who has difficulty in hearing all that is said will look at the speaker's lips to aid their comprehension. This facility is not open to the pupil with a visual impairment, and is another reason why the teacher should speak with clarity.

Salt (1986) suggests that auditory training is an important area that needs to be developed in all children, and there seems to be little doubt that effective listening skills are particularly valuable to children with a visual impairment.

Listening skills in the early years

Listening is not the same as hearing. The child may *hear* a sound without either understanding or comprehending it but Heinze (1986) states that the act of *listening* involves several steps. According to Welsh and Blasch (1980) the child develops auditory perception by:
- becoming aware of the sound;
- discriminating one sound from another;
- identifying the source of the sound;
- attaching meaning to the sound;

There are many simple listening games that can be used with young children to encourage careful listening and develop auditory memory, and some of them need little preparation. 'Chinese whispers' is the traditional game where a message is whispered from one child to the next around a circle. Another popular listening game is for the teacher to read a short story asking the pupils to clap each time a key word is repeated. In 'The shopping game' each child repeats the sentence 'I went to the shop and I bought ...'. Each participant then adds an item to the list and the next player has to repeat the whole list before adding their own 'purchase'. It is important to arrange the rules of the game so that the child with a weak auditory memory or poor listening skills is not eliminated when they fail to remember the list. This would result in the child always sitting out, and not having a chance to practise and improve their skills (Mangold 1982). Activities like this can help young children to develop listening skills in an effective and enjoyable way.

Higher listening skills

Harley *et al.* (1979) maintain that when listening to a text the pupil with a visual impairment needs to be taught strategies which will enable them to:
- discover the main ideas;
- recognise a sequence of events;
- predict outcomes;
- remember details from a complicated text;

- recognise stated or inferred cause and effect;
- 'recognise pivotal words that are cues to sequence, contrast, cause and effect';
- distinguish between fact and opinion;
- 'appreciate shades of meaning expressed by various words';
- make value judgements;
- 'evaluate the source of the information';
- 'adjust the pattern of listening and thinking to the type of material and listening purpose';
- 'select and summarise material pertinent to the listening purpose'.

Active listening is specified as a key skill in the National Curriculum for English (see Chapter 23). Trowald (1978) introduced the term 'auding' to describe the sophisticated process of active listening akin to the studying of a text in reading. Passive listeners can quickly lose concentration and are generally less efficient than active listeners in their ability to retain what they have heard (Nolan and Kederis 1969).

Aldrich and Parkin (1989) developed an active listening technique which uses self-assessment questions (SAQs) which they suggest are particularly effective for comprehending lengthy passages on tape which contain factual material. The self-assessment questions are embedded within the text at intervals of at least one minute to help the listener to focus their attention and remain on task. It is suggested that this technique improves recall of the targeted factual information. SAQs should be carefully structured to ensure that the key information is brought to the pupil's attention. At critical points in the text, answers to questions might be included as a further measure to keep the student actively involved and focused.

Accelerated and compressed speech

The average rate for print reading aloud is 120 wpm but the listener can process speech at a much faster rate than it is normally delivered (Aldrich and Parkin 1989). The student who is visually impaired can exploit this ability by using variable speed tape recorders to speed their listening. With practice, listening speeds approaching, or even exceeding, average silent print reading rates (250 wpm) can be attained (Salt 1986). This ability can enable students in further and higher education to process large amounts of study material efficiently.

The disadvantage of some variable speed recorders is that as the speed of the tape is accelerated, the pitch of the speaker's voice rises and the listener finds it increasingly uncomfortable to listen to. Aldrich and Parkin (1989) found that the female voice, with its initial higher pitch, was particularly difficult for listeners to comprehend when played at higher speeds. In Compressed speech the speed of reading is increased but the original pitch is restored by means of a pitch control device and the words are electronically sampled and shortened without loss of intelligibility. Research by Foulke and Sticht (1969) found that with this method speech of 150 wpm could be increased to 275 wpm without affecting comprehension, although Mangold (1982) suggests that for most pupils comprehension diminishes rapidly when speeds are increased above 300 wpm. Students will need to be trained to make effective use of accelerated and compressed speech, but the benefits make it a worthwhile investment of time and expense.

Tape-recorders

A variety of standard and modified cassette recorders are used by people with a visual impairment in the United Kingdom. Perhaps the most popular specialist cassette recorders are those produced by General Electric and adapted by the American Printing House for the Blind (APH). The APH 3-5194 is a robust four-track desk model with speed control and voice indexing facilities. It has a built-in microphone and rechargeable battery and mains adapter. A feature of the machine is the tactile markings on the control switches and a window in the cassette compartment which allows users to feel with their fingertip whether the tape is playing. The APH Handicassette is a more compact machine which has most of the features of the 3-5194 but in addition has a built-in pitch control and electronic compression for speeded speech. Both machines conform to the format used by the Library of Congress and give access to the 60,000 pre-recorded titles offered by Recordings for the Blind in the USA.

Four-track machines are particularly useful for study through tape. They are more efficient than conventional recorders in that they allow four tracks to be recorded on each cassette in comparison with the two tracks of the conventional recorder. Most machines developed specifically for use by people with a visual impairment have a tone indexing facility which allows signals to be inserted onto the tape which are audible when the tape is fast forwarded or rewound. A variety of tones can be used to enable the listener quickly to find the start of sections or to locate key information in the recorded material. Best (1992) describes a more advanced technique for use on four-track recorders in which material is recorded on the first track and the parallel track is used to index key points in the text and to store verbal notes about the text. He compares this to writing notes in the margin of a page.

Standard pocket memo recorders can also be a useful aid for making lists or quick notes. They offer a range of features at a variety of prices. The most sophisticated are voice activated (they record only when a person is speaking), have variable playback speed control and tone indexing facilities.

Regularly updated fact sheets on cassette recorders suitable for users who are visually impaired can be obtained from the Employment Development and Technology Unit at the Royal National Institute for the Blind.

Making recordings

There is a wide range of pre-recorded study materials available from sources such as the Royal National Institute for the Blind Student Tape Library. New material for recording can be posted to an express reading service which records texts for clients on request. However teachers are sometimes required to make their own recordings for individual students and Best (1992) suggests the following simple strategies which can improve results considerably.

- Try as far as possible to cut down background noise.
- Use the pause button to begin and end recordings (to avoid the distracting noises of the record buttons being pressed and released appearing on the tape).
- Use a separate microphone. (An external microphone is usually of better quality than the built-in device.) For the best results the microphone should be placed on a stand, 20 to 30 centimetres from the speaker.
- Stand the recorder and microphone on a piece of carpet or felt to absorb vibration and make a simple screen from thick card or an old curtain to block extraneous sounds.
- Speak clearly and evenly in a relaxed and well modulated tone. Pitch and volume are important and the speaker should avoid speaking quickly and maintain a constant speed.
- Read and edit the text before beginning the recording. Where the original text is illustrated, it may be necessary to provide tactual diagrams, tables or maps to accompany the tape-recorded material.

In addition, Hartley (1990) suggests that materials should be carefully structured and sequenced when presented in a taped format. The addition of a summary or abstract of the taped material at the beginning of the recording is often useful and the addition of headings, introductions and questions may also help the listener. If the listener is referring to a brailled text or a diagram, a signal (such as the ringing of small bell) might be added during the recording to denote the point at which the page should be turned. Chapman and Stone (1988) point to the need to obtain copyright before transferring printed materials on to tape.

The acquisition of listening skills is a key development for children with a visual impairment and, with careful teaching, these skills can be nurtured and developed for use across all areas of the curriculum.

Chapter 16

The Development of Literacy through Touch

Stephen McCall

Introduction

The subject of literacy through touch is a complex one, and this chapter is designed to provide the person who is new to the field with basic information about the nature of tactile codes and about issues relating to the development of literacy skills in children and young people who are blind.

The chapter will also review some of the resources for reading and writing available to children who access the National Curriculum through predominantly tactile methods.

Reading through touch

The braille code

The vast majority of the estimated 19,500 children with a visual impairment who read and write use print, but there are an estimated 850 children who use braille as their primary medium for learning (see Chapter 2).

Louis Braille published the first draft of his code in 1829 when he was only 20 but Braille's code wasn't adapted for use in Britain until 1870, and between 1830 and 1870 a bewildering variety of codes were used in the teaching of touch reading. As Armitage (1886) later described it

> The usual plan ... was for someone who was in comparative ignorance of what was done by others to start a new system which was taken up by philanthropists, who had still less knowledge of the subject. Subscriptions were raised, and the Babel of systems was increased by a fresh one.

Some of the codes such as *Alston* were based on raised line versions of the print alphabet, while others such as *Frere* and *Lucas* were of an arbitrary design. There was bitter rivalry between the proponents of the various codes (Ritchie 1930) but what gave braille the edge over its rivals was the fact that it was the only available code which could be written easily: a simple frame and stylus was all that was needed to produce hard copy.

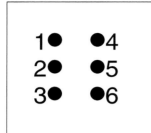

Figure 16.1   The Braille Cell

Braille's system is based upon a 'cell' of six raised dots arranged like the six on a domino (Figure 16.1).

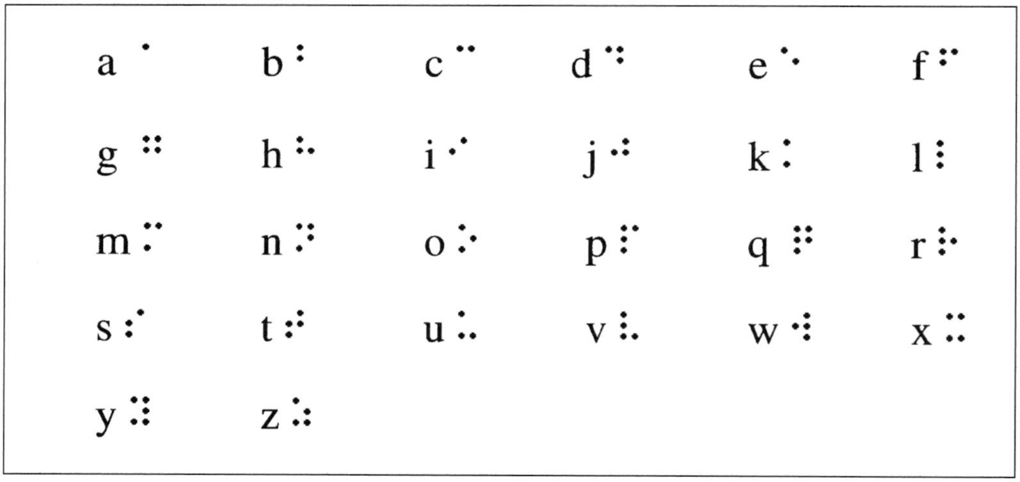

a •   b ⠃   c ⠉   d ⠙   e ⠑   f ⠋

g ⠛   h ⠓   i ⠊   j ⠚   k ⠅   l ⠇

m ⠍   n ⠝   o ⠕   p ⠏   q ⠟   r ⠗

s ⠎   t ⠞   u ⠥   v ⠧   w ⠺   x ⠭

y ⠽   z ⠵

Figure 16.2   Braille: the letters of the alphabet

Letters are made up from combinations of dots from the basic cell (Figure 16.2).

The 63 possible combinations of dots allowed by the arrangement of the cell are used not only to develop an alphabet and punctuation but also to create signs for whole words and for groups of letters called 'contractions'.

There are two grades of British braille. Grade 1 comprises the alphabet and punctuation signs while Grade 2 is a complex code containing 189 contractions.

Grade 2 braille has special signs for common letter combinations such as AR, ST, ING, SION, TION, ITY and for frequently used words such as AND, FOR, TO, IN, WAS. Some words appear in a shortened form, for example 'receive' is RCV. These contractions are governed by a complex system of 126 rules. Contracted braille was introduced to save space (braille is a very bulky medium) and to help touch readers read more quickly.

The vast majority of the touch reading material in Britain is published in Grade 2 braille and almost all children are taught to read using reading schemes that introduce contracted braille from the start. In addition to the literary braille code, there are special codes for curriculum subjects such as music, mathematics, science and modern languages.

Reading through braille

Even though it is essentially a shorthand code, braille seems to be an intrinsically slower reading medium than print. In a survey of schoolchildren in England and Wales, Williams (1971) found that the average reading rate of children varied from 78 words per minute (wpm) at 11 years to 103 wpm at 16 years, just under half the reading rate of print readers who are fully sighted. Interestingly though, she found little difference in the comprehension rates between print and braille readers.

Nolan and Kederis (1969) suggested the main reason that braille is a slower medium than print is that the processes by which braille readers recognise words are fundamentally different from those used by print readers. While the eyes of an efficient print reader can take in several words at a single fixation, the finger can only make out a single cell at a time. The process of reading braille is one of building up sense from a sequence of signs as the finger passes rapidly over them in succession. By comparison, the recognition of print words by sight is virtually simultaneous. While children who read braille do learn to move from conscious character-by-character word building to a recognition of sequences of letters and words, it appears to be a slower process than achieving whole word recognition in print.

The nature of the braille code itself presents readers with a number of challenges which are additional to those faced by children learning print. The letter shapes in braille are less distinctive than those in print alphabet, for example, the letters D, F, H and I are rotations of the same basic shape (Figure 16.3). It is often difficult for readers to distinguish between the upper and lower positions of signs within a cell (Figure 16.4). There is very little redundancy in Grade 2 braille and many of the signs carry several meanings, for example the sign for 'was' can also mean 'by', 'close quotes' or 'the degree sign' depending on its context (Lorimer 1990).

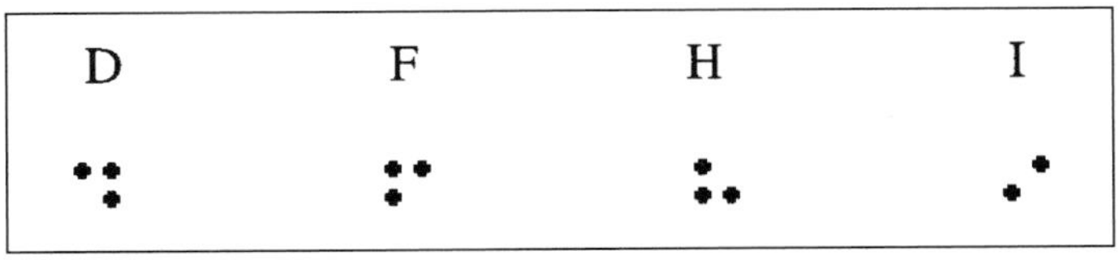

Figure 16.3

Figure 16.4

Some authors have concluded that learning to read through braille is a more challenging process than learning to read through print, but nevertheless Henderson's assertion that braille is 'the most effective graphic tool in existence for communication by individuals who are blind' (Henderson 1974) still holds true.

There has been a popular misconception, for at least three decades, that braille as a medium will be made obsolete by advances in technology, but in fact braille technology has increased the availability of braille. Programmes which can quickly translate print files into Grade 1 or Grade 2 braille for downloading to braille embossers are now widely available at affordable prices for a wide range of desktop computers. Recent legislation is also likely to reinforce the rights of people who are blind to information in braille; for example the Disability Discrimination Act (1995) obliges employers to provide information in an accessible form for customers and employees who are blind. For many people who are blind this preferred form will be braille, because braille offers all the conveniences of working from hard copy. Unlike communication systems which rely on listening, such as tape or synthesised speech, the braille reader is in complete control of the text and can vary the pace of reading according to the complexity of the material, reviewing or scanning the text as necessary without being dependent upon the availability and reliability of technological aids.

Approaches to the teaching of reading through braille

The success of children in learning to communicate through braille is determined to a great extent by the teaching expertise that is made available to them. Teachers' own enthusiasm for braille, their knowledge of the code and of the perceptual and cognitive processes of braille reading and writing, and their familiarity with techniques for the teaching of reading, will be key factors (Olson 1981).

Approaches to the teaching of reading in the United Kingdom have been the subject of intense debate in recent years. The arguments are complex but in simplistic terms there are two rival schools of thought. On one side are those who regard reading as essentially a skills-centred, decoding activity where meaning is built up from an understanding of letters and the component parts of words. The words are combined into sentences and the sentences make up the story. In this 'bottom up' approach the key tools of instruction are often graded readers with a carefully controlled vocabulary and an emphasis on phonics.

On the other side of the debate are advocates of a 'linguistic' approach which says that children should be taught to read and write in the same natural way that they develop their oral language. The story is the starting point of instruction and the purpose of reading is to derive meaning from the text. Reading should be relevant and meaningful from the start and children should be encouraged to use their knowledge of language and experience to predict meaning (Rex *et al.* 1994). As a starting point, children are often encouraged to develop their own personalised reading materials which are used as the basis of their reading development and writing is commonly integrated into the reading experience. Children are encouraged to read general interest books or stories selected for their relevance, interest and attractiveness. The reading process and learning style might involve cooperative reading groups, and the teacher has a role as a facilitator of reading and writing.

While linguistic approaches have had some impact on the development of reading for children with a visual impairment who used print, particularly in those mainstream schools where linguistic approaches predominate, it has had relatively little impact on the teaching of braille in the United Kingdom. Most children who are learning to read and write through braille are taught in special schools or specialist resource bases where there is a tradition of braille teaching and a consensus of how braille should be taught (see Chapter 22). Approaches to early instruction in braille reading and writing in these settings are usually based upon the use of contracted braille from the start, and use graduated basal readers such as *Braille for Infants* (AEWVH 1986) and *Take Off* (AEWVH 1990) which have a strong phonic element, a controlled vocabulary and fixed order of introduction of braille contractions.

Traditionally teachers in the United Kingdom laid emphasis on developing additional 'pre-reading' skills for children who read through touch. For example the teacher's handbook (AEWVH 1987) that accompanies the *Braille for Infants* reading scheme offers guidelines for the teaching of braille at pre-school and infant level and identifies four areas as being of particular importance in 'considering a child's readiness to read'. These areas comprise motor development, auditory skills, language development and reading awareness.

'Motor development' is defined in terms of activities designed to promote wrist flexibility and finger dexterity, two-handed coordination, light finger touch, tactile perception and line tracking skills. 'Auditory skills' include the development of auditory discrimination, sequencing and rhythm. 'Language development' is concerned with promoting 'concrete understanding' of the language the child hears and uses, and developing through concrete experiences 'concepts' such as 'same and different, big and little ... up and down, left and right.' 'Reading awareness' includes the activities which introduce children who are blind to the concept of reading, such as the labelling in braille of objects in the house. Parents are advised to learn braille and to read to children from books in print and braille.

While the importance of these activities continues to be acknowledged in British schools, they are now more likely to be considered within a broader framework of literacy (McCall and McLinden, 1996) rather than as indicators of a child's readiness or lack of readiness to read.

Transferring from print to braille

The child who has been an accomplished print reader and needs to transfer to braille because of deteriorating vision or a sudden loss of sight, clearly has different needs from the young child who is using braille to learn to read. The loss of sight, whether it happens after a gradual deterioration or a sudden accident, inevitably requires a period of readjustment. There is a danger that in some cases students may come to view braille as the final acknowledgement that their sight is irretrievably lost and will consciously or subconsciously reject attempts to introduce it (McCall 1994), and the timing of the introduction of braille needs careful consideration. While young children are able to learn to read braille at their own pace, students at secondary school may be facing the pressures of preparing for public examinations and there will be a sense of urgency about introducing braille.

In these circumstances the student's motivation is probably the key determinant of success in braille. A situation where the student has sufficient vision to read print under extreme magnification, but finds that it is too slow and laborious a process to meet the demands of the curriculum, can sometimes be resolved by waiting until the student recognises the need for the more efficient method of access that braille offers. Some teachers argue that the decision about when to embark on learning braille is the student's decision, others argue that sometimes it is sometimes necessary to make the decision on the student's behalf, pointing to the fact that some students who are initially reluctant to start braille quickly develop into enthusiastic and accomplished braille readers once they have been introduced to its advantages. Students may benefit from professional counselling in coming to terms with the issues of readjustment before braille is introduced (see Chapter 14).

The choice of materials for students who transfer from print to braille has improved dramatically in recent years with the publication by the RNIB of three reading schemes. *Spot the Dot* (Fitzsimons 1988) and *Braille in Easy Steps* (Lorimer 1988) are both intended for children at secondary school and offer a graduated introduction to reading of Grade 2 braille. They contain pre-reading exercises and provide extensive materials for reading practice. *Fingerprints* (Berry 1992) is designed for 16–25 year olds. It introduces both reading and writing and while it allows for independent study, it assumes that the reader will have some access to tutorial support.

The mechanics of braille reading

We've already seen how braille reading rates are slower than those for print reading. In order to minimise this disadvantage, there has traditionally been a strong emphasis on the development of efficient reading techniques. Although braille readers exhibit a range of different hand techniques, analysis of the best touch readers suggests that there are some general principles which children and young people can be encouraged to adopt.

It is generally recommended that children should work on a firm and flat reading surface which is just below elbow level so that their arms can move freely. If the reading materials are placed square on, or at a slight angle to the edge of the table, children are less likely to lose their place when transferring from one line to the next. The best readers usually adopt an erect, but comfortable and relaxed position.

In order to ensure that the finger pad is making maximum contact with the braille letters, the hands need to be arched slightly with the fingers at an acute angle to the reading surface, Ashcroft and Henderson (1963) suggest that an angle of around 30° allows the optimum contact.

To achieve the lightness of touch and the smooth scanning movements exhibited by the best readers, it is usually argued that the weight of the hands should be borne by the muscles of the forearms and not by the fingertips and that the wrists should be relaxed.

There is enormous variation in the way that people use their hands and fingers to read braille and there is considerable disagreement in research findings about which is the best hand or finger for braille readers to use. Most readers establish a preferred hand and finger early on and touch readers most often use their index or middle fingers. Right-handed people sometimes find it easier to read with their left hand and vice versa. The best readers can sense braille with fingers on either hand and make use of additional fingers in their reading to ensure the hand travels straight along the line and to detect when the end of the line is approaching. The quickest readers develop the ability to use both hands in partnership, with the right hand reading the second half of a line while the left finds the next line and reads the first part of it as soon as the right hand finishes. This technique is difficult to master fully but the majority of children can be encouraged to use the weaker reading hand to supplement the work of the dominant hand.

Assessment of braille

The best teachers are constantly making informal assessments of children's performance in braille reading and writing throughout the curriculum. Experienced teachers are often able to identify areas for improvement through their observation of the children's work; however more formal approaches to assessment can sometimes be useful in identifying starting points for instruction and monitoring performance over a period.

Simple checklists such as those provided in Olson (1981) and Harley *et al.* (1987) can be used to monitor the child's mastery of the mechanics of braille or for identifying gaps in the child's knowledge of the braille code.

In the United Kingdom, the Neale Analysis of Reading Ability has been recently re-standardised for use with blind children (Greaney *et al.* 1994). This is a comprehensive assessment of reading performance for children between the ages of seven and 13 which provides age norms for accuracy, comprehension and reading rate and is arranged in parallel forms which allow for subsequent re-testing.

Reading through Moon

Moon is a tactile code based on a simplified raised line version of the Roman print alphabet. It was invented in 1847 by an English clergyman, Dr William Moon, and was widely promoted in Britain, Australia and the United States until it gradually lost ground to braille. The Moon characters are large and bold compared to braille and Moon has survived in the United Kingdom as reading medium for those elderly blind who are unable to master braille (Figure 16.5).

Although the number of adult readers of Moon is small, its production continues to be supported by the RNIB and the National Library for the Blind. There has been a revival of interest in Moon in recent years sparked initially by the introduction of a mechanical Moonwriter (Tobin and Hill 1984). Research has been undertaken into its potential as a medium of communication for children and young people with a visual impairment and additional difficulties who are unable to learn braille (McCall and Stone 1992). The RNIB has recently published a children's reading scheme called *Mooncats* (McCall *et al.* 1996) for use by children. Furthermore, a support and advice centre for parents and professionals wishing to find out more about its application has recently opened at Rushton Hall, an RNIB special school in Northamptonshire for children who are visually impaired and have additional learning difficulties (McCall and McLinden, 1996).

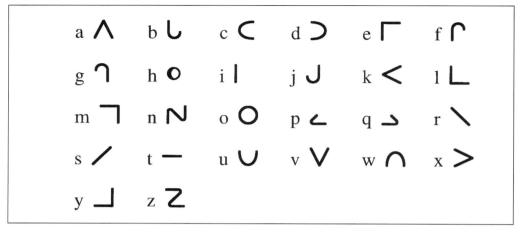

Figure 16.5

Moon appears to have some intrinsic advantages for children who need to learn through touch but are unable to use braille. The fact that it is a is a line-based code means that in the initial stages of instruction, the characters can be enlarged without affecting their legibility. Moon makes use of few contractions, and because it has some resemblance to the print alphabet it is relatively easy for sighted adults to learn.

However, like braille, the Moon alphabet is made up from a small number of basic shapes which rotate to provide different characters. This can be seen in letters such as L, E, Y, M. These rotations can confuse new learners and a carefully structured teaching approach is required. There is, as yet, no mechanical writing device which allows children and young people with additional difficulties to write Moon easily.

There is a wide range of children who are blind and who have additional learning difficulties. Their potential for achievement in communication and literacy varies greatly according to the degree and nature of their abilities and disabilities. Helping these children to develop the early skills which may lead towards literacy will be an increasingly significant challenge for educators in the coming years.

Writing tactile codes

Braille

About 25% of adult braillists still make use of the stylus and hand frame for taking notes, but mechanical braille writing devices have been available for more than a century. In schools in the United Kingdom the Perkins braille writer is still probably the most commonly used device for writing. The Perkins is a mechanical writer which has six keys, each key corresponding to a dot in the braille cell. When the keys are pressed down in the appropriate combination raised letters and signs are embossed onto on a sheet of manila 'braille paper' which is fed manually into the machine (Figure 16.6).

In recent years a variety of electronic braille writing devices have been introduced into schools which also make use of the six key format for input. Output may take the form of synthetic speech or a constantly renewable (refreshable) tactile display on the machine itself. The machines vary considerably in sophistication and price. Most electronic braille writing devices are 'paperless' allowing the user to store text in the machine's own memory for subsequent transfer.

When hard copy is required most of these machines can be connected to peripherals such as standard printers or braille embossers. When the braille text is downloaded from the machine to a conventional printer, a program in the braille writer automatically translates the braille into print. Some of the 'paperless' braillers have built-in disc drives and store text onto disks or random access memory (RAM) cards compatible with personal computers (PCs). These 'paperless' machines have the advantage of being light and portable, some weighing only 16 ounces, and most can operate from the mains or rechargeable batteries.

Figure 16.6   Writing braille with a 'Perkins'

At present there is a debate on the question of the appropriateness of teaching older children to use dedicated braille writing devices as their main medium for recording information. Some teachers argue that children who are educationally blind should be taught to touch type using a conventional qwerty keyboard in primary school, and to develop skills in word processing using the same computer technology as people who are fully sighted. At secondary level many children do use conventional laptop and desktop computers with adaptive software and synthesised speech as their primary means of writing and storing information.

Voice recognition software that enables users to input text into personal computers through speech is already available and while at this stage it is unsuitable for classroom use, it is intriguing to speculate that ultimately the spoken word may become the standard input system for sighted and blind users alike.

Moon

The Possum Moonwriter is a mechanical device developed primarily for people who have lost their vision as adults and who read Moon. Effective use of the machine requires well developed motor skills and is generally unsuitable for children and young people with additional difficulties.

The RNIB have recently introduced a Moonframe which is a small plastic grid for writing Moon characters by hand onto a plastic sheet called 'german film'. Although the Moonframe is designed primarily for simple note taking by the elderly blind, it may be useful for some children and teachers. A Moon Wordbuilding Kit is also available through the RNIB which enables children and teachers to construct words and simple sentences using Velcro-backed plastic tiles embossed with Moon letters which can be attached to a small frame.

In recent years a number of Moon fonts have been developed for use on desktop computers. Moon text can be typed onto the computer screen and then downloaded through a standard printer onto paper. Moon is then photocopied onto 'swell' paper and passed through a stereo-copying machine and raised (see Chapter 18).

Conclusion

As Rex *et al.* (1994) observe, much of the methodology in literacy instruction with children who are blind has evolved from common practice and received wisdom rather than from research-based knowledge:

> some of the common instructional practices in teaching literacy to children who are blind may not be the best practices. The truth is that professionals in the field of blindness simply do not know.

Classroom-based research into the way that children who are blind develop skills in literacy may help to resolve some of this uncertainty. One thing is certain however, whether working with young children or late beginners, there can be few more fascinating or rewarding activities for teachers than introducing children to reading and writing through touch.

Chapter 17
Mobility and Independence Skills

Juliet Stone

Introduction

The extent to which people are able to care for themselves and travel independently determines, to a large extent, the quality of their lives. Young people who have severe visual impairments may require specific intervention and carefully planned curricula if they are to reach their potential in independent living. The first part of this chapter considers the skill of independent travel and the second part discusses the issues surrounding the learning of self-help skills.

Mobility and orientation

In the survey carried out by the Royal National Institute for the Blind (Walker *et al.* 1992), it was discovered that over 40% of children aged 12 years and over and who have a visual impairment never go out alone. There is clearly some connection here with another fact which they discovered, that only a quarter of children with a visual impairment have had any mobility training at all. This section discusses the ways in which a visual impairment affects the ability of children to travel independently and suggests ways in which this ability can be encouraged and developed.

Terminology

Independent movement and travel within the environment require two abilities. The first is usually referred to as **orientation**, which involves having an awareness of space and an understanding the situation of the body within it. Good orientation means being able to answer the questions: Where am I, where do I want to get to and how do I get there? (See Hill and Blasch 1981.) The other requirement is **mobility**, which is the ability to move oneself without coming to any harm. Safe travel involves being able detect hazards and take avoiding action. In order to do this, children may use a long cane or people who are sighted as guides (Figure 17.1). Young adults in addition may use guide dogs or an electronic aid.

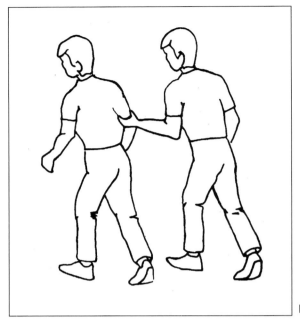

Figure 17.1   Sighted guide

Provision of mobility education

For children who are visually impaired, orientation and mobility must be viewed as integral parts of the child's total development and learning. It is not simply a process of mastering a set of skills that can be taught in a few weeks or months. Within special schools for the visually impaired, mobility programmes are offered to most pupils who need them. In mainstream schools the availability of instruction is patchy. Some resource centres and advisory services provide excellent programmes, while others are unable to provide any access to mobility specialists. Statements of special educational need and individual education plans should always include a reference to mobility skills and to the provision of mobility teaching where appropriate. Parents and teachers can help with the instruction of basic mobility skills, but a mobility specialist is required for some of the higher order skills, such as long cane travel in towns.

Why are mobility and orientation so important?

The ability to move in and around the environment can affect the individual psychologically, socially, emotionally, economically and physically. Koestler (1976) said, 'the loss of power to move about freely and safely is arguably the greatest deprivation inflicted by blindness'.

There is a direct connection between movement and learning. It is through moving within our environment that understanding of the world is developed. Children who are visually impaired may be severely restricted in the variety and quantity of opportunities to experience and explore the world for themselves. There is a danger that children's knowledge of the world around them comes secondhand, only perceived through what they are told and what they read. If children are able to move independently their world expands and they are exposed to a far wider range of real experiences. This will feed into all their development and learning, including their language, literacy and understanding of concepts.

Another important aspect of independent movement is that it facilitates social interactions. It is usually in the wider community that new social contacts are made. The confidence to meet friends, to go shopping or go to discos opens up many social opportunities.

Inevitably, moving around independently involves problem solving and risk taking. Understanding danger, assessing risks and taking responsibility for your own welfare is an important part of personal development and the raising of self-esteem.

A visual impairment can impede free, relaxed and speedy movement and it is this type of movement which develops posture, improves the muscle tone in the legs and feet and improves the walking gait. A lack of movement retards good physical development and conversely, poor physical development will prevent coordinated movement. Mobility specialists comment that they often need to initiate a programme to improve fitness levels in their pupils before they are able to undertake formal mobility training. The writer worked with one young lady of 15 who had a severe visual impairment. She was so unfit that she was unable to walk for a hundred yards without losing her breath. The mobility training was slow, not because she was incapable of learning, but because she had to keep stopping to rest.

Travelling independently is one of the prerequisites for employment (Hill 1986). While it is true that it is possible to find paid employment working at home, these are often dull, repetitive jobs which are poorly paid. One of the most important needs for all of us is social interaction and again, for many of us, our employment is one of the main channels for this. In the past, academic qualifications were seen as a guaranteed route to employment for young people with visual impairments; however, in some cases, young people were leaving colleges and universities with good qualifications, but their lack of mobility skills left them virtually unemployable.

Even for people who do not need travel for their employment, an inability to travel independently can mean that any journey becomes an expensive proposition. Taxis have to be used instead of trains or buses, and this may well limit the number of journeys that can be made outside the home.

Children who are blind

The problems of orientation and mobility for children and young people who are congenitally blind are very different from those who lose their sight later in life. Children who are born with a visual impairment have very considerable problems in forming correct concepts of their own bodies, and their mental map of the world and their own position in it may be very limited. Concepts such as those of distance may be particularly difficult for them to grasp. Education in mobility should start in the very early years and continue throughout the child's school life and beyond.

Children with low levels of vision

Until recently, the mobility of children and young people with low vision had received little or no attention. The scarcity of trained mobility teachers in schools, particularly in mainstream schools, means, unfortunately, that in many cases this is still true. It is important that pupils with low vision should be assessed in their ability to travel independently. It is also essential that this assessment takes place in an unfamiliar environment. The way that youngsters move in and around an environment that they know well, such as their school, is no indicator of how they will function in a strange locality. Some children will have reduced distance acuity or field loss which will seriously affect their ability to travel safely and confidently. Others may have difficulties with adapting to light and dark. Pupils with photophobia, who seem to move around confidently on a cloudy day, may experience difficulty on a bright, sunny day. When the sun is behind them, they may navigate a route across the school campus easily; the reverse route, facing the sun, may leave the pupil nervous and confused. If distance vision is reduced the use of landmarks may be restricted. Many pupils with a visual impairment have poor depth perception, and may trip up on a kerb or 'see' changes of depth which are actually shadows.

Children whose condition causes double vision need specific training to cope with their faulty visual images. Other difficulties for the pupils with low vision include identifying street names, house or bus numbers and destination signs.

Pupils with eye conditions which cause night blindness, such as retinitis pigmentosa, need special consideration. They may well be seriously restricted in their ability to get about in the evenings or at night. Some of them may be unwilling to admit, even to themselves, that problems exist, preferring to make excuses as to why they do not wish to go out in the evenings. This can seriously affect their leisure and social activities. Pupils with conditions that may cause these difficulties should be assessed on their mobility in poor light. Although mobility training for pupils with reduced vision will differ from that for pupils who are totally blind, the importance of this training cannot be overemphasised.

Additional difficulties

Mobility and orientation education programmes should be a key part of the curriculum of those pupils who are visually impaired and who have additional complex difficulties. Even if children are immobile, they can be helped to develop an understanding of the space around them and their routes across and within it, as they are carried or pushed in wheelchairs. These children need to be given time to explore their surroundings, to feel the radiators along the corridor and process other aural or olfactory clues. If they are able to indicate which turn to take at a junction, they increase the control they have over their lives and their environment. It will also help to develop their problem solving strategies and expand their knowledge of the world. It is important that all staff, including therapists, are aware of the current objectives of the orientation and mobility programme and of the terminology which is being used. The aim of the programme will be the same as for any child, to progress along the continuum of understanding, control and independence (Figure 17.2).

Figure 17.2

Personality

There is no doubt that the personality of children and young people greatly affects their attitude to travelling independently. Mark, a boy of 16 with an outgoing personality who had been blind from birth, described a visit to a large pop concert at Sheffield. Describing the journey to the sports stadium, Mark recounted how he became separated from his two friends with whom he was travelling, about three quarters of a mile from the venue.

> 'That threw me a bit', he said, 'because I hadn't really been taking much notice of where we were. But a group of other kids came along, and I guessed they were going to the concert as well, so I just followed them.'
> 'What would have happened if they had just been going to the pub?' I asked.
> His quick retort was, 'Well, I'd have been late for the concert.'
> 'Did you find your friends?'
> 'Yes, they were waiting at the gate for me.'

He appeared to have found the whole experience, including standing in the middle of a packed crowd for three hours during the concert, great fun. It will be readily appreciated why this young man took so easily to independent travel and why other young people, more shy and reserved, may find it more difficult. Many of the personality factors which make for successful mobility, such as assertiveness, a sense of humour and the ability to stay calm can all be encouraged in children. Developing these abilities is a cross-curricular issue which involves all members of staff.

Motivation

The most important factor in all children's learning is motivation, and this is certainly true of mobility and orientation programmes. For the baby who moves to get to the toy that has gone out of reach or for the young person who wants to go to the town centre to buy the latest record, it is the reason to move that is important. Children who are visually impaired miss many of these motivational factors. A blind baby who has dropped a toy may not realise that the toy still exists and can be reached.

Young children can unintentionally be discouraged from moving by parents and others who may bring toys to them rather than stimulating and supporting them to move to the toys. Sometimes sufficient time and care is not taken to discover what will motivate the individual child or young person to move. Unless children are motivated to move early in their lives, it may be very difficult to motivate them as they grow older. The children who have been actively encouraged to move, explore, develop and satisfy their curiosity will have a willingness to face the challenges that will come later.

Self-help and independence skills

McCall (1990) defines two sets of skills in this area: 'living skills' and 'interpersonal skills'. These two groups can be further subdivided as follows:

Living skills

- eating
- food preparation
- hygiene/personal grooming
- money management
- house care

Interpersonal skills

- communication
- relationships
- sexuality/sex education
- assertiveness
- etiquette

The basics of feeding, dressing and hygiene can be introduced in early childhood as part of the daily routine of the family. Encouraging young children to put their toys away can be the start of instruction in home management. The need for education in these skills will continue into the school years, but the demands of the National Curriculum often mean that finding the time for the learning and teaching of independence skills is difficult. This is particularly the case in mainstream schools, where the cross-curricular possibilities for teaching these skills may not be fully appreciated.

Assessment of daily living and social skills

It is important that information and advice based upon a careful assessment of children's achievements and needs in these areas are included in the official statements of their special educational needs. Many guidelines, assessment procedures and checklists have been published for parents and teachers to use to help identify a pupil's individual needs.

Careful observation of children at work and play will also reveal any difficulties which children are experiencing in these areas, and observation in a variety of settings can help to assess whether the child is able to transfer the skills they acquire to a new situation.

There are a number of possible reasons why children who have visual impairments fail to develop appropriate self-help or social skills, for example:

- instruction is not given in language which is appropriate to the child's level of development;
- the child has not yet mastered the coordination and fine motor skills required for the skill;
- the skill is inappropriate to the child's culture.

Teaching self-help skills

Transference of self-help skills can be a difficulty for some children and wherever possible, skills should be taught *in situ*. For example, feeding skills and table etiquette are best taught at meal times, the selection of clothes at dressing times and so on. The demands of time in the home and in school do not always allow for this, but as a principle, the more relevant the learning situation, the easier it is for children to acquire the skills. Care should also be taken to ensure that the activities are developmentally as well as chronologically appropriate.

Task analysis

A common approach to the teaching of many self-help skills is the use of task analysis. This involves breaking down a skill into a sequence of easily managed stages. An example of this is the following breakdown of the skill of making a cold drink using powder and liquid (Best 1986):

1. locates cup
2. locates spoon
3. locates jar of powder
4. moves jar to cup
5. unscrews lid from jar
6. places lid on surface
7. holds spoon correct way up
8. places spoon in powder
9. lifts filled spoon out of powder
10. relocates cup
11. moves spoon to cup

12. puts powder in cup by tilting spoon
13. puts spoon in cup
14. locates jar top
15. replaces jar top
16. replaces jar in appropriate position
17. locates jug
18. moves jug next to cup
19. lines up spout with cup
20. pours liquid into cup
21. stops pouring when sufficient liquid is in cup
22. returns jug to appropriate position
23. locates spoon
24. stirs drink with spoon
25. places spoon in appropriate position
26. lifts up cup to drink.

Task analysis facilitates the teaching of skills in the following ways. Firstly it identifies the particular sub-skills which the pupils may need to learn before the whole task can be achieved. Consider step 20 in Best's sequence, 'pours liquid into cup'. Children who have played with water from an early age will have already mastered this skill and it can be skipped over, but pupils who cannot pour liquids may need to practise this skill separately before incorporating it into the sequence of the whole task.

Equipment

The availability of appropriate equipment can make the learning of self-help skills easier for children. Standard equipment, carefully selected and adapted to meet the needs of individual children, is appropriate in some situations. Specialised equipment, designed specifically for people with visual impairments is essential in others.

For example using a black non-stick saucepan for heating milk or presenting steak and salad on a white plate makes the foodstuffs easier to see. Standard washing machines, microwaves and so on can be made easier to use through the addition of large print, braille or other tactile labels and instructions. Clothes for young children which have zippers rather than hooks and eyes are easier to fasten.

Specialist equipment is available from many sources, including the RNIB and the Partially Sighted Society, and includes items such as liquid level indicators and labels bearing the names of colours in braille which can be stitched onto the inside of clothes to help with colour coordination. It is important that pupils understand the principles (such as contrast) which determine the choice of equipment. When, as young people, they move away from home and away from the carefully planned living and learning environments found in many schools, they may need to apply these principles to their new situations, at college or in their first bedsits.

Problem solving

Any teaching programme in the area of self-help skills should provide strategies for problem solving. Problem solving is an essential skill and can be developed during any teaching session through questions such as the following.

- What other ways could you do this?
- If you lost your potato peeler, what could you use instead?
- What would be a good way to sort clothes for washing?
- What colour plate would help you to see this food more easily?

Students will find their own solutions to their problems. One young man always chose scampi and chips if eating in a restaurant, as he felt confident at being able to manage this meal with as he put it, 'a certain amount of dignity'. Giving the pupils the opportunity to think about and discuss problems will enable them to meet new challenges with confidence.

Teaching interpersonal skills

Children or young people who have severe visual impairments usually need help in understanding the importance of the interpersonal skills which come more naturally to their peers. Huebner (1986) lists some of the visual elements which affect social interchanges: 'appearance, dress, facial expressions, body posture and positions, gestures, eye behaviours'.

Children and young people can be helped to increase their understanding of these elements. For example, they need to appreciate that by turning their faces towards a speaker or by changing their body positions, they can facilitate their interaction with other people. They need to realise that there are unwritten rules about how close you can stand to other people without making them feel uncomfortable. The closeness that is perfectly natural in a crowded underground train is very unnatural in an empty restaurant! The decision about whether to use this knowledge and skill is up to the individual, but at least the choice will be an informed one.

The school and college curricula can be used to develop social skills. The personal and social education (PSE) curriculum is obviously one area that lends itself to raising these issues, but drama, dance and movement, language and environmental studies can all be used to raise the students' awareness and increase their self-esteem and confidence.

There is insufficient space in a short chapter such as this to discuss other important areas, such as sexuality and sex education, and child protection programmes. Huebner (1986) emphasises the importance of allowing children and young people to develop the feelings they have about their own sexuality. A visual impairment, however, precludes much of the learning that can take place without very specific intervention and families may feel unequal to the task of sex education. Teaching materials specifically for children and young people with visual impairments are scarce and some schools are only now beginning to face up to their important role in this area.

Parents, carers and schools, colleges and services all need to work together to ensure that our young people are given the opportunity to experience the dignity of being in control of their own care and to make informed decisions.

Conclusion

This chapter has raised many of the issues involved in independent living for children and young people and has stressed the importance of this area for their lives.

Encouraging independence in children and young people with visual impairments is the responsibility of all who work with them. It should feature in early intervention programmes as a gateway to learning, and it should permeate all curriculum areas in schools.

ACCESS TO THE CURRICULUM

There are four chapters in this section and each one develops the theme of access and entitlement to the mainstream curriculum for pupils with visual impairment. In addition to providing advice about the preparation and organisation of pupils' work, wider issues of concern to managers and governors are raised, relating to the provision of appropriate access technology and the adaptation of the school environment.

The first chapter discusses the ways in which materials can be adapted for the pupil who relies predominantly on tactile learning methods. The advantages and disadvantages of various systems for producing diagrams are considered in some detail to enable the reader to make informed decisions about the options which are available.

The development of efficiency in personal organisation and time management are essential if children with a visual impairment are to meet the increasing demands of the curriculum as they progress through school. Effective study skills can be encouraged in the early years of learning and refined in further and higher education. Chapter 19 raises issues about independent learners and the working relationship between children and those who support them.

Chapter 20 considers the potential barriers to learning for children or young persons with a visual impairment and describes how many of them can be overcome through the use of access technology. The author draws on case histories to indicate the practical ways in which technology can be applied effectively to learning.

The final chapter of the section discusses the issues surrounding the adaptation of the working environment for pupils with a visual impairment. It draws upon government recommendations for the design of classrooms and buildings and upon examples of good practice from schools and colleges throughout the United Kingdom.

Chapter 18

The Preparation of Raised Diagrams

Heather Mason and Christine Arter

In this chapter we seek to define some of the principles for the production of effective tactile materials using methods available to most teachers, and to raise issues relating to the skills required by pupils with a visual impairment to interpret these materials successfully.

Children who are educationally blind need a range of sophisticated skills in order to interpret the tactile representations, maps, and diagrams that feature in academic work and in aspects of the special curriculum such as mobility.

The National Curriculum increasingly requires teachers to use primary source materials such as charts and illustrated manuscripts, and many of these will have to be adapted into a form that touch readers can access. Pupils who have low vision may also need tactile materials to supplement information gained through the visual channel to enable access to the full curriculum.

Tactile perception

The term **tactile** is used primarily to refer to passive touch such as the sensation of the back against the chair, while the terms **tactual**, **tangible** and **haptic** usually refer to active exploratory and manipulative touch such as a person might use to check the texture of piece of fabric.

Research in this area would seem to suggest the following general principles.
1. Tactual skills need to be taught in a systematic way from a very early age.
2. Tactile information is processed sequentially and a mental image of the whole is built up gradually through an accumulation of its parts.
3. The development of tactual skills is influenced by other considerations such as the extent of the development of short-term memory, spatial abilities, fine motor skills and search and scan techniques.
4. Most tactile diagrams require explanation and introduction before they can be used in a meaningful way. Teachers need to allow time to help children to make sense of tactile diagrams, particularly in the early stages of interpretation, and may need to provide students with brailled or tape-recorded notes and instructions.

5. Three-dimensional representations are very difficult to portray in a two-dimensional tactile form. Children who are congenitally blind may have no appreciation of the visual conventions of scale and perspective.

6. Strategies that make print diagrams clearer, such as enlargement may make recognition more difficult when applied to tactile diagrams.

7. Tactual qualities, for instance texture and hardness, are relatively easy to discriminate while discrimination of shape requires a more systematic approach to the detection of critical features.

It cannot be assumed that children with a severe visual impairment are more adept in exploring through touch than their peers who can see. Contrary to commonly held beliefs, children who are blind do not have improved tactual or auditory acuity (Warren 1994). Some young children who are blind are 'tactile defensive' and avoid the sensation of unfamiliar textures. They may require a carefully sequenced learning programme to encourage them to explore and discriminate between different textures and to scan and search tactile materials.

Teachers need to be aware that the methods that children who are blind use to obtain information from diagrammatic representations are quite different from those used by children who are fully sighted. The child who has sight is able to obtain an immediate visual impression of the whole and then scans the diagram to assimilate the detail. The child who is blind absorbs the information in a reverse order, gradually searching and scanning the material build up a mental picture of the whole. This complex process may need to be supplemented by oral explanation and guidance to aid their interpretation of the material.

Throughout the primary school years, materials of gradually increasing sophistication should be presented to the children who rely upon touch to help them to develop skills in interpretation. They will need to be introduced to techniques that will enable them to use tactile materials successfully. For example the child needs to learn techniques for scanning such as the following.

- Spreading the fingertips of both hands across the top of the page and then running them down the page, to gain a general impression of where textures, lines and labels are located.
- From reference points at the periphery, the fingers of each hand move in a clockwise spiral motion until the centre of the page is reached.

The principles of tactile representation

Before producing tactile materials for students it is important to consider these questions.
- What experience has the user had in the use of tactile representations?
- What information is the student meant to gain from the diagram?
- Can the same information be provided in a simpler form, for example in notes, or through feeling a model, an artefact or a real object?

- Is the information the student needs already available in the text? Is the diagram redundant?
- How can the print diagram be simplified without losing the relevant information?
- How can the print diagram be modified to make it more significant to a touch reader?
- Will it be better to break down the information in a complex print diagram into two or more simple tactile diagrams?

Producing materials can be a complex process, and adopting the most appropriate approach can save an enormous amount of preparation time. In making decisions about which technique to employ, an important consideration is whether the material being produced will have a one-off use, or whether it will become a resource that will be used many times. In the latter case it will be worth investing the time and effort to assemble in advance a high quality master worksheet using tactile materials such as wire and sandpaper. The master worksheet can be copied repeatedly using a thermoforming process and stored away for use on later occasions. However if the material is to be used just once it may be better to employ a quicker format to present the concept to the pupil. For example, it may be possible to draw the diagram directly onto german film (a thin plastic sheet which produces raised lines when a pointed instrument is drawn across it; available from the RNIB) in the student's presence. This approach can incidentally help the pupil to understand the process of how tactile pictures, maps or diagrams are built up.

Those who are new to the production of tactile materials often make the mistake of adhering too closely to the original print format. When adapting a maths worksheet which requires the young child to count a number of sweets for example, it is unnecessary and unhelpful to try to faithfully reproduce the shape of the fussy sweet wrappers. Simple rectangles are easier for the child to count and equally significant as representations of candy.

Teachers often face a series of dilemmas when producing tactile materials. For example, sometimes details are included in the print illustrations which are purely for visual decoration. In a story where the main character has freckles, should these be included in the accompanying tactile picture? When the character is actually called 'Freckles' the child will certainly need to know what freckles are, and it could be argued that they should be included as a part of the picture. In most cases however the minor detail of freckles would add clutter to the picture and should be omitted.

Perspective in pictures poses another problem. Since in many ways perspective is a purely visual convention, it could be regarded as an unnecessary complication. Edman (1992) suggests that perspective is best avoided in tactile representations. Some teachers would argue that the inclusion of perspective introduces to the child the idea that for people who are fully sighted the further away an object is, the smaller it appears. An understanding of perspective may be useful for subjects such as geography, where diagrams showing hill or mountain ranges and river courses are often used. Without this understanding, it may be difficult for the child to interpret a picture in which people appear to be the same size as a house or a tree.

There is no single set of conventions that is used consistently or universally in the production of tactile diagrams. Two skilled practitioners may reproduce the same print diagram in totally different formats, using a range of different textures and symbols. Unless students have been exposed to diagrams which represent a range of techniques and styles they may be at a serious disadvantage when confronted with tactile materials produced by external agencies as part of a standard assessment tasks (SATs) evaluation or a GCSE examination.

Attempts have been made by a number of countries to develop a consistent approach to map production. For example, in Scandinavia it was agreed that the sea should always be represented by embroidery canvas. In the UK the Royal National Institute for the Blind produce the Nottingham Map Kit which incorporates various plastic symbols and shapes to represent prescribed features on mobility maps. Even though it is not possible to produce tactile materials that are consistent on an international basis, it should be feasible within a secondary school, for example, to develop a consistent approach across separate subject areas. With planning it should also be possible to obtain consistency between the secondary school and its primary feeder schools. In the case of infant and primary schools too, agreement could be reached over conventions for depicting the characters in a reading scheme, for example.

The mechanics of tactile representation

Labelling
Braille labels take up far more space than print labels. A braille label consisting of two braille cells needs a space of at least 12 mm by 16 mm.

When using braille labels on tactile materials there are a number of points to note.
- Keep braille labels to a minimum – use a key.
- Place labels in the centre of area symbols.
- Place labels horizontally.
- Use 'rub-down' transfers (Mecanorma) to reproduce braille letters for use on swell paper (see below); do not produce braille dots freehand.
- In some instances consider adding labels in braille that do not appear on the print version in order to clarify the diagram.

Making keys for diagrams
Consistency in the use of keys in diagrams is essential. Obviously the key should feature the same textures and symbols used on the map or diagram itself. Edman (1992) also suggests the following.
- The title of the diagram should appear first in the key.
- The symbols used should be provided in a column on the left side with braille descriptions placed directly opposite.
- The key should be provided on a separate sheet attached to the map, or included on

a facing page. If the key is given on the same sheet it could be mistaken as part of the map or diagram and may cause confusion.

- If letters or numbers are used to refer to items in the print diagram, the braille version should use consecutive numbers (or letters preceded by the braille letter sign) ordered from the top to the bottom of the diagram.

Choosing materials

Tactile diagrams can be produced in several ways. Collage, a common technique, uses an assortment of materials such as sandpaper, wire, string and textured wallpaper. The materials are cut to the appropriate shape and applied with adhesive onto a backing material. Collages have limited durability and may be bulky and difficult to store safely, the parts which are in relief may become flattened and glued features may peel off whilst in storage.

Vacuum forming

It may be better to treat diagrams produced in the collage format as masters which can be cheaply reproduced using a vacuum forming process on a specialist machine such as a *Thermoform* (Figure 18.1). The Thermoform contains a grill which heats up. The master is placed face up on a tray or **platen**, and a sheet of plastic material called **braillon**, is placed on top of it. A frame is then placed over the sheet and clamped into place to produce an airtight seal. Care must be taken to ensure that the master and braillon are the same size and that both fit under the metal frame with no gaps around the edge of the frame. The platen

Figure 18.1   A Thermoform

is then passed under the grill. As the braillon heats up it begins to soften and a suction pump draws air out from under the sheet, pulling the heated braillon down onto the master and forming a plastic relief copy of the original.

If either the master or the braillon are not placed correctly on the platen and there is a gap, air cannot be drawn out to form a vacuum and the copy will lack sharpness. A margin of approximately 1.5 centimetres should be left around the edges of the master copy. Many teachers make the mistake of working right up to the edge of the master with the result that information at the edge of the braillon sheet is lost. It is necessary to practise regulating the temperature of the machine since poor copies result when the temperature of the grill is too high or too low.

This process can also be used to reproduce sheets of braille text. Braillon has a number of advantages as a reading medium: the sheets are durable and suitable for outdoor use, the braille dots will not be rubbed smooth, and damaged braillon sheets can be replaced easily if the master has been retained. A disadvantage is that many touch readers find braillon less comfortable than braille paper as a medium for reading at length.

The Thermoform is an expensive piece of equipment, but once the initial purchase has been made, maintenance costs are low and multiple copies can be quickly reproduced using braillon, which costs only a few pence for each sheet. Various qualities and thicknesses of braillon paper are available. The Thermoform machine has a counter to monitor the number of copies made – a useful feature when producing large numbers of copies.

Summary of advantages and disadvantages of using the Thermoform

The advantages of the Thermoform are:
- the Thermoform machine requires minimum maintenance;
- multiple copies are relatively cheap to produce;
- copies are robust and suitable for outdoor use;
- the process is able to reproduce 'piling' or relief;
- symbols have sharp edges and good definition.

Its disadvantages include the following:
- masters are very time consuming to produce';
- production methods may require special kits, glues etc.';
- masters cannot be photocopied for duplication at other centres';
- masters cannot be easily updated or corrected';
- braillon copies are not easily visible for the child with low vision who wants to supplement tactile information';
- considerable space is required for the storage of both masters and braillon copies';
- 'producers' need training to perfect skills.

Using microcapsular materials

Tactile materials can also be produced using microcapsular or 'swell' paper and a heat fuser. The master version is produced in a clear, black outline line on white A4 paper. This is then photocopied onto the microcapsule paper, which is a special paper coated with microscopic plastic capsules containing alcohol. The microcapsule paper is then exposed to a heat source (120–125°C). The black lines absorb more heat than the white areas of the paper and the microcapsules under the black lines expand causing the lines to swell and rise. As microcapsule paper is expensive and budgets for its purchase are often limited, it is essential to plan its use carefully.

The raised black lines contrast well with the white background to allow the pupil with residual vision to supplement the information they have received through touch.

A limitation of the process is that it is not possible to create a diagram which incorporates variations of relief. Moreover, small symbols tend to have rounded edges and lack the clarity and definition of those produced by the vacuum forming process. Copies may have a limited lifespan and may become flattened after heavy use. Symbols can be scratched off and may be shortened by exposure to strong sunlight and rain. The method is perhaps best suited for the production of items such as simple graphs, pie charts, electrical and logic circuits, outline shapes of objects, scatter diagrams, mathematical constructions, uncluttered maps and simple apparatus diagrams. This process is an important method of production of the Moon reading code (a raised line alternative to braille).

Summary of the advantages and disadvantages of the microcapsular system

The advantages of this system are:
- masters can be prepared relatively easily and quickly using permanent marker pens or standard printers;
- the process does not require the purchase of special consumable symbols (such as the Nottingham Map Kit, see above) or complex crafting skills;
- masters can easily be amended or updated;
- masters are easily stored because they are standard A4 size and have no relief;
- masters can be photocopied for use in other schools, centres;
- the black on white images are useful for students with low vision;
- it is possible to braille directly onto the tactile copies;
- master diagrams can be designed and stored on computer;
- commercially available sheets of transfers, such as Letratone, Meconorma and Alfac, can be used to create symbols of a professional quality which are consistent in size, shape and intensity;
- mistakes in preparation of the master copy can be corrected with a commercial correction fluid such as *Tippex*.

This disadvantages of the microcapsular system are:
- the cost of the heat fuser;
- the high cost of microcapsule paper;
- the process does not allow layers to be created; thus variations of relief are very difficult to achieve;

- small symbols or closely drawn lines may lack sharpness and definition;
- copies are not robust, becoming smooth after regular use and cannot tolerate exposure to rain or strong sunlight;
- symbols can be scratched off by fingernails;
- perspiration on readers' fingers can make the surface feel 'tacky' and the ink can leave black traces on the finger;
- A4 paper does not easily fit into standard braille folders;
- Not all photocopiers are able to photocopy onto microcapsular paper – check first!

Safety issues

Both the microcapsule and vacuum forming processes produce fumes, so they should only be used in well-ventilated areas. The Thermoform machine becomes extremely hot and should be carefully located to avoid accidental burns.

Why use tactile representations?

In this chapter we have raised some of the issues surrounding the production of tactile representations, and the reader will be aware by now that it is a time-consuming and labour-intensive process. However, well-produced materials of this kind are essential resources in the education of children who rely upon touch as a learning medium, and the effort of producing these materials can be easily justified in that:

- pupils with a visual impairment are entitled to full access to the same curriculum materials as their peers who are fully sighted;
- diagrams often present complex information in a simplified form and enable learners to work with a greater degree of independence;
- the tactual skills developed in the exploration and processing of tactile materials may transfer to other areas of academic study and to daily living skills.

The ability to produce effective tactile materials and to instruct pupils in their use is an essential competency for teachers of children and young people who are visually impaired.

Chapter 19
Study Skills

Rory Cobb

Introduction

Study skills can be defined as the 'appropriate techniques for completing a learning task' (Gall *et al.* 1990) and include skills in gathering, storing and retrieving information, time management, the organisation of materials and the efficient use of study aids. These skills become increasingly important as children move through school and they translate directly into employment skills.

Children who are visually impaired require effective study skills for the same reasons as children who are fully sighted: to undertake learning tasks efficiently and to achieve their full academic potential. Many of the individual strategies which they need to employ are also fundamentally the same, a point borne out by recent research (Erin *et al.* 1993). This chapter sets out to identify the main features of effective study skills and to suggest how children who are visually impaired may best be encouraged to develop them.

Time management

All children who are visually impaired require additional time to access and understand information. A range of strategies can be employed to address this issue, and will vary according to the age of the student and the demands of the curriculum. Some of these strategies, particularly for younger children, may involve intervention by teachers and other adults to control the demands on a child's time, for example by modifying or rescheduling the work expected of them. Older children, however, need as far as possible to be in control of their own work, and for them the development of independent study skills becomes increasingly important.

Good study skills involve a combination of two factors: a grasp of the key skills and the ability to employ them efficiently to maximise achievement. For students who are visually impaired efficiency is essential. The visual medium dominates communication in everyday life because of its immediacy and versatility. Accessing information through sound, touch or reduced vision is, in most cases, inherently less efficient. Study skills and time management skills therefore hold great significance for students who are visually impaired, as means of minimising the impact of this shortfall.

The development of these skills is not a discrete activity which can be timetabled into the school day; it is an integral part of the way in which children should be encouraged to think about their work and the demands which it makes on their time. Planning ahead, setting your own deadlines and not leaving things to the last minute are standard time management strategies which apply to all learners. However, children who are visually impaired need to understand that the factors which make up the time equation for them are likely to be different, because many tasks are likely to take them longer to complete in the first place. Understanding and accepting this fact is an essential part of their development as learners.

Accessing information in alternative media

Most children with a visual impairment will require their work to be presented in a non-standard medium such as large print, braille or audio tape. For these children the immediacy of visual information is wholly or partially absent. Whether they rely on touch, hearing or imperfect vision to access information, their ability to locate and retrieve relevant data is inevitably reduced.

A simple explanation of the reasons for this may be found in an analogy from the world of computers. Access to information by the standard visual route is like parallel communication between a computer and a printer: large amounts of information are transferred simultaneously. Access to information via braille, audio tape and (depending on its size) large print is more like serial communication between the two devices: one piece of data at a time in a fixed order. It is not only inherently slower but also very much less flexible.

To minimise the problem, children who are visually impaired need to be taught the most effective methods of gaining access to information they require. The specific access strategies which teachers should encourage will vary according to the medium being used and will be discussed in more detail in other chapters. Typically, however, they might include strategies such as the development of a procedure to identify the information contained on a tape before listening to it, or using the contents of a braille book to locate a summary before embarking on lengthy reading of a whole chapter. It is worth noting that the exercises to test comprehension and reference skills which are commonly used to develop study skills in children who are fully sighted may need to be adapted to make them relevant to the idiosyncrasies of the alternative medium being used by the child who is visually impaired. Teachers should not assume that the skills required in such exercises are necessarily the same.

Recording information

Many children who are visually impaired record information in different ways from their peers, employing typing or braille skills and using specialist technology. The development of these skills is often seen as a parallel to the development of handwriting in children who are fully sighted, but the comparison is limited. In order to write in braille, children have to master a highly contracted code; typing is a skill that is learnt in addition to, not instead of, braille or handwriting. The additional workload involved in mastering these writing skills is considerable and reduces the total time available to children and teachers for the development of other skills. These differences in methods of recording also have some practical implications. Saving information onto disk and printing it later is standard office practice but does not fit readily into the work pattern of most primary or secondary schools. Whereas a pencil or pen is all that a child who is fully sighted needs to undertake almost all recording activities in school, pupils who are visually impaired may need to use several different instruments, for example a stylus for drawing diagrams on plastic film, a Perkins brailler, or a word processor.

Work will often be recorded on single sheets rather than an in exercise book. Whether their medium is print or braille, children who are visually impaired need to develop good housekeeping strategies to keep this work accessible and manageable, such as numbering and titling all pages, keeping all work in clearly marked files and in a standard order, and keeping tapes and computer disks clearly labelled and stored. Consistency is again the key to success; if you have a severe visual impairment and cannot find the right file at the right time the consequences in terms of additional time and effort to resolve the problem are considerable.

Motivation and concentration

Most children with full sight who master the art of reading and writing reach a point where the activity itself becomes automatic and subconscious. Children who are visually impaired may reach this point either much later or not at all. Reading and writing tasks, especially those in which there are frequent changes of activity, will often prove difficult, not because the content is beyond the level of the child's understanding but because it is difficult to record. It can often be hard for children who are visually impaired to maintain their interest and concentration over an extended period of time because of these technical complications. The visual stimuli which are so often used in school textbooks to make the presentation interesting and varied also cause difficulties to students who are visually impaired. If they are modified and retained in the large print or braille versions they can prove time consuming to read and give little real benefit, but if they are removed altogether the remaining text lacks the variety of the original.

Most learning tasks take longer for people with a visual impairment; not for any reason connected with their cognitive ability but simply because of the greater time it takes for them to access and record the relevant information. It is worth considering ways in which tasks requiring sustained attention can be made more accessible. One general strategy that teachers can employ is to scale down tasks to make them equivalent in demand to those undertaken by students who are fully sighted, or to break them down into more discrete and structured parts. For example, a maths homework might be reduced to 15 questions which test the same skills as the 20 expected from other pupils.

Use of adult support

A failure to provide differentiated tasks, which take account of the problems of time and access to information, may overload a child who is visually impaired or force an unhealthy dependence on adult intervention.

Many children who are visually impaired will receive support in school from a classroom assistant or support teacher whose role it is to assist them in gaining access to the content and activities of lessons. There is a danger that the adult will take responsibility for organising the work in order to ensure that the child completes on time and does not fall behind. In this way the child who is visually impaired may cover the content of the curriculum but fail to develop many of the key incidental study skills. In the long run it is preferable for children to manage learning tasks independently, even if the tasks have to be modified in some way, than to become dependent on adult support as a key to success. Differentiating tasks, by reducing content, simplifying or removing visual information or rethinking activities to reduce the importance of visual skills and clues, is vital if children who are visually impaired are to retain control of their learning. For example, the use of 'vision friendly' means of presenting information such as complex flow charts, maps or diagrams should be considered carefully in relation to the objectives of the lesson. If the skill of interpreting information in this way is not one of the objectives being tested it may be possible to present the content in a different, more accessible way (for instance as a list of figures or a written summary) which enables a pupil who is visually impaired to study it without the need for adult intervention.

Where the use of adult support is a necessary and appropriate strategy to ensure access to the curriculum, it is important to achieve a balance. In practical activities involving issues of safety, as far as possible the role of a classroom assistant should be to oversee the work rather than to undertake it directly. Where direct involvement is essential the assistant should encourage the child to take the initiative in organising the work.

Forward planning

Providing resources for children who are visually impaired so that they can work independently alongside their peers who are fully sighted involves a considerable amount of foresight on the part of teachers and support staff in identifying the tasks and materials which may require modification.

Children also need to develop specialist skills in planning ahead for their work. For example, braille is a bulky medium and most books are split into a number of volumes. It is not just a case of taking the right book to lessons but of taking the right volume of the right book. Similarly, children need to prepare the specialist equipment which they will require in lessons; for example children who use electronic note-taking devices will have to check the battery power and format the floppy disks on which they store their work. Most personal devices of this kind do not incorporate a printer and further planning will be needed to ensure that work is printed out at regular intervals and in time for relevant lessons.

The school life of many children who are visually impaired is considerably more regimented by such considerations than that of their sighted peers. Some may develop more effective skills of self-organisation as a result; however, it should not be assumed that children who are visually impaired have more of a natural inclination to do so than any other children. Some children who are visually impaired develop misguided expectations, believing for example that it is somebody else's responsibility to collect their books and equipment for lessons. It is important to establish a routine in which the responsibilities of the pupil are clearly defined. While it is the duty of support staff to provide pupils who are visually impaired with the skills of self-organisation needed to manage their work independently, pupils must also learn for themselves the consequences of a failure to carry out their own responsibilities.

Reading and independent note taking

The additional effort and time which children who are visually impaired may have to expend to complete reading and writing tasks make it important that they develop effective strategies for identifying and extracting relevant information from their reading. Whereas the SQ3R approach ('Survey Question Read Recall Review') approach to dealing with new text is appropriate for children who are fully sighted, the process might be too time-consuming for children who are severely visually impaired. One solution can be to provide a list of structured questions as signposts for their reading. This not only encourages more purposeful reading but also helps to break up the task of assimilating text which may not be relieved by illustrations or diagrams because it has been transcribed into braille or onto tape. Providing material on tape as well as in written form may help some students to concentrate more effectively by reading along with the tape.

One of the most efficient means of accessing information in print is through the use of a person who is fully sighted who reads out text on request. Children need to learn to apply the same techniques which they would employ in their own reading to appraise a book's potential value, and need skills in guiding their reader to the parts of the text that will be of most use.

Organisation and storage of materials

A most important factor for encouraging the development of independent learning skills in students who are visually impaired is a familiar and ordered working environment. From an early age children should be encouraged to maintain a consistent pattern of organising and storing their learning resources so that they can locate these unaided. This will require the provision of suitable shelving and desk space, with appropriate labelling in braille or large print. Primary school classes lend themselves to the creation of a structured and consistent environment more readily than secondary schools, where children are usually required to move from room to room on a regular basis. However, where children do change classes frequently, the principles of consistent layout can still be adopted in the central resource base where children store their work and equipment.

Use of reference materials

The ability to locate and retrieve information using a range of reference tools is becoming an increasingly important skill at every stage of education and across the range of curriculum subjects. Recent developments in information technology (IT), especially in the area of CD-ROM, have considerably improved prospects in this area for individuals who are visually impaired. With specialist software, most IT applications are now accessible through speech or large character displays and data stored on computers can be located and read independently by users who are visually impaired. While this is a significant step forward in providing equality of access, technology seldom offers a complete solution. Accessing information technology through speech or large character displays is a considerably more complex process than the conventional approach. It remains the case that most children who are visually impaired will require some modification of tasks requiring extensive searches of reference materials held on disk if they are to complete them within a reasonable time.

This is even more apparent in the case of traditional reference skills involving the printed word, for example in the use of dictionaries or encyclopaedias. The fact that very few reference works of this kind are available in braille or large print is only partly explained by the relative cost of producing them for a small number of users who are visually impaired, their impracticability is a more significant factor. The difficulties of dealing with a full-scale dictionary in braille, for example, are substantial. The user is required to locate the appropriate volume from the many (possibly up to 20 in number) into which the braille version has to be split. The user then has to search methodically through each page heading to locate the correct page, before working through all the entries on the page to find the word concerned. Although this process is similar to that undertaken by print readers, each stage will take the touch reader considerably more time and effort. The end result is that the effort required becomes disproportionate to the value of the outcome. This is not to suggest that students who are visually impaired cannot learn or should not be taught independent reference skills. It is important, however, to recognise that their efficiency threshold in such tasks is likely to be considerably lower than that of students who are sighted. In such circumstances it may be appropriate to consider modifying the task itself to reduce it in scale (for example, using a simplified word list rather than a full dictionary) or to encourage the student to access the relevant information using an alternative strategy, for example by employing a sighted reader.

Working in the classroom

The importance of a child's education lies not only in achieving the product but also in experiencing the process. There is a danger that in the quest to ensure that children who are visually impaired complete the work, the difference between the quality of their educational experience and that of other children is overlooked. Wherever possible, children who are visually impaired should be able to work in class in the same manner as those around them: on their own or in a group as appropriate. Clearly there are significant areas of the curriculum where additional adult intervention is unavoidable, but adult support should always be justified in terms of the demands of the activity, and not used as a means of compensating for the child's poor study skills or the teacher's lack of preparation.

The challenge to support staff is to ensure that relevant materials are available in the appropriate format before the lesson begins, and that the child has been briefed in advance about any complexities which may be encountered. The child needs to be able to read and write competently using either low- or high-technology devices, but the child also needs the organisational skills to manage efficiently the technical resources required. In addition to these 'technical' requirements, children need to develop the confidence to speak up for themselves in order to represent their own needs to teachers.

In research activities children who are visually impaired can work in a group with children who are fully sighted and have equal input into designing the activity and identifying useful avenues of investigation. Depending on their level of competence with technology, they may also be able to access specific information through a CD-ROM or similar device on behalf of the group. Where the effect of their visual impairment substantially limits their ability to locate information efficiently they can hand over to others in the group to undertake this aspect of the work. Working together in this complementary manner is the key to successful teamwork and in many areas, such as touch typing or listening skills, a competent student who is visually impaired may have more to offer than most children who are fully sighted.

Working as part of a group also serves to underline the importance of interdependence. Both at school and in adult life there are many activities where a person with a visual impairment will benefit from sighted assistance, regardless of how independent they are. The ability to recognise this fact, accept it and integrate it into one's life is a measure of coming to terms with disability. Children who are visually impaired should be taught to view help from people who are fully sighted as part of a reciprocal relationship to which they themselves are required to make a significant contribution. In short, they should be encouraged to view themselves as full members of the group, where the assistance provided to them is given because of who they are and not out of a sense of duty or pity for their disability.

Educational visits

Educational visits form a significant part of all children's education. Children who are visually impaired should be able to participate in these visits as far as possible on equal terms with other children. Wherever possible, the place to be visited should be checked out in advance to assess its suitability and to work out the potential for non-visual access. If given advance notice, staff at museums and other educational sites are often very willing to accommodate the needs of a visually impaired individual; for example, by taking items out of display cases to be touched or by allowing pupils behind cordons. Consider also ways in which pupils can record their findings independently while on visits; perhaps by the use of a pocket memo tape recorder from which they can write up notes later. Educational visits should be positive experiences which introduce children who are visually impaired to new challenges and which reinforce their sense of independence and self-esteem.

Summary

Effective study skills are essential to the educational success of children who are visually impaired. One of the difficulties of nurturing effective study skills is the fact that responsibility for teaching them belongs partly with all teachers and wholly with none. This often leads to a lack of consistency across the curriculum, and it is essential that a clear lead on study skills is given by staff with a specialist understanding of visual impairment. Tasks and activities should wherever possible be designed or modified to encourage children to become independent learners, instead of requiring them to work mainly through a sighted intermediary. At the same time interdependence with other sighted students and adults should also be recognised as a valid and necessary strategy for managing some of the demands of the visual world. The development of effective study skills enables children who are visually impaired to demonstrate and experience positive achievement in school and to develop a range of skills and strategies which will serve them well throughout their adult lives.

Chapter 20
Access through Technology

Stuart Aitken

Introduction

In the early 1980s the first text to braille, screen reading computer entered UK classrooms when the BBC workstation was converted for use by pupils with visual impairment (Spragg 1984). Around the same time, similar developments took place in North America, using Apple II and PCs, and also in Scandinavia and other countries. Since their introduction, the choice, range and power of access technologies benefiting people with visual impairment has grown exponentially. Now 15 years later libraries can be accessed on the other side of the world, essays can be written by speaking to a personal computer, discussions may be held with others who have a shared interest regardless of where they live, and it is possible to corresponded with friends in privacy – provided they have the right software, hardware, phone lines and have bills their bills.

The term 'educational technology' is used throughout this chapter, partly because the latter term roots the technology within an educational context more than other near-equivalent terms such as 'information technology' or 'microelectronic technology'. Also the term 'educational technology' is used here in the same sense as by Bozic in chapter 35, emphasising the continuity between the technology offered to pupils who have the single impairment to vision and that for pupils with visual impairment who are multiply disabled. Discussion of other issues emphasises the continuity between solutions for visually impaired pupils with or without additional impairment, for instance the identification of suitable technology and review of its use within a cyclical process of assessment (see Chapter 35 for further details). In this chapter the discussion is focused more on pupils without additional impairments.

Curriculum demands

The basic requirements of educational technology have changed little since the early 1980s. Aitken and McDevitt (1995) argued that any curriculum places the following demands upon the young person who is visually impaired, and therefore also requires the appropriate educational technology to fulfil these demands.

- Access information, for example by reading; without adaptation, the printed page is inaccessible to a person who is blind.
- Express oneself, for example in writing; the personal letter, note, essay or report often cannot be written by hand.
- Drawing; in art classes pupils who are visually impaired may wish to appreciate the drawings of others, and to have their own drawings and paintings appreciated (Hinton 1992).
- Manipulate symbols; mathematics, science, music and, to a lesser extent, foreign languages, may require access to special sets of symbols.
- Communicate personally; interaction with other people may be affected, especially if additional impairments are present (see Chapter 17).
- Manipulate and control equipment; for the pupil who is visually impaired an abstract task may be made still more abstract, and difficult to conceptualise.
- Move around safely; avoiding obstacles at a school entrance, which was designed by architects at a time when disability was not a consideration, can be a serious hazard for someone with a visual impairment.
- Engage in the activities of daily living; for instance the blind person is placed at a serious disadvantage using bank auto-teller facilities. Although the technology is already available to solve some of these telecommunications problems, few companies provide the facilities (Gill 1996).

In any school subject, most tasks will require one or more of the skills listed above. Each of these requirements represents, to some degree, a barrier to learning for someone who is visually impaired. Educational technologies offer a means of overcoming these barriers to learning and unlike most other methods (such as the services of a personal reader), educational technologies foster independence. Although it has provided opportunities to help overcome barriers to learning, the introduction of technology has also presented problems to learners. We will consider examples of both.

For the pupil or student with visual impairment, educational technology offers access through sight (for instance enlarged print and graphics), sound (for instance speech synthesis), or touch (such as converting text to braille).

Problems addressed by educational technology

Given the wide range of educational technology that is available, why do children and young people who are visually impaired still experience difficulties in accessing the curriculum using these methods? As is often the case, the devil is in the detail. Although technological solutions are available, many additional factors need to be considered in order to make the most effective use of them. We consider in more detail four of the aforementioned requirements of educational technology.

1. Accessing information

For many years non-technological solutions, including human or personal reader services, have offered access to the inkprint page. The advantage of technology is that it provides a means of accessing information which is less dependent on the goodwill of others.

Two main areas will be considered: first the technology used by pupils themselves to access information, and second, the technology used to indirectly support the pupil's access to information, through curriculum sharing, in-service training and access to specialist support.

Educational technology offering direct pupil support

As long ago as the early 1970s Lindqvist and Trowald (1971) identified key problems experienced by children and young people with visual impairment in accessing information. The eight most important factors (after Lindqvist and Trowald, 1971 and further adapted from Aitken and McDevitt, 1995) were:

1. getting study material on time
2. finding one's place in talking books
3. keeping up with papers and journals (for further and higher education students, especially)
4. reviewing study material before exams
5. comprehending descriptions of figures and tables
6. utilising dictionaries and encyclopaedias
7. working with photocopied material
8. maintaining concentration while listening to talking books.

Advances in technology have brought improvements in many of these areas. It is now possible for students to access a wide range of up-to-date journal articles through the Internet or other specialised services. These articles can then be downloaded to a personal computer to be read by a screen reader through speech, magnification or braille. Economies of scale have reduced the price of optical character reading (OCR) machines and scanners, to a level which some schools can afford. For many people with visual impairment an OCR, used in combination with a scanner reading system, represents a major advance in personal independence, allowing them to read correspondence and personal papers in private (Sullivan 1993).

CD-ROMs can store large sets of archived material, making it possible to access dictionaries and encyclopaedias without the need for the tens of metres of shelf space required to hold bound braille volumes. Hybrid CD-ROMs, containing both electronic and spoken versions of the same text, are even now beginning to replace the talking books traditionally recorded on cassette tapes. A problem that faces people with a visual impairment in accessing CD-ROM is that most commercially available titles contain linked text, graphics and sound which can complicate access to the information required by the person who is visually impaired. While we await access to broadband communications, through cable, satellite and microwave, an interim solution could be to use CD-ROM technologies to store information for later access. CD-ROM writers/ recorders are now available for around £1500 making it feasible to write curricular materials onto CD-ROMs at relatively low unit cost.

Educational technology offering indirect pupil support

Video-conferencing is used routinely in some countries. For instance, in Scotland two more geographically remote regions have developed an electronic infra-structure which allows staff to share curriculum materials using a bulletin board system (BBS) as well as video-conferencing to allow staff to attend meetings without leaving their office. Similar facilities existed at Perkins School in the USA several years ago, allowing staff to attend meetings without leaving their bases. Video-conferencing can allow specialist teachers to maintain contact with pupils. One peripatetic teacher of a pupil with visual impairment had to attend a meeting some miles away, which required her to be absent for four days. The pupil was shocked to be phoned by her teacher on the first day at 9.15 am, and each day thereafter, and to be asked to open up her work on the computer for correction, sharing the screen through 'electronic whiteboarding' then switching seamlessly to speech to discuss her work.

Common to the success of these 'information superhighway' projects has been an emphasis on high quality content and the need to establish firm cooperative working relationships before embarking on electronic forms of communication. Traditional interpersonal communication became a firm base on which to develop narrow band and intermediate band technologies. Success in using the information superhighway will require clear understanding of the need for integration of human elements with technical objectives.

Unfortunately, innovation in technical solutions has not so far been matched by innovative approaches to capital investment. In the few rural locations which have been able to secure investment in these technologies, one of the spin-offs has been that the existence of these solutions has then acted as a magnet to small businesses, encouraging them to relocate. Government funding of the infrastructure within rural locations would, at least in part, lead to further investment. Cost-effectiveness should be considered in terms of cost–benefit relationships, rather than simply looking for what is the cheapest option.

There are potential benefits in connecting schools to broadband networks for curriculum delivery, in-service training and for some aspects of administration. At this stage however, the technology is beset by problems caused by lack of agreed standards, inequality in provision and proliferation of information providers with little understanding of how to present information in a form accessible to pupils and students who are visually impaired.

Other factors identified by Lindqvist and Trowald (1971) as important to pupils accessing information have become more problematical as a result of advances in educational technology. Indeed for at least one of the factors, that is comprehending descriptions of figures and tables, the increased power, scope and penetration of educational technology has itself resulted in greater disadvantage for the pupil who is visually impaired. A detailed discussion of this is provided in the section on drawing.

In recent years one of the most significant advances in the human–computer interface (the way the user operates the computer) has been the graphical user interface (GUI). For the computer user who is fully sighted, GUIs offer a much simpler environment, reducing the number of complex key presses that have to be remembered. Instead of interacting with the computer via the keyboard, GUI systems have a pointing device (usually a mouse), which is used to point at, and interact with, visual images on the screen.

The increasing use of visual information introduced by GUIs places the visually impaired user at a disadvantage. Modern GUI systems are extremely visual, and very difficult to adapt for people who cannot see a screen. (For a full discussion of the problems presented by GUIs, see Edwards 1991.) Applications such as outSPOKEN for the Apple Macintosh, which uses keyboard commands to control the mouse and navigate the screen, opened up the possibility of blind people being able to access computer systems which use a heavily visual interface. Morley (1995) describes the Windows interface for PCs, helping people who are visually impaired to appreciate the concepts underlying the use of icons, windows, mouse and pointers.

2. Expressing oneself in writing

A wide range of input systems are now available which enable the pupil who is visually impaired to write text. Some are based on braille input, others use alphanumeric keyboards with software to convert text into braille, often in combination with speech synthesis as a means of reviewing what has been written. Writing for a sighted audience of teacher, family and friends presents obvious difficulties to a pupil with visual impairment. What is perhaps less obvious is the precise nature of the difficulties presented. Based on the work of Odor *et al.* (1988), Aitken and McDevitt (1995) showed how different forms of writing place different demands on the writer who is visually impaired, in terms of speed, vocabulary and editing.

Table 20.1 summarises this account, indicating in which particular education sector each form of writing predominates, and identifying the broad category of technology which often proves helpful. One reason primary school pupils with a visual impairment generally receive less exposure to educational technologies is that the effort of learning new technologies often outweighs the benefits received. But as the demands for writing increase, these benefits can become substantial. Problems arise when the changing demands of writing tasks are not anticipated in curriculum planning.

Voice recognition

The increased memory, storage capacity and processor speed of computers have advanced voice recognition technologies enormously and have reduced their costs. To obtain maximum benefit, however, users need to pay careful attention to 'training' the computer

Table 20.1   Comparison of demands made by different forms of writing

	Speed	Vocabulary	Editing	Education sector	Potential impact of technology
Letter writing	Under writer's control	Under writer's control	Minimal	Primary school	Low
Taking notes	Controlled by other person's rate of speaking	New, frequent errors	Complex	Secondary school and further/ higher education	High, e.g. pocket braille machines with speech output
Essay/report writing	Under writer's control but high demands	Mostly writer's but less familiar	Complex	Secondary school	High, e.g. desktop computer with access software

to recognise their voices. Attainment of over 90% accuracy only follows constant review and update of the voice recognition system over a period of several months. While voice recognition has applications within a commercial and home setting it will, at least for some time to come, not be widely available within schools.

Pupils using voice recognition technology have to divide their attention between speaking at the correct rate and in the right tone of voice, checking what has been written, editing the text and then returning to speaking. It will be some time before these problems are sufficiently resolved so as to bring voice recognition technologies into everyday classroom use. At that point other questions will arise, not least as to whether such technologies will be allowed in examinations.

Nisbet and Kerr (1996) reviewed the use of educational technology within formal testing and examination settings, describing how technology can be used to help students to participate in written exams. They identified several ways in which students who are visually impaired or students with other special needs can undertake examinations. Methods included the provision of extra time, the use of a reader and/or scribe, large print,

Table 20.2   Strategies used in examination conditions (Nisbet and Kerr 1996)

	Blind	Partially sighted
Braille (+ extra time)	6	0
Large print (+ extra time)	9	75
Scribe + reader	2	9
Word processor	1	0
Extra time only		21
Total	**19**	**113**

(Data do not total exactly as some information was not available)

Terms 'blind' and 'partially sighted' as used in source data different colours of paper, and raised diagrams. Part of their analysis involved a review of all pupils who were visually impaired who undertook examinations in Scotland in 1993. The analysis of these results is shown in Table 20.2.

Clearly, at the time of the study educational technology was not used routinely in examinations; for instance, there is only one recorded instance of a word processor being used. This situation is changing, not least because exam boards are now beginning to state a preference for pupils to undertake exams independently without the support of an adult (Nisbet and Kerr 1996). This change means that examination boards will have to rethink their requirements, since many of the tools used routinely in the classroom by pupils who are visually impaired, such as spell checkers, accelerated writing techniques and grammar checkers, are prohibited under current examination regulations.

3. Drawing

The increased availability of personal computers revolutionised the presentation of information. Three of the earliest developments were:
- spreadsheets which allowed people routinely to perform complex calculations;
- word processing which released people from laborious editing through cutting and pasting scraps of paper;
- desktop publishing which resulted in a huge increase in the inclusion of illustrative material within inkprint versions of books and other documents.

Of these developments, the last has perhaps had the greatest impact upon people with a visual impairment. Desktop publishing may enable attractive presentation, but each figure or other graphical item has to be interpreted by the visually impaired person. Verbal descriptions of these features can become so complex that pupils and students frequently may not able to understand their significance.

For the sighted person, appreciation of spatial relations and visual concepts is perceptual, that is direct and immediate. The person with residual vision has to spend more time visually scanning the illustration, relying on memory to build up an appreciation of the contents and spatial relationships of the elements in a picture. In addition, an illustration may contain images for which the child has no concrete referent. While the interpretation of pictures and other graphical material is a perceptual exercise for the pupil who is fully sighted, for the pupil who is blind or has only residual vision it becomes a complex, cognitively demanding task.

Until recently, people converting print into alternative forms were instructed 'that no parts or aspects of the figures should be left out' on the basis that if the student who is fully sighted is able to access the material so too should a student who is visually impaired. Only recently has this belief changed. It was realised that the interpretation of graphical materials is not only hard to follow: what one does not comprehend, one will probably not remember (Greene 1987).

Several strands of research (for a review, see Myrberg, 1978) provide simple principles for converting diagrammatic inkprint information into other media, for example: 'comprehension will be adversely affected when description is longer than about one minute', or 'avoid recursive sentence structure'. 'Avoid use of visual metaphors' (after Myrberg 1978).

Interestingly, the same issues regarding interpretation have arisen as technologies have advanced in other areas, for example:

- concerning raised diagrams which faithfully reproduce every curve, line of perspective and other painter's cues (Gibson 1950);
- the proliferation of research into finding a means of reproducing in every detail a tactile representation of the computer screen's graphics;
- in deciding which graphical information presented via the World Wide Web (WWW) should be converted to enhanced visual, auditory and/or tactile form.

The argument has been dominated by the belief that, in order to be effective, auditory and tactile information must convey the same quantity of information as visual information. An alternative approach is to focus on the nature of the information that should be conveyed, rather than the quantity. Myrberg's identification of key principles suggests a different direction for technical developments.

4. Manipulating symbols

An understanding of sets of symbols is necessary for pupils to progress in maths, sciences, music and (to a lesser extent) foreign languages. We will concentrate here on the issues raised concerning mathematical symbols. During the early stages of primary school these are limited to numbers and simple calculation signs. As maths becomes more complex and science is introduced, the representational task becomes formidable. Symbols may be positioned above, below, at a diagonal to or at the centre of other symbols or groups of symbols, and even the sizes of symbols can transmit information. At present a person who is skilled in both maths and braille notation is needed to translate symbols from their visual form with the high degree of accuracy that is demanded. Unlike text translation, in which an accuracy rate of 94% in translating from visual to braille or speech is perfectly adequate for all but the most demanding circumstances, a translation success rate of 94% would not be sufficient in maths: it would lead to the wrong answer.

Although existing text to braille translation software often has the capacity to produce mathematical symbols by utilising a range of special procedures, substantial training is needed before teachers and others feel confident in using such systems. Significant advances will be necessary before automatic translation is available which will allow non-mathematicians and/or non-braillists to produce maths in a tactile and/or auditory form through a computer.

A feature which mathematical symbols have in common with tactile diagrams is a problem referred to as 'chunking'. When people skilled in maths and science look at a mathematical equation, they see not only single symbols but also the general grouping or pattern of the problem or equation. Current conversion systems, whether based on synthesised speech or braille, only allow equations to be analysed serially, making it hard to comprehend more complex expressions.

The final issue to be discussed concerning mathematical symbols shows how advances in educational technology are changing not only the content of the curriculum but also the order in which that content is learned. In the past five years graphical scientific calculators have been introduced to the National Curriculum in England and Wales and within the 5–14 Curriculum in Scotland. Whereas in the past, pie charts, histograms and bar graphs would have been taught later in the curriculum, these are now being introduced at an earlier stage. These graphical forms can make it easier for children who are fully sighted to grasp mathematical ideas, but the diagrammatic representation may place children who are visually impaired at a disadvantage. It is of course possible to convert the visual image into a tactile one. However, as we have seen interpretation of tactile drawings is not just a perceptual task but also a cognitive one for the pupil who is visually impaired.

Summary

Educational technology offers many advantages to the pupil with visual impairment, who previously depended far more on other people in order to gain access to the curriculum. At the same time as presenting new opportunities, technological advances used by visually impaired people to access the curriculum may in themselves present new difficulties and challenges.

Chapter 21

The Learning Environment

Christopher Lewis and Hugh Taylor

Introduction

Over the lintel of the first school built for myopes in the United Kingdom was inscribed the motto, 'Reading and writing shall not enter here' (Lowenfeld 1974). While this epigram is not an entirely a fair reflection of educational practice in the school, it does serve to illustrate the enormous changes in educational practice regarding children with low vision. Discoveries by ophthalmologists, educators and psychologists have not only informed educational practice but have also influenced the design and development of learning environments for pupils with a visual impairment.

Schools and colleges for the visually impaired which are entirely purpose built include Henshaw's College (Harrogate), Northwood Sunshine House (Middlesex), Clapham Park School (South London), Priestley Smith School (Birmingham) and the RNIB College, (Loughborough). Most of the specialist schools and colleges for the visually impaired have modern purpose-built sections grafted onto older buildings. The Royal School for the Blind Wavertree, (Liverpool), and RNIB New College (Worcester) for example have undergone extensive rebuilding in the 1990s.

As we approach the end of this century more children with low vision are taught in mainstream schools. There is a debate about the extent to which educational buildings should be adapted to meet the needs of the visually impaired. Clearly, pupils need to be independent enough to operate sometimes in conditions which are not specially adapted but at the same time they should not be hampered by an unsuitable learning environment; they have a right to adaptations that will ensure that they can access the curriculum as efficiently as possible.

It is not the purpose of this chapter to enter this debate in any great detail. It is hoped that the following suggestions about the adaptation of buildings will be seen as reasonable ways of maximising educational opportunities for pupils and students with a visual impairment.

There are five main considerations in the organisation and adaptation of buildings for pupils and students who are visually impaired:

- the general layout of the building
- the working space required by individual pupils and students
- the specific adaptations for individual subjects

- the provision of facilities for the production and storage of materials and equipment
- the adaptation of lighting

General layout

The pupil or student with a visual impairment can understand the general internal layout of a building more easily if it is logically arranged. For example primary schools might be arranged with a natural progression of classes according to age down a corridor or around a reception/hall area. The Sunshine House School at Northwood is a good example of a special school planned on these simple but effective lines. In secondary schools, specialist teaching areas are easier to locate and access if they are arranged in subject clusters e.g. science/humanities/arts.

It can also be useful for pupils with a visual impairment to have access to a tactile or large print map or plan at the entrance of the school, so that information about the layout of the building can be learnt from a set starting point. Such systems can help pupils with visual impairments to formulate a mental map of the building which can be reinforced by training from mobility staff.

From a safety point of view, it is desirable for key features of the building to be highlighted through decor and/or specialist lighting. For example internal support columns could be painted distinctively to alert pupils with low vision of their presence in otherwise open areas. It is also important to ensure that there are no overhangs or protrusions on staircases, corridors or in classrooms that could cause injuries. Protrusions at head height are particularly dangerous for children who are blind as they escape detection by the standard body protection techniques adopted in indoor mobility. Design Note 25 (Department of Education and Science (DES) 1981a) recommends that 'doors should be fitted with closures and open against a wall rather than into a room' although the authors also note that an open door can sometimes be a very useful aid in orientation because of the change in acoustic quality it affords. Windows which project into walking areas are also hazardous, horizontal or vertical sliding windows being preferred.

In corridors and hallways, radiators should be recessed. If this is impossible then they should be highlighted in different colours. Floor surfaces should be matt to avoid glare. Barker *et al.* (1995) suggest that 'high glare floor finishes are to be avoided because, by reflecting both natural and artificial light they can distort environmental images'. Changes in floor level should be indicated to students well in advance. This can be achieved with changes in floor textures or colour. Some buildings in mainstream schools have marker lines painted around corridor floors to act as route guides for pupils with a visual impairment. Contrast may also be used to distinguish parts of the environment (Figure 21.1)

Goldsmith (1976) recommends particular attention to acoustics in buildings for use by people who are totally blind. Design Note 25 (DES 1981a) describes how, in the open areas of buildings, reflected sound can 'provide necessary information to judge changes in

Figure 21.1   Contrast between floor edges and walls and doors. A distinctive tactile symbol is used to identify each classroom.

direction and obstruction'. Barker *et al.* (1995) recommend that in classrooms ambient noise levels should be kept to a minimum so that students who are blind can benefit fully from auditory information.

In gaining access to the building, it is important that the student with a visual impairment can walk safely to the front entrance without having to negotiate hazards such as traffic, bollards or overhanging trees or shrubs. It should be possible to enter the building without having to mount steps or avoid columns supporting a canopy. A ramped approach with automatic sliding doors is ideal, if money permits. Floor tiles with raised patterns can also provide useful cues to orientation around entrances. Building Bulletin 77 (1992) suggests that in all buildings in which pupils who are visually impaired are educated 'careful consideration should be given to appropriate warning and alarm systems and to means of escape'. These considerations are an essential part of the school's health and safety policy and may well be a point of focus during Ofsted inspections.

Working space for individual pupils and students with a visual impairment

Whether the pupils who are visually impaired are educated in a mainstream or a special school, consideration must be given to their main working areas. Arrangements for pupils at primary level are often easier because they are likely to spend most of their time in one classroom. A feature evident in a number of schools for visually impaired children, especially in classrooms for nursery/reception children, is a split level or mezzanine arrangement. This may be part of the structural design or take the form of a wooden playhouse with steps leading to a raised play area. The small scale of these rooms appeals to young children as they are literally child-sized, but also enables them to form the concept of a room, including the ceiling, which they can reach to touch. Examples of the two types are in the Royal School, in Liverpool and Shawgrove in Manchester (Figure 21.2).

Figure 21.2   The mezzanine style wooden playhouse at Shawgrove School, Manchester. Note the child-sized proportions of the 'upper' and 'lower' rooms.

At secondary level, consideration may need to be given to adapting a range of subject rooms if the students with a visual impairment are to have access to a broad and balanced curriculum. The points outlined below apply to most pupils with a visual impairment.

Whether the pupil is visually impaired or blind, it is likely that they will need more room in which to work. The student's work surface will need to be large enough to accommodate bulky braille texts or large print materials in A3 size. The student who is blind may need room accommodate a braille writing machine, a tape recorder, a braille desktop computer or other specialised equipment. The pupil who has low vision may require a raised desktop or reading stand, task lighting and room for magnifying devices such as a closed circuit television (CCTV).

It will need to be borne in mind that pupils who have additional disabilities may also need space for their wheelchairs and standing frames. Some children will have special assistants or support teachers who will accompany them in lessons, and thought needs to be given to the demands they will make on workspace.

In both special and mainstream schools, consideration will have to be given to the safe and secure storage of specialist equipment. Building Bulletin 77 (1992) outlines the need for small rooms appropriate for individualised work such as tuition in braille. These 'withdrawal' rooms are also useful for visiting therapists, and are invaluable at the time of Standard Assessment Tests and public examinations such as GCSE and A-Levels, where an amanuensis can work uninterrupted with individual pupils. Although the Bulletin refers only to special schools, the principle also applies equally to mainstream schools.

It is important for special schools, or mainstream schools with units where a significant number of pupils who are visually impaired are being educated, to have an area which can be used by visiting ophthalmic experts to assess vision, undertake refraction, prescribe low vision aids, and talk to pupils, parents and school staff. Special schools are likely to use a nurse's room that is equipped with Snellen charts and blackout. However in a mainstream setting where space may be critical, a withdrawal room can be utilised with a portable Snellen chart and a mirror. An advantage of ophthalmic staff seeing pupils in school is that they can advise on adaptations within the building where the pupil is working. These rooms can also be suitable areas for parents and teachers to meet for annual reviews or other consultations.

Adaptations for specific subjects

Further adaptations will be required for subjects such as science, design technology, art and PE which have a strong practical element. Design Note 25 (DES 1981) states that in areas where technology and art are taught, there must be good definition by colour and lighting of any machinery which has moving parts not covered by guards, a good example being a potter's wheel.

In science and food technology areas, Barker *et al.* (1995) recommend the addition of a raised hardwood edge to worktops to contain spills. In food technology rooms they recommend that continuous fitted work surfaces and fitted appliances should be used. Cookers and washing machines should have control settings with tactile markings (set horizontally rather than vertically). Some modern microwave ovens and washing machines are also available with speech facilities for students with visual impairments.

In all working areas, electrical plugs should have safety handles and the floor surface should be non-slip. Variations in the floor texture can be used to alert pupils that they are nearing a work area. The colour and type of worktops should be chosen to maximise the visibility of items of equipment placed on them and also to minimise glare. Cookware, crockery and equipment should be chosen to maximise this contrast. Centres such as those run by the Disabled Living Foundation have specially adapted rooms that illustrate these modifications to good effect.

In science laboratories and technology areas, hidden non-glare strip lighting can be installed above work surfaces, under cupboards and shelves, so pupils do not stand in their own light when undertaking practical tasks.

In music rooms, a backscreen projector can be used to project notation. Pupils who have low vision can then read the visual display without occluding the light source when getting close to the screen. In all teaching areas a mobile black or white board is useful, provided that it is placed in appropriate light to avoid reflection. The most important feature of these boards, however, is that they are kept clean in order to maximise contrast.

The physical exercise (PE) areas should be well lit with no sources of glare and should have a non-slip floor. Particular attention should also be given to contrast and simplicity when marking out playgrounds. Some special schools have swimming pools specially adapted for the visually impaired, and adaptations include lighting which prevents the scatter of glare from the water. This is particularly helpful to pupils who are photophobic and have to remove their photochromatic or dark glasses prior to swimming. Special attention is given to the acoustics in these pools and other adaptations include non-slip flooring and stippled tiles near the water's edge (Figure 21.3).

Figure 21.3   Non-glare lighting, non-slip flooring and stippled tiles, at Priestley Smith School swimming pool, Birmingham.

Building Bulletin 77 (1992) also suggest that consideration needs to be given to library areas and the facilities which are required to store the bulky braille and large-print books and the audiovisual hardware needed to support the students' independent research, which could include CD-ROM facilities. In the future schools may require soundproofed areas where students with a visual impairment can dictate text into a voice activated computer (see Chapter 20).

Reprographics area

Both Bulletin 77 (1992) and Design Note 25 (1981a) stress the need for a room where audiovisual equipment can be repaired by a technician and an area where braille, large-print materials and tapes can be produced for pupils. The reprographics area will require facilities for photocopying, thermoforming, and book production as well as recording facilities for both tape and video. Reprographics equipment, which may include print scanners and computerised systems for the production of braille materials, need to be sited in a spacious, well lit and preferably soundproofed area with the appropriate electrical fittings. This area might also be used to store braille and print learning materials. In all areas where students with visual impairments are being educated there may be very expensive specialist equipment and schools need to ensure that rooms in these areas are secure and that this specialised equipment is regularly serviced.

Lighting for students who are visually impaired

Barker *et al.* (1995) state that, 'the human visual system depends on light to operate' and use the phrase 'no light – no sight.' In assessing the lighting requirements of pupils who are visually impaired there are two main considerations:

- the overall level of ambient lighting in classrooms, corridors and halls
- the 'task' lighting required by individuals to maximise their use of near vision while studying.

Jay (1980), Design note 25 (1981a) and Barker *et al.* (1995) all state that, as a general rule, the visually impaired require twice the normal level of lighting in circulation, amenity and study areas. All areas should be illuminated by glare-free lighting and Hopkinson (1973) and Barker *et al.* (1995) warn that harsh lighting can cause shadows that can be visually confusing.

Both artificial and natural light need to be controlled to ensure that the appropriate level of lighting can be delivered to the right part of the classroom. Some pupils who are visually impaired (such as those with photophobia) will need reduced illumination, while other pupils will prefer high levels of lighting for maximum contrast. Natural light can be controlled by louvres, blinds and tinted glass and ambient artificial lighting can be controlled by dimmer switches fitted to ceiling cluster lights.

Priestley Smith School, in Birmingham, was the first school in the world to be purpose-built for the partially sighted. It was erected shortly after the 1944 Education Act which introduced the term 'partially sighted' rather than 'partially blind' (see Chapter 1). Following revised ophthalmic opinion concerning sight saving, architects and designers were anxious to build an environment which would encourage pupils to use their vision rather than conserve it. The ceilings contain glare-free lighting which can be adjusted to illuminate particular areas within a room. The building design incorporates clerestories and careful attention was given to the decor, windows and blinds (Figure 21.4).

At Clapham Park School in South London, architects used natural and artificial lighting in such a way that, 'it contributed to the normal expression of the building so gaining the additional benefit of assisting the child to find a relationship between the environmental situations that he/she encounters at home and upon leaving school' (Banting 1971).

Design Note 25 (DES 1981a) alerts architects to the need to avoid harsh contrasts and specula reflections in designs for special schools for children who are visually impaired, as many of the students in the school are likely to be wearing glasses and will be vulnerable to glare or halation. A high level of ambient light enhanced by the use of appropriate decor is recommended. Barker *et al.* (1995) urge that walls are painted in pastel shades with a matt surface and Jay (1980) asserts that titanium white is best for ceiling areas.

Figure 21.4 Lighting and blinds in a classroom at Priestley Smith School, Birmingham.

The floor surfaces should be 'plain without optically confusing patterns and no gloss finish to glare or to dazzle' Barker *et al.* (1995). Fittings such as doors, switches, sockets and handles should be painted in contrasting colours to highlight their presence. The only time the use of gloss paint is recommended by Jay (1980) is for window frames and surrounds, which should be painted glossy white. This is to 'soften the contrast between the bright sky seen through the window and the frame itself'. Windows should be kept scrupulously clean and Hopkinson (1973) warns that dirty window surfaces can not only reduce the amount of light but also cause perceptual distortion.

Consideration also needs to be given to 'task lighting'. Jay (1980) describes how a high level of light required for reading can be provided by a relatively low-powered light source mounted close to the task. For pupils with optic atrophy or dystrophies of the retina, such increased localised illumination is required to maximise contrast. The Partially Sighted Society produces a portable 11 watt adjustable reading lamp. Because the bulb is fluorescent the surface of the lamp remains cool and students can work close to it in safety. By reducing visual fatigue, task lighting can dramatically increase a student's ability to sustain close work.

Sensory rooms

Specialist schools for pupils who have severe, or profound and multiple learning difficulties often contain a sensory curriculum room. Building Bulletin 77 (1992) explains that these rooms offer a range of stimulatory experiences involving sight, sound, smell and touch. In these sensory stimulation rooms there are various controllable light sources and sometimes ultraviolet lights are used to stimulate visual responses. Best (1994) warns that staff using such facilities should contact services for the visually impaired or the local education authority (LEA) to establish the health and safety policy regarding the use of ultraviolet light.

Signs

A simple but important adaptation in buildings used by students who are visually impaired is that of signs and notices. These need to be simple and consistent and, as Barker et al. (1995) advocate, they should be an integral part of the process of planning the building and environment. They suggest that signs for children who are visually impaired should be well lit, preferably white on a dark background, and 1.4 to 1.6 metres above floor level. Tactile signs or symbols should be set at a consistent height and position on doors, cupboards, etc. In the most modern buildings, talking signs can be found in lifts and entrance foyers. A good example of the use of signs is to be found at Henshaw's College in Harrogate.

Conclusion

Empowering children to appraise their environment and to voice realistic changes which will meet their needs successfully is an important task for the teacher.

Teachers and others who have accompanied children with visual impairments on residential or day trips to unfamiliar places will be aware of the difficulties which children encounter in a totally unfamiliar environment. However, these children and young people with visual impairments are adaptable; they can learn to cope in unfriendly physical environments. The key to success is often the social environment and if there is a welcoming and positive attitude to pupils who are visually impaired, then there is a high probability that the difficulties in the environment can be overcome.

THE MAINSTREAM CURRICULUM: PRINCIPLES OF ACCESS

The National Curriculum was introduced as a result of the Education Reform Act of 1988 and was revised after the Education Act of 1993 (DfE 1993). The Act provided for the establishment of a National Curriculum for the core subjects (maths, english, science and technology, including design and technology and information technology) and other foundation subjects (history, geography, art, physical education, music and a modern foreign language) to be taught in England and Wales. The National Curriculum applies to pupils of compulsory school age in maintained and grant maintained schools in England and Wales. It is divided into four Key Stages as shown in Table S1:

Table S1 Key Stages of the National Curriculum for England and Wales

	Pupil age	Classes
Key Stage 1	5–7 years	Years 1–2
Key Stage 2	7–11 years	Years 3–6
Key Stage 3	11–14 years	Years 7–9
Key Stage 4	14–16 years	Years 10–11

There are prescribed programmes of study for each subject and each Key stage, which set out what pupils should study and attainment targets set out the expected standards of pupil achievement. Eight 'level' descriptions give the standards of performance that most pupils are expected to achieve.

The National Curriculum Orders stress the importance of providing pupils who have special educational needs (SEN) with 'appropriately challenging work' (DfE 1995a). It allows some flexibility for pupils with SEN, allowing teachers to respond to the student's specific needs. The National Curriculum may be modified, and where appropriate it may be disapplied, for pupils with SEN.

Whenever reading about the teaching of children with a visual impairment, or when talking to teachers who work with the visually impaired, the subject of time is a constant, recurring theme. It is well documented that children with a visual impairment work at a slower rate, when compared with their peers with full sight (Chapman and Stone 1988, Harley *et al.* 1979, Mason 1995). The child with a visual impairment needs hands-on experience to develop a full understanding of concepts and to compensate for a lack of incidental learning. They need a full programme of visits and the opportunity to handle artefacts to gain a greater understanding. Instructions and descriptions need to be clear and precise, and care needs to be taken to ensure that pupils have a full understanding of the language and terms used. All of these aspects will involve an increase in the amount of time required to cover all areas of the National Curriculum.

The National Curriculum is comprehensive and lays down a vast amount of work that needs to be covered. Specialist curriculum areas required by pupils who are visually impaired, such as mobility, typing, training in the use of residual vision, listening skills, study skills and self-help skills, compete for time in the already crowded school day.

Materials may need to be produced in an enlarged or tactile form, and all information should be carefully and clearly presented. The teacher needs to plan well in advance to make sure that materials are readily available to the child, and to ensure that appropriate equipment is available when required, across all areas of the curriculum.

Initially, when the National Curriculum was introduced, many teachers felt some degree of concern at their loss of independence in choosing what they were going to teach, and when and how they were to teach it. However, when the National Curriculum was fully implemented it was generally welcomed because it was felt that it allows all pupils full access to a broad and balanced curriculum (DES 1985), and it also ensures progression. The special school curriculum had long been criticised as being too narrow and restricted (Brennan 1985), and practice has shown that the implementation of the National Curriculum has not resulted in banal teaching. Teachers have re-examined what they teach, and why and how they teach it.

Chapter 22
English

Christine Arter

English has an identity of its own as a separate and distinct subject area, but it also features in all other curriculum areas. English is often taught in different ways in both primary and secondary schools. In primary schools English teaching may be integrated and encompass many areas of the curriculum, while in secondary schools it is generally taught as a separate subject, often by a specialist teacher (Department of Education and Science (DES) 1989b).

The aims of the English curriculum

The Cox report (DES 1989b), which pre-dates the National Curriculum, set out formal proposals for statutory attainment targets and programmes of study for English, and suggested that

> The overriding aim of the English curriculum is to enable all pupils to develop to the full their ability to use and understand English. Since language can be both spoken and written, this means the fullest possible development of capabilities in speaking, listening, reading and writing.

Spoken and written language play a vital role in the growth of understanding and the ability to organise experiences.

Teachers would generally agree that the teaching of English should enable pupils to become competent across a wide range of skills. For example children should learn to speak in standard English as well as non-standard English, in order to communicate with a wider group within society. Furthermore teachers seek to develop within their pupils an understanding of the different ways in which meaning is conveyed by the spoken and the written word.

The role of English in the curriculum

The Cox Report summarises a number of commonly held views about the role of English in the curriculum:

- The 'personal growth' view: there is a relationship between language and learning, and literature is important in developing children's imagination and appreciation of the aesthetic.
- The 'cross-curricular' view: all teachers are teachers of English and have some responsibility to help the child to use and understand the language.
- The 'adult needs' view: all aspects of English teaching help the child to prepare for the demands made later in adult life.
- The 'cultural heritage' view: children should have access to the literacy legacy of their country.
- The 'cultural analysis' view: English should lead the pupil to understand and appreciate their own cultural environment and that of the wider world.

The English National Curriculum

When the English National Curriculum was introduced following the Education Reform Act of 1988, the initial reaction of many teachers was one of apprehension.

With the passage of time it has become apparent that the imposition of the structured approach to the teaching of English has not resulted in the dull or uninspired teaching that many feared, but has led teachers to re-examine what they teach and why. Some teachers may now cover topics not previously taught, and in this way the English curriculum has been enriched.

The English National Curriculum (DfE 1995a) states that teachers should respond to the needs of those children who have special educational needs (SEN), and should provide SEN pupils with 'appropriately challenging work at each key stage'. This chapter seeks to discuss some of the ways in which teachers of children with a visual impairment can ensure full access to the English National Curriculum for their pupils.

Programmes of study: speaking and listening

This programme of study is central to the teaching of English; however, it does present some difficulties for the pupil with visual impairment.

Listening skills

It is stated in the programme of study state that 'Pupils should be taught to listen carefully and to show their understanding of what they see and hear by making relevant comments' (DfE 1995a). The development of listening skills is especially important for the child with a visual impairment, and a structured teaching programme will be necessary to encourage the development of good listening skills and listening comprehension, enabling the child to listen, understand and appreciate the variety of material that should be available in Key Stage 1, and throughout their life. (For a full discussion of listening skills refer to Chapter 15.)

Language development

The development of language in the child with a visual impairment has provoked considerable debate. Wills (1978) suggests that the child's restricted early experience usually results in delayed language development. McGurk (1983) states that in language acquisition the blind child 'follows the same path to communicative competence as his sighted peers' but 'takes longer'. Others believe that the blind child takes a different route to language development. Fraiberg (1977), for example, describes this as a 'long and circuitous route'. However the language of many children with a visual impairment shows no obvious differences from that of their peers who are fully sighted.

Cutsforth (1932) suggested that the language of children who are educationally blind may be intrinsically less meaningful than that of their peers who are fully sighted. His research found that when a blind child was asked to name an object and to describe one quality of that object, 48% of congenitally blind children responded giving words that described visual qualities. Cutsforth concluded that such 'verbalisms' lead to 'incoherent and loose thinking'. This view has been challenged by other writers (Warren 1977, 1994, and Wills 1979), who point to the fact that sighted people often use words for which they have no first-hand experience. Scott (1982a) described gaps in understanding of concepts by a child with a visual impairment, as 'black holes'. Scott suggests that the child may use the correct language to discuss the concept but any sustained discussion will reveal that the child lacks true understanding. The opportunity for the child to handle objects and explore them tactually, will aid the development of concepts. Careful explanations of objects is also important (Barraga 1976, Norris 1972).

It is felt to be important for the teacher to examine each of the key stages of the National Curriculum closely and to consider how they may be adapted to make access easier for the child with a visual impairment.

Key Stage 1

The programme of study states that 'Pupils should be taught conventions of discussion and conversation, for example, taking turns in speaking,' (DfE 1995a). This is a skill that needs to be taught to the child with a visual impairment. Turn taking in this context is often dependent on visual clues. Those taking part in a discussion will see from body language and facial expressions, when other members in the group wish to contribute. They will await their turn to contribute with their own comments. It is not always an easy skill to develop or use well. It is an especially difficult skill for the pupil with a visual impairment to learn. For example if the pupil is determined to contribute to a discussion they may find themselves interrupting others or dominating the conversation, because they are unable to utilise visual clues to help them time their interjections appropriately.

They will be unable to use visual clues to help them to establish that it is time to stop speaking and let someone else take their turn in the debate. Such a situation may mean that the pupil will be rejected by peers because their behaviour is felt to be unacceptable. It is possible therefore that this aspect of speaking and listening may be an area of difficulty for the pupil with a visual impairment, however Workman (1986) suggests that appropriate verbal intervention by the teacher can encourage peer interaction.

Key Stage 2

As the pupil progresses through the programme of study it is expected that they should develop the skill to 'express themselves confidently and clearly' (DfE 1995a).

Many pupils with a visual impairment experience some difficulties in interacting with others. Early experience may have provided the child with fewer opportunities to mix freely with peers. They may have been sheltered and overprotected (Tobin 1992). This may in turn result in fewer chances to develop social skills and to learn to communicate readily with their peers.

These points are discussed in greater depth in other chapters of this book (see Chapters 10 and 11), however the effect of these factors should be kept in mind when considering the teaching of speaking and listening to all pupils with a visual impairment.

In an integrated setting in either a primary or secondary school, the visually impaired child may find themselves isolated from their peers by working with an adult who provides support. Unless support staff are carefully deployed, such a situation might prove a difficulty and indeed a disadvantage for the pupil. Group work may be used to encourage the student with a visual impairment to develop the confidence to express themselves. Some skilful adult guidance and intervention may be required in the group situation to foster true group interaction, whereby the pupil with a visual impairment makes an equal contribution. Speaking and Listening is an area of the curriculum where the child with a visual impairment has the same role to play and has equal status in the group and can therefore make a good contribution. It is the duty of teachers and support assistants to ensure that the child participates fully in this important area of the curriculum.

Key Stages 3 and 4

As the child grows and moves on to the higher stages of the National Curriculum they will be required to develop a range of sophisticated skills.

The Speaking and Listening programme of study suggests that the pupil should 'be taught to use gesture and intonation appropriately' (DfE 1995a). Such communication skills are usually learnt incidentally by most children. Gestures can be seen and imitated and may accompany a distinct tone of voice. The child who is fully sighted will observe both and will be able to synthesise the information to gain a fuller understanding of the situation. Such incidental learning may not be possible for the child with a visual impairment, who may need to be taught to look at the person to whom they are speaking. This is an obvious and important social skill which develops naturally in the sighted child. However, for the child with a visual impairment, constant reminders will often be necessary until the skill becomes an automatic response. It is not going to be an easy task for the pupil to learn how to use gestures naturally and appropriately. Drama lessons may provide the opportunity for the pupil to practise and develop these skills.

The National Curriculum demands that pupils be taught to 'identify the major elements of what is being said, and to distinguish tone, undertone, implications and other indicators of a speaker's intentions'. At this level of complex communication, much is often conveyed through body language and facial expression. This information may not be available to the pupil with a visual impairment, and they will need to work much harder and concentrate more fully on the tone and implications of what is being said. Many pupils with a visual impairment may experience particular problems because of their lack of the visual feedback which informs the fully sighted about how their verbal contributions are received. The Speaking and Listening programme provides the opportunity for teachers to help pupils develop effective communication skills.

Reading

Again the general requirements of the English National Curriculum are commendable, and state that pupils should:

- 'read accurately, fluently and with understanding;
- understand and respond to the texts they read;
- read, analyse and evaluate a wide range of texts (DfE 1995a).

However, there are some areas of potential difficulty for the child with a visual impairment.

Key Stage 1: reading

For many children with a visual impairment reading can be a slow and laborious task. This may mean that it will be difficult to motivate the child and to encourage them to read an 'extensive range of children's literature' (DfE 1995a).

The child who has low vision and reads print, may only be able to see part of the word at a time, and may find it impossible to scan a word or a line of print. This problem will be exacerbated if the print is enlarged by photocopying or by the use of a closed circuit television (CCTV). It may take longer for the pupil to locate the correct page in their book and then to find the line of print. When the child looks away from the text, perhaps to write, it will take them longer to relocate the line they are reading. Such problems will make it harder for pupils with a visual impairment to attain the reading speeds achieved by their fully sighted peers (Best 1992). It is well documented that the blind reader reads at speeds that are well below those reached by sighted readers. Harley *et al.* (1987) state that the average braille reader reads two or three times slower than a print reader. They suggest that an average print reader can achieve speeds of up to 179 words per minute (wpm), while the braille reader (of secondary school age) averaged speeds of only 86 wpm.

The inviting and attractive layout and illustrations of modern children's books may be a cause of difficulty and confusion for the child with low vision. The text is often printed over a coloured picture, making it very difficult for the child with a visual impairment to locate and decipher the print. Amusing and attractive fonts may also be a source of difficulty for the pupil with a visual impairment who is best able to read a clear, bold, serif free text.

Conversely, many braille books are visually and tactually dull. Fortunately this problem is gradually being addressed as more books with interesting tactile illustrations, such as the *Take Off* scheme and Ladybird *Well Loved Tales* are now produced by the RNIB. 'Clear View' books which incorporate the brailled text into a print book, will allow the blind child to share a book with their siblings and peers who are fully sighted. (Details of where these books may be obtained are given at the end of the chapter.)

When the child who is fully sighted enters school they will already have learnt many early reading skills. For example they will have learnt how to open the book at the front and how to turn the pages. They will have observed many of the conventions of print; for example, that print is usually written in lines, that books have titles, pictures and page numbers. Even those children who have had limited opportunities to have stories read to them, will have gathered much of this information from the television and from looking at books, however briefly. Much of this incidental learning, that is taken for granted by teachers of children who are fully sighted, will need to be taught to some children with a visual impairment.

After years of controversy, the importance of phonic knowledge in the development of reading has been laid down in Key Stage 1 of the English National Curriculum, where it is stated that children should possess a knowledge of phonics, a wide sight vocabulary and be able to use syntax and contextual cues (DfE 1995a). The child who is blind and is learning to read through braille usually reads words letter by letter or cell by cell, using letter sounds. If the child has a poor auditory memory or poor auditory sequencing they may find it difficult to learn to read using this approach. For the sighted child experiencing this difficulty, more emphasis could be placed upon visual sequencing and memory to develop a sight vocabulary. This option is not available to the reader who is blind.

It is harder for the child with a visual impairment to use either contextual or syntactic cues. They usually read more slowly and may have forgotten the beginning of the sentence before they have reached the end. They are unable to quickly scan back to check a word they have read, and for the child with a visual impairment it will often be difficult, if not impossible, to use pictures to help them understand the text.

By prescribing that the child should be exposed to an extensive range of literature, the English National Curriculum has by implication endorsed the view that children should read 'real' books (Campbell 1995). Perhaps by also stating that the child should develop a phonic knowledge, the English National Curriculum is also implying that reading schemes are a useful tool when teaching children to read. Many teachers would agree that a variety of appropriate methods should be adopted when teaching children to read.

For the blind child reading braille, access to 'real books' is not easily achieved. The common approach to teaching braille reading suggests that children should be introduced to the braille code in a systematic way. The braille alphabet, contractions, word signs and abbreviations are introduced gradually and children are usually not asked to read words that contain such conventions until they have been taught (Olson 1981). As a result the child who is blind is not able to access a variety of books at Key Stage 1. This option is only available to the child when they have acquired a wide knowledge of the braille code.

Key Stages 2, 3 and 4: reading

At later key stages the student is expected to read a wide range of literature and should be provided with the opportunity to 'read extensively'. The pupil should be reading 'more challenging and demanding texts' (DfE 1995a). All of those working with the child with a visual impairment would happily concur with this approach, however there are areas of concern. For example at Key Stage 3 the National Curriculum demands that a pupil should read pre-twentieth-century literature. Such texts are extremely lengthy with archaic vocabulary and long involved sentences, and braille versions may run into several volumes. The reading of novels by authors such as Dickens or Hardy, would be a daunting task for the student reading braille, or for the child who reads using a CCTV or enlarged text.

Lorimer (1977) emphasises the importance of training to help braille readers improve their reading skills. This is vital, but it places yet more demands on the pupil and time must be found for this additional training.

Consideration should be given to putting some of the reading materials on tape to ease the burden for pupils with a visual impairment. Advanced listening skills will need to be employed at this stage to enable the pupil to make full use of this approach (see Chapter 15). However for pupils working at the higher key stages the availability of taped materials or brailled texts may be a problem. The time-consuming preparation of these materials may prove an enormous burden for both teaching and support staff.

Increased emphasis at these stages, is placed upon the importance of finding information from books. Pupils should be taught to use scanning and skimming techniques when reading for information. These are not easy skills to learn and they will be especially difficult for the pupil with a visual impairment. The reader who is blind will be able to use these techniques, but again it will be difficult, demanding much effort for them to acquire the skills. Olson (1981) gives some useful ideas about how to encourage a pupil who reads braille to develop these skills.

Writing

The general aims of this area of the National Curriculum for English are to develop writing which displays:
- 'compositional skills – developing ideas and communicating meaning to a reader, using a wide-ranging vocabulary and an effective style, organising and structuring sentences grammatically and whole texts coherently;

- presentational skills – accurate punctuation, correct spelling and legible handwriting;
- a widening variety of forms for different purposes.'

The development of compositional skills and writing in a variety of formats would appear to be readily achievable by the child with a visual impairment. However limitations in the pupil's access to a range of written material may make it more difficult for the child with a visual impairment to write to the required standard.

At Key Stage 4 pupils are required to annotate texts. Annotating a text involves skills such as highlighting parts of the text and making notes in the margins. Pupils who are blind may approach the task by making and using braille notes, but this is far from ideal. This task is extremely difficult for both the child using braille and the pupil with low vision, and places them at a great disadvantage.

Reaching the required levels for spelling and handwriting may also prove challenging.

Spelling

The English National Curriculum places emphasis on the importance of accurate spelling. However, many pupils with a visual impairment experience some difficulty in this area (Arter and Mason 1994, Norris 1972). These difficulties would appear to be due to a number of factors. The child with a visual impairment has had limited incidental exposure to the written word and therefore has less opportunity to learn the correct spelling of a word from an early age. For example, the spelling of some words may be learnt from advertising slogans on hoardings and television adverts.

The importance in spelling of the ability to remember the visual pattern of a word has long been acknowledged (Peters 1967). Poor vision may mean that children with a visual impairment have difficulty in retaining the visual pattern of a word, because they see only part of a word, or a few letters at a time. Specific eye conditions, such as nystagmus, make fixations difficult and may result in a blurred image on the retina. All of these factors will make it difficult for many children with low vision to learn to use even a large print dictionary quickly and efficiently. It will be a more demanding task for the child with low vision to achieve a high and accurate standard of spelling (Arter and Mason 1994).

The pupil who uses braille may experience many of the same problems as the child with low vision. They will not have been exposed incidentally to the written word and spellings to the same extent as their peers with full sight. Children who are blind are often not introduced to braille books until they start school, and are unlikely to have much early experience of the written word. Children who are blind encounter an additional challenge with spelling because they have to remember word signs, contractions and abbreviations when using the braille code to write. They also need to learn the spelling of a word in full when using print to communicate, perhaps when using a word processor. This amounts to a double workload for the pupil who is blind.

Handwriting

This programme of study is obviously not appropriate for the braille user, who will be disapplied in this aspect of the National Curriculum. It is however considered to be an important skill for the blind person to learn to sign their own name (Chapman and Stone 1988). Young children who are blind usually derive a great deal of pleasure from signing cards they have made for parents. The development of this skill will enable them to become more independent adults, allowing them to personally sign cards, forms or cheques as an adult, and to sign documents which confer legal status.

For the pupil with low vision, the skill of handwriting is often difficult to learn and improve (Arter *et al.* 1996). Poor vision may result in poor hand–eye coordination, making it difficult to control the writing tool. The child may find it difficult to see how a letter is formed, and the use of a CCTV to demonstrate letter formation is sometimes appropriate. Children with low vision need one-to-one supervision to ensure that they are forming letters correctly and are not developing bad writing habits which are difficult to overcome at a later stage. In order to see what they are writing, some children may need to peer very closely at the page. The use of an adjustable work surface may help to overcome the problems often associated with poor posture. Many children with a visual impairment find handwriting difficult and become frustrated at their poor performance in this area. They may also find it especially difficult to read their own handwriting.

The English National Curriculum Key Stage 1 advocates that the child 'should be taught the conventional way of forming letters' and should 'build on their knowledge of letter formation to join letters' (DfE 1995a). This skill is referred to through the later key stages as the child continues to 'develop legible handwriting in both joined up and printed styles' (Key Stage 2). Some writers suggest that the child with a visual impairment should be taught to write using a joined style (Chapman and Stone 1988). The flow of the style means that the child does not continually lose their place and have to spend time relocating their place. Peters (1967) states that spelling ability is improved by learning a cursive script to join letter strings together. Other writers suggest that the teaching of the cursive script should be delayed until the child is able to reproduce letters legibly and is able to recognise the cursive script in print (Arter *et al.* 1996, Bishop 1971).

At Key Stages 3 and 4 the pupil 'should be taught to write with fluency and, when required, with speed'. As in all other areas of the curriculum, the child with a visual impairment finds it very difficult to complete work quickly. Since so many pupils with a visual impairment find it difficult to write well and at speed, and to read their own writing, the skill of typing or word processing should be taught as soon as possible. The English National Curriculum does refer to this possibility at Key Stage 1. 'Pupils should have opportunities to plan and review their writing, assembling and developing their ideas on paper and *on screen*' [Author's emphasis]. This is an important skill for the pupil with a visual impairment, and its importance continues to grow in this technological age.

Assessment and examinations

Both Standard Attainment Tests (SATs) and General Certificates of Secondary Education (GCSEs) place a high demand on the pupil with a visual impairment. All the tasks the child is required to complete involve a great deal of reading and comprehension. The effort of prolonged concentration causes fatigue, and often the child has insufficient time to complete the work, in spite of time extensions. This point is endorsed by the research of Hull and Mason (1993), who found that braille users took three times longer to process information than did their fully sighted peers.

For younger children with limited reading experience, the layout of the page may be unfamiliar and confusing. For example text has been presented in SATs using a newspaper layout. If adverts are given as the focus of a task, the design and layout may make it difficult for pupils to locate and access information. Pupils with a visual impairment cannot quickly scan a text and it will certainly take them longer to assimilate the information. Where pictures are used, the blind child is given extra text to provide some of the information presented in pictorial form. This means that the child has even more text to read. At higher levels the child is also required to write at length. With an enlarged exam paper the child who has large handwriting finds the space given for them to write their answer is often insufficient. Many teachers are aware that their pupils are placed at a great disadvantage when being assessed.

Conclusion

It is vitally important that the child with a visual impairment, like all other pupils, should have the opportunity to experience the full range of the English curriculum. It is felt that 'competence in English is important, both in its own right and to enable pupils to gain access to and benefit from the other areas of the National Curriculum (DES 1989b). The Cox Report makes the assumption that 'virtually all children will travel along broadly the same path in English, but some will move more quickly, and further than others (DES 1989b).

There is no reason why the child with a visual impairment should not succeed at a high level in this area of the curriculum. With careful and informed teaching practices and well prepared teaching materials, the child should make the same progress as their fully sighted peers; however for many of these children the additional effort they will need to make in order to achieve at these levels is quite considerable. They will need help, encouragement and support.

Acknowledgements

Thanks are extended to colleagues Nick Bacon, Pat Everest and Kay Malin for their support and encouragement.

Useful addresses

Clear Vision Books are available from Clear Vision, Linden Lodge School, 61, Princes
  Way, Wimbledon, London SW19 6JP
Take Off Books and *Ladybird Well Loved Tales* are available from: RNIB, PO Box 173,
  Peterborough PE2 6WS.

Chapter 23
Mathematics

Sue Clamp

Introduction

The ability to solve problems is at the heart of mathematics. Mathematics provides a means of communication which can be used to illustrate, to interpret, to predict and to explain. However, it is only 'useful' to the extent to which it can be applied to a particular situation, and it is the ability to apply mathematical understanding in a variety of other curricular areas, such as science, food and design technology, geography and environmental studies, business studies and world of work, which makes it such a vital subject in the National Curriculum. The task of the mathematics curriculum is to enable each child with a visual impairment to develop the skills and understanding for adult life, further study and training, and ultimately for employment. Every young person is entitled to the high quality teaching illustrated in Figure 23.1.

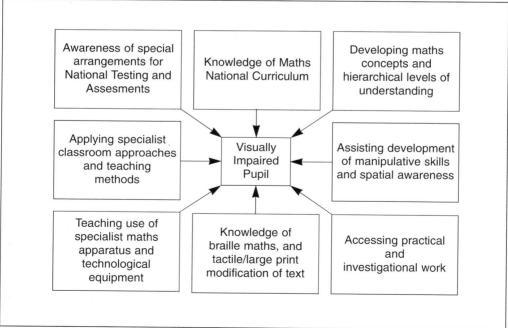

Figure 23.1

Mathematics in the National Curriculum

Mathematics is a 'core' subject, and is compulsory throughout the education of all pupils aged 5–16. The hierarchical learning structure of mathematics within the National Curriculum (DfE 1995a) is based on the progression from Level 1 through to Level 10 at four Key Stages. As you can see from Figure 23.2, the hierarchical levels in the National Curriculum allow a degree of overlap across the Key Stages (K.S.) and across the Year groups.

National Curriculum Key Stages

			Levels										
			1	2	3	4	5	6	7	8	9	10	
P	K.S.1	Year 1											
R		Year 2		Levels 1–3									
I													
M	K.S.2	Year 3											
A		Year 4			Levels 2–6								
R		Year 5											
Y		Year 6											
S	K.S.3	Year 7											
E													
C		Year 8					Levels 3–8						
O		Year 9											
N													
D													
A	K.S.4	Year 10					Levels 2–6						
R		Year 11											
Y													

Figure 23.2

The content of the mathematics curriculum is divided into programmes of study (PoS) within four attainment targets (ATs):

AT1: using and applying mathematics

AT2: number and algebra

AT3: shape, space and measures

AT4: handling data.

(The algebra part of AT2 is not introduced until Key Stage 3.)

These programmes of study and attainment targets provide the basis upon which teachers must plan their teaching. Schemes of work contain details of mathematical topics, themes and activities which thread across and through the elements of the programme of study, and provide the cohesion and progression essential for effective teaching and learning to take place.

Teachers of the visually impaired have to modify and adapt the content of their schemes of work to meet the specific visual needs of their pupils. Differentiation according to academic ability must also be given careful consideration. Progression through the mathematics National Curriculum levels will vary according to the pupil's:

- intellectual ability
- spatial awareness
- manual dexterity in relation to practical work.

These variables indicate the likelihood of a greater variability between levels in attainment targets because of visual impairment. Whereas a child who is fully sighted will usually be at the same level for each AT, a child with a visual impairment might be at Level 2 in AT3 (shape, space and measures) but at Level 4 in AT2 (number and algebra) and schemes of work should take account of such anomalies.

Mathematical concept formation in pupils with a visual impairment

Most pupils follow Piaget's five stages of intellectual development (Child 1973) but, because children with a visual impairment lack one source of sensory input their perceptual processes are different. Children who are fully sighted learn to perceive objects in their entirety, and observe them in relation to their environment; a child with a visual impairment cannot view objects in such entirety, and move from parts to the whole. The lack of vision reduces the effectiveness of the tactile sense, or distorts the visual input, so that many children who are visually impaired seem to function in mathematics primarily at the concrete and functional levels of intellectual development. The formal operational stage is Piaget's final phase where the child moves from concrete to abstract ideas. Some pupils might never reach this formal operational stage in their school career, while others may easily make the transfer.

The breadth of mathematical concept development is usually related to the breadth of perceptual experiences. Consequently, pupils with a visual impairment are often slower to acquire mathematical knowledge than their sighted peers for reasons such as those suggested by Clamp (1978):
- the lack of natural mathematical visual stimulation;
- the limiting effect of visual impairment on cognitive functions;
- the underdevelopment of specific mathematical concepts;
- the complexity and slowness of tactile material/large print as a working medium;
- the difficulty of completing individual practical investigational work within a limited time frame.

Of course, there is considerable variation in the rates at which all children acquire mathematical understanding, and it seems desirable that the teaching of mathematics to the visually impaired is introduced at the same level, and, as near as possible, at the same time as to children who are fully sighted. All mathematics within the National Curriculum falls into six basic conceptual areas:

1. Seriation
2. Classification
3. Discrimination

4. Comparison

5. Distance and time

6. Geometry.

These are distributed amongst attainment targets 2, 3 and 4. As mathematical learning is hierarchical it is vitally important that the basic lower level concepts are fully understood before attempting to move on to a higher level task. Often, if a mathematical concept has not been introduced and learned at the maturational stage at which it is ready to be learned, it is lost.

Seriation

When children who are fully sighted enter school, they have already incidentally acquired some concepts such as seriation. Basic to the understanding of number is an understanding of the conservation of number (that is, the number remains the same in quantity, even with a transformation in the objects to which it is applied). Children who are fully sighted can easily see a number as a whole, for instance 6 chairs, 6 cups, 6 knives, 6 bottles, sets of 6, but children who are visually impaired may not be able to grasp the property of '6', '8' or '12', for instance, so easily. Much practice must be given to developing seriation skills of quantity, with emphasis on 'more' or 'less', matching, counting, comparing, etc.

Classification

Classification skills are easier for a child who is fully sighted to acquire experientially. For example when shopping a sighted child can see that some articles are 'dairy products' and some are 'sweets', and in the street the child can distinguish large dogs and small dogs at a quick glance. The child who is blind has to touch and smell to classify objects, and may not have had the opportunity to experience this kind of incidental learning in the everyday environment. Children who lack practical experiences such as these may function at a much lower level mathematically. It is important that a child who is blind has access to formal and informal learning experiences to develop the important basic skills of classification.

Discrimination

Teachers cannot assume that a child with a visual impairment understands the concepts of 'same' and 'different'. Some pupils who are blind have never encountered the discrimination of objects, and need experiences with everyday articles, such as spoons (wood, metal, plastic, teaspoons, desert spoons, serving spoons and so on) or footwear (ladies' and gent's, children's, sandals, trainers, lace ups, buckles, slippers, flip-flops) or brushes (hairbrushes, nail-brush, toothbrush, brooms). A child will need many matching and sorting activities with real objects of different sizes, shapes, textures and weights before they can move into a more abstract level of discrimination, such as sorting triangles, circles and rectangles.

Comparison concepts

The ability to use the mathematical language of size, width, length, height or weight is vital for the child who is visually impaired. Activities involving comparisons between large and small, rough and smooth, hard and soft, tall and short, light and heavy, all help to develop such concepts.

Distance and time

Mathematical problems which directly or indirectly involve the concept of distance are particularly difficult for the child with a visual impairment. The concept of perimeter or 'all the way round' may be absent, as a result of the child's inability to view something as a 'whole'. The measurement of objects with a touch horizon (hand/arm span) in the classroom, such as the desk surface, window, sorting trays, books or cupboard doors, could help the children to grasp the idea of individual parts fitting together to make a 'whole' object or surface. The concepts of perimeter, surface area, and even volume, could also be simply introduced by this method.

Because of their restricted movement, children who are blind generally have a poor grasp of distance–time relationships. Children might estimate distances by walking and considering the length of time taken; for instance 'how long does it take to walk from the gym to the classroom?' Often, a deficiency in grasping relative distance prevents the older pupil from making maximum use of tactile maps, scale drawings and diagrams involving direction.

Geometry

With regard to geometrical concepts, plane (that is, two-dimensional) geometry is far easier for pupils with a visual impairment to comprehend than solid three-dimensional geometry, because they are accustomed to examining one aspect of a thing at a time. To assimilate the 'wholeness' of a solid shape by tactual methods is far more complex than a total visual inspection. As poor spatial awareness may be a problem, mastery of geometrical concepts beyond a basic level is often very demanding and specific activities involving the use of a 'search' strategy to help develop geometrical concepts are essential.

Difficulties in mathematical understanding

Historically, the teaching of mathematics has always been considered a source of frustration in the education of the visually impaired. Past research by the Americans Hayes (1941), Nolan (1964), Brothers (1972) and Lewis (1970) consistently suggested that pupils who were blind or partially sighted were achieving levels in arithmetic 20–50% below their sighted counterparts.

Clamp (1988) used tactile and large print versions of the Chelsea Diagnostic Tests (Brown *et al.* 1985) in number, fractions, measurement and algebra with 114 pupils aged 11–15 with a visual impairment, and compared their levels of understanding to sighted children of the same age.

These diagnostic tests are based on a Piagetian framework, but do not assume that intellectual development is rigidly tied to chronological age. They are not only concerned with children's mathematical understanding, but also identify the type of understanding that is missing. The Chelsea hierarchical levels of understanding range from Level 0 to Level 4. Table 23.1 illustrates their connection with the Piagetian stages and the Mathematics National Curriculum.

Table 23.1 Relationships between the levels of understanding in the Chelsea Diagnostic Tests, Piagetian stages and National Curriculum Levels

Piagetian stages	Chelsea levels of understanding	National Curriculum Levels (Mathematics)
Sensorimotor	Level 0	Level 0
Preconceptual	Level 1 (Stage 1)	Level 1
Intuitive	Level 2 (Stage 2)	Levels 2, 3
Concrete operations	Level 3 (Stage 3)	Level 4
Formal operations	Level 4 (Stage 4)	Levels 5–10

Clamp's research (1988) confirmed the pattern of previous decades, that, on average, children who are visually impaired are from 16 to 25% behind their peers who are fully sighted.

This research showed that 66.6% of the 11–12-year-olds tested had little appreciation of the division or multiplication of whole numbers, and of these, 36.6% were unable to make a coherent attempt at addition or subtraction problems. With regard to fractions the most noticeable feature was that the proportion of pupils with a visual impairment who passed each item ranged from 16 to 35% fewer than pupils who were fully sighted in the same age group. Measurement items illustrated that 62.9% of the 13–14 year olds who were visually impaired did not even reach Level 1 for understanding of length, perimeter, area and volume. In algebra, the overall achievement patterns for all the 14–15-year-olds tested was similar. All pupils found the algebra difficult, but the Level 2 results for the pupils with a visual impairment were 7.3% better than the results for their counterparts who were fully sighted.

Figures 23.3–23.6 show the distribution of the hierarchical levels of understanding for visually impaired and sighted pupils.

In short, the overwhelming impression obtained through Clamp's 1988 research is that mathematics, with specific reference to the four topic areas of number operations (AT2), fractions (AT2), measurement (AT3) and algebra (AT2), is a very difficult subject for most pupils with a visual impairment. The survey also shows that understanding improves only slightly as the pupils get older. Generally, fewer than 50% of secondary pupils who have a visual impairment can deal with the demands of Stage 1 and Stage 2.

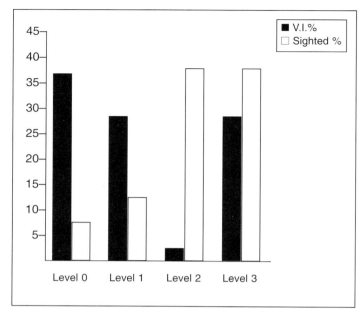

Figure 23.3   Number operations; 11–12-year-olds.

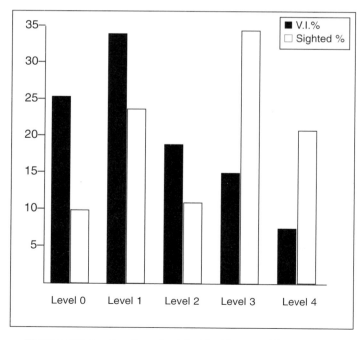

Figures 23.4   Fractions test 1; 12–13-year-olds.

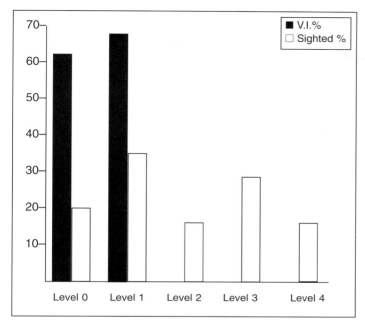

Figures 23.5   Measurement; 13–14-year-olds.

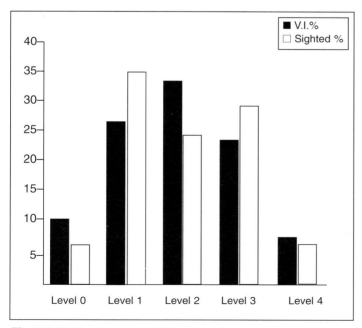

Figures 23.6   Algebra; 14–15-year-olds.

Classroom approaches and teaching methods

Cockroft (Department of Education and Science (DES) 1982) recommended that 'Mathematics teaching should include opportunities for:
- exposition by the teacher
- discussion between teacher and pupils, and between pupils themselves
- appropriate practical work
- consolidation and practice of fundamental skills and routines
- problem solving, including the application of mathematics to everyday situations
- investigational work.'

A pupil with a visual impairment is also entitled to these opportunities. The specialist teacher has to provide access to a variety of classroom approaches. Some basic teaching points which should be remembered when approaching mathematics both at primary and secondary levels are listed below.
- Forward planning: it is essential that all work required for pupils is prepared well in advance.
- Individualisation of approach: the differences between pupils in the type and extent of visual impairment necessitate individual teaching techniques, differentiated by use of colour and textures, size of print, thickness of lines and availability of models.
- Concreteness in teaching: verbal substitutions are totally inadequate for teaching about the use of money, going shopping, weighing everyday items, measuring objects, making fractional parts, exploring geometrical shapes. There is no substitute for 'hands-on' experience in real-life situations. Pupils should not be expected to share apparatus or materials.
- Teaching by units: use every opportunity to experience the topic in its totality. Cross-curricular themes can include geographical and science data recording, calculations of the amount of materials required to construct design technology frameworks, and so on.
- Investigational work: this can prove extremely difficult, and 'discovery' mathematics will be 'guided discovery' for the majority of pupils.
- More discussion of topics will be required to compensate for the lack of incidental visual mathematical input in the environment.
- Diagrams in textbooks need to be carefully selected and suitably modified. It is not sufficient to reproduce or enlarge *ad hoc*. Tactile and large print diagrams need to be:
  - appropriate in size
  - clear and uncluttered
  - good in definition.

Figure 23.7 shows how a diagram and associated table could be modified for use by a pupil with a visual impairment (Britten 1984).
- For many topics where tactile representation is required additional input will be necessary, for instance verbal explanations of diagrams.
- Specific strategies need to be taught for recording work in braille, computation in

mental arithmetic, diagram exploration, three-dimensional work and the use of specially adapted mathematical equipment.

- In graph work the teacher must ensure a permanent record is made of the pupil's graph when mapping pins, thread, rubber bands or Flexicurve have been used; this can be done using a spur wheel.
- It must be constantly remembered that much of what is assumed knowledge for children who are fully sighted must be specifically taught to a child with visual impairment.
- Tasks appropriate for a seeing child (for instance, reflection and rotation) might appear unsuitable for the child who is visually impaired but, because of their inclusion in the Mathematics National Curriculum, they must be attempted with appropriate adaptation

The mathematics braille code

The mathematics braille code should be introduced as appropriate, and should be presented in accordance with the rules of the Braille Authority of the United Kingdom (*Braille Mathematics Notation* 1987). The different aspects of the National Curriculum must be considered when introducing pupils to mathematical braille. These broadly divide into:

1. number
2. units and measurement
3. algebra
4. shape and space
5. data handling
6. other: set notation, matrices, subscripts.

A child who is blind must not be taught mathematical braille through dictation; ready prepared examples should be available as terms of reference for all levels of ability. Teaching mathematical skills is the priority, teaching mathematics braille is secondary.

Mathematical braille must be accurate: a slipped dot or a reversal can mean the difference between a correct or totally incorrect answer, such as 5 or 9, 66 or 44, 10 or 18. Methods of recording work need to be established early in the primary school and should continue to be taught in a systematic way throughout the senior school. Because reading or writing in braille can be 50% slower than working in print (Harley 1979), it may be acceptable for pupils to complete a smaller number of examples, provided they can demonstrate an understanding of the task. Worksheets produced in braille for the less able should use double line spacing and Grade 1 code if necessary. All GCSE work in Key Stage 4 should be produced in accordance with the GCSE examinations specifications.

Mathematical braille is complicated, and there are many areas of possible confusion as shown in Figures 23.8 and 23.9.

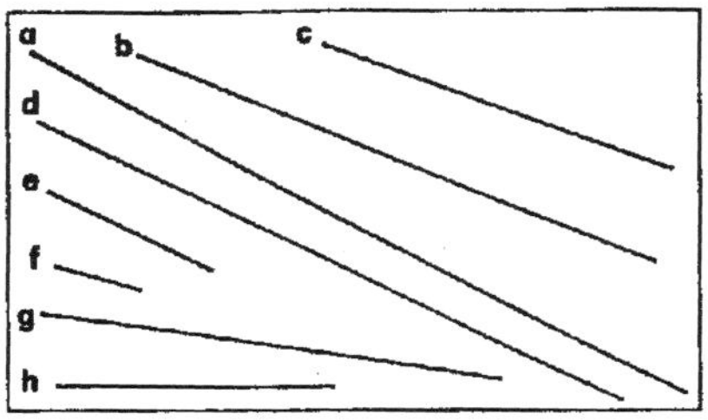

Copy this table. Do not fill it in yet:

line	estimate	measure	difference
a	cm	cm	cm
b	cm	cm	cm
c	cm	cm	cm
d	cm	cm	cm
e	cm	cm	cm
f	cm	cm	cm
g	cm	cm	cm
h	cm	cm	cm

Original diagram had red
lines on a pink background

Diagram Modifications	Table Modifications
i) x $1\frac{1}{2}$ size	i) x 2 size
ii) re-aligned horizontally	ii) more space within boxes
iii) thicken lines	iii) thicken framework
iv) clarify letters	iv) clarify letters

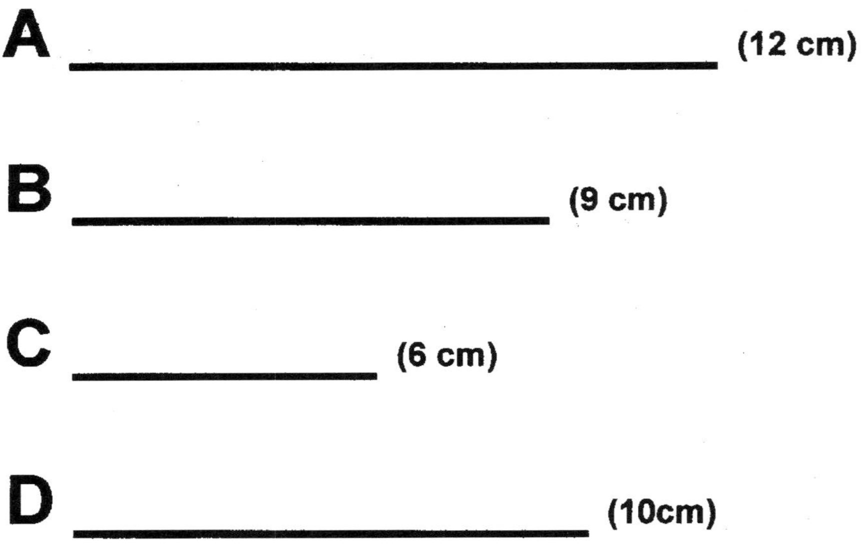

A _____ **(12 cm)**

B _____ **(9 cm)**

C _____ **(6 cm)**

D _____ **(10cm)**

.... **and** so on

Figure 23.7   The diagram shown (top left) was modified to the form shown in the bottom half of the figure (Britten 1984).

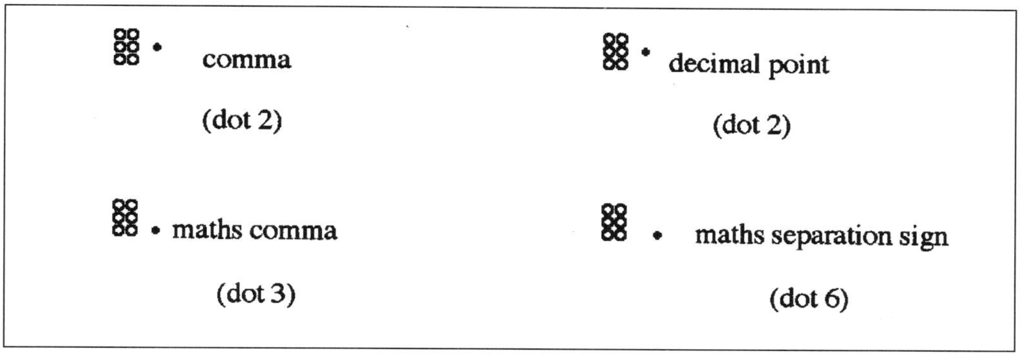

comma
(dot 2)

decimal point
(dot 2)

maths comma
(dot 3)

maths separation sign
(dot 6)

Figure 23.8

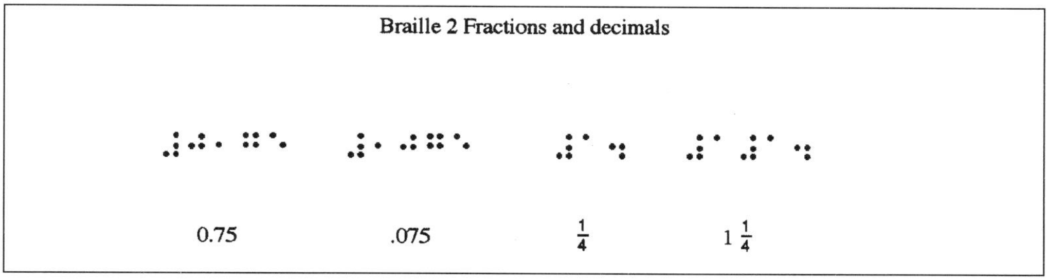

Braille 2 Fractions and decimals

0.75   .075 $\frac{1}{4}$ $1\frac{1}{4}$

Figure 23.9

Calculations which are set out vertically in braille can cause confusion; it is better to use a linear method as shown below.

$$
\begin{array}{r} 61 \\ + 22 \\ \hline 83 \end{array}
\quad \text{becomes} \quad 61 + 22 \quad = 81 + 2 = 83
$$

$$
\begin{array}{r} 442 \\ -31 \\ \hline 411 \end{array}
\quad \text{becomes} \quad 442 - 31 \quad = 412 - 1 = 411
$$

$$
\begin{array}{r} 421 \\ \times\,3 \\ \hline 1263 \end{array}
\quad \text{becomes} \quad 421 \times 3 = 1200 + 21 \times 3
$$
$$
= 1200 + 60 + 3
$$
$$
= 1263
$$

$$
264 \div 3 \quad \text{becomes} \quad 3\,)\overline{264} \atop 88
$$

In algebra the use of letter signs, power signs, simple curved brackets, square brackets, division signs, and so on, can cause confusion.

Total competence in the mathematics braille code up to examination level is a necessity for specialist mathematics and secondary support teachers working with braille users, in either a special school or in a mainstream setting.

Practical work

Prior to the 1970s, 'mathematics' teaching to pupils with a visual impairment consisted mainly of pure number work and mental arithmetic. Since the compulsory inclusion in the mathematics curriculum of measurement, perimeter, area, volume, bar charts, line graphs, pie charts, coordinates, geometry, data handling and investigational coursework, the emphasis on practical work has more than doubled. Figures 23.10–23.13 show examples of pupils engaged in appropriate practical tasks.

The development of fine motor skills is crucial for the successful completion of most practical activities. Hand and arm manipulative skills involved in mathematical activities include the following.

- Picking up small objects like cubes. It helps to have flat shapes such as coins, presented on a non-slippery surface such as a 'Dycem' mat or within a raised-edge sorting tray.
- Using drawing equipment such as german film, rubber mat, ballpoint pens and fragrant felt tip pens.
- Using stencils and templates for drawing inside or outside a framework.
- Using measuring equipment, for example:
1. rulers for
   − finding and identifying tactile markings
   − holding still while measuring or drawing lines
   − reverse counting from a measured mark.
2. metre stick or trundle wheel for
   − marking a repeated metre distance
   − managing the excess centimetres.
3. tape measures for
   − recognising 1-cm, 5-cm, 10-cm markings
   − coping with the 150-cm flexible length.
- Putting items into a balance pan for weighing activities.
- Pouring liquids from one container into another and the use of funnels.
- Exploring two- and three-dimensional shapes by feeling along edges, corners and surfaces, comparison of solid shapes and development of search strategies.
- Assembling and dismantling mathematical apparatus, such as Multilink cubes or prisms, Clixi and Geostrips.
- Using geometrical equipment, such as protractors, compass, callipers.
- Using graphical apparatus, such as graph boards, mapping pins, rubber bands, spur wheel.
- Using a talking calculator: familiarity with keypads for pupils who are totally blind.

Practical work is an integral part of the National Curriculum. Most pupils enjoy participating in this aspect of mathematics, and for pupils with a visual impairment, the practical element is an essential part of the learning process. Their perceptual level of development is most likely to be at the concrete stage and they need practical experience

Figure 23.10 Practical work for AT3 (shape, space and measures, Level 1): longer than, shorter than: using real strips of wood.

Figure 23.11 Practical tasks for AT3 (shape, space and measures, Level 2): measuring up to 100 cm, using everyday objects.

in order to assimilate any new mathematical concepts (see Figure 23.14; AT1 using and applying mathematics).

Assessment and testing

Key Stages 1, 2 and 3

In 1996 it became compulsory for all pupils in England and Wales to be tested in mathematics at the end of Key Stage 1 (7-year-olds), Key Stage 2, (11-year-olds) and Key Stage 3 (14-year-olds). Pupils with a visual impairment were included in this national

Figure 23.12 Activity for AT3 (shape, space and measures, Level 1): weighing, heavier than, lighter than 1kg, using fresh fruit and vegetables.

Figure 23.13 Practical task for AT4 (handling data, Level 5): plotting results of pebble survey on german film grid paper.

testing. The controlling examining body, the SCAA (Schools Curriculum and Assessment Authority), set the tasks and tests according to the content of the mathematics National Curriculum.

Within the general documentation distributed annually by SCAA on assessment arrangements, a section headed 'Special Arrangements' outlines additional considerations for pupils with a visual impairment. These include varying the scheduled national timetable, allowing extra time, using a reader, amanuensis or transcribers, using special apparatus and models, the provision of test papers in enlarged print, modified print, braille or on tape, and the early opening of papers to check the contents. Some of these

Figure 23.14 Practical work for AT1 (using and applying mathematics, Level 1): capacity, and taller and shorter than, using familiar everyday containers.

special considerations are also made available to candidates with a visual impairment by the GCSE (General Certificate of Secondary Education) examination boards in Key Stage 4. Original test papers are modified by highly experienced mathematics teachers of the visually impaired in collaboration with the test agencies, examination boards and SCAA, before being contracted out to various large print and/or brailling agencies prior to dispatch to the schools and special units.

Key Stage 4

Key Stage 4 covers the last two years of compulsory education (14–16 years). It is unique in that the assessments lead in most cases to the nationally recognised GCSE qualification. The content is the same for all syllabuses and examining boards are not allowed to deviate from the mathematics National Curriculum. Non-GCSE candidates can work towards a Certificate in Educational Achievement.

GCSE coursework

The requirements for GCSE Mathematics coursework present potential problems for both pupil and teacher. These can be identified as follows.

- Restriction in the choice of appropriate topics, for example:
  - surveys
  - planning a holiday/day trip/party
  - designing and making a mathematical game
  - designing and making a clock based on a geometric shape
  - 'redecorating' a bedroom
  - dice/card probability
  - investigating 'eggs in a box'.

- Lack of availability of resource material in large print and braille, such as train timetables, route maps, holiday brochures, furniture catalogues, wallpaper books.
- Pupils are less likely to be able to travel independently to do individual coursework research, for instance visit travel agents for holiday project information or visit DIY stores.
- It takes the pupil with a visual impairment more time to complete tasks. Generally, if a piece of coursework was designed to cover 10 lessons for a child who is fully sighted it will take a child with a visual impairment at least 15 lessons.
- Moderation/transcription of assignments for example:
  - external moderators cannot read braille;
  - pupils have fulfilled coursework requirements in braille so they should not have to redo the coursework in print for external agencies;
  - teachers do not have the time to transcribe coursework assignments, although the use of computers with speech and print output could be used by pupils, provided that appropriate software is available.

However, there are some positive aspects of GCSE coursework for example it:

- gives the pupil the opportunity to produce work at their own level outside stressful examination conditions;
- allows the development of oral, written, practical, investigational and problem-solving skills, which are essential to mathematical understanding;
- encourages the application of mathematics to everyday situations;
- develops the ability to reason logically, to clarify, to generalise, and to prove a hypothesis.

Conclusion

Lack of visual experiences impedes concept development and for pupils who have a visual impairment all aspects of mathematical concept formation rely on the consolidation of experiences mediated by the use of real objects and appropriate relevant language in everyday situations. Limited spatial awareness and poor manual dexterity may delay the development of geometrical, graphical, and time-distance concepts. Pupils with a visual impairment need to acquire specific mathematical concepts sequentially and in a systematic way as mathematics is a hierarchical learning process. 'A learning hierarchy identifies a set of intellectual skills that are ordered in a manner indicating substantial amounts of positive transfer from those of a lower position to connected ones in a higher position' (Buckle 1986). As the curriculum has become more practical, investigative, constructive and more individually creative, it has in fact become more labour intensive for the student who is visually impaired and also for the teacher who has to provide suitable mathematical experiences to facilitate understanding in these active learning situations.

While the developmental path followed by pupils who are blind and visually impaired is the same as that of other children, research shows they may lag behind their seeing peers. The biggest single factor affecting the teaching of mathematics to children who are visually impaired is the extra time needed for understanding, in all areas of the mathematics National Curriculum.

The specialist teacher requires an inordinate amount of skill to provide full access to the mathematics programmes of study. They have to be providers of plentiful opportunities to help pupils move from passive, to active, to creative learning within the modern framework of mathematical education.

Information about mathematical apparatus is available from the author.

Useful addresses

Braille Mathematics Notation (1987), Braille Authority of the United Kingdom. This is available from: RNIB, Bakewell Road, Orton Southgate, Peterborough, Cambridgeshire PE2 OXU.

Braille Mathematics Notation (Simplified Version, Part 1) 1995. This is available from: Peter Southall, Dorton House School, Seal, Sevenoaks Kent.

GCSE Examination Specifications (VIEW/RNIB – GCSE Joint Council Guidelines 1995/6). Available from: Joint Council for the GCSE, 6th Floor, Netherton House, 23–29 Marsh Street, Bristol BS1 4BP.

Schools Curriculum and Assessment Authority (SCAA), Newcombe House, 45 Notting Hill Gate, London W11 3JB.

NEAB GCSE Coursework Guidelines. Assessment Criteria and Exemplar Material. Available from: Northern Examination Assessment Board, Orbit House, Albert Street, Eccles, Manchester M30 0WL.

AEB Coursework Guidelines. Available from: Associated Examining Board, Stag Hill House, Guildford, Surrey GU1 5XJ.

WJEC Coursework Guidelines. Available from: Welsh Joint Education Committee, 235 Western Avenue, Cardiff CF5 2YX.

Chapter 24
Science

Steve Minett

Introduction

When some secondary school students were asked recently about the practical work which they carry out during their science course, one of them replied 'The practical makes it more interesting. Doing something yourself, exploring yourself, you feel in control more. It all slots into place when you've got the results and you plot the graph. It makes you more confident, getting things right.'

This answer helps to illustrate the unique interdependence between the theoretical and the practical which distinguishes science from other subjects in the curriculum. The student's answer also conveys a sense of achievement and developing confidence, of being in control, and of ownership and success.

What the answer does not convey is the fact that this student is blind, uses braille as a working medium, and has no residual vision to rely on when carrying out experimental work.

Clearly, pupils with a visual impairment are entitled to a science curriculum appropriate to their individual abilities and needs, but the delivery of the science curriculum presents teachers with obvious challenges. These may arise directly as a result of the visual loss; for example the pupils may be unable to read writing from a board at the front of the classroom, or to see clearly the diagram displayed by the overhead projector. Other challenges may be less obvious: for example, how might teachers convey information about topics which are outside the pupil's experience, such as the design of a suspension bridge or the appearance of an elephant? Guidance on general issues such as communication and language, access to resources and materials, and the production and use of diagrams will be found in other chapters of this book. This chapter will concentrate on the issues surrounding the successful delivery of the practical aspects of the science curriculum. Experimental work in science provides valuable opportunities for pupils with a visual impairment to explore their own environment, and to interact with it in a planned and controlled way, but visual impairment can often be wrongly seen as a barrier which prevents access to practical work.

When planning a practical activity for a pupil with a visual impairment, the first essential requirement is to decide its main purpose. If it is to provide **experiences** to illustrate and support theory (for example studying a model of a plant, the action of a mineral acid on a carbonate, or a transverse wave on a slinky spring) then clarity, guidance and understanding are the important factors. There is no requirement for independent working, and help and support can be given so that the student fully understands what is going on. In principle, this is a personal equivalent of a teacher demonstration.

Alternatively the practical activity may have independent working as its main purpose, either as an **exercise** in which skills are learned and mastered, or as an **investigation** which is planned and carried out independently by the student using these skills.

For students to feel that they are working independently and are in control, they must have already mastered some basic skills; for example they should be able to measure the temperature of a liquid in a beaker, or to measure the length of the shoot of a growing plant. These are the enabling skills without which no practical work can be carried out, and are referred to in this chapter as **technical skills**. This chapter suggests that, by planning practical exercises so that a carefully chosen repertoire of technical skills is learned and mastered in sequence as the course progresses, pupils who are visually impaired can work independently, confidently and successfully in science. In addition, it is to be hoped that the manual dexterity and spatial awareness which is acquired will be transferred to practical tasks both in other subjects and in everyday life.

It is of course neither necessary nor even desirable for every student to be able to work independently in every area of practical science. Just as unnecessary detail is removed when planning a tactile diagram, and text is carefully edited before production in large print or braille, then independent practical activities can be chosen so that the technical skills required reflect the ability and interest of the student as well as the apparatus available.

The special nature of science

Science is different from other subjects. In the secondary school some of these differences are immediately obvious to all students: a science laboratory is not at all like an ordinary classroom, and the demonstrations and experiments make the lessons quite different from say English or History. The lesson content is real, in that the pupils explore and interact with their own environment, study plants, animals and materials at first hand, measure electric currents and control chemical reactions. This link with the real world is of special value to a child with a visual loss, as Lowenfeld (1974) illustrates:

> Education must aim at giving the blind child a knowledge of the realities around him, the confidence to cope with these realities, and the feeling that he is recognised and accepted as an individual in his own right.

Practical work provides concrete experiences through handling specimens and models, stretching materials, pushing and pulling, weighing and pouring, moving and measuring, heating and cooling, and so on. For children and young people whose experience of their environment has been limited and whose understanding of it has been confused by visual impairment, these practical opportunities, followed by discussion and interpretation, can clarify and strengthen children's 'knowledge of the realities' around them in a way which other curriculum subjects cannot.

The interdependence of theory and practice makes science different from other subjects. Students with a visual impairment can gain particular benefit from the concrete experiences which support the theory, from the confidence which they can gain from the mastery of a repertoire of practical skills, and from the independence which comes with ownership and the sense of control.

Science in the National Curriculum

The programmes of study for science in the National Curriculum provide the framework within which pupils of compulsory school age learn and develop an understanding of three main subject areas: 'life processes and living things', 'materials and their properties', and 'physical processes'. There is also a list of requirements which apply across the whole programme of study for each key stage, grouped under headings such as 'science in everyday life', and 'health and safety'. Programmes of study must be taught to 'the great majority of pupils ... in ways appropriate to their abilities' (Department for Education (DfE) 1995d). It is expected that schools will make provision for pupils who need to use, for example, 'non-sighted methods of reading, such as Braille...' or 'technological aids in practical and written work'.

Some aspects of the programmes of study are clearly perceived as problematic for children with a visual impairment. The documentation on the teaching of the subject of light says that 'Pupils with visual impairment should be supported in gaining as much access as possible to the Light sections of the programmes of study.' Through the key stages, the concepts related to light are gradually developed, from light sources, light and dark, seeing, opaque materials, shadows, reflection, refraction, dispersion, colour, diffraction, total internal reflection, and properties of electromagnetic waves to communication systems. With careful planning, the standard equipment available for optics work can be used by almost all pupils, if conditions are arranged to enable pupils to make best use of their residual vision. This might involve controlling the ambient lighting by the use of blinds and providing a single source of light of appropriate intensity against a dark background material. In these conditions even the smallest degree of functional vision is sufficient to locate a beam of light from a ray lamp in an investigation of reflection, and if a pupil has no residual vision then a light-sensitive device such as a light probe allows experiments on shadows, materials, sources, reflection and refraction to be carried out quite satisfactorily.

The decision about the length of time spent on any particular area of science may be dictated by the individual's degree of vision and interest. For example, the topic of refraction (which naturally leads into lenses and optical instruments) may be of special interest to a student with visual impairment for whom low-vision aids are part of everyday life, whereas it may seem dull and irrelevant to someone with no sight, who might feel that other systems of communication, radio waves, electromagnetic radiation and related areas are of more relevance. Similarly, the importance and relevance of the topic of 'colour' will also depend on the individual student.

Pupils with a visual impairment have an entitlement to the full science curriculum, but may need carefully planned support in order to gain access to it, and it may be desirable to emphasise some areas of the subject while giving less weight to others.

The aims of practical work and the types of activity which can achieve them

The National Curriculum has placed experimental and investigative science firmly at the beginning of the programme of study for each key stage as the first step towards the knowledge and understanding required in the three traditional areas of the subject. Although the practical requirements are listed in detail, there has been no significant attempt to list the aims of experimental work, a surprising omission considering the cost of this work to schools in terms of time and resources.

This chapter is not the place for a detailed discussion of these aims, but a number of authors have published work in this area, including Hodson (1990, 1992), Lock (1988), Tamir (1991), White (1988), Woolnough (1988).

The following aims are suggested as a framework for the planning of a practical course for pupils with a visual impairment.
1. To motivate, stimulate interest, and promote self-esteem through success.
2. To teach scientific skills, and to encourage their use in investigative work.
3. To provide experiences which give a feeling for basic phenomena and illustrate theory.

The first aim suggests that practical work should be purposeful, interesting and achievable. For students with limited sight it is particularly important that while the work is carefully planned to allow for success, it still offers an element of challenge.

The second aim recognises that while practical skills are likely to be more challenging for students with a visual impairment to learn, they are essential in any independently planned and executed investigation.

The third aim recognises that a true understanding of scientific concepts is based on concrete experiences. These experiences are of particular value to students who are blind or visually impaired and provide a foundation for the teaching and discussion of more advanced concepts.

Types of practical activity

Practical activities may also conveniently be divided into three categories: exercises, experiences and investigations (see Woolnough and Allsop 1985). Although experiments may be designed to fulfil more than one purpose, this simple classification is a useful planning device.

Exercises are used to develop and master technical skills. Students may need guidance and assistance when learning the skills, but some exercises can also offer opportunities to refine independently skills which have been taught.

Experiences are guided and structured practical activities which may illustrate a point of theory or a feeling for a basic phenomenon. As much support should be given as is needed to ensure that the student has fully understood the experience and there is no ambiguity. An experience is teacher-directed and may take the form of a simple experiment, for example touching the cone of a loudspeaker as the sound is made louder. There is no attempt at independent working and the student is guided through the experience which often focuses on just one specific idea.

Investigations give the students opportunities to plan and carry out their own experiments using the technical skills they have mastered in exercises. They are directed by the students themselves who should feel they have ownership of the experiment and that they are working independently. Successful work of this nature can give motivation and confidence.

Scientific skills: using a system of technical skills to structure practical work

Even a small repertoire of technical skills can enable the student to carry out independent experiments and investigations. Here are a few examples of simple technical skills:
- measuring length using a ruler (for example when measuring leaves of plants in biology)
- assembling and adjusting a metal stand (to hold a flask in chemistry)
- connecting a battery pack (to an electrical circuit in physics)
- transferring 10 cubic centimetres of liquid using a syringe
- plotting points on a graph grid
- measuring mass using a top-pan balance.

There is no strict definition of a technical skill, but it normally involves the use of apparatus. The way the skills are acquired will vary according to the apparatus available and the abilities of the student. In some cases the apparatus will need to be carefully chosen or adapted in some way, for example a standard metre rule may be used provided it is white with large print figures, or labelled in braille; the top-pan balance may need to have a large display or speech output.

A list of technical skills for a student or group of students with visual impairments may be written to cover a course, key stage, year, subject area or topic. The list may include reference to mobility skills, for example the ability to collect a power pack from a rack or to collect graph paper and graph drawing kit from a cupboard. There are some other basic skills which are likely to be included in any list and involve the ability to measure length, time, and mass, and to use standard laboratory apparatus.

To take a simple example let us consider the area of 'physical processes' where pupils are to be taught 'how extension varies with applied force for a range of materials' (DfE 1995d). The teacher is likely to support the theory by offering a range of *experiences* related to physical properties of materials, including handling, stretching and bending different materials, such as Plasticene, polythene, copper, rubber, wood, glass, tin and silicone putty. These experiences are guided and discussed, with no need for the student to work independently, but rather to relate the experiences to terms such as 'strong, soft, brittle, flexible, and so on'. As an exercise, the teacher may ask the student to load a steel spring and to measure its extension (a simple Hooke's Law experiment).

The list of technical skills associated with this work might include:

- collect metal stand, boss and clamp
- collect metre rule
- assemble and adjust metal stand
- use slotted masses and holder
- measure length using a metre rule
- plot points on a graph grid.

If these skills have already been mastered, the experiment may be carried out quite independently by the student. If the skills are part of an *exercise* around the use of the steel spring, then one of the other materials can be *investigated* independently, for example by loading a strip of polythene sheet or an elastic band. When this area of work has been covered and the appropriate skills have been mastered, further independent investigations become possible. For example the bending of a loaded cantilever can be tackled.

Modern technology can facilitate the development of technical skills, for example with appropriate software a computer can deliver the display from an electrical thermometer, balance or voltmeter in speech or in large print. Wherever possible students should be given opportunities to collect and process data in science using information technology.

There is a dearth of apparatus specially designed for use by students with a visual impairment, and it is fortunate that many standard items can be employed if they are carefully labelled in print or braille. The work of Harwood (1968), Stephenson (1968), Toriyama (1985) and Wexler (1961) provides many valuable suggestions for adapting equipment. Even a small degree of residual vision is invaluable in experimental work, but with ingenuity, most areas of practical science can be tackled successfully by students who are totally blind. Key items of equipment for these students will include a light-sensitive device such as a light probe, a talking thermometer, and a means of measuring mass, electric current and potential difference.

When students have mastered a repertoire of technical skills, they know what they can do, and are able to work independently, confidently and safely.

Barriers to access

In the space available it is not possible to do more than give a few further pointers when considering the delivery of science in the National Curriculum to pupils with a visual impairment. Factors which will affect teaching approaches will include the nature of the educational setting, the degree and nature of the visual loss and the age and ability of the pupils, the facilities and resources available and the availability of classroom support. Nevertheless, some suggestions are summarised below.

- *Teaching and class discussion.* Use clear language based on ideas within the pupils' own experience, supported where possible by practical experiences.
- *Audiovisual material.* Provide pupils with individual copies in the appropriate medium, read out what is written on the blackboard slowly and clearly, provide additional commentaries when using a video-recorder or television.
- *Printed material.* When preparing text or diagrams, edit ruthlessly to remove all superfluous material; aim for brevity and clarity.
- *Theory.* Ensure that all new concepts are based on concrete experiences, wherever possible carried out as guided and supported practical work in the laboratory.
- *Teacher demonstrations.* Allow access to as much visual information as possible, and support with descriptions, diagrams, and handling of the apparatus.
- *Safety.* Carry out a risk assessment for all practical work. Classify all practical activities so that experiences are carefully guided and supported, and exercises employ clearly defined technical skills which the student learns and masters. Vet and supervise investigations planned by the student to ensure the skills required have already been mastered.
- *Residual vision.* Encourage the maximum use of residual vision in practical work.
- *Mobility.* Regard independent mobility as a technical skill. Teach students the route from the workplace to sink and the location of essential items such as the waste bin, cupboard for power packs and so on.
- *Laboratory layout.* Define routes which should always be kept clear (but it is not necessary for the student to have access to all parts of the room).
- *Special equipment.* Provide the special apparatus appropriate to the nature and degree of visual loss. Choose the most appropriate ordinary equipment and adapt it.
- *Medium of work.* Ensure that the student is using the most efficient medium for receiving and storing and recording information. (This may be pen and paper, typewriter, brailler, a computer incorporating a word-processor with a large display or speech output, or possibly an audiocassette recorder.) Remember that the speed of working can vary enormously and the teacher should be aware of this when issuing material to be studied.
- *Graphs.* Present graphs in the most appropriate form, for instance on paper (with a suitable grid), on german film, on a graph board, or on computer.
- *Assessment.* Ensure that pupils have mastered the relevant technical skills before they are asked to plan and carry out an investigation.
- *Manual dexterity and spatial awareness.* Remember that some pupils with visual impairment will have additional cognitive or physical difficulties which may affect performance in these areas and will need regular practice to improve these skills.
- *Classroom support and intervention.* Focus support on experiences and technical skills

so that students can investigate without the need for intervention, and without reliance on a sighted person.

• *Group practical work.* In group activities ensure that the pupil who is visually impaired has a clear idea of what is going on and knows what contribution to make. Identify an appropriate technical skill, for example make the student responsible for timing or measuring temperature.

Age and ability range

It is hoped that many of the ideas discussed in this chapter will be relevant for students of all ages, from Key Stage 1 to further and higher education.

In Key Stages 1 and 2, the major context for the programmes of study is 'science in everyday life'. At this level, much of the work is experiential and the practical activities are not designed to take place in a laboratory. Part of the programme will naturally take place in the classroom with appropriate objects and materials, but other locations within the local environment can be used, including the school grounds, streets, parks, woods, and educational facilities such as museums and houses. These activities may consume a considerable amount of time but will bring benefits at a later stage when abstract concepts are developed at a higher level. Without these experiences, the pupil may not have the background knowledge and understanding needed to continue with more advanced work on materials in Key Stages 3 and 4, or to plan scientific investigations successfully in this area of the subject. A structured practical approach such as this can make learning science both meaningful and stimulating for young pupils, and with careful planning it is possible to introduce simple investigations which give some independence to the individual as well as generating and maintaining enthusiasm.

Summary

The relationship between theoretical content and practical work gives science a special place in the curriculum, and gives it special value to pupils with a visual impairment. Practical work provides experiences on which theoretical concepts can be built and developed, and allows opportunities for successful and independent work which can generate interest, motivation and confidence.

By focusing on the aims of practical work in science, in particular by providing experiences to support theory, and by developing specific technical skills (the practical skills which enable students to use scientific equipment in experimental work), the course can be structured so that all students can work safely and independently irrespective of age, ability and degree of visual loss, and can gain their full entitlement to an education in science.

Chapter 25
Humanities

Christine Arter, Pat Everest and Stephen McCall

Introduction

The study of history and geography presents specific challenges to children with a visual impairment. Most children arrive at school with some awareness of the historical past derived from incidental exposure to visual media such as paintings, photographs, television and architecture, but it cannot be taken for granted that children with a severe visual impairment will have had the same opportunity for incidental learning. Similarly, the sense of the structure and scale of the physical environment, which children who are fully sighted gain immediately from a glimpse of a distant range of hills or a river valley, may be slow to develop in children with little or no sight. This chapter seeks to offer practical suggestions as to ways in which access to the themes set out in the National Curriculum programmes for geography and history (DfE 1995a) can be achieved by children with a visual impairment.

Resources

As has been suggested in many of the previous chapters, children with a visual impairment derive particular benefit from schemes of work which are planned to incorporate concrete experiences. Clearly it is not possible to convey all learning through 'hands-on' experience; for example children cannot tactually explore the lighted fire and cooking spit during a visit to a medieval manor house. In much of their learning, children with a visual impairment will be relying heavily on the teacher to provide clear explanations and to allow time for questions and discussion (Chapman and Stone 1988). Nevertheless, history and geography both provide opportunities for practical study through a variety of resources.

The National Curriculum (DfE 1995a) specifies the use of documentary evidence such as photographs, maps and diagrams, and in history, stresses the importance of referring to original source documents. There are important principles which can be used to guide the selection of source materials for children with a visual impairment. For example pictures or photographs that are used should be clear and well defined, and children with a visual impairment often find black and white photographs and pictures more accessible than colour prints. A closed circuit television (CCTV) may be required to help children to examine materials which contain fine detail, and colour CCTVs will be essential for some applications such as the examination of Ordnance Survey maps. The selection and adaptation of materials is a time-consuming process and careful forward planning is required to ensure that materials such as maps, worksheets, photographs and diagrams are presented in an appropriately adapted form (see Chapter 18).

Radio programmes are useful sources of information for the study of history and geography, and Schools Radio presents topics directly related to the National Curriculum. Television programmes too provide excellent source material but may need to be supplemented by teacher commentary in places where the programme relies solely on images to convey meaning. The teacher will need to arrange to pre-record and preview the programme, to prepare a careful introduction to the programme and to offer appropriate and timely intervention during the session. For children with low vision, careful consideration should be given to the child's seating position and some children will need to be very close to the screen. Some children may need to adopt unusual and uncomfortable postures to make best use of their residual vision to watch the television programme and it may be necessary to build in short breaks to enable the child to sustain concentration. Where programmes are very long it may be possible to select only the key parts of the broadcast for the lesson.

Museums and art galleries are becoming increasingly aware of the needs of children with a visual impairment (see Chapter 30) and, provided they are given advance notice, some will allow children to examine displays or sculptures by touch. Many large museums have school services and offer private sessions for classes of children in which they will provide a selection of artefacts relevant to the topic the children are studying. Some provide classrooms where the children can handle the items and discuss them with an expert, but these services usually have to be booked well in advance.

When planning visits or field trips, teachers are required to comply fully with the health and safety policy of the school and local education authority and the conditions of the school's insurance cover. Parental permission must be sought before the child is taken out of school, and care must be taken to follow simple safety procedures. Children with conditions such as glaucoma, asthma or epilepsy may require regular medication and teachers will need clear instructions for the administration and storage of medication before embarking on a visit. Additional precautions will be necessary in some cases. For example if a child has a condition such as high myopia or glaucoma where there is an increased chance of retinal detachment (see Chapter 5), the child should obviously not be put into situations where jolts or knocks to the head are likely. Warning signs of complications can take the form of severe headaches or sudden clouding of vision and teachers and other helpers should be alert to possible symptoms.

Educational suppliers such as History in Evidence (address at end of chapter) now provide copies and facsimiles of costumes and artefacts, and museum shops are another useful source of materials. A collection of resources within the school is an invaluable asset for studying history or geography in the National Curriculum, but because of the expense, most schools will need to build up collections gradually. It may be possible to persuade some parents to make facsimiles of items such as Victorian toys or period costumes and loan or donate them to the school. Some parents may even be prepared to donate original artefacts.

The History National Curriculum

The History National Curriculum defines five key elements:
- chronology
- range and depth of historical knowledge and understanding
- interpretations of history
- historical enquiry
- organisation and communication.

These key elements are developed through programmes of study, for example in Key Stage 2

> Pupils should be taught about important episodes from Britain's past, from Roman to modern times, about ancient civilisations and the history of other parts of the world. They should be helped to develop a chronological framework ... They should have opportunities to investigate local history and to learn about the past from a range of sources of information.' (DfE 1995a)

Among the study units at this stage are: life in Tudor times, Victorian Britain, Britain since 1930, Ancient Greece and local history. At Key Stage 3 there is an emphasis on changes in the 'economy, society, culture and political structure of Britain from the early Middle ages to the twentieth century'.

Some children with a visual impairment will be slower to develop an awareness of the past than their classmates and will need opportunities for exposure to history in the environment through carefully designed practical experiences.

Visits to buildings and sites such as stately homes, castles and churches provide enjoyable, exciting and stimulating opportunities for historical enquiry. Some buildings of historic interest organise special school visits where children can dress up in period costume and can take part in role play. This approach enables children to ask and answer questions and record information about the daily routines of the household such as the preparation of food, and it gives an insight into the roles of the different members of the household. Museums such as Hartlebury Museum in Worcestershire, provide the opportunity for children to take part in a school day as it would have been in Victorian times. Children are able to compare the ways of life at different levels of society by finding out how rich and poor children spent their days, and to relate this to their own lives. Such visits can be immensely valuable but a high pupil/staff ratio is required to ensure that the child with a visual impairment has access to the careful guidance and explanation necessary to gain the maximum benefit from the experience.

A visit to a castle can be a rich learning opportunity about life in Tudor times, for example, for a child with a visual impairment. The child who is fully sighted can quickly learn a great deal about a castle from one of the many books available on the subject in most school libraries, but only by visiting a castle can a child who is blind start to develop a meaningful understanding of its nature. A child who is blind may read or be told that a castle is built of stone. The child's concept of stone may be associated with the small stones found in the garden and only by feeling and exploring the size of the blocks of stone used in building a castle, walking around the perimeter of the castle and exploring its hall, chambers, battlements and spiral stone staircases, will they develop some understanding of its scale. The drawbridge and the moat provide additional fascinating areas for study and further research.

The National Curriculum specifies the study of local history so it is important for the teacher to carry out a thorough investigation of what is available in the locality and to use local resources to their full potential. Information about earlier times can often be gained from place names, street names, and the names of houses and pubs within walking distance of the school. Sometimes the occupants of local houses of interest are happy to talk to children about the history of their house and show them items of antiquity that they have uncovered. There may be a local history trail and these are usually carefully set out and can often be followed without the need for prior booking. Local churches can be another extremely useful resource and some will be able to provide a guide to talk to a class. Children are usually able to tactually explore features of the building, including tombs, pillars, carvings and furniture or to make brass rubbings. These visits and field trips can be used to develop learning across many areas of the curriculum such as art, maths, and information technology and indeed geography and history themselves can be combined for younger pupils and taught using a cross-curricular approach.

Family photographs, letters and personal reminiscences also provide useful source material for a study of more recent history. Older relatives, such as grandparents or aunts and uncles are often willing to come into school to talk about life at home in their childhood, or relate their wartime experiences, or talk about the changes in technology and transport in their lifetime. Many homes will have items of historical interest that can be brought to school, such as ration books, watches and old money, to add to the children's understanding of a topic.

Other areas of the National Curriculum, such as drama, music and dance have an important part to play in fostering understanding. Radio drama series produced by the BBC are useful for bringing to life scenes from the past; for example there are programmes covering the plague of Eyam and the history of the Tower of London. Dance, music and song can be used to develop historical themes and even PE lessons can provide insights into the past: for example children can be helped to recreate 'drill' lessons as they would have been taught in Victorian times and experience the discipline of not being allowed to talk in lessons!

Design and technology lessons can be used to make costumes or models appropriate to the period being studied. For example children can build models of Viking or Tudor ships or the teacher can demonstrate steam powered models when the Industrial Revolution is being studied. Toys and games appropriate to the period can lead to animated discussion, and recipes appropriate to the times can be cooked and sampled.

There are many colourful and attractively designed commercial publications for use in the study of history at school, which often convey information in a story format describing the lives of children of the times. Some may need to be adapted before they can be used effectively by children with a visual impairment (see Chapter 10).

Stories and poems from the past, such as Greek myths and legends and Aesop's fables are another very useful tool to help develop an understanding of Ancient Greece in pupils with a visual impairment.

Pupils with a visual impairment studying History in the secondary school will be required to read extensively from textbooks and original source materials in order to select, analyse and deploy information to reach conclusions about the reasons for events and changes. At this stage, use can be made of tapes (see Chapter 15) to provide an alternative means of access and to reduce the fatigue of studying. The student will benefit from study skills such as efficient note taking to record their work in a form that will make revision for examinations easier (see Chapter 19).

The Geography National Curriculum

The History National Curriculum prescribes the topics which are to be studied but the Geography National Curriculum (DfE 1995a) presents programmes of study under broad themes. At all key stages the themes include the following.

- *Geographical skills*. (These include the ability to observe, question and record, and to communicate ideas and information.) Pupils must be taught to use geographical terms, to undertake fieldwork activities, follow directions, make plans and maps, use globes, maps, plans and atlases, identify major geographical features, and to use secondary sources such as pictures, photographs, books, videos, and a CD-ROM encyclopaedia. At Key Stage 3 pupils are also expected to select and use appropriate graphical techniques to present evidence.

- *Places*. At Key Stage 1 pupils are expected to study two localities, that of the school and one that will provide a contrast to the local area. At Key Stage 2, three areas are to be studied, including the wider local area and a contrasting area in the United Kingdom and another in either Africa, Asia, South or Central America. In Key Stage 3, two countries other that the UK should be studied. Pupils may study from prescribed lists and must choose a developed and a developing country.

- *Thematic study*. At Key Stage 1, the quality of the environment should provide the basis for study. At Key Stage 2, four themes should be covered including rivers, weather, settlement and environmental change, and at Key Stage 3 nine geographic themes should be studied, including tectonic processes, geomorphological processes, weather and climate, ecosystems, population, settlement, economic activities, development and environmental issues.

Geographical skills

Since many children with a visual impairment will have had fewer opportunities for incidental learning, it is important not to make assumptions about what the child understands but to build upon the skills and knowledge that the child has already acquired. In the area of map work for example it is possible that the child with a severe visual impairment may not have come across the examples of maps or plans that children who are fully sighted commonly find in print books or on television.

For the younger child the first step towards understanding plans may be to arrange objects on a tray and to discuss their relative position using terms such as 'beside', 'above', 'below', 'left' and 'right'. The child may then be asked to reproduce the layout using concrete objects before moving to pictorial, two dimensional representations of the objects. The child's knowledge could then be extended to plan the classroom, the school corridor, their bedroom at home and then the wider environment of the school. The terms 'left/right' and 'top/bottom' can be replaced later by an introduction of the points of the compass.

Once the basic foundations have been laid it is possible to move on to the larger topic of map work, working outwards from the school locality to the map of the British Isles and beyond. Skills in using maps and a compass can be practised on school visits. As was noted earlier, visits provide excellent opportunities for cross-curricular study in the humanities, for example walks along canal tow paths can be the basis of a study of the history of transport or of the development of settlements. Geography can also be used to support the development of skills in mobility and orientation for the child who is blind and the teacher can work closely with a mobility officer to reinforce the child's knowledge of direction, and ability to interpret maps and to identify key features on routes.

The Geography National Curriculum (DfE 1995a) demands that from Key Stage 1 children learn to 'record, and to communicate ideas and information'. Young children with a visual impairment often find recording large amounts of information in a written form to be an arduous task and charts and diagrams may be used to record information that children have gathered. Art work can also be used, for example a collage of the Amazonian rain forest, or a poster depicting causes of pollution will provide an effective means of recording what has been learnt. From Key Stage 2 onwards, the Geography National Curriculum states that information technology (IT) should be used to record work and many children with a visual impairment will have already possess sophisticated skills in areas such as word-processing which they will be able to employ to effect.

The theme of places

For the primary school child this topic may include a number of concepts found in the area of thematic studies. For example the topic of local geography will involve visits to local shops, places of work or parks. Transportation networks including roads, railways and canals can usually be studied locally and there may be a nearby airport. Local geographical features can help to provide a basic understanding of concepts that can then be applied to a wider study of the United Kingdom and other countries and continents. For example a trip to the local park can help to formulate ideas about the best place to build a home settlement. Important factors such as water, food and fuel supplies, building materials, defence, a well drained fertile soil, communications and transport can be discussed with reference to real features. A frieze could be made in art lessons to show the perfect place for a settlement and models and maps could be used as a means of recording work.

Once basic concepts have been grasped and understood it is possible to make comparisons with different environments. It is important to relate new information to ideas that the child is familiar with, moving from the familiar to the unknown. This approach is particularly important for some pupils with a visual impairment who may have been afforded fewer opportunities to explore their local environment than their peers.

When studying an unfamiliar country the child might be first encouraged to seek answers to practical questions such as the following.

- How far away is it?
- How long would it take to get there?
- Could we travel overland?
- What clothes would we take if we were going there on holiday?
- What would the food be like?

Themes could be developed across subjects, for example the child could learn about the country by listening to local music or playing indigenous instruments. Science lessons could be used to grow plants from the seeds of fruit grown in the country such as avocados, and melons. When studying the rainforests, visits to locations such as botanical gardens can enable pupils to gain some experience of the atmosphere of a rain forest and the type of plants that grow there. Education officers from zoos sometimes visit schools and give children the opportunity to hold and feel exotic animals. In art and design and technology lessons children can make ethnic jewellery, woven fabrics, musical instruments and models of houses, and in English lessons children can be introduced to stories of life on a sailing ship or a journey on a stagecoach to inform their study of transport and communication.

At Key Stage 3 studies become more focused. For example in their study of population, settlement and economic activities, students may be expected to undertake surveys at a centre of tourism and to ascertain the number of tourists in comparison with local inhabitants and to analyse the type of shops and businesses found there. Some field trips will lend themselves to work at different key stages, for example the rate of the flow of a stream may form part of the work when studying rivers at Key Stage 2 and geomorphological processes at Key Stage 3.

Older pupils will require sophisticated tactile skills to be able to interpret the more complex range of maps and diagrams they will meet at secondary level (Figure 25.1; also see Chapter 18). As in the study of History, the use of taped material can be considered where extensive reading is required.

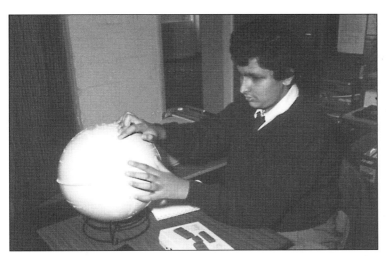

Figure 25.1

Specialist teachers and the humanities

For both history and geography, curriculum groups, comprising specialist teachers from a range of mainstream and specialist provision for the visually impaired across the country, meet regularly under the auspices of VIEW (the professional body for teachers of the visually impaired; see below), to represent the interests of students with a visual impairment with regard to developments in the National Curriculum and public examinations. They also help to develop specialist teaching approaches, for example the geography group has recently developed conventions for the tactile adaptations of symbols on Ordnance Survey (OS) maps. The groups also provide feedback to SCAA (the national body with responsibility for curriculum and assessment) about the appropriateness of the National Curriculum requirements for children and young people with visual impairment. Some group members are involved actively in the transcription of examination papers into braille for examination boards, and these groups have become significant and influential sources of advice for the examination authorities in this specific area of special educational needs.

The VIEW group also provide a forum for advice about the requirements of the different examination boards at GCSE. There is a disparity between examination boards in the adaptations and substitutions they will allow in examination papers. For example, for some examination boards OS map work questions are compulsory, while with others they are not. While teachers in special schools for the visually impaired can often enter students for the examination board of their choice, teachers supporting children in mainstream schools are often restricted to the board which the school chooses for the rest of their students.

Conclusion

The humanities offer children with a visual impairment opportunities to develop their understanding of their community and their heritage and to provide them with insights into their environment. History and geography also offer children with a visual impairment opportunities to develop important specialist skills, such as orientation and mobility and the use of technology, within a framework of requirements common to all children.

Useful addresses

History in Evidence, Unit 4, Park Road, Holmewood, Chesterfield S42 5UY.
VIEW, York House Annexe, Exhall Grange School, Wheelwright Lane, Ash Green, Coventry CV7 9HP. Tel: 01203 361127.

Chapter 26

Modern Foreign Languages

Carol Gray

Introduction

Modern foreign languages were traditionally regarded as subjects appropriate for study only by the more able. During the last two decades provision has extended dramatically, and the National Curriculum Orders in England and Wales now include a modern foreign language as a foundation subject for all pupils from the age of 11 to 16. This raises questions about staffing, resources and methodology, particularly in the light of current recommended teaching practice with its emphasis on visual input to convey meaning. This chapter discusses some of these issues and their implications for pupils with a visual impairment.

Languages for all

Modern foreign languages were traditionally a high status subject, deemed to be accessible only to the most able (Bovair and Bovair 1992). Attitudes and methodology have changed, and a modern foreign language is now included as a foundation subject of the National Curriculum in England and Wales for Key Stages 3 and 4: 'studying a foreign language is perceived to be important for all children, both in terms of practical and vocational benefits and in terms of receiving a rounded education' (SCAA (Schools Curriculum and Assessment Authority) 1994).

Although the National Curriculum Orders (Department for Education (DfE) 1995c) include foreign languages only up to age 16, the Dearing review identified 'unanimous support, among parents and employers, for pupils to begin to learn a modern foreign language at primary school' (SCAA 1994). The 1996 report on the review of qualifications for 16 to 19 year olds also emphasises the importance of language learning at post-GCSE level (Dearing 1996).

Schools providing specialist education for more able pupils with visual impairment have a long tradition of modern language teaching (Nikolić 1986). Certain schools catering for pupils with complex difficulties have resisted and a small number may continue to do so (Lee 1991). The consensus of expert opinion is, however, that 'in most cases exposure to Modern Foreign Languages is beneficial' (National Curriculum Council (NCC) 1993), even for pupils with severe learning difficulties (Lee 1991).

What can languages offer?

Greater vocational mobility and increased opportunities for tourism and leisure are the most commonly cited reasons for learning a modern foreign language. Further benefits of opening up language learning to pupils of wide ranging ability are well documented throughout recent literature (CILT 1996, Deane 1992, Fox and Looney 1993). Pupils who have experienced learning difficulties are given the opportunity for a fresh start, without the 'negative connotations of other curriculum areas where they have already failed' (Asher *et al.* 1995). Several authors make reference to the potential here for the enhancement of pupils' self-confidence and self-esteem (Nikolić 1986, Woods 1995).

The National Curriculum Order for Modern Foreign Languages consists of a list of procedures and opportunities which must be given to the child, such as the opportunity to express opinions on topics of interest, to work in pairs or groups or to take part in creative and imaginative activities. The contexts within which such activities must take place are identified as five 'areas of experience': everyday activities, personal and social life, the world around us, the world of work, and the international world. Work in the modern languages classroom should consist of 'listening, communicating, working with partners and in groups, co-operating, being exposed to new experiences, learning about other people' (Woods 1995). In theory, 'as a subject modern foreign languages can be tailor-made to meet the needs and interests of pupils' (Watkins 1995). In reality, the content of lessons is largely determined by the GCSE examination boards or by local certification schemes which aim to provide non-examination candidates with a sense of progress and achievement.

The language used in the beginners' class for modern foreign languages is simple and concrete, with great efforts made to establish and reinforce meanings. Pupils learn how to say their names, ages and addresses, describe their family, learn the names for various classroom items and instructions. Learning is placed within familiar situations and contexts. The decontextualised language of the secondary curriculum which can disadvantage pupils with a background of experiential deprivation, is thus avoided.

The main emphasis in the early modern language class is upon listening and repeating, followed by a gradual movement towards independent use of the language without the support of a model. The emphasis on listening and speaking can put the child with a visual impairment at an advantage by comparison with fully sighted peers (Nikolić, 1986):

> No matter what their educational level, the visually handicapped often display a marked talent for learning foreign languages. This seems to be the result of a particular aural sensitivity and the memory training which forms part of the rehabilitation process.

This is echoed by Couper who refers to the 'enhanced aural, concentration and memory skills' of pupils with a visual impairment (Couper 1996). There is evidence that modern language work can contribute to the development of pupils' skills of listening and concentration (Bovair and Bovair 1992, Nikolić 1986, Hurrell in Trafford 1994; see also Chapter 15).

Since new input is primarily accessed aurally and the skills of listening, speaking, reading and writing are given equal weighting, at least half of pupils' work should be assessed independently of literacy skills; coursework can be produced on tape rather than paper. During the early stages, reading and writing are regarded as reinforcement skills rather than as means of access and assessment.

When reading and writing are introduced the initial process is slow and careful, starting with the copying or transcription of individual words. Time and space are made for close concentration on the spelling of individual words and phrases, which may benefit pupils who have particular difficulty in these areas. Continuing attention is given to the sounds of the words and to the relationship between sound and shape.

Frequent reference is made in the literature to the possibilities which language work offers for the rehearsal of essential basic concepts; language learning can be 'used to recycle things already taught elsewhere' (Fawkes 1995a, see also Deane 1992). Basic numeracy is reinforced (Higham 1993), as are spatial concepts such as direction and map reading (Lee 1991, Thomas and Nichols 1991). Such work can also provide a safety net for pupils whose lack of experience in such areas has not been recognised (Higham 1993).

Life skills and life experiences can also benefit greatly: the aim of language learning is for pupils to be able to survive and to communicate their needs in the countries where the chosen language is spoken, thus a wide range of life skills are revisited. Topics vary from meeting people and initiating conversations through ordering food and drink in French cafés to shopping at the local supermarket, catching buses and trains and filling up the car with petrol. Evidence shows that some pupils lack the English vocabulary for such activities (Gray 1997). Personal hygiene routines and health care are also included among the many areas covered in a languages course (Higham 1993). Since 'the teaching of modern languages lends itself to a multisensory approach' (Bovair 1995), much of this learning is accompanied and reinforced by the miming of actions, singing, chanting, moving around the classroom following directions or interviewing peers, role-playing or real acting with props, or the smelling and tasting of foods and drink, thus encouraging the development of self-help and mobility skills.

On a broader level, language learning can be said to develop 'skills for work', such as politeness, helpfulness and inventive thinking (Bovair and Bovair 1992). Moreover, the development of social skills and interpersonal relationships form a major feature of the current communicative style of language teaching (Fawkes 1995a, Fowler 1989, Lee 1991). Teachers of pupils with visual impairments often testify to the sometimes serious difficulties which their pupils experience in such social skills, and the literature emphasises that pupils with a wide range of special educational needs 'frequently have poor relationships, both with other pupils and with adults' (Ramasut 1989).

Which language?

The predominance of French in the UK education system as a whole is a 'historical accident' rather than a result of rational decision making (Department of Education and Science (DES) 1987, Phillips and Filmer-Sankey 1993). There are frequent references in the literature to 'the 'considerable difficulties' of French in the early stages of learning' (Phillips and Filmer-Sankey 1993), mainly based on the phonology of spoken French, that is, its pronunciation and the interrelationship between the spoken and the written forms (Fowler 1989, Westgate in Phillips 1989). Given the difficulties which many of our pupils experience in reading and writing, and in spelling in particular, this factor needs to be considered. German pronunciation, vocabulary and intonation present fewer problems (Fowler 1989, Phillips 1989, Phillips and Filmer-Sankey 1993), and the spoken forms of Spanish are deemed to be 'much closer and more systematic than that of French (Fowler 1989, Rouwe in Phillips 1989).

Low-ability learners have also been found to be particularly negative in their attitudes towards French' (Kenning 1993, Phillips and Filmer-Sankey 1993), with the highest proportion of pupils finding the foreign language both easy and enjoyable was found among those pupils learning German (Phillips and Filmer-Sankey 1993). Not withstanding potential difficulties in providing adequate staffing and resources, such research demonstrates the need to consider carefully the choice of first foreign language for all children, perhaps in particular those with a visual impairment.

Difficulties in implementing the National Curriculum

The teaching of modern foreign languages to pupils with a visual impairment is not without its difficulties and its implications for teaching techniques, staffing and resources.

The conveyance of meaning

A major aspect of work in the modern languages classroom is that while other curriculum areas use communication to teach the subject content, modern foreign languages use content to teach communication (see Corder 1966). Non-verbal methods of communication play an essential part in the teaching of meaning, and in most language classrooms 'the visual sense plays a dominant though not exclusive role' (Couper 1996).

The difficulties raised by this for pupils whose eyesight is not adequate for picking up visual clues is compounded by current emphasis on use of the 'target' language (Department of Education and Science/Welsh Office 1988). It is generally accepted that pupils need to have maximum exposure to the new language and to experience it as a valid means of real communication. Nevertheless, even researchers who acknowledge that 'use of the target language in the classroom should become the norm rather than the exception of everyday practice' (Asher 1993) are concerned about the possible consequences for pupil understanding and the dangers of 'verbalism'; 'pupils can perform quite adequately in certain oral language functions without actually having a very definite idea of what they are saying' (Asher 1993, see also Corder 1966). Teachers are largely dependent upon 'visual techniques to teach meaning' (Corder 1966) such as real objects, flashcards, the overhead projector, gesture, mime, facial expression, pictures and cartoons. Literature on the teaching of modern foreign languages to pupils with special educational needs advocates the use of visual support for the learning and remembering of words, such as Kim's game, noughts and crosses, hangman, board games and the use of realia, pictures and mobiles. Deprived of these support measures, the teacher of the child with a visual impairment needs to seek new ways of facilitating target language use without detriment to the conveyance of meaning.

Resources and materials

As in all subject areas, the resources available to teachers today are highly visual in impact. Textbooks are colourful and cluttered, often with a fragmented layout which can be confusing even for pupils who are fully sighted. Meaning is often conveyed in visual terms by the use of pictures, diagrams and maps. The preparation of adapted materials for use in class by pupils with a visual impairment is dealt with in detail by Price (1993, 1994a) and Couper (1996) This is, however, a time-consuming process, and pupils using such adapted resources are deprived of many opportunities for incidental learning and increased motivation from the peripheral information provided by the original (see also Chapter 18).

Emphasis is placed in the National Curriculum Orders upon the use of authentic materials from the countries and communities concerned, such as teenage magazines and newspapers. The simplified versions of magazines, brochures, tickets and menus which we produce have, to a large extent, lost their contact with the original culture. In addition, our necessary intervention severely reduces the opportunities for pupils to choose their own reading materials for pleasure as recommended by the Orders. Although this issue affects the availability of all reading materials (Stone 1995, 1995a), the implications of restriction within language work are more severe.

Reading and writing skills

The potential difficulties of reading and writing across the curriculum for pupils with a visual impairment are widely acknowledged; it is difficult to skim and scan texts, to transfer back and forth between a written text and a set of questions, to locate specific sections of a text quickly, and to combine the skills of reading and writing or listening and writing. Such difficulties can be compounded with a new language. Ways must be found for pupils to practise these skills, however, as 'some authors have found that the main trouble lies in the less frequent contact the visually impaired have with the written form' (Nikolić 1986).

A specific practice of language lessons which can present problems for pupils with slower than average reading speeds is that of reading while hearing in order to reinforce the relationship between sound and shape. The National Curriculum emphasises the need for 'mixed skill' activities in the classroom, that is, activities combining two or more of the four skill areas of speaking, listening, reading and writing, so that the listening and speaking tasks at which pupils may well excel become complicated by the addition of reading and writing (Couper 1996).

Print readers may have particular difficulty with 'authentic' foreign handwriting in resource materials. In addition the emphasis on the use of authentic materials leads to the inclusion of menus, timetables, brochures, cinema schedules and so on, with various sizes of print, keys to interpretation and with a fragmented layout. Accents and umlauts are often indistinct and need to be highlighted.

Braille users are presented with a more uniform format, but have additional difficulties to cope with as each language has its own contracted system. To simplify this, modern foreign languages are taught in Grade 1 braille with the inclusion of the necessary signs for accented characters, umlauts, and common word symbols. This emphasises the spellings of words, but there is still ground for confusion as for example the sign for 'ch' in English reads 'au' in German and 'â' in French, and similarly 'wh' reads as 'sch' or 'û'. The small amount of authentic material which is available in braille from the countries concerned cannot be used as this is written in contracted braille. Students at sixth form level and beyond either have to learn the new braille codes for themselves or become dependent upon taped recordings.

Access to reference materials

A particular area of concern for pupils with a visual impairment is that of meaningful access to dictionaries. Given the difficulties experienced in skimming and scanning, consultation of a dictionary becomes a major obstacle for both print and braille users. Wordlists for GCSE have been produced in braille and large print by the Manchester Service for the Visually Impaired (Price 1994b) and are also available on disk so that words can be added. However, the range of vocabulary available in them is necessarily restricted and more advanced learners are without access to adequate resources. Volunteer readers who are fully sighted are often the only viable alternative: 'rather than representing a skill developed by the student, using a dictionary involved a frustrating degree of dependence on other people for these pupils' (Couper 1996). The implications of this are particularly worrying given the move towards allowing dictionaries to be used in language examinations. Speaking computers and moving braille displays may help, but what is really needed is a full and efficient hand-held speaking dictionary with acceptable pronunciation.

Using IT where appropriate

Although pupils with a visual impairment may rely on computers for interaction with the curriculum and many have quite good keyboard and general information technology skills, much of the commercial software available for language learning and reinforcement is heavily visual in nature. Speech synthesisers which are available for word processing vary in their ability to produce modern languages (Couper 1996), and moving braille displays, although commonly used in France and Germany, are expensive. CD-ROMs can provide reading materials accompanied by sound versions, though teachers will need to select very carefully to ensure that the visual element included is not overly dominant.

Assessment procedures

Assessment procedures used by examining boards inevitably both reflect and affect current teaching practice. The Modern Languages Curriculum Group (address at the end of the chapter) has negotiated a standardised pattern of adaptations across examining boards which includes the reduction of the visual element by simplification of advertisements and other pictorial stimuli, omission of unnecessary and potentially misleading detail from textual sources and the production of large print papers on A4 rather than A3 to make them more manageable for pupils, particularly those using a CCTV. It must be remembered, nevertheless, that pupils who are fully sighted are often able to obtain clues as to meaning from the visual elements of materials such as drawings, and the emphasis given in different sizes and boldness of type. Such adaptations may well thus increase the language difficulty of the tasks for the child with a visual impairment and adapted questions may be necessary to enable pupils to demonstrate their true language ability (Price 1993). Listening comprehensions can become a major feat of memory without the option of taking notes as an *aide-mémoire* during listening. The extra time given to complete examinations is necessary but it makes enormous demands on stamina and concentration. As new examinations begin to reflect the teaching style implied by the National Curriculum Order further problems will be encountered; the heavy emphasis on target language use will necessitate an even greater reliance upon visual stimuli. Such assessment strategies may well be difficult to adapt and any alternatives used will change the nature of the task, potentially making it more difficult linguistically.

Coping in specialised settings

Clearly where the majority of pupils are likely to experience varying degrees of difficulty with visual presentation, the challenge is to reduce the importance of this element without detriment to the conveyance of meaning. A limited range of vocabulary and ideas can be introduced by the use of tactile objects as well as by smell, taste and sound effects, but care must be taken to ensure that all pupils fully understand what they are experiencing (Price 1994a); in a relatively large class this may not be feasible. Nikolić recommends the use of objects, models, relief maps, diagrams, and all kinds of recorded sounds (Nikolić 1986).

Most teachers admit to using more English than they would like, in order to convey meaning. It may be necessary to use 'code-switching' until pupils begin to build up an initial degree of comprehension; this consists of using the target language, repeating in English, then again in the target language and gradually withdrawing English support as pupils learn meanings. Such a procedure is often frowned upon in language teaching circles as it can confuse rather than clarify (Nikolić 1986); however, in situations where the highly visual presentation required by consistent target language use is inappropriate, it is arguable whether the alternatives would be any less confusing. Language teachers in any setting tend to use a mixture of languages (Neil 1996).

Within a specialised setting there will inevitably be a greater emphasis on the use of auditory clues (Price 1993). As mime, gesture and facial expression may not be accessible, these need to be supplemented by the use of cognates (that is, words similar to equivalents in the mother tongue because of common stems, such as Hund for dog (hound), Mutter for mother, Tochter for daughter, and so on), and also clearer speech, emphasis being given to words or parts of words which are already known to the pupils and tone of voice. Individual pupils can be asked to interpret for the whole class; such comprehension checks are essential in any language class to avoid verbalism, but are perhaps even more important where pupils' vision prevents them from picking up the subtle visual clues which aid interpretation.

Many authors advocate the use of physical response in order to internalise language (Couper, 1996, Woods 1995), a possibility with particular relevance for pupils who need to develop their orientation and mobility skills. Acting out role-plays and dramatised dialogues (Nikolić 1986) also helps pupils to put language into context and practise patterns, as do games and quizzes (Kenning 1994). An active, multi-sensory approach is encouraged, involving (CILT 1991):

> ... rhythmic chanting, rap, chain-games, mini-lab, recorded diaries, reporting back to another group, simple interviews, surveys, repetition exercises requiring a physical response, e.g. couple a word with an action, repetition where each member of the group 'owns' one word (Mexican wave) ... (Carty and Crow 1991)

Many of these and similar activities can be adapted for use in a specialised setting with pupils who have a visual impairment.

The National Curriculum Council also emphasises the benefits of singing and rhymes for pupils with special needs (National Curriculum Council 1993), and 'many teachers have long recognised that songs are an invaluable support to language learning' (Carty and Crow 1991). There are several recent collections of simple songs available which have been especially written (Fawkes 1995b, Collins and Borgwart 1996, Robb and Geoghegan 1995, Wahl 1993) and pupils can be encouraged to make up their own songs or rhymes to build up patterning.

Another possibility which may increase pupil motivation as well as providing a context to aid understanding and give meaning to learning is that of the negotiation of content. Watkins refers to 'the importance of beginning with the pupils' ideas and interests as "springboards" and building on these' (Watkins 1995; see also Holmes 1991). Such negotiation will inevitably be in English, but if it sets the context for pupils to understand what they are learning and ensures that they are learning what they feel is relevant, the benefits will far outweigh the disadvantages.

One potential advantage of the specialised setting has been the extension of the GCSE cycle from two to three years; it is unfortunate that not all schools are able to provide this facility.

Coping in mainstream settings

In a mainstream setting adaptations for pupils with a visual impairment will require careful coordination. In an ideal situation, materials for use in class are discussed with the support team well in advance, so that modified versions or appropriate alternatives can be produced before the lesson and the teacher made aware of potential difficulties and strategies to overcome them. Members of support services often find the adaptation of sighted materials a daunting task, and few are in the privileged position of the Manchester Service with access to publishers' disks (Gray 1997).

The support provided for pupils with various kinds of special educational needs in language learning is variable (Woods 1995), and that for pupils with a visual impairment are no exception (Couper 1996, Gray 1997). Some pupils in mainstream schools are accompanied to all lessons by classroom assistants or specialist teachers, whereas for others priority is given to support in lessons where there are potential safety risks such as science. Constant support may be advantageous in terms of understanding lesson content and gaining access to the core of the curriculum, yet it may restrict socialisation between peers which is one of the main advantages of the modern languages classroom. It may be more appropriate for the class and its teacher to be fully briefed and supported to integrate the child into all classroom activity. There is a fine balance between ensuring maximum access and encouraging independence rather than learned dependence.

Certain schools specialising in the integration of the visually impaired provide extra tuition in a resource base to support the mainstream classroom experience; however there are not always staff in the resource base who can cope with the language work. Whenever help is given, the particular circumstances of language support need to be considered (Lee 1991):

> the kind of help needed in the foreign language classroom was different and there was clearly a need for the special needs teachers to be provided with some INSET [in-service training] in order to increase their confidence in French and German.

Support staff can be allocated to a beginners' class to learn alongside the students (Bovair 1995). Fortunately there does seem to be a growing determination on the part of modern linguists themselves to make their subject accessible to all pupils whatever their needs (Gray 1997).

Real learning: the trip abroad

One of the main emphases in the National Curriculum Order for modern foreign languages is on the use of language for real purposes; the programme of study states that: 'Pupils should be given opportunities to come into contact with native speakers in this country, and, where possible, abroad' (DfE 1995a). In specialist settings, exchanges can be arranged with similar schools abroad, where the specific needs of pupils are likely to be catered for (see Gray 1988). Many mainstream schools organise exchange visits and trips abroad, and pupils with a visual impairment often take part (Gray 1997). Particular problems may need to be addressed; given the low incidence of visual impairment and society's perceived image of helplessness, trip organisers may have a difficult task convincing partners and potential hosts of the viability of the idea. Funding will need to include the provision of a suitably qualified teacher, though care must be taken not to limit the child's exposure to the new culture by reducing contact with native speakers. Much of the experience of visiting a foreign country and engaging with a new culture is visual, as is incidental language learning from the recognition of signs and notices. These factors will need to be addressed by competent and understanding staff. The importance of funding such ventures cannot be underestimated, as 'in life skills the trip abroad could be seen as equivalent to ten weeks of learning' (Lee 1991; see also Thomas and Nichols 1991, and Gray 1988).

Summary

There appears to be a consensus that the vast majority of pupils, whatever their ability, can benefit from the study of a modern foreign language, not least as an opportunity for success in a different curriculum area and a chance to rehearse basic social, educational and life skills within a new medium. The emphasis in current teaching methodology on speaking and listening and upon communication as the prime aim can be an advantage for pupils whose most reliable channel of input is aural.

The same methodology can, however, present major problems for precisely such pupils because of its heavy reliance upon the visual element to support comprehension and memory. Teachers in both mainstream and specialised settings need to be aware of the implications of this and imaginative enough to adapt their teaching style to encourage maximum access.

Consideration needs to be given by curriculum managers to the choice of language to be offered, and the provision of adequate support for both pupils and teachers, as well as to the desirability of funding and staffing visits to the appropriate country, both to provide a real-life context to justify the learning process and to offer pupils an invaluable experience in terms of their social and life skills.

Useful address

For further information about the VIEW Modern Languages Curriculum Group, contact Rory Cobb, RNIB New College for the Blind, Whittington Road, Worcester WR5 2JU.

Chapter 27
Information Technology

Jane Sutcliffe

Introduction

The status of information technology (IT) within the National Curriculum is enhanced by a new emphasis upon the use of IT within all areas of the curriculum. Pupils are now given opportunities to use IT as tools to solve problems and to support their learning. IT skills are introduced within a context which will help them understand how information impacts upon the commercial and industrial world and the home. There is an expectation that all children will become familiar with a range of IT applications and will develop the skills necessary to use them.

This increasing emphasis on integration of IT within all subject areas has particular significance for children with special educational needs. IT is an enabling mechanism which allows pupils to take more control over their learning by promoting independence, and providing access to areas of the curriculum where visual impairment is often thought to present barriers (Chapter 21). IT can also promote equality of opportunity by allowing access to a varied and differentiated curriculum in the primary and secondary years and in later stages when working towards employment and further study.

The Code of Practice on Identification and Assessment of Special Educational Needs (DfE 1994), states that in supporting children with special needs of whatever nature, schools are expected to investigate the technology requirements of the child. It insists that provision of the most appropriate technology is made for the individual and notes that inappropriate provision will constitute an additional barrier to learning.

Assessment

The information required to identify accurately the most appropriate technology will include an understanding of the individual's level of attainment in diverse areas such as mobility and orientation, hearing, motor skills, reading and writing media, movement and body posture, hand–eye coordination, visual and auditory perception, literacy and numeracy. The individual's general development and learning patterns will also need to be taken into account.

In assessing the needs in this area of children with a visual impairment other key considerations will include: the immediate and long-term teaching objectives; the effects of the individual's eye condition; the implications of visual impairment, and the presence of other impairments or disabilities. These are now discussed in more detail.

Clear definition of both the immediate and long-term teaching and learning objectives

A word processor which provides basic facilities for editing and formatting may meet educational and visual needs in the primary and early secondary years, but from Key Stage 4 onwards more sophisticated equipment which is compatible with that used in the workplace will be required to prepare students for employment or further and higher education. The Code of Practice (DfE 1994) states that the child should be able to use appropriate technology throughout the curriculum and at home, and that provision should take account of movement from one part of the school to another. This may be an easier task in Key Stages 1 and 2 when most subjects are class-based, but may be more difficult from Key Stage 3 onwards when different subjects are taught by subject specialists.

An understanding of the issues surrounding the effects of the eye condition

Visual loss lies on a continuum, from total blindness to vision which can be improved to normal standards through the use of spectacles (see Chapters 6 and 7 for further information). Information about a child's eye condition enables some general predictions to be made about the most appropriate size of print for the child or the child's reaction to glare, but there are inherent dangers in making decisions about technology based upon the eye condition alone.

An appreciation of the implications of visual impairment and how these affect the learning situation

The achievement of children with a visual impairment will be influenced by many factors, such as the severity of the visual impairment, the extent of early intervention, the supportiveness of the family environment, motivation, opportunities for exploration and the quantity and quality of the practical experiences they have enjoyed. Visual impairment can present potential barriers to learning such as reduced access to printed material, or difficulties with reading and writing. The difficulties are sometime due to the intrinsic nature of media such as braille or Moon (see Chapter 16), or they may arise because the children's visual impairment prevents them from seeing the correct formation of letters, or from reading back text accurately.

An understanding is also required of the effects of visual impairment on developmental areas such as perception, concept formation, memory, independence and organisation skills, spatial skills, fine and gross motor skills and directionality, many of which are vital to the efficient and effective use of information technology (see Chapter 3).

An awareness of the possibility of additional needs caused by the presence of other impairments or disabilities

The OPCS (Office of Population Censuses and Surveys) survey (Bone and Meltzer 1989) found that 83% of children identified as having a visual disability had an additional disability such as hearing or speech impairment, epilepsy or diabetes. These may have an additional effect upon the learning process and some may render inappropriate access technology such as speech synthesis.

By matching knowledge of the needs of the pupil to an awareness of the range of relevant devices, recommendations can be made to provide the most appropriate technology.

Staff awareness

For access technology to be successfully integrated into all areas of the curriculum there has to a 'whole school policy' which is understood and supported across the curriculum.

There is a wide range of equipment for pupils with a visual impairment ranging from 'low tech' solutions such as braille labels, to the more technical software and hardware solutions such as voice synthesis and character enhancement, talking dictionaries, computers with braille keyboards and braille displays, and touch-sensitive concept keyboards (such as the Nomad).

Access software packages which run alongside off-the-shelf programs can be powerful and complicated tools which have to be learned in conjunction with the applications software. Facilities within screen enhancement programs allow for a wide variety of print sizes, fonts, colours, and options for stability, cursor stability and isolation of portions of the screen. Speech synthesis enables the user to customise the output to a preferred gender, speed and tone of voice, and there are other facilities to enable the reading of punctuation and capitals, or allow the user to control the output from certain portions of the screen. These common forms of access technology have their own difficulties and it is sometimes assumed, incorrectly, that the addition of a voice synthesiser or screen magnifier will enable a pupil with severe visual impairment to work in exactly the same way and at the same speed as their peers who are fully sighted. Most pieces of access software contain barriers of their own, such as the following.

- Screen magnification suffers from the same difficulties as any form of magnification: it only allows a 'keyhole' view of the tasks in hand.
- On default settings speech synthesisers often speak too much, have voices which are difficult to understand, or are able only to speak in lines rather than sentences, reproducing many words which are inflected and pronounced wrongly.

As technological developments continue, facilities such as speech synthesis and text enlargement are becoming integral parts of standard computer programs and in some circumstances the facilities of standard programs can be used instead of expensive alternatives. The rate of change in technological advances can itself cause additional difficulties. Updated versions of software may no longer be compatible with previous versions, or may require higher specification computers. The requirements of learning to operate different versions of facilities and commands places increasing demands on a child who may already have a steep learning curve to contend with.

Whatever type of IT is used, it will have to be tailored to the individual (Figure 27.1). The decision regarding suitable and appropriate equipment will depend upon an appropriate assessment, but may ultimately end in a compromise between the potential of the equipment and the needs of the child. Inevitably, the equipment bought to meet the needs of one child may not be suitable for use by another.

Figure 27.1

IT and the National Curriculum

In this section each of the key strands within the IT Orders of the National Curriculum is considered and specific areas of concern are highlighted.

Strand 1: opportunities to investigate IT

The basis of this strand is the exploration and examination of IT and its usage in everyday life.

The expectations teachers have of children with a visual impairment may differ from those they have of children who are fully sighted. The child with the visual impairment may, in fact, have a more diverse range of experiences with information technology than sighted peers. Everyday life for such children may require the use of a wide range of resources such as talking clocks and scales, or computers and microwaves with synthesised speech. Groenveld (1993) believes that children with a visual impairment are not children from whom something has been taken away, instead they have perceptions and experiences which are uniquely their own and which need to be shared and developed.

The National Curriculum provides opportunities for the successful integration of information technology devices employed by children with special needs. Closed circuit televisions (CCTVs) provide children with low vision with a means of accessing print, maps and diagrams; the use of such equipment in the learning environment also enables children who are fully sighted to benefit. Specialist adaptations such as Anglepoise copy holders, and large monitors, antiglare screens, large character keycaps are helpful for all children.

Strand 2: communicating and handling information

This strand is concerned with the various ways computers can be used to process and communicate ideas and information using textual and numerical data, graphical representation, pictures and sound.

For the child with a severe visual impairment, the ability to handle information is determined primarily by its presentation and accessibility. Textual and numerical information is most commonly accessed via speech synthesis and screen enhancement. The design of these environments determines the efficiency with which children are able to access a computer program.

Touch typing skills are essential for a child with a visual impairment where a QWERTY keyboard is being used to manipulate data. Time should be devoted to developing these skills at an early age to ensure that a computer is viewed as a natural aid to communication. Adapted keyboards can help meet individual needs. (Alternatives include braille or Dvorak or Maltron keyboards or keyboard overlays for children with reduced manual dexterity.) Keyboard skills allow the child to maintain a level of competence and independence and also enables packages with graphical user interfaces (GUI) which are specifically designed for use with the mouse, to be used effectively with keystrokes instead of the mouse pointer. This approach will go some way to helping those pupils who are unable to see the display icons and those who experience difficulties with spatial skills.

Word processing requires skills such as scanning, visual discrimination, hand–eye coordination and the mastery of simple navigational controls which allow the user to move around the text. Applications such as spreadsheets and databases also require students to understand more complex spatial concepts such as cells, columns, rows and fields, and cause and effect relationships.

A word processor can become an important aid for children who write very slowly or who have difficulty reading back their own writing. For the learner with any kind of visual impairment proof reading will be a laborious task and while the use of voice synthesis or enlarged text can be helpful, pupils need opportunities to employ these adaptations across the curriculum in order to consolidate them into their repertoire.

Programs such as word processors, spreadsheets and databases often have fast find functions (find, search or Goto facilities) which overcome difficulties with searching and skimming. Standard packages often allow changes in screen size and style of font, and spell checkers, while not a complete solution for pupils with reading, writing and spelling difficulties, have distinct advantages and can be used with voice synthesis. Other facilities may allow the insertion of borders to aid orientation on screen and the use of different colours to provide a visual separation between different functions or areas of the screen. While text enhancement involving justification, emboldening and changing type fonts, is not specifically prescribed by the National Curriculum, in examinations and in the workplace young people will often be required to create appropriate page displays.

The National Curriculum requires the use of graphs to communicate ideas and to display information. A person who is fully sighted derives information from a diagram at a glance; the diagram can be seen in its entirety and comparisons can be drawn quickly and easily. Children with a visual impairment may find even simple graphical representations (such as a bar graph or pie chart) to be inefficient methods of receiving or presenting information because they cannot easily achieve an overall view of the data. Alternative methods of presentation, such as lists or tables, are often more accessible. In deciding how to present information, the learning objective of the task is a vital consideration: is it to develop the skills needed to output information in pictorial format, or to present information in the most convenient format for the child?

The appropriateness of communicating ideas and information through pictures, for example by the use of painting packages, has to be addressed when working with children who have a visual impairment. Many packages which enable the creation or importation of graphics allow very limited access through speech synthesis. If screen magnification is used, perception of the whole picture may become difficult as the enlargement process may distort the image by breaking it into pixels: the higher the magnification, the more distorted the image becomes.

Equipment such as CD-ROMs allow access to vast amounts of text and information, but often contain graphics and video clips which are of little use to pupils with a visual impairment unless there is additional print/audio information to support them. For the same reason, the Internet, at the present stage of development, is not wholly accessible to all people with a visual impairment.

Strand 3: controlling and modelling, measurement and monitoring

Vision plays an important role in the development of spatial concepts. Some information such as an understanding of the position of the body in relation to the environment, and information about directions and distances, can be gained through senses other than vision. This strand of IT can provide children who are blind or have low vision with experience of spatial concepts.

Control can be implemented in three basic ways:

- switches which will involve navigating an object around a screen, for example, movement through a maze to reach a goal;
- tools such as a buffer box which allow the user to program a sequence of instructions to control models or devices;
- programmable robots such as a Roamer or a Pixie which move around the floor as instructed.

All three control techniques provide the opportunity to develop skills which are vital to the development of a child with a visual impairment. In this sense, IT employs many of the same skills used in physical education, mathematics and geography, and develops expertise required in areas of the special curriculum such as mobility and orientation.

However, this third strand of the Information Technology Orders tends to cause the most difficulty because it necessitates the purchase of additional specialist equipment (floor turtles, buffer boxes, input and output devices, monitoring and measuring equipment) and it also demands time for the in-service training of staff. Once the equipment is mastered however, only minor modifications or adaptations may be required to make it accessible to a child with a visual impairment, such as the addition of tactile markings or large print labels for identification, or perhaps the substitution of a buzzer for a lamp.

This strand also requires the use of models or simulations and the ability to generalise. Tobin (1994) suggests that children with a visual impairment are often poorer than their peers at activities which require them to make assumptions and generalisations because of their limited visual experiences.

Software often employs highly complex three-dimensional graphics to illustrate simulations and models. While these may provide an attractive and stimulating on-screen learning environment for the child who is fully sighted, such graphics can constitute an inaccessible and meaningless barrage of information to the child with a visual impairment. In such instances, the statement of access might acknowledge that the provision of non-sighted methods of acquiring information may be more appropriate.

The introduction of sound has made many applications accessible to pupils with a visual impairment, and has emphasised the role of listening skills as a 'critical avenue to learning' (Heinze 1986) especially with the use of digitised voice output in place of synthesised speech.

Access technology has also to be considered in the light of issues such as staff training, resources and environment. Training for both teaching and support staff is vital to ensure that access technology will be integrated into all areas of the curriculum. In fact, the Code of Practice (DfE 1994) states that schools should provide training in the use of appropriate technology for the child, his or her parents and staff, so that the pupil is able to use that technology across the curriculum at school and, wherever appropriate, at home.

Conclusion

Effective inclusion of a child with a visual impairment relies not only upon the provision of appropriate access and adaptive technology, differentiated to reflect individual learning needs and abilities, but also on the administration and day-to-day management of the learning environment. The development of the IT capability of the child across the curriculum takes place when there is:
- an effective school policy
- appropriate allocation of resources
- full assessment of the needs of individual pupils
- training for all members of staff.

Chapter 28
Music

Sally-Anne Zimmermann

Introduction

This chapter traces a path through the National Curriculum for Music for England and Wales, raising points about its implementation which are worthy of special attention when working with students who are visually impaired.

If students who are visually impaired are delighting and thriving in all the manifestations of musical education in and out of school, they will be participating on an equal footing in group activities which involve debating, planning, rehearsing, leading and being led, sharing and receiving. Music can promote self-confidence, nurture aspirations and give satisfaction, in solo and group work.

For most students for whom sound, not vision, is their main sense, music as a receptive medium provides a rich source of pleasure. However music is also an expressive medium which provides these students with opportunities for active creation, often at a standard which is at least the equal of their fully sighted peers.

Music plays a large part in most adults' lives. The vast majority are listeners but an increasing number are also performers and some are composers. The opportunities for employment in the arts and leisure field connected with music are extensive and vital to the country's economy. Yet little of this musical involvement can be directly attributed to the formal general music education of the UK. For children in school in the 1960s class music was probably a rather staid experience of singing and playing the recorder or xylophone. Those destined for music degrees acquired their skills by attending instrumental lessons at local Saturday music centres, while those respected by their classmates sneaked off to generate huge decibel levels with electric guitars and amps. For children in school in the 1970s and 1980s, class music was probably a rather unstructured time of group negotiations 'sharing' with the class jangles of sound that bore little relation to 'real' music. The advent of the National Curriculum has provided for the first time a common framework for school-based musical activities, to which all children are entitled. It is clear however that the development of musical skills begins in earliest childhood.

Early years

The babbling and cooing, jabbering and gurgling of infants who can see, is immediately appealing to adults who respond by repeating the child's sounds, smiling and making eye contact. The child takes the lead in this communication which is a key stage in the development of language. Infants who are visually impaired also need to enjoy these multi-sensory, sound-led activities, and adults need to be given reassurance that a lack of visual response does not mean that their children do not want to share in this intimacy of sounds (Nielsen 1992, Stern 1985).

The toys which very young children who are visually impaired use and love most are often ones that make exciting sounds. When selecting instruments and objects to stimulate a young child's sound sense, carers should consider what kind of sound they make and how that sound is controlled and varied. An untreated wooden shaker, a skin drum and a metal bell provide richer sound rewards and are more interesting to feel than many plastic instruments. Everyday objects such as kitchen utensils can provide early opportunities to develop and refine awareness of sound. Games which involve noting how the same toy makes different sounds in different rooms and parts of rooms, or activities which encourage children to reach out for the sound-source, can foster the development of skills essential for independent mobility and exploration beyond the immediate environment.

Even from an early age, children who are visually impaired can learn to manipulate cassette recorders, videos and more sophisticated technology. A posting-box tape recorder can give hours of listening pleasure while developing dexterity and fostering control over sound.

The first complications in music education may occur when the child who is visually impaired joins music sessions in the nursery and early years group. Sharing nursery rhymes and simple musical games is easier when the child can see the subtle visual clues which signal when to begin and to finish. Vision helps children to concentrate on music games by providing quick explanations for extraneous sounds of, say, the child crying in the corner and the traffic outside. However with some forethought musical solutions can be found to these problems. For example, musical cues, such as instrumental introductions and unsubtle slowing down at the end of pieces, sometimes give clues to the structure; verbal explanations of the causes of distracting sounds can help the child with a visual impairment to ignore them.

When percussion instruments are first introduced in the nursery, children who can see, often immediately deduce how they can be made to produce sound and even predict the kind of sound from the instrument's overall appearance. They will usually automatically decide on how to hold the instrument and if they are in any doubt as to effective ways of playing it, they can sneak a look at those around. A child who is blind will need time and help to explore an unfamiliar instrument, and should receive it early when the instruments are being distributed.

Teachers usually devise strategies for giving out instruments, perhaps rewarding those who are sitting straight by giving them instruments first but at the end of the lesson the collecting up of instruments is often a scramble. It can be bewildering to a child who is visually impaired when the instrument suddenly disappears without explanation as it is grabbed by a classmate. It makes sense to allow the child with a visual impairment to distribute and put the instruments away and learn where they are stored. This can provide an opportunity for exploring the range of instruments and making choices about what they would like to play.

Music at Key Stage 1

The National Curriculum in England and Wales requires pupils to control vocal and instrumental sounds, perform with others, compose and pass on their musical ideas, listen to different sorts of music and respond to the music they hear. This curriculum is fully accessible to pupils who are visually impaired, provided that they are confident about what is expected of them and have been set clear tasks. Students who are visually impaired often excel in the appreciation of the musical elements of pitch, duration, dynamics, tempo, timbre and texture. Their increased reliance on memorising event by event in time, can make it easier to grasp musical structure. Special considerations for children who are visually impaired will include attention to body posture in singing and playing. Musical tasks can be simplified at this stage for example unrequired notes might be taken off the glockenspiel or xylophone, with explanation. When playing these musical instruments one hand can be used for the beater while the other finds the notes to be struck.

At Key Stage 1, music is often presented through other curriculum areas. It is common for mood and character in music to be described by movement, for example. While this is a valid, exciting exercise, the child who is visually impaired is not able to rely on copying the most able children in the class which is the means that other children rely upon to achieve the subtle class standard. Work with partners involving holding hands and taking turns in copying the partner's actions can provide a creative solution to this challenge.

Interpreting symbols relating to sound through touch, or with reduced visual field or acuity, is going to differ from the instant and comprehensive looking by sighted peers. Where accessible scores are made to represent sounds, using raised shapes and different textures, for example, children who are visually impaired may need more time to explore them. The meaning they attach to the symbols may vary considerably from their peers. To perform from them, verbal description and memorising will usually be necessary, (see Ockelford 1996b).

Music at Key Stage 2

By Key Stage 2 singing is well established, and the National Curriculum encourages singing songs in parts. Rounds are particularly popular with children and often follow on easily from playground action songs. Rounds provide an easy introduction to harmony, and can help to tighten up on pitch and rhythm; a child who is visually impaired may need a physical prompt to know when to enter the song. At this stage, the curriculum orders stress the context of performance and seek to develop in students the skills required to communicate effectively with other performers and the audience. For a child who is visually impaired, getting onto the stage at the end-of-term concert, finding instruments and locating the other members of the group may be more stressful than the performance itself. Clear instructions about individual and whole class responsibilities and regular rehearsals can help overcome the fear of performance.

As composition becomes more independent and more sophisticated, reliance on group memory becomes risky and the need for reliable methods of recording musical ideas grows. A braille user might wish to jot down a few cues using a Perkins braille writer. For example pitches could be represented by braille letters. If rhythm is to be shown as well as pitch, the length of 'held notes' could be shown by cells of lowest case literary C (see Ockelford 1996b).

Markers on instruments can unobtrusively speed up the location of notes, for example, the middle C on keyboards might be marked with a piece of Velcro or with braille Dymo tape. Main function keys on keyboards, such as the volume control, can be similarly textured, and a quick reference card can be written in braille to explain the function of other keys.

Many children spend considerable time listening to music on tape or CD and the wish to find favourite tapes and tracks can be a motivator for the use of braille or print coding of the cassettes, discs and their containers, and can develop organisational skills in storing and locating their possessions at home or at school.

Music at Key Stage 3

Usually at age 11, children in England and Wales transfer to secondary education. The new school will have specialist music teachers and music will be a distinct lesson in the timetable, delivered in a separate music room.

During Year Seven the new children will perhaps start with work on rhythm and be given some tests to gauge musical experience and competence. At the beginning of most lessons, the whole class will work together. Formal musical notation is introduced, and class singing is regulated by many subtle gestures and facial expressions from the teacher who drifts or strides around the class. In this situation it can be difficult for the child who is visually impaired to display his or her gifts confidently.

The lesson may then move on to group work. The noise level increases and the student relying on hearing, may find the environment extremely confusing. Without visual cues, entering into a debate with colleagues is tricky; it is easy for the student who is visually impaired to take the extreme role of leader or of the most passive member, rather than playing an equal part in this rather artificial sharing of artistic creation currently favoured in education. Ironically, while peers may be scared most when it comes to sharing their efforts by performing to the rest of the class and to the tape recorder, this might be the easiest time for the student with a visual impairment, when all else is quiet and the plan for the next few minutes is clear.

At this stage the students who are visually impaired need to have music represented in appropriate symbols. Before adapting notation, teachers need to be clear about what symbols are required. If the rest of the class are studying duration and looking at the rhythmic elements of stave notation, it may only be necessary to present a braille user with the braille rhythm notation in the passage. If rhythm is represented in print by blocks of relative sizes, then a cubarithm board with cubes can be a useful alternative for the braillist. For a student who has low vision, it may be that the material presented on the white board for the whole class just needs to be ready in advance on a separate sheet of appropriately coloured paper. Suitable task lighting and a music stand for enlarged photocopies can also help to make the material accessible. When notating and recording compositions, groups can be encouraged to choose symbols that can be interpreted by everyone in the class; perhaps by presenting materials in bright colours. This might form the basis of a class discussion about the different ways music can be transcribed and the effect this might have on performance techniques.

The international system of braille music notation, invented by Louis Braille, presents stave notation in a code based on patterns of raised dots. Few people in this country use it, most learn the music that they play or sing by ear from tape. Reading staff notation is itself a very specialised skill. Few people can 'hear in their head' what they read from the page without some kind of sound clues. In print notation notes are recognised by their relative position on the stave with further instructions around these five lines. Notes and all other information in braille are presented sequentially in a single line. Instrumentalists who are blind need their hands to hold and play their instrument, so any tactile notation has to be memorised first. In the mainstream setting, no one else is likely to be using braille music so who is going to share this language? At present, it usually falls upon the specialist instrumental teacher to learn and teach braille music (Watson 1994).

Enlarging notation using a photocopier may help students who have low vision but music on A3 size paper easily becomes cumbersome and the enlarged gaps between symbols make the music more difficult to read. Small amounts of music may be written out by hand for the student or a computer notation package can be adapted to reduce the space between the enlarged symbols (Ockelford 1994a).

Increasing use is made of keyboards, computers and recording equipment at this key stage and issues of access arise for students who are visually impaired. Computers in many music departments may not be compatible with those used by students with a visual impairment, and even where they are, the adaptive software necessary for independent access may not be installed in the music room. That said, there is considerable interest in making music technology available for independent use by all people who are visually impaired from beginners to professionals. Currently, the most readily available source of information is on relevant World Wide Web (WWW) pages (Page 1995).

Music at Key Stage 4 and beyond

Special arrangements are made to enable candidates who are visually impaired to fulfil the examination requirements at General Certificate of Secondary Education (GCSE) and Standard Grade. Indeed, for students under pressure in other curriculum areas because of the time required to deal with written material, music can be a liberating option to select.

Coursework in both composing and performing can be wholly sound-based, with the necessary background information given on tape. In the final listening paper, most examination boards read the questions on to the tape and all boards allow extra time to respond. All boards permit the use of amanuenses. Alternatively, candidates may use braille, word processors or write answers by hand.

Only an elementary knowledge of staff notation is required of candidates at GCSE level, even though many will have already developed advanced skills in this area. Although it may seem surprising that knowledge of staff notation forms a very small part of the examination, it is worth remembering that very little of the world's music is notated and that much of the art of those musical cultures which do use notation is in the interpretation that lies beyond the written symbols.

For GCSE syllabuses which include a classical set work, piano reductions of the score and other modifications, such as annotation of specific passages with highlighter pen, may make otherwise inaccessible written material manageable.

A-level music examinations are also accessible to candidates who are visually impaired, although some mode of access to western classical scores is required for the history and harmony papers. Braille scores for a range of the works set for study are available from the RNIB. The International Baccalaureate is gaining popularity as an advanced examination in the UK because it puts more emphasis on direct listening and sound production than the current A-level syllabuses.

Extracurricular work in and out of school

It is often the non-statutory, non-timetabled activities that turn a school from a place of learning to a community. While the regular timetable for a student who is visually impaired can be extremely demanding and tiring, it would be wrong to deprive any student of the opportunity to join voluntary groups, and in most schools music groups form the backbone of this extracurricular activity.

Involving a child who is visually impaired in a recorder group (or any other instrumental group in the western tradition) might require extra effort from the tutor and some minor modifications to lesson delivery, such as establishing clear distinctions between experimental practice times and times when the group are meant to be playing altogether. Encouraging the student who is visually impaired to show the support teacher what he or she has learnt might be a positive way of checking on progress. Although the use of books of notation may feature at an early stage in these groups, most pupils learn by waiting to hear the piece and copying the most able in the group. Experience of working by ear might give the student who is visually impaired an advantage in playing in these circumstances.

When the music to be performed becomes too complex for casual memorisation, there are several possible strategies. Taping the music to be learnt is one route. Teachers usually introduce a new piece to the class by playing it through, phrase by phrase. The teacher might then sing the piece or particular ensemble line, naming the pitches and exaggerating any particular articulations such as slurs and dynamics. In either case the visually impaired student can record this part of the session on cassette and play it back later, pausing where necessary. The student might sing with the tape until the piece is memorised and then work with the instrument independently of the tape.

Another possibility is to provide students with staff notation and explanatory notes to accompany it. Alternatively Clearvision music books (where the original print text is visible and the braille equivalent produced on clear plastic alongside or over the top) can provide the opportunity for sighted and non-sighted students to work from the same material.

Not all popular musical ensemble activities require notation or require the lead of a silent conductor. The Caribbean steel pan has only been in existence for 50 years but its influence in schools in England in particular has been enormous. The art and craft of the steel band is completely aural (although European lack of trust in something undocumented has led to the introduction of a variety of pan notations). Gamelan orchestras are led by the drummer in league with the player of the largest gong. There are also genres of music in which, once a structure has been established, musicians improvise. Approaches which embrace a broader musical experience have often thrived in schools where the traditional curriculum has proved unsuccessful.

Instrumental teaching

Whether delivered through private lessons in out-of-school time or by visiting peripatetic specialists employed by the school, instrumental teaching is an established part of education in the UK. All instruments are suitable for students with visual impairments, although concern is sometimes expressed about the appropriateness of stringed instruments for braille users because of the possible harm to the sensitivity of the finger-tips. Happily this anxiety is unfounded because the area of the fingerpad used for braille reading is different from that used in either plucking or pressing down strings; the coarsening of skin on the finger pad would only interfere in extreme cases with braille reading. Most braille readers develop a slight callous on their fingertips through reading braille in the normal course of reading and this does not appear to affect their reading skills.

With some instruments, such as the violin, a pleasing sound is only going to be obtained if a player adopts the correct body posture and, particularly if the student is educationally blind, the teacher may wish to manipulate the student into the correct posture. Clearly teachers will need to explain what they want to achieve and obtain the student's permission before touching the student.

Conclusion

Music has been traditionally seen as a natural pursuit for people who are visually impaired. There are indeed singers and instrumentalists, who have achieved international fame in all genres. Many blind people around the world earn their living as musicians, but for most people who are visually impaired, playing or singing alone or with others is a most satisfying hobby, and a social skill which opens many social opportunities (Dykema 1986).

Chapter 29
Physical Education

Christine Arter and Kay Malin

Physical education (PE) is unique in the curriculum in that it focuses on the body and provides learning experiences in which bodily movement plays a significant part. Through a variety of enjoyable and creative activities it can develop physical competence and promote physical development in the areas of stamina, strength, suppleness and coordination. Children can work independently, with a partner, and in a group, and can develop skills of cooperation, communication, and teamwork. PE can initiate an awareness of the importance of a healthy lifestyle and the necessity to be active, lively and dynamic in order to keep fit and healthy. It also has an important part to play in the raising of self-esteem (Lawrence 1987).

PE allows pupils to develop their skills in a safe environment at their own speed, with adult support available when it is needed. It promotes skills of personal organisation and responsibility to others and allows for competition within regulated settings.

It is often argued that pupils with a visual impairment need to experience a wide range of activities to improve their health and fitness, since many pupils tend to lead passive lifestyles and have poor levels of fitness (Blessing *et al.* 1993, RNIB 1993). Scott (1982a) stresses the importance of PE in raising muscle tone and counteracting poor posture and obesity. It can also help to improve the coordination and spatial awareness necessary for success in mobility programmes.

PE can help to enrich a pupil's leisure through cultivating an understanding and enjoyment of sport as participants or spectators. Many visually impaired children or young people follow television and radio coverage of athletics, tennis, rugby and many other events and some regularly attend games and events. Unless children who are visually impaired have had the opportunity to try a variety of activities in their PE lessons at school, they may harbour basic misapprehensions about the nature of games. For example, children may listen to the rugby commentary on the radio and be able to discuss the game with friends afterwards; however, unless they have actually handled a rugby ball they may well think that it is round like other balls. Until they have used a rugby ball themselves they will be unfamiliar with the irregular way in which the ball bounces.

To share fully in events which capture the national imagination, such as track and field events in the Olympics, the child who is visually impaired will need some understanding of the equipment and terminology used in that sport. For example the pupil needs to explore the shape of a javelin, to discover what it is made of and how heavy it is, and to have the opportunity to learn how to propel it through the air. The same is true for putting the shot. The child needs to be aware of the weight, size and shape of the shot to understand the explosive energy that is needed to putt the shot into the air.

In ball games such as basketball what does it mean to start the game with a 'jump ball'? Unless it has been explained, the child may not understand the concept of a 'touch down' or of 'scoring a try' in rugby or taking a 'throw in' in soccer. Children with a visual impairment may need to be given information through practical experiences that children who are fully sighted will have learnt incidentally.

Even when children with a visual impairment are unable to achieve a high level of skill in a particular game, or are unable to participate in the full game situation, an understanding of the skills and practices involved is invaluable. Most activities can be adapted and developed without losing the competitive element which most children enjoy. At any level of participation a positive approach can ensure that pupils experience success and enjoyment and with the right opportunities some children who are visually impaired will realise the highest standards of achievement in sport.

Basic principles

Safety

The National Curriculum (DfE 1995a) in the section covering general requirements, addresses safety issues in physical education. It is stated that to ensure safe practice, pupils should be taught:

- to respond readily to instructions;
- to recognise and follow relevant rules, laws, codes, etiquette and safety procedures for different activities or events, in practice and during competition;
- about the safety risks of wearing inappropriate clothing, footwear and jewellery, and why particular clothing, footwear and protection are worn for different activities;
- how to lift, carry, place and use equipment safely;
- to warm up and recover from exercise.

Teachers are reminded that:

Many activities in physical education are, by their very nature, potentially hazardous. They offer opportunities to challenge children's skill, initiative, and courage and therein lies part of their appeal and value. Children learn new skills and ways of moving in new environments, and learn to make judgements to avoid or cope with colliding, falling or stumbling.

Although it is teachers who are ultimately responsible for those in their charge, it should be their aim to make children increasingly aware of safety and of the need to minimise risks so that pupils can become responsible for their own safety and that of others. (Department of Education and Science (DES) 1981)

Safety considerations are vitally important when teaching PE to all children. When working with pupils who are visually impaired, teachers and support assistants need to take account of additional factors.

The child needs to be made aware of the dimensions of the space in which they are working and if necessary should be given the opportunity to explore the area before lessons commence. This will help to increase the child's confidence.

Teachers working with pupils who are visually impaired should address pupils by name and give clear instructions, and should use their voice to keep contact with the pupil, offering regular encouragement and explanations about what is happening (Walker 1992). Vague instructions such as 'stand over there' or 'near that line' can serve only to confuse the pupil with a visual impairment. Instructions need to be precise, for example 'take three steps to your left' (Wood 1985). It may be helpful to liaise with other professionals such as the child's mobility officer to ensure that appropriate, uniform language is used when teaching movement-related activities.

While some pupils with a visual impairment are diffident in PE, others may be over-confident and may be unaware of possible dangers. For example if they climb apparatus without fear, it may simply be because they are unaware how high they have climbed and of the consequences of a fall.

The teacher needs access to clear information about children's eye conditions and other medical circumstances (Walker 1992). In some eye conditions such as Marfan's syndrome, or high myopia (see Chapter 5) there is a danger that a collision will detach the retina. Medical advice should be sought about the degree of risk. Some children must take care to avoid knocks to the head and are advised for example, not to dive in the pool when swimming. It may be necessary for some children to wear a protective helmet, in addition to the usual protective equipment. It is important, however, to avoid, wherever possible, making the child feel exceptional or different. This will become more of a dilemma at the secondary school. The teacher will also need information about other medical conditions, such as heart defects, where the child must avoid over exertion. Some children may have a range of disabilities attached to a particular syndrome. The teacher needs to know whether the child's eye condition fluctuates; in some cases the child's vision may vary from day to day. The child too needs to take some responsibility for their own learning. They should be encouraged to inform teachers of difficulties they are experiencing and to say that although they were able to see a marker in the PE lesson last week, they are not able to see it today.

Teachers need some general guidance about children who wear spectacles. Often children will choose not to wear their glasses for certain activities such as gymnastics, where they may be a hindrance and of limited use. In other activities such as jogging, the child may find that the wearing of glasses is beneficial. Usually children are able to make a sensible judgement about when to wear their spectacles, but the school medical officer should be consulted if there is doubt.

In the final analysis, it is the duty of the teacher to ensure that they have all the relevant and most up-to-date information to safeguard the well-being of their pupils (BAALPE 1995).

The environment

The teacher of students who have visual impairments will need to be made aware of the way in which the environment can affect their pupils' performance. For example the teacher must be mindful that inappropriate lighting levels, or the sun shining on to a highly polished hall or gym floor, may result in uncomfortable or even painful glare for the child who is photophobic.

Similarly when working outside in the playground the child with photophobia may find it difficult to work in full sunlight, and may be unable to locate the teacher, the equipment or the other children in the class. The playground surface itself may reflect sunlight and make it difficult for the child to hit or to receive a ball. Wherever possible, the shaded areas of the playground or playing field should be used. The children should be placed so that they stand with their backs to the sun or strong light sources such as floodlights.

Adaptation of equipment

Some specialist apparatus such as balls containing bells or bleepers can be purchased from suppliers such as the RNIB, but standard equipment can often be easily adapted. For example shot can be inserted into footballs through the valve to make them audible to a pupil with a visual impairment, and sometimes a local sports shop can be persuaded to adapt footballs in this way. Bells can also be pushed into airflow balls of various sizes to make them appropriate for pupils.

Brightly coloured tape or stickers can be added to equipment to ensure that it will standout against the background. For example bright tape may be added to skittles or cones make them more clearly visible.

Coloured rubber spots on the floor can define a pathway or a starting position and because they are flush to the floor they are therefore much safer to use than hoops, which can fly up or slide if trodden on accidentally. Judicious use of contrast can also make help to make the environment more accessible. Light mats can be used on dark floors to define areas and dark lines on a light surface can make playing areas clearly visible.

Simple modifications can also be made to implements. For example hockey sticks can be marked with Velcro denoting where the handle should be held to maintain a correct grip. A mark on the top of handle can help children to check quickly that the face of the stick is correctly positioned.

Hitting a ball hard and true can bring enormous satisfaction. Children with low vision can often achieve an accurate strike with a ball that is larger than the regulation size and brightly coloured. Children who are blind can participate in team games such as rounders, softball or base ball with the use of a ball stand. A ball stand is made from a piece of tubular rubber on a rigid rubber stand, and can be adjusted to suit the height of any child (see Figure 29.1). The ball stand can be used to teach the correct action for striking a ball with a bat. The child needs to be shown how to transfer body weight from the back to the front foot as the arm swings through to add momentum to the striking action. The child can place their own ball on the stand, at a distance to suit their own swing, and can then hit the ball from the top of the stand.

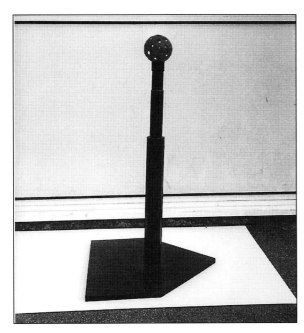

Figure 29.1

Equipment will almost invariably need modification to make it user friendly for the beginner who is visually impaired. For example hurdling-type activities can be practised using sponge or rope barriers to prevent the pupil from banging their knees or shins. They may be used with the younger child to develop rhythmic jumping movements to promote good coordination. Lightweight high-jump bars and crash mats for landing also make jumping activities very enjoyable.

Gymnastics

In gymnastic activities too, the use of colour, texture and contrast can be exploited to the advantage of children with a visual impairment. Gymnastic tables for example are now available with padded tops in a variety of colours and textures.

Bar boxes can be marked with coloured tape so that each individual bar can be readily identified. The edges of wooden benches can be painted to help pupils with poor figure/ground perception to define the edge of the bench in relation to the gym floor (Figure 29.2). Bright yellow or white markings have been found to be successful in this context.

Clear, high-contrast marking on walls can be useful in aiming games, and a contrasting colour behind the wall bars will help pupils to locate rungs and is particularly helpful if the rungs are unevenly spaced.

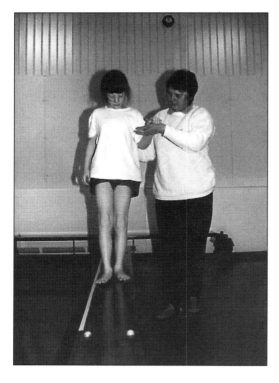

Figure 29.2

It is recommended that pupils are allowed to explore gymnastic apparatus in advance of a set task. If more than one piece of apparatus is used (Figure 29.3), for example if a mat, box and bench are to be linked together for use in a sequence, it is important to ensure that the child can identify starting and finishing points and can anticipate the sequence.

Equipment needs to be stored carefully so that the child can gain easy access to it and help put it away at the end of the lesson. Lightweight modern gymnastics equipment makes it possible even for primary age children to set out equipment (BAALPE 1995). Routines encouraging careful tidying away of equipment should be taught, so that items of equipment are not left out where they might prove a hazard to other pupils, particularly those with a visual impairment (RNIB 1993).

Athletics

Children with a visual impairment can participate safely in athletics provided standard safety procedures are followed. For example when practising throwing events such as the javelin or the shot, the following rules should be enforced:

- allow a clear time gap so that the first participant is clear before the next child takes their turn;
- throw from behind a line or a rope on ground;

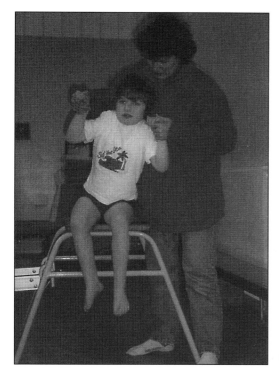

Figure 29.3

- all throw in the same direction;
- throw one at a time;
- only collect equipment when instructed to do so by the teacher and then return behind the line;
- keep responsibility for your own equipment;

Special care must be taken to ensure that pupils with a visual impairment both understand and observe the rules for safety that apply in all events in athletics.

The teacher will need to be aware of the additional potential hazards that face pupils with a visual impairment who could for example, easily injure themselves by running into a javelin angled into the ground.

Games

In games which involve the use of bats, sticks or racquets, the teacher will need to explain safety issues clearly and specifically, and should ensure that the child understands the need for clear space before swinging the bat.

Scott (1982a) states that games involving a moving ball are difficult for pupils with a visual impairment, and Bishop (1971) suggests that individual games are more appropriate than team games for these children. However the writers feel that with appropriate assistance, children with visual impairment can participate successfully in team games.

Most children for example could participate in rounders with the use of a ball stand, a ball which is large, brightly coloured and audible and a runner who runs with the child when the child scores.

None of these suggested adaptations would have any detrimental affect on the enjoyment of the players who are fully sighted. Cricketers who are visually impaired participate regularly in their sport in well established national league competitions. Other sports such as golf and five-a-side football also have internationally recognised codes to enable sports people who are visually impaired to participate.

Goalball is an interactive, recreational ball game for children and adults with a visual impairment which is played in many schools around the world. Fully sighted and visually impaired players can enjoy the game together and are able to compete on an equal basis since all participants wear eyeshades. The court is approximately the size of a volleyball court and is marked with tactile line markings. Goals are the full width of the court. A ball with a bell is used, approximately the size of a basketball but heavier and with less bounce. There are three players in each team, who wear hip, elbow and knee pads. Players start the game in a V formation, and the ball must be rolled across the surface of the court. The object of the game is to score the maximum number of goals in a seven minute period. (For further details of associations which provide sports, outdoor and adventure activities for people who are visually impaired see Chapter 31.)

Schools are usually able to offer pupils in Years 10 and 11 a wide choice of activities such as trampolining, ice and roller skating and running. Sports such as these may be enjoyed throughout life and will help to maintain high levels of fitness (Department of National Heritage 1995). They may also enhance social opportunities as pupils get older (Scott 1982a).

Swimming

The PE National Curriculum requires that children should be able to swim 25 metres unaided at Key Stage 2. Swimming is an excellent sport for children with a visual impairment because it helps to develop strength and stamina (Chapman and Stone 1988).

In mainstream education, pupils often have limited opportunities to swim on a regular basis. Children with a visual impairment are likely to need frequent tuition which provides individual instruction to model stroke techniques. For this reason many special schools for the visually impaired have their own swimming pools and afford pupils the chance for regular swimming lessons and recreational swimming. Children with a visual impairment in mainstream schools may need to join a local swimming club or attend regular lessons in the local pool.

Safety considerations are of paramount importance in this area of the curriculum. It is essential that a qualified swimming instructor has an overview from the side of the pool, and is able to watch of all of the group or class. Some local education authorities insist that both 'spotters' at the pool side and those teaching swimming, are fully qualified swimming instructors. If the child with a visual impairment is part of a large mainstream class, it may be advisable for an additional instructor to be given sole responsibility to watch over that pupil, particularly if the pupil has additional disabilities. The area of the pool in which the pupil is working needs to be clearly defined with markers, and lane markers might be necessary. Those pupils lacking in confidence may need one-to-one support in the water, as well as buoyancy aids. Children with a visual impairment will need to understand the layout and dimensions of the pool and should have the opportunity to work and play in confidence in a controlled environment.

Dance

Children who can see, watch and copy others, and learn to refine their own movements by observation (Scholl 1986). Pupils with a visual impairment may need individual help to build and model their movements. Listening to a teacher 'talking through' a movement can be a baffling experience for a child with a visual impairment. The instruction 'stretch into a star shape' may mean absolutely nothing in terms of body shape to a child who is visually impaired. When a teacher or support assistant uses a 'hands on' approach to help a child work through a particular movement, they must first obtain the child's consent and explain what they are going to do before touching the child. Younger children are usually happy with this teaching method, but the adult needs to know the older child well to use this approach to help the child to adopt the correct body position.

The use of music often enhances the enjoyment of dance. It can be used to create a mood, explore feelings and to build a relationship between children in a group or partner situation. The voice may also be used in an expressive way to help to extend the child's movement vocabulary. The way in which a word is pronounced may aid understanding, for example, 's-t-r-e-t-c-h' or 's-l-o-w-l-y'.

Dance can help a child's spatial awareness but again clear explanations about the 'shape' of the dance, where other children in the group are, and what they are doing are vital. The teacher's voice link with the child is essential in this type of activity.

Assessment

The end of Key Stage descriptions (DfE 1995a) can be used as guidelines for assessment, and should be considered in relation to games, gymnastic activities and dance at Key Stage 1. At Key Stage 2 the six listed areas comprise games, gymnastic activities, dance, athletic activities, outdoor and adventurous activities and swimming. The teacher should consider what the pupils know, what they understand and what are they able to do. Gathering this information can be time consuming, but it is essential in order to inform future teaching and thus to ensure progression.

Schemes of work should be designed to build upon the child's acquisition of skills and techniques, their body awareness, movement vocabulary and their understanding of the specific activities set for each key stage. Safety aspects can be incorporated into the scheme of work and aspects of health and fitness should also be included in each unit. Opportunities for cross-curricular work abound in this area and the PE curriculum can be easily linked to other work on health, diet and how the body works.

Conclusion

> Sport can provide lessons for life which young people are unlikely to learn so well in any other way. Lessons like team spirit, good sportsmanship, playing within rules, self-discipline, and dedication will stand them in good stead whatever their future holds. (Department of National Heritage 1995)

The implementation of a balanced PE programme for pupils with a visual impairment may not be easy to achieve, but pupils should have opportunities and access appropriate to their own abilities, difficulties and attitudes (DES 1991).

Useful addresses

British Blind Sport (BBS), Director, 67 Albert Street, Rugby, Warwickshire CV21 2SN. Tel: 01788 536142. BBS produce a magazine entitled *Target*.
British Blind Sport Goalball Subcommittee, Roger Clifton, 54 Hatherley Road, London E17 6SF.
RNIB Leisure Service Sports Information Packs. RNIB Leisure Service, 224 Great Portland Street, London W1N 6AA.

Chapter 30
Art and Design

Miranda and Colin Brookes

Introduction

The purpose of this chapter is to consider the properties of art which are of particular relevance to young people with a visual impairment and how they can gain access to them. Art in the National Curriculum 'is to be interpreted as "art, craft and design" throughout' (Department for Education (Dfe) 1995b) and includes '...drawing, painting, printmaking, photography, sculpture, ceramics, textiles, graphic design [and] architecture'.

Generally, this chapter will seek to show how art can help to develop attitudes, perceptual sensitivities, understanding and skills which can enrich many aspects of life. As the majority of young people with a visual impairment are taught in integrated settings there will be an emphasis on showing how art can be taught successfully to young children with a visual impairment within the whole class setting.

The first section deals with practical considerations for teachers. The second section addresses some theoretical considerations as we seek to clarify the values and purposes associated with art education for pupils with a visual impairment. Following this, aspects of artistic development and visual impairment are considered and finally, reference is made to accessibility to art education through language. These theoretical considerations will be summarised in three tables, accompanied by brief explanations.

Practical considerations

Health and safety

Health and safety considerations are crucial and obviously local authority guidelines must be adhered to in the use of all specialist materials, tools and processes. Clear, detailed, sequenced instructions supported by a demonstration (preferably hand over hand) are required to enable a young person with a visual impairment to use the wide range of equipment safely.

The classroom environment

In many subjects, and art is no exception, the practical considerations of the learning environment initially seem to dominate. All pupils need to be fully aware of how the room and its contents are organised and laid out, and those arrangements should remain reasonably constant to aid orientation and allow safe mobility.

In art, as in other practical subjects, there is a need for additional time to enable young people with visual impairment to access, understand and then apply the necessary skills to the task, but the acquisition of these technical skills can sometimes dominate the learning process. Task analysis can enable a balance to be achieved between learning to use materials and tools correctly and understanding art concepts. Some tasks, for example accurate measuring, may take a disproportionate amount of time for a student with a visual impairment. However, once a level of competence has been achieved in measuring, then pre-cut labelled lengths of dowel can be used as 'unit rulers', enabling the student to spend more time on other areas of a task.

Resources

Physical

The learning environment can be made stimulating for all the children in the class through displays of a broad range of reference materials, artefacts and artworks. Natural objects, manufactured objects designed for a range of functions, and materials from a variety of cultures can be put on display within easy reach so that students with visual impairments can touch and explore the displays independently. Shelves should be clearly labelled (in braille or print in appropriate sizes and fonts) and two-dimensional work should be displayed at eye level, and mounted on a contrasting coloured background whenever possible.

Reference material for art might also include books, photographs in black and white or colour, prints and pictures. These can be accessed with low vision devices, and together with television and video can provide opportunities to study areas that may be difficult to access at first hand.

Information technology

A desktop computer with Internet and CD-ROM facilities enables students to 'tour' galleries around the world and receive an almost infinite range of information. An increasing number of CD-ROMs are available on both individual artists and galleries. These are often interactive and have facilities for detailed enlargement and speech. For example, the Michelangelo (EMME Interactive) CD-ROM allows students to appreciate the artist's life and work in the context of the events at that time. There are numerous colour photographs from all over the world of Michelangelo's art, and his major works are analysed with reference to his achievements in the arts. The CD-ROM includes speech, music, videos and puzzles to engage and challenge the student.

Computer aided art and design (CAAD) is a generic term sometimes used to describe the visual images which can be created on computer. Various open-ended paint programmes and scanned image transfer facilities are available (Mathieson 1993). Images or designs can be created on the screen and transferred to other materials and processes.

The software can enhance the scale, detail and contrast of the design to increase access. For some young people with a visual impairment, manipulating a keyboard and 'mouse' may be easier and more appropriate than using traditional art materials. The National Council for Educational Technology (NCET; address at the end of this chapter) will give help and advice, especially in the area of software.

Specialist resources

There are a broad range of approaches which enable people with a visual impairment to gain an understanding of paintings and sculptures. Although their relevance is often difficult to assess, tactile diagrams produced through a vacuum-forming process are potentially useful. Some representations of artworks are available with accompanying tape descriptions from The Living Paintings Trust (address at the end of this chapter), and there is currently a project to make this resource more accessible and suitable for children. The paintings are represented using a bas-relief technique with a raised edge but young people who are visually impaired will need extensive experience with tactile diagrams before they can make sense of these depictions.

Raised drawings which are based on visual conventions such as perspective, or which depict scenes unrelated to a child's experience can be potentially confusing. An example of this would be a depiction of a Victorian street scene with terraced houses going into the distance. To a child who is blind the houses may simply appear to get narrower and smaller for no apparent reason. Another confusing convention is the use of symbols, for example a 'V' shape for a flying bird.

It may sometimes be more appropriate to use a three-dimensional model to clarify the relationship between the various features in a design. For example when describing, within the Diwali story, the journey of Ramu and Sita into the forest, it is possible for the young people to appreciate that the key figures are always depicted larger than less significant figures or features, regardless of their location. The pupils can then begin to understand that perspective is a Western convention and that it is not necessarily applied in art throughout the world. In addition they can appreciate the importance of art as a story telling device.

A wide variety of materials need to be available and accessible to ensure that an appropriate approach or technique is available to every child. An extensive selection of papers, card and fabric, model making equipment such as wire, wood (especially dowel and balsa), clay, stone and plaster (including Modroc) can enable a young person to appreciate the vast range of qualities available and build up their own vocabulary of techniques and approaches.

Various implements are available to enable a young person who is blind to draw raised lines. For example a special plastic, known as 'german film' produces a raised line when a pointed implement is drawn across it. Sheets of german film are available from the RNIB. The RNIB also sells spur wheels which produce raised lines of various heights and textures when drawn across manila paper. Some children prefer to draw using a pencil; their designs can then be etched from the reverse using a tracing wheel, or raised with a Minolta machine (see Chapter 18). Tactile reference points can help children maintain a mental image of the proportion or composition of a picture. For example, when a child is drawing a face, they can be encouraged to feel their own faces and appreciate where the eyes are positioned in relation, say, to the top of the ears. By orientating the individual features, the whole begins to take shape and make sense to the children.

Low vision devices, such as colour closed circuit televisions, and appropriate environmental and task lighting can enable some children with small amounts of residual vision to see colours and other details. Colour enhancement through overlays can also help some young people to appreciate an image.

Social resources

The most stimulating resource available in an art room is often other students. The discussions of their work between the young people can offer insights and understanding of concepts within an atmosphere of trust and openness that may not be available to the same extent in other disciplines. Students with a visual impairment need to know who else is in the room and what they are doing, so that they can participate in the sharing of ideas and approaches that can inform, enlighten and delight.

Public resources

Visits to galleries, museums and other places where original artworks can be accessed are essential resources. These are especially useful when young people are able to touch and explore the exhibits, and some galleries have specific collections that can be handled by visitors. For example, New Walk Museum in Leicester has a range of 'handleable' examples of painting, sculpture and costume design which inform students about the skills, processes and approaches involved in their production.

'Artists in residence' schemes often enable pupils to work alongside, or with, professional artists and can offer wonderful opportunities for understanding some of the wider implications of art. Artists who are funded by local arts associations and councils will often make visits to schools on request.

Theoretical considerations

Values and purposes associated with art education

Broadly, the justifications for art education can be separated into the 'instrumental' and the 'intrinsic'; Eisner (1972) described these respectively as 'contextualist' and 'essentialist' justifications. The 'instrumental' approach justifies Art Education in terms of the benefits it can provide for individuals such as assisting their general development, or for its therapeutic effects. In this case the product is of secondary importance. The second of these justifications emphasises the 'intrinsic' value of art, irrespective of what other purposes it can be said to serve.

The values and purposes for art implicit in the programmes of study in the National

Curriculum (DfE 1995b) could be said to include both intrinsic and extrinsic justifications and include:

- The development of visual perception
- Creative, imaginative and practical skills
- The expression of ideas and feelings
- The ability to record observations
- Visual literacy...[responsiveness]...to ideas, feelings and meanings communicated in visual form
- An appreciation of tactile elements, including...[formal elements of design] ...images...and artefacts.

In order to make National Curriculum Art more accessible and relevant to young people with a visual impairment, a number of the values and purposes suggested immediately above need to be re-interpreted.

For example 'the development of visual perception' needs to be interpreted in a broader sense to include the range of senses other than vision through which art can be experienced. 'Visual literacy' needs to be considered as 'perceptual literacy' in which the young person with a visual impairment can appreciate the significance and meaning in artworks through the interactive engagement of all their perceptual systems.

Young people with visual impairments should not be excluded from the opportunities of the subject because National Curriculum Art happens to have a restrictive emphasis on the visual.

Table 30.1 Nature of the perceptual ranges that may potentially be directed toward phenomena including art

Potential interactive perceptual range	Direction of attention
Orientational – locating	Relative body position, direction, scale, motion/stillness by reference to experience of forces of gravity and inertia, muscular position – weight, acceleration and deceleration...
Visual – seeing	Light, direct from various sources and reflected: its intensity, structure, duration and colour (including the reflected light structure of patterns, images and lettering)...
Tactile – touching/grasping/ feeling	Surface qualities, textures, 'patterned' arrangements (including braille), temperature, conductivity, hardness and resistance, softness, solidity, plasticity, pliability Quality of surrounding features off atmosphere, e.g. clammy, damp, dry, etc...
Oral/auditory – hearing and speaking	All features of sound; language, heard and spoken...
Olfactory – smelling	Odorous qualities

The content and form of this table are based on and modified from the table of perceptual systems in J. Gibson (1996) *The Senses Considered as Perceptual Systems*. Westport, Connecticut: Greenwood Press, p. 50

The perception of art

The concept of 'perceptual systems' (Gibson 1966) provides a valuable and extensive basis for reflecting on the perception of art which is particularly, although not exclusively, applicable to young people who are visually impaired. One of the extraordinary qualities that art possesses is the range of ways in which it can be perceived. Table 30.1 summarises the information that can be derived from each perceptual system.

Figure 30.1

Figures 30.1 and 30.2 show a child who is blind using a range of perceptual systems to explore a copy of an Etruscan sculpture of a horse. In Gibson's analysis, the significant features of the sculpture that the child is drawn to will include the following.

- Orientational: the scale, weight and comparative position of the horse's body parts.
- Tactile: the temperature, hardness, surface qualities such as ridges and indentations including patterned indentations, vibration when the surface is tapped.
- Auditory: the particular resonance of bronze.
- Oral: the language used to describe perceived features of the sculpture through a 'commentary' on their qualities. This information enables us to appreciate some of the qualities of the materials involved as well as their sculptured form.
- Olfactory: the smell of oxidising bronze. The aromas that are especially a part of the physical and material properties of art can provide a vivid source for enhancing the experience of art. For example, the distinctive smell of paint or clay, of paintings and sculptures including environmental and land art, or the odorous aura of interiors of architecture, such as galleries and cathedrals.

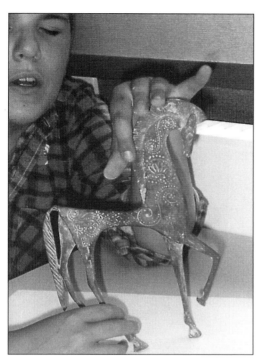

Figure 30.2

The properties of art

The child's involvement with the sculpture of the horse can also be analysed from another perspective which would seek to define the experience in terms of a theory of the properties of art. For further information on this approach see Burgin (1986), Brookes (1992), Hanfling (1992), Marcuse (1978), Osborn (1978), Sheppard (1987) and Weitz (1966). Table 30.2 summarises some of the main theories of art and the properties that they elaborate.

The properties of art that were explored can be grouped as follows.

- *Imitational:* the representation of the horse and its components (head, neck, mane, body, legs, hooves, and so on).
- *Expressive/emotional:* the affective response to the elements of the horse which are emphasised; for example the strength of the limbs, in itself and in comparison with the delicacy of the head and the tension given by the mane.
- *Formal:* the 'extended' flatness of the sculpture and patterned treatment of the surface.
- *Aesthetic:* engagement with the qualities and style of the artwork; its possible meanings and significance in 'art, myths and legends'.

Figure 30.3 shows the same copy of an Etruscan horse during a 'hand over hand' demonstration supported by clear, sequenced instructions.

Figure 30.4 shows how a range of perceptual systems were used when the same child was asked to design a garden and produce a model of it in clay. The significant features included the following.

Table 30.2   Theories of art and properties entailed

Theories of art	Aspects of art which are emphasised	Material and physical properties of art
Imitational	Mimetic, representing, standing for or symbolic of some thing, narrative or event – actual, imagined, ideal, spiritual ...	Materials Tools and equipment Processes: how made generally Technique: how made in particular
Expressivist/emotional	States of feeling 'expressed' or conveyed by/through artworks and experienced by perceivers...	All made to function as media in the production of art
Formal	Elements of design – mass, shape, colour, tonality, surface qualities, texture ... and their treatment via media	
Functional	Utilitarian, practical purposes; serving 'functions'	
Art and its 'aesthetic dimension'	Non-practical considerations – interest in/attention to/ engagement with quality, form, style, meaning, etc. and significance of artworks for their own sake ...	
Art as an 'open concept'	Art as 'dynamic' and changing over time with cultures – not constant or fixed but creative and persistently challenging...	

- *Orientational:* the scale, weight and location of the plants, stones and clay within the 'garden'. The 'garden' was arranged with a view to making areas of sunshine and shade, through the position of plants and seating.
- *Tactile:* the surface qualities of the plants, stones and clay, their organisation and arrangement.
- *Auditory:* the sound (rustle) of the plants when moved, this included the contrast between the various seed heads and leaves.
- *Oral:* the child's description of perceived features.
- *Olfactory:* the plants were chosen for their odorous qualities.

The range of materials, tools, processes and techniques which were used in the

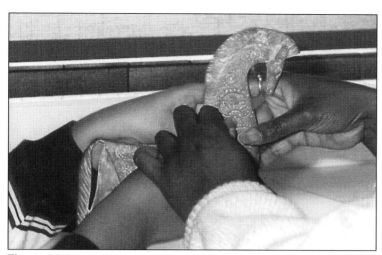

Figure 30.3

production of the artwork (refer to Table 30.2) included:

- *Materials:* clay, stones, and plants.
- *Tools:* scissors and a skewer were used to cut and position the plants, a knife and wooden pottery tool were used to sculpt the clay.
- *Processes:* various construction processes were employed.
- *Techniques:* included building and joining clay, as well as fixing a range of materials into different surfaces.

Figure 30.4

Artistic development and visual impairment

Assumptions about learning apparent in the Art National Curriculum document (see 'Programmes of Study for Key Stages' and 'End of Key Stage Descriptions'; DfE 1995b) seem to based on the notion that through learning, individuals move towards an increasingly conscious and purposeful approach to art. In this growing consciousness and critical engagement, they are expected to develop and refine practical skills, knowledge and understanding, and become more able to account for their production of and responses to art.

Many accounts of general artistic and aesthetic development have focused on the visual element in perception and its relationship to cognition, emotion, or 'affect', and moral development, within social and cultural contexts (Warren 1984). Examples of such accounts would include Cox (1992), Gardner and Perkins (1989), Levi and Smith (1991) Parsons (1987) and Thomas and Silk (1990). In an account of artistic development in people who are visually impaired, Blagden and Everett (1992) emphasised the significance of the 'conceptual' in both explaining approaches to teaching and in interpreting the work of their students. When the degree of attention normally given to the 'visual' aspect of artistic development is extended to all perceptual systems, new valuable insights become apparent.

Perceptual development provides a basis for aesthetic development and an increasing capacity to discriminate properties of art. In all perceptual systems, this would involve moving from the simple and unitary to the complex and multiple. Such developing capacities will influence the development of practical, manipulative skills in making and investigating (Attainment Target (AT) 1) as well as in knowledge and understanding (AT2).

To teach art to a person with visual impairment is to help them actively to build as highly differentiated perceptions as their interactively operating perceptual systems will allow.

Art education and language

Art criticism often entails the following phases: description, analysis, interpretation and evaluation (see Smith, 1968). These phases comprise a coherent approach to criticism which has been used successfully in art education for some time. Talking and writing about art and its properties helps to establish and refine the concepts which help to inform perception. The phases can be summarised as follows:
- 'Description' involves relating what is 'perceived' in as open and unprejudiced a way as can be managed. A kind of 'inventory' or list is made to 'register' the objects, features and properties to which attention has been drawn.
- Following description, 'analysis' entails efforts to discern relationships, connections and interactions between and among the features and properties described.

- 'Interpretation' is concerned with attributing meaning and significance to that which has been described and analysed, with a view to gaining and/or refining understanding.

Throughout these three stages the idea of postponing judgement is implicit, and this allows the observer to remain open to potentially valuable and insightful alternative interpretations.

Lastly, 'evaluation' involves making judgements about the quality and significance of the object(s).

Table 30.3 seeks to synthesise the theoretical considerations outlined in this chapter, which can provide a structure for the teaching and learning of art in the National Curriculum for all pupils including those who have visual impairments. It can be used as a path to plan activities and as a checklist to monitor them.

Table 30.3 Summary: perceptual range that may potentially be directed toward phenomena and art; theories of art and properties emphasised; material and physical properties; access through language; art attainment targets in the National Curriculum (NC)

Potential interactive perceptual range	Theories of art and properties	Material and physical properties of art	Access through language	Art NC attainment targets
Orientational – locating	Imitational	Materials Tools and Equipment	Description Analysis	Attainment Target 1: investigating and making
Visual – seeing	Expressivist/Emotional Formal	Processes	Interpretation	Attainment Target 2: Knowledge and understanding
Tactile -touching/ grasping/feeling	Functional	Techniques All as media	Evaluation	
Oral /Auditory – speaking and listening	Art and its 'Aesthetic Dimension'			
Olfactory – smelling	Art as an 'Open Concept'			

This table can be used to help to structure teaching and learning in the Art National Curriculum for *all* pupils and especially young people who are visually impaired. It can be used as a path and/or checklist by moving through the content of the five columns.

Conclusion

It is naive to suggest that art is an exclusively visual subject, despite the emphasis in the National Curriculum. The 'artworld' (Dickie 1974) and its audience have much benefit to gain from those whose perceptions of the world and artworks do not necessarily emphasise visual properties. The very 'openness' of art presents possibilities for pupils with a visual impairment and their teachers which need to be realised and pursued; access to the Art National Curriculum is but a starting point.

For additional information and advice on the teaching of art, public examination bodies and exhibitions, please contact ADVISE (Art and Design Visual Impairment Special Education; address below).

Useful addresses

ADVISE (Art and Design Visual Impairment Special Education) – c/o Education Officer, RNIB.

Living Paintings Trust, Queen Isabelle House, Unit 8, Kingsclere Park, Kingsclere, Newbury, Berkshire RG 20 4SW.

NCET (National Council for Educational Technology), Milburn High Road, Science Park, Coventry CV4 7JJ.

Tel: 01203 416994; email (Enquiry desk@ncet.org.uk).

Chapter 31

Extracurricular Activities

Angela Beech and Brian McManus

Introduction

By school age, children with visual impairments are often developmentally several years behind their peers who are fully sighted, in walking, running and playing.

No child's educational needs are entirely met by the school curriculum. Most schools realise this and provide a variety of extracurricular experiences which can be either structured or unstructured. The opportunities that children with visual impairment have for spontaneous involvement in community life, such as the chance to play freely in the garden or street with a group, or to run down to the local playing fields and watch others, may be stifled (Wood 1979).

Given the appropriate encouragement and assistance, 'there is no type of extracurricular activity, whether it be sailing around the world or going across town to the movies, that cannot be pursued successfully by some visually impaired person' (Conway *et al*. 1982).

The value of extracurricular activities

Extracurricular activities can bring benefits which will help all youngsters. The activities can:

- promote confidence and self-worth
- develop social skills
- make positive use of leisure time
- promote a healthy lifestyle
- broaden knowledge through a range of experiences.

Purposeful involvement outside of school time can also help to meet the specific additional needs often associated with a visual impairment.

As can be seen in Chapter 29, concerns are often expressed about the physical fitness of youngsters with a visual impairment. 'Because of their tendency to be less active than their sighted peers, they need physical activities to avoid the poor muscle tone, poor posture and obesity that are too often present in visually impaired students' (Scott 1982a). The AEWVH and RNIB Working Party (1991) suggested that youngsters who are visually impaired tend to be, 'less fit than their sighted peers, as they have usually had fewer opportunities to run around and play'.

While the physical education curriculum will seek to address some of these problems, participation in physical activities out of school can help students appreciate that such activities are not confined to school but can be incorporated into a healthy lifestyle which makes positive use of leisure time. Such activities can also help to develop independence and self-confidence by improving the individual's spatial awareness, orientation and mobility skills, gross motor coordination and posture, and can increase self-confidence.

Exercise is often seen as beneficial in reducing anxiety and promoting a sense of well being. While all children experience anxiety and frustration at some time, children with special needs may be more prone to these feelings. This becomes most evident during the teenage years when issues of relationships and status come to the fore. The availability of leisure time activities allows for personal expression and social relaxation. Extracurricular activities are, of course, not confined to exercise and sport and the same advantages can be gained from participation in less physically demanding pursuits.

The development of skills in daily living is another area of need for children with a visual impairment which extracurricular activities can meet. Many of these children will benefit from the opportunity to practise these skills under supervision at school camping trips where skills can be mastered without the pressure of time that is often experienced during lessons. Great pleasure and self-esteem can be derived from successfully completing household chores, carrying out simple repairs and organising one's own shopping trips.

Leisure-time pursuits can also facilitate social integration. Some children will often be found alone and while every child needs some opportunities for personal peace and quiet, it is common for children with a visual impairment to spend long periods alone listening to music or reading a book. It can often be difficult for these children, especially those who are more timid and less confident, to initiate contact with a group or an individual and many will take the safer option of sitting alone until someone comes to them. A variety of organised activities, such as quizzes, board games, discussion groups, cosmetics and beauty care sessions, party games and discos can bring children together and encourage the development of their interpersonal skills in an enjoyable way.

Special interest groups or clubs after school also allow children to develop their existing areas of expertise. If a child has a talent for music or computer programming, they can be actively encouraged to nurture that ability. Expertise in any field can be utilised as a route to social status and may even help to improve career prospects.

While children with a visual impairment are just as capable and talented as their sighted peers, it is evident that the nature of that visual impairment can impose some constraints on their ability to fulfil their potential. A programme of extracurricular activities can present the structure within which their skills can be learned and developed.

Sport and special interest clubs

Sport and special interest clubs have traditionally had an important role in provision for children after school. They provide opportunities for children to develop knowledge and expertise in areas of particular interest to them. These clubs are often located at the school and organised by the schoolteachers. Sometimes they may be run by outside agencies which make use of the school's facilities, and others will be completely independent of the school. They all share an interest in developing their particular activity and in introducing it to as wide an audience as possible.

Schools are often limited in the range of activities they can offer, because of constraints on time, money and the range of expertise available. Specialist centres and clubs can offer pursuits ranging from judo to ocean yacht sailing and provide all the necessary equipment. What they may lack, however, is a knowledge of the needs of children with visual impairments. For example, a child with a visual impairment who shows ability in gymnastics could be introduced to a local gymnastics club. But if the gym instructors are not aware of such issues as: the medical details of the child's eye condition; the necessity for appropriate lighting; the need for good contrast on certain apparatus; the difficulty in judging distance; the limitations of demonstration as a teaching method, and the importance of precise language in instruction, then the child could be at a disadvantage or even in danger.

Teachers of the visually impaired who are alert to the interests and talents of their pupils encourage participation in out-of-school clubs and associations. Clubs which are hoping to cater for children with special needs should seek the advice of the youngsters' teachers, or other suitably qualified adults, to ensure that they are fully aware of the extent of those needs so that the children can benefit from their expertise in a positive and safe manner.

Outdoor pursuits

The National Curriculum requires that children have experience of outdoor activities as part of their physical education entitlement. In practice, such experiences cannot usually fit within the constraints of the daily school timetable and must be catered for outside school hours. In this way activities such as canoeing, sailing, horse-riding and mountain-work, bridge the gap between curricular and extracurricular activities (Figure 31.1).

Figure 31.1   Students studying a tactile map in preparation for water ski-ing.

People with a visual impairment derive the same fun, adventure and sense of achievement as a fully sighted person from outdoor pursuits. Some challenges, such as pot-holing may actually favour a beginner who is used to working more with senses other than vision. In some activities, aids such as braille and audible compasses, tactile maps and electronic sights will be helpful, but the most useful aids whether climbing, golfing or hiking, are invariably a guide who is sighted and an experienced, qualified instructor. Provided standard safety requirements are in place and there is an understanding of the particular needs of the individual and a willingness to adapt, no activities come to mind in which people with a visual impairment cannot participate.

Health and fitness

It is important that young people are introduced to those activities that they will want to continue to enjoy during their holidays and after they have left school. Children who are reluctant to be involved in sports or team games can work towards cardiovascular fitness in many ways. Facilities in most communities will include the following.

- Leisure centres. Most now house a fitness suite containing multigyms, running machines, steppers and static bicycles, all of which provide excellent opportunities for people with a visual impairment to keep fit.
- Swimming pools. Swimming is an ideal way to perform aerobic exercise and to build up stamina.
- Dance and aerobic classes. These provide a social occasion to keep fit with friends.
- Jogging and running clubs. These meet regularly and match members of similar abilities to train together.
- Gymnastic and trampolining groups. These are often based in local schools. Both of these activities help to develop strength, suppleness, posture and orientation skills.
- Rowing clubs. These are perhaps less widespread, but coxed-rowing is an activity which enables people with a visual impairment to participate on level terms, and as a team member, with their peers who are sighted.

Pupils who are introduced to such activities during their schooldays may leave school with both the knowledge and the confidence to continue to participate and to maintain a healthy lifestyle.

While the activities above are within the capability of most people with a visual impairment, it must be stressed that it is vital for instructors to be fully aware of all the implications of the particular visual condition of the student.

Recreational and social activities

A youth club affords a setting where a young person with a visual impairment is able to participate in a mutually enjoyable activity with peers who are sighted, and to develop friendships based on common interests.

Hobbies do not necessarily have to be based around physical fitness, but can involve art and craft activities such as pottery, weaving, model making, jewellery and collage work, while others can be concerned with the performing arts including drama, singing, playing musical instruments or disco dancing. Opportunities to learn to play popular board games such as Trivial Pursuits, chess and Monopoly can also add another dimension to the use of leisure time within the family. (Braille versions of Monopoly and other board games are available from the RNIB.)

Interest groups which give teenagers the chance to learn about cosmetics, beauty care and fashion can be of particular value to girls with a visual impairment. (The Body Shop produces an audio tape about makeup for people with a visual impairment.) However, in this age group boys, too, need the chance to keep abreast of trends in fashion. Both boys and girls enjoy popular table games like snooker, pool and table football, and being able to practise in a comfortable situation, with coaching, can give them the confidence to join in these games in pubs and other social settings as they get older.

An advantage of the youth club situation is that it enables adolescents of both genders to mix freely and to develop relationships; a role which is made more difficult when the ability to make eye contact across a crowded room is taken away. The skill of the adults in creating situations that allow for introductions to be made in an informal and relaxed manner is of great importance.

Youth club groups often organise visits to the theatre, theme parks, discos, quiz nights and other local youth clubs. These are often arranged by committees of youngsters within the club. These committees can offer children with a visual impairment an excellent opportunity to extend their range of experience and develop their organisational skills.

Adults working within a youth club situation should not be unduly anxious at having a young person with a visual impairment as a member of the club. In some activities a higher ratio of adults or smaller activity groups may be needed to accommodate the young person with a visual impairment, but wherever possible youngsters should not be restricted and should be actively involved in discussions and choices of activity options.

It is important that any member with a visual impairment is not a passive follower, but an active participant in all aspects of youth club life.

Facilitating involvement in extracurricular activities

A young person who has a visual impairment need not be disadvantaged in their chosen area of participation because of their lack of sight. However, there are a number of indirect influences which may restrict their access to extracurricular activities.

Information about courses and events is more often than not, presented in a format which may be difficult for youngsters to access. Unless information is purposely disseminated in braille or large print, someone with a visual impairment may have to rely upon a second-hand account from a reader who is fully sighted. Information which is presented as posters for example will be lost to a person who cannot read the poster or does not even know it exists.

Knowing that a course is available is one thing, reaching it is another. If you are not a car driver or a cyclist you may be able to use public transport but buses seldom stop immediately outside the course venue, and even if you decide to take a cab, which can be an expensive option, there still remains the problem of finding your way into the activity room. Family and friends are usually the most important source of assistance as they operate in the same environment as the youngster and the local facilities. Schools have, perhaps, an equally important responsibility in providing information about local courses in an accessible form and in establishing links with local, national and international organisations.

Voluntary associations for the welfare of the visually impaired, which exist in most districts, often provide evening and weekend courses and can also help individuals to overcome problems with transport to other venues.

Local clubs, either in the school vicinity or in the home environment, will often go to great lengths to enable people with special needs to become active members in their organisation.

National agencies, such as the RNIB and British Blind Sport, provide information in a range of formats about courses and 'Have-a-go' days which they run in all parts of the country throughout the year. In turn, their courses and competitions often allow for an individual to become involved at an international level in sports and other leisure pursuits. (A list of addresses of national agencies in the UK is given at the end of the chapter.)

Important considerations regarding children with visual impairments

Staff training sessions delivered by specialists which involve the use of blindfolds and simulation glasses, can enable organisations to gain some understanding into the world of the visually impaired and build up confidence by overcoming the fears and misconceptions concerning visual impairment.

Instructors need information about the factors which will affect the child's performance and safety. This information should cover details such as the nature of the present condition, the degree of residual vision available and the age of onset of the impairment. A young adventitiously blind person with a visual memory may need different support from a child who is congenitally blind. In some activities, a total lack of vision may be less of a challenge than coping with an unpredictable, fluctuating eye condition.

Most young people with a visual impairment are able to take a full part in extracurricular activities. However, for eye conditions where there is a danger of retinal detachment (see Chapter 5), or where there is a dislocated lens or increased eye pressure, activities such as diving, trampolining, weightlifting and collision sports (such as rugby) should not be undertaken without the approval of an ophthalmologist.

Further information on the implications of eye conditions for physical activities can be found in Chapter 5. Fluctuating eye conditions cause unpredictable and unstable levels of vision and allowances have to be made for this.

A reduced field of vision can affect the ability to judge distances accurately, and greatly reduces the amount of information that would otherwise be available via peripheral vision.

Albinism not only causes visual problems, but also requires extra care to be taken when working in sunlight to avoid burning of the skin.

The wearing of spectacles has to be taken into account. Some people need to wear their glasses during all activities, including football and swimming, and this has a bearing on the safety of other participants.

Many eye defects are the result of a more general medical condition and, therefore, some people may have, in addition to poor eyesight, associated problems of hearing loss, obesity, diabetes, epilepsy, weak joints or motor problems.

As Hanninen (1975) states:

> The Specialist Teacher can help the student to select appropriate activities and provide assistance in the initiation into these experiences by interpreting the students' abilities ... as well as providing aid in acquisition of necessary material and equipment.

Young people with a visual impairment need to feel safe and have confidence in the abilities of the adults assisting and directing activities. They need encouragement, stimulation and interpretation, appropriate physical contact, role models, friendships and respect for their individuality and views. Chapter 29 provides additional information on the adaptations and modifications of equipment, areas, organisation and procedures that may be necessary to enable these students to participate fully in extracurricular activities (Figure 31.2).

Figure 31.2 Theory into practice! There is no substitute for experienced instruction.

Summary

Extracurricular activities are vital to fill the gaps that the school curriculum and the more informal learning experiences of the home background do not provide for children. This is true for all youngsters, but it is especially pertinent in relation to those with special needs, who may have more 'gaps' to fill than their peers. These 'gaps' are often not directly caused by visual impairment itself, but rather by the lack of opportunity that is afforded the child.

Those with the responsibility for the provision of extracurricular activities must ensure that children with a visual impairment are not merely allowed to join in, but are encouraged and guided to make the fullest possible use of their abilities. They should also remember the advice of Buell (quoted in Hanninen 1975).

> Do not too much regard bumps, rough scratches or bloody noses, even these may have their good influences. At worst, they affect only the bark and do not injure the system like the rust of inaction.

Useful addresses

Activity holidays

Details of group activity holiday courses are available from: RNIB Leisure Service, 224 Great Portland Street, London W1N 6AA. Tel: 0171 388 1266.

Merlin Activity and Adventure Courses, 120 Allerton Road, Liverpool L18 2DG.

The Calvert Trust, Adventure Centre for Disabled People, Little Crosthwaite, Keswick, Cumbria, CA12 4QD.

Archery   Grand National Archery Society Disabled Archery Co-ordinator, National Agricultural Centre, Stoneleigh, Kenilworth, Warwicks CV8 2LG. Tel: 0203 696631.

Blind Sport   British Blind Sport (BBS) Administrative and Development Officer 67 Albert Street, Rugby, Warwickshire. Tel: 0788 536142

British Sports Association for the Disabled (BSAD), 34 Osnaburgh Street, London NW1 3ND. Tel: 0171 383 7277.

Canoeing   British Canoe Union, John Dudderidge House, Adbolton Lane, West Bridgford, Nottinghamshire NG2 5AS. Tel: 0602 821100.

Chess   Braille Chess Association (BCS), Hon.Sec. Mr S. Lovell, 7 Coldwell Square, Cross Gates, Leeds LS15 7HB. Tel: 0532 600013.

Duke of Edinburgh's Award Scheme   Guilliver House, Madeira Walk, Windsor, Berkshire. Tel: 0753 810753.

Football   British Football Association for the Visually Handicapped, (BFAVH), Chairman, 1 Malvern Close, Prestwick, Manchester M25 5PH

Girl Guides   Girl Guides Association, 17–19 Buckingham Palace Road, London SW1W 0PT. Tel: 0171 834 6242.

Goalball   Goalball Association, 51 Farnway, Darley Abbey, Derbyshire DE3 2BQ. Tel: 0331 559172

Golf   English Blind Golf, 93 St Barnabas Road, Woodford Green, Essex IG8 7BT. Tel: 0181 505 2085

The Golf Foundation, 57 London Road, Enfield EN2 6DU. Tel: 0181 367 4404

Guide Dog Adventure Group (GDBA), Hillfields, Burghfield Common, Reading, Berkshire RG7 3YG. Tel: 0734 835555

Gymnastics   British Amateur Gymnastics Association, Thames Valley College, Wellington Street, Slough, Berkshire SL1 1XT. Tel: 0753 534171

Holidays for the Disabled, (Young Disabled on Holiday), 12 Ryle Road, Farnham GU99 8RW. Tel: 0252 721390

Ocean Youth Club, The Bus Station, South St., Gosport, Hants. PO12 1EP.

Outward Bound Trust (HQ Office), Chestnut Field, Regent Place, Rugby CV21 2PJ. Tel: 0788 60423

Rambling   The Ramblers Association, Secretary, 1–5 Wandsworth Road, London SW8 2XX. Tel: 0171 582 6878

Riding   Riding for the Disabled Association (RDA), Secretary, Avenue R, National Agricultural Centre, Kenilworth, Warwicks CV8 2LY. Tel: 0203 696510

Rowing   Amateur Rowing Association (Rowing for the Disabled), 6 Lower Mall, Hammersmith, London W6 9DJ. Tel: 0171 748 3632

Sailing   The Cirdan Trust, RYA teaching establishment, Fullbridge Wharf, Maldon, Essex.

Jubilee Sailing Trust, Test Road, Eastern Docks, Southampton SO1 1GG. Tel: 0703 631388

Scouts   Scout Association, Gilwell Park, Chingford, London E4 7QW. Tel: 0171 524 5246

Ski   British Ski Club for the Disabled (BSCD), 'Springmount', Berwick St John, Shaftsbury, Dorset SP7 OHQ

Swimming   Amateur Swimming Association, Secretary, Harold Fern House, Derby Square, Loughborough, Leics LE11 0AL. Tel: 0509 230431

Tandem   The Tandem Club, Liasion Officer for the Visually Handicapped, Worlds End House, 56 High Street, Green Street Green, Kent BR6 6BJ

Trampolining   British Trampoline Federation Ltd., Secretary, 146 College Road, Harrow, Middlesex HA1 1VH. Tel: 0181 863 7278

Water-Skiing   British Disabled Water-Ski Association (BDWSA), The Tony Edge Centre, Heron Lake, Hythe End, Wraybury TW9 6HW. Tel: 0784 483664

Yachting   Royal Yachting Association (RYA) Seamanship Foundation, Director, 22/24 Romsey Road, Eastleigh, Hampshire SO5 4AL. Tel: 0703 629962

Youth Hostelling   Youth Hostels Association (England and Wales), Trevelyan House, 8 St. Stephen's Hill, St Albans, Herts AL1 2DY. Tel: 0727 55215.

CHILDREN AND YOUNG PEOPLE WITH MULTIPLE DISABILITIES AND A VISUAL IMPAIRMENT

Although projections for the total number of children in the United Kingdom with a visual impairment suggest little change in the next 20 years, the *proportion* of children entering the education system with disabilities in addition to a visual impairment is expected to increase. This increase has major educational implications for both service delivery and teacher training.

These children do not present as a homogeneous group and the *New Directions* report (RNIB 1990) suggested that the only common link between these children may be the visual impairment. Teachers of children with a visual impairment often feel 'deskilled' when faced with a child with multiple disabilities, and some even question whether their role should encompass work with this population. Specialist training courses for teachers of children with a visual impairment have attempted to address this issue by incorporating more appropriate course content into their courses and second level training is now available for teachers of children with a visual impairment who work in the area of multiple disabilities.

The education of these children draws on knowledge from a number of fields including visual impairment, multisensory impairment and learning difficulties. It is not possible to provide here all the information and expertise a teacher working with this group will require. There are however important principles relating to the education of children with a visual impairment which need to be understood. The aim of this section is to provide an introduction to these principles and to consider in particular the educational implications of a visual impairment for children with multiple disabilities.

Chapter 32

Children with Multiple Disabilities and a Visual Impairment

Mike McLinden

Introduction

This chapter provides an introduction to the population of children described as having multiple disabilities and a visual impairment (MDVI). Following a brief historical overview the following areas are considered: the population, the nature and causes of multiple disabilities and current research issues relating to the population. The chapter concludes with a discussion of the role of parents and professionals working with these children.

Historical background

Recent legislation

In recent years there has been increasing recognition that children with multiple disabilities and a visual impairment constitute a distinct group with a unique set of educational needs. Prior to the Education (Handicapped Children) Act of 1970 (Department of Education and Science (DES) 1970), children now described as having profound or severe learning disabilities may have been classified as 'ineducable' and were consigned to the care of local health departments or residential hospitals.[1] The 1970 Education Act introduced the category of 'severely educationally subnormal' and for the first time embraced these children into the education system. However, the classification of children into categories according to their primary 'handicap' tended to restrict the recognition of the other problems the child might have (Gulliford 1987, Muldoon and Pickwell 1993). 'Mental handicap' tended to be viewed as the primary disability and usually took precedence over additional sensory impairments in decisions about educational placements.

The 1970 Education Act was significant in that all children, regardless of disability, came under the supervision of local education authorities (LEAs). Children with severe disabilities were labelled as 'educationally severely subnormal' (ESSN), although this description was later changed to 'educationally subnormal (Severe)'. This category included children who were described as 'multi-handicapped and visually impaired' (MHVI).

Children within the MHVI population were educated mainly in special schools run by LEAs or voluntary organisations (see Chapter 1). Although staff may have been qualified in the education of children with ESSN, it was rare for them to hold a qualification in teaching children with a visual impairment. Pupils with the most profound disabilities formed a category within the ESSN group. These children, who commonly presented with additional severe physical disabilities and sensory impairment, received their education in a unit within the school usually described as the 'special care' class. During the 1970s the needs of these pupils began to be addressed for the first time within an educational framework, which included an appreciation of the importance of assessing individual needs and of planning an appropriate curriculum to meet those needs.

The Warnock Report (DES 1978) recommended that in education the idea of categories of 'handicap' should be replaced by a consideration of the *needs* of the individual. The subsequent 1981 Education Act (DES 1981) adopted the recommendations of the Warnock Report and introduced the concept of 'special educational needs'. Under the terms of the Act a child was considered as having special educational needs if he or she had a significantly greater difficulty in learning than the majority of children of his or her age (Subsection 2a). Through a 'Statement of Special Educational Need' the specific needs and requirements of each individual and the curricular provision required to meet those needs could be identified.[2]

The 1988 Education Act and the introduction of the National Curriculum again led to debate about the educational status of children functioning at early levels of development. The first versions of the National Curriculum did not take account of the needs of children within this population, and as a result many teachers questioned the applicability of the National Curriculum to the pupils they taught. It is fair to say that subsequent government documents and publications together with recent revisions to the National Curriculum following the Dearing Review (Dearing 1994), have addressed these issues and have secured the place of these children within an educational framework common to all pupils throughout the UK.[3]

Ware (1994) concludes that, subject to certain conditions being fulfilled, the National Curriculum now has the potential to provide all children 'with a curriculum which is both broad and relevant'. Chapter 37 considers in greater detail approaches to the curriculum for children with multiple disabilities and a visual impairment.

Population

National surveys: general

Although current data relating to the population of children with multiple disabilities in the United Kingdom are limited, the results of recent national surveys suggest that:
- individuals with one impairment are statistically more likely to have a second impairment;
- the likelihood of an individual having other impairments increases as the learning disability becomes more severe (Kelleher and Mulcahy 1986).

The study by the Office of Population Census and Surveys (OPCS), *Surveys of Disabilities in Great Britain*, was commissioned by the Department of Health and Social Security in 1984 to help plan benefits and services. The surveys provided information on the number of people with disabilities, and included reference to children (Bone and Meltzer 1989, Meltzer *et al.* 1989, Smyth and Robus 1989). Using an ICIDH format[4] the OPCS surveys suggested that 3% of children aged 5–15 had severe disabilities (Bone and Meltzer 1989). Approximately one-third of these children (36%) had one disability, and the remainder had two or more disabilities which often occurred in distinct patterns (Loughran *et al.* 1995).

National surveys: visual impairment

Although accurate statistical evidence prior to 1992 is limited, estimates of the number of children described as having additional/multiple disabilities had increased from 39% in 1959 to 50.6% in 1970 (Griffiths 1979). With the influential report of the Vernon Committee, *Education of the Visually Handicapped*, reporting a 'strong indication of a rising prevalence of dual or multiple handicap among children of school age.' (DES 1972).

The RNIB survey (RNIB 1992) provided the first detailed national picture of the population of children with a visual impairment. A sample of 285 pupils aged 3–19 provided data on a range of issues, including medical treatment and advice, daily living and mobility, schooling, employment, leisure and holidays.

More than half of the children (56%) in the study had one or more additional disabilities including impaired hearing, speech and language difficulties, physical disabilities, and learning difficulties. A number of key points relating to children with additional disabilities were highlighted by the survey.

- Children with poor sight were found to be more likely to have additional impairments, especially in the areas of communication (hearing and speech), physical integrity and mental functioning.
- By the age of 1 year the additional disabilities had been identified in over 50% of the sample.
- By the age of five the additional disabilities had been identified in 80% of the sample.

Taken as a whole, the RNIB data suggested there were two distinct groups of pupils with a visual impairment within the UK:

- a group of children with a visual impairment and no additional disabilities;
- a larger group of children with a visual impairment and with additional disabilities.

The findings of the 1992 survey suggested that pupils with a visual impairment and additional disabilities do not form a homogeneous group, 'for whom a common curriculum and common teaching methodology will be easy to devise and implement' (RNIB 1992).

'The survey on visually impaired pupils in the United Kingdom by Clunies Ross and Franklin (1996a, b) provides the most recent national data relating to children with a visual impairment and is based on returns from heads of LEA visual impairment services. The survey sought to establish the ages and distribution of the population of children known to Visual Impairment Services and requested details of children considered to have multiple disabilities together with information about the criteria the services used to identify this population.

Table 32.1 provides a summary by age of the number of pupils known to the LEA Visual Impairment Services.

Table 32.1   Numbers of children with a visual impairment only (VI) and with multiple disabilities and a visual impairment (MDVI) in England, Wales and Scotland in 1995; adapted from Clunies-Ross and Franklin (1997)

Age	VI	MDVI	Total
11 to 15+	4336	2297	6633
5 to 10+	6432	2961	9393
under 5	1911	1433	3344
Total	12679	6691	19370

In addition, 1369 pupils aged 16 to 19 were identified by local education authorities. Of these, 798 were reported as VI and 571 as MDVI.

Over one-third of the total population of children with a visual impairment identified by Heads of Services in LEAs were described as having 'multiple disabilities'. In general, the results of the survey indicate inconsistency in the definitions of 'multiple disability' offered by the services. For a number of Services, for instance, children were described as having 'multiple disabilities' if they were receiving their education in a school designated for children with severe learning difficulties or physical disabilities. In the descriptions they offered, vague references were frequently made to 'learning difficulty' and 'developmental delay', highlighting the difficulty of obtaining reliable data in the absence of nationally agreed criteria for defining the population.

National reports

A number of reports commissioned by the Royal National Institute for the Blind in recent years have made significant contributions to identifying the needs of children and adults within the UK who have multiple disabilities.

An RNIB study of services to adults described as 'multihandicapped visually impaired' (MHVI), resulted in the report *Out of Isolation* (RNIB 1987). The report states that the overall effect of multiple 'handicaps' on an individual 'varies according to their relative severity and the way in which they are combined'. A distinction is made between individuals who are 'congenitally multiply handicapped', and those with one or more acquired additional 'handicaps', with each sub-group considered to have slightly different needs.

New Directions (RNIB 1990) was produced by an RNIB working party set up to consider the needs of children and young people described as 'multihandicapped visually impaired'. The report estimated that there were approximately 6000 children and young people in the age range 0–19 years in UK, 'whose additional disabilities, physical, sensory, mental or behavioural, are severe enough in themselves or in combination with their diminished vision, to interfere with normal development or education'.

New Directions found a number of relatively distinct groups within the population. A 'core group' of children with the most severe disabilities is described, although it is acknowledged that even within this group there will be a considerable range of ability and potential. Two other sub-groups are identified within the report as warranting special attention: children who are deaf-blind, and those with degenerative diseases.

Nature of multiple disability

Definition of disability

The term 'disability' is defined by the World Health Organization (WHO 1980) as 'one of the possible consequences of an impairment and is conceived of as lack of ability to function within the range considered normal for most human beings' (Tobin 1994).[5]

The concept of 'disability' is often described in terms of the individual's degree of functioning with or without assistance or aids and/or in terms of the individual's developmental skills as expected for age (British Association for Community Child Health (BACCH) 1994). It is defined in the Disability Discrimination Act (1995) as: 'A physical or mental impairment which has a substantial and long-term adverse effect on a person's ability to carry out normal day-to-day activities' (Disability Discrimination Act 1995).

Estimates of the prevalence of disability depend on the definition of disability which is adopted, and on the threshold which is used to distinguish disability from non-disability (Martin *et al.* 1988; see Figure 32.1).

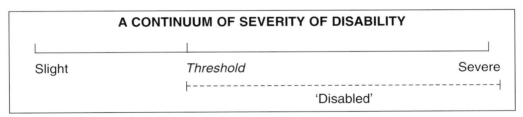

A CONTINUUM OF SEVERITY OF DISABILITY

Slight   *Threshold*   Severe

'Disabled'

Figure 32.1   (Adapted from BACCH 1994)

One difficulty with this model, is that disability is not a static or uni-dimensional concept with an easily recognised threshold. The threshold can vary according to the person's age, the stability of the condition, the nature of the additional disabilities and so on. A more useful approach might be to consider that an individual's way of functioning is a result of the interaction between the disability and his or her environment (Weddell 1981). Disability, especially as it relates to children, can be seen therefore as the result of a complex, interactive process 'which is discerned in relationship to the abilities of the developing child and not, as when it is used in adult life, to the static model of an 'able' adult'. (BACCH 1994).

The definition of disability which is used in the Children Act (DES 1989c)[6] has been criticised as being of limited practical value (Hutchison 1995). In an attempt to offer a more useful replacement, an interdisciplinary working group has made recommendations for a definition of disability as it relates to children (BACCH 1994). This proposal includes:

- a statement about the age a child becomes an adult

- the dimensions of disability[7]
- the threshold of severity[8]
- an indication that the disability is long-lasting
- an acknowledgement that objective measures of disability must be added to the effects of environment if loss of social role (disadvantage) is to be assessed (Hutchison 1995).

Multiple disabilities

The essential feature of 'multiple' disabilities is the fusion or interaction of the disabilities and their *combined* influence on development. The term is used by Orelove and Sobsey (1991) to refer to individuals with:

- 'severe or profound learning difficulties
- one or more significant motor or sensory impairments and/or special health care needs'.

The prefix 'multiple' or 'multi' is commonly used to highlight the synergetic effect of the combination of the disabilities and emphasises the interactive or multiplying effect which exceeds the sum of each individual disability (Best and Brown 1994). In discussing the way combinations of impairments may influence overall development, Hogg and Sebba (1986) use the term 'association of impairments'. Rather than considering 'primary', 'secondary' or 'additional' disabilities, it is suggested that combinations of conditions be given equal weight in order to 'emphasise the totality of development and show how any given area will interact with others to condition the pattern and course of development'.

In discussing learners with 'multi-sensory impairment', Best and Brown (1994) use the term to describe a *situation* rather than a 'condition', the situation being characterised by an individual being unable to:

- gather sufficient information from the environment to learn independently
- make sufficient use of the environment to function independently.

Ashman and Conway (1989) demonstrated that to differing degrees, children with severe or profound learning difficulties have particular difficulty in separating relevant cues from irrelevant aspects of the environment. In addition children within this population have been found to have problems in retaining information in short- and long-term memory so that it can be incorporated into existing knowledge of the world. This in turn disrupts the processing of information and their ability to organise problem-solving responses to a situation (Muldoon and Pickwell 1993).

Kiernan *et al.* (1982) highlight the interference in the basic abilities of early communication in children with severe and profound learning difficulties, which include making eye contact and attending to and interpreting facial expressions and body gestures. This interference affects the interactive relationship with parents and carers who consequently may be unable to understand the child's needs or intentions (Beveridge 1989). Factors affecting the development of early communication are considered in further detail in Chapter 33.

It has been shown that some 'additional' disabilities may be remediable either by direct intervention or by more efficient management and/or understanding of the visual impairment as it relates to the individual child (McKendrick 1991). The adult working with these children will therefore need to have not only a knowledge of the normal pattern of child development but also some understanding of the potential impact on early development of a severe visual impairment. In addition, an overview of the development of other groups of children with special educational needs will provide a useful framework for appropriate intervention and programme planning.

Causes of multiple disabilities

Developments in medical science have resulted in a changing pattern in the population of children entering the education system. Many children with multiple disabilities who thrive today would not have previously survived infancy. Special care baby units together with improvements in medical screening techniques and genetic counselling have resulted in fewer cases of children being born with conditions that were once relatively common, such as, Down's syndrome, or spina bifida, or those conditions resulting from the mother having rubella during pregnancy.

Increasing numbers of children are now entering the education system with a range of highly complex medical conditions which require facilities for tube feeding, and overcoming breathing difficulties and severe epilepsy. A number of those children appear to have brain function which is limited to controlling the autonomic systems responsible for basic bodily functions. Such complex medical conditions challenge educators to provide a curriculum which can appropriately meet these children's needs.

Relatively little is known about the prevalence or causes of visual impairment in pupils with severe and profound learning difficulties although 'as a group they may have a wide range of problems in which visual disorders figure significantly' (Muldoon and Pickwell 1993). This high incidence of visual problems can be explained in part by the close link between the foetal development of the eye and brain with damage to the brain of the foetus possibly resulting in damage to the eye.

Approximately 70 conditions have been listed which are either genetically transmitted or result from disease and cause severe or profound learning difficulties (Evans and Ware 1987). Of these conditions 25 have severe visual disorders associated with them as specific characteristics, while others feature visual disorder associated with an overall neurological dysfunction (Muldoon and Pickwell 1993). There is, for instance, a high incidence of visual problems in children with cerebral palsy (Goble 1984). The incidence of hyperopia, optic atrophy, cataract and nystagmus within this population is also greater than in normal populations (Fantl 1964, Muldoon and Pickwell 1993).

The most common causes of severe visual impairment in children with severe learning difficulties are (Warburg 1986):
1. cortical visual impairment
2. optic atrophy
3. retinal disorders

4. cataract

5. malformation of the eyes.

A number of children with severe learning difficulties may well have visual disorders which have not been identified, and their abilities may consequently be underestimated.

Table 32.2 provides a summary of data concerning 423 children collected by a visual assessment team in the UK over a period of 14 years, and illustrates the spectrum of eye conditions and associated disorders.

Table 32.2   Spectrum of eye disorders in 423 children with visual impairments: data collected by a visual assessment team, 1975–1989. (Adapted from McKendrick 1991.)

Eye condition: order of frequency	Associated disorders
Cortical visual impairment	Global delays/cerebral palsy
Congenital cataract	Developmental delays/hearing loss
Optic atrophy	Hydrocephalus
Malfunction of the eye	Microcephaly Congenital malformations
Retinopathy of prematurity(ROP)	Developmental delays

Research issues

It has already been shown that children with multiple disabilities and a visual impairment do not form a homogeneous group. Consequently there are particular difficulties in applying established research methods such as the use of matched sample groups. Practice in teaching has evolved from a variety of sources, and the effectiveness of these approaches has seldom been evaluated or monitored.

Knowledge of the development of children with multiple disabilities and a visual impairment is still limited and is usually based on:

- individual case studies
- work with children with a visual impairment and no additional disabilities
- comparisons with normal child development.

The true extent of the visual function of a child with multiple disabilities is frequently unknown and may vary depending on the child's general health and physical condition. As a result guidelines for working with this population often offer only a general framework for appropriate intervention.

Warren (1994) advocates an 'adaptive tasks' approach to research in the area of visual impairment, based on the assumption that 'the variables that are related to visual impairment are simply additional sources of variance in the development of children', and must be considered along with those which are evaluated when 'accounting for the development of sighted children'. Development is viewed as being determined by 'the complex relationship among the child's environments, the child's developing abilities and characteristics, and particularly how other people respond to the child's disability' (Warren

1994). This approach can inform practice not only among those engaged in research within the field but also among parents and professionals working with the children.

Role of parents and professionals

Children with multiple disabilities frequently present 'an immense challenge to professionals responsible for their education' (Orelove and Sobsey 1991). Each adult working with a child with multiple disabilities has an important role in ensuring that the child is able to make sense of the environment using appropriate information from a range of sensory channels. In attempting to provide the child with a balanced understanding of the environment, the adult will need to structure an appropriate learning environment which can be both reactive to the child's actions and responsive to the child's needs (Bell 1993).

Adults working with a child with multiple disabilities and a visual impairment will need to understand both the educational implications of the visual impairment and the general developmental patterns of children with a visual impairment in order to interpret accurately the behaviour of that child. In particular, difficulties may be created by 'lack of a true understanding by care-givers of the effects of visual impairment' (Best 1986), which may result in unrealistic or low expectations. Even in the absence of additional disabilities, a severe visual impairment may result in a developmental lag during the first few years of life, and evidence from children who are congenitally blind and have no additional disabilities, suggests that a lag of 18 months may be typical at 6 years of age in some areas of development (Best 1986).

Early identification of the children is clearly of crucial importance in order to ensure appropriate intervention. An RNIB working party report (McKendrick 1991) considers the work of the visual assessment team (VAT) in the UK, and highlights the importance of the accurate assessment of a child's:
- functional vision
- developmental/educational status
- additional disabilities.

The report recommends that each VAT should consist of a stable, multi-disciplinary core group which includes:
- a consultant paediatrician or senior clinical medical officer
- a specialist educational psychologist
- an advisory teacher of children with a visual impairment.

In addition the team should be supported by a social worker, appropriate therapists and if possible, an orthoptist. An ongoing parental contribution is considered to be essential in the assessment and decision making process.

It is clear that the needs of children with multiple disabilities cannot be considered in isolation from the more extensive needs of the family as a social group. Caring for children with disabilities inevitably results in changes in family roles, and this may produce additional tensions and conflicts. What parents want for their child may be quite different from the goals identified by professionals. Any assessment of the child, therefore, will need to consider not only the child's individual educational needs, but also the needs of the child within the wider context of the family group.

To ensure that children with multiple disabilities and a visual impairment are able to live as full and normal a life as possible, *New Directions* (RNIB 1990) identified a number of principal needs including:

- early identification and diagnosis of visual impairment
- accurate assessment of performance and abilities
- appropriate formal education from the earliest possible age
- training in making full use of residual vision
- access to a wide range of expertise.

It is clear from this summary that both parental and professional expertise is required in the assessment process. Parents and professionals have a pivotal role in determining the individual needs of each child and in planning appropriate intervention if the child's potential for further development is not to be underestimated.

Summary

There has been increasing recognition of the educational needs of children with multiple disabilities and a visual impairment in recent years.

There has been a reported increase in the proportion of children with multiple disabilities entering the education system: this can be attributed in part to advances in medical expertise. There is a high incidence of visual disorders in children with profound and severe learning difficulties.

Children with multiple disabilities and visual impairment do not form a homogeneous group: the only common link may be a visual impairment. The diversity of needs found within the population of children with multiple disabilities has major implications for future research in the area particularly relating to assessment, evaluation of intervention programmes, surveys and so on.

Parents and professionals have an important role to play in understanding the individual needs of each child so as not to underestimate his or her potential for further development.

Notes

1. The 1944 Education Act required LEAs to provide education for children according to age, ability and aptitude. The categories of 'handicap' outlined in Sections 33 and 34 of the Education Act included: blind, partially sighted, physically handicapped and educationally subnormal. The 'Handicapped Pupils and Schools Health Regulations', in 1945, defined 11 categories of handicap which were modified to 10 in 1953 (Solity and Raybould 1988).

2. The notion of a continuum of learning difficulties was suggested in the Warnock Report to reflect the wide range of special educational needs to be found in the population. It was estimated that 20% of all children may have special educational needs at some point in their schooling with some 2% having significant special needs which are profound and long term. The term 'severe learning difficulties' (SLD) replaced ESNs, and 'Profound and multiple learning difficulties' (PMLD) was introduced to describe those children in 'special care'.

3. At an early stage of the Dearing Review, two fundamental principles were established; (i) all children have an entitlement to participate in the National Curriculum; (ii) the revised National Curriculum should be accessible and relevant to pupils with special educational needs (SCAA 1996).

4. 'ICIDH format' refers to the International Classification of Impairment Disability and Handicap, which was published by the World Health Organization (WHO) in 1980.

5. In the WHO definition, the term 'impairment'; refers to a loss or abnormality of an organ or of some part of the physiology or anatomy of the organism. The term 'handicap' is used to describe a possible consequence of a disability (Tobin 1994).

6. The following definition of disability is used in the Children Act: 'A child is disabled if he is blind, deaf or dumb or suffers from a mental disorder of any kind or is substantially and permanently handicapped by illness, injury or congenital deformity or such other disability as may be prescribed.'

7. The following 11 dimensions of disability are suggested by the BACCH: locomotion, fine motor, personal care, continence, hearing, vision, communication, learning, behaviour, physical health, consciousness.

8. It is suggested each dimension is coded along four degrees of severity: mild, moderate, severe, profound.

Chapter 33
Development of Early Communication

Helen Hendrickson

Introduction

Children with multiple disabilities and a visual impairment encounter diverse challenges in their development of communication skills. Complex sensory, physical and cognitive impairments may make conventional means of interpersonal communication inaccessible to, or inappropriate for this population. The aim of this chapter is to explore the nature of pre-verbal communication development in children with multiple disabilities and a visual impairment. Particular emphasis is given to the role of the communication partner in promoting the optimal development of each child's communication skills.

Background

Communication is one of the ways through which we receive information about our environment, and is a primary means by which we act on the environment. The ability to communicate is 'an essential part of life, a necessary means for participation in society, and an essential ingredient for the development of self worth and dignity' (Butterfield 1991). There is increasing recognition of the importance of developing communication skills within educational intervention (Rogow 1988), with communication being described by Aherne and Thornber (1990) as 'a cross curricular skill which is transferable, chiefly independent of content and can be developed in different contexts across the whole curriculum'.

In considering the impact of a visual impairment on early communication development, research evidence suggests that the visual impairment of itself does not mean that a child will necessarily experience severe communication difficulties. McGurk (1983) suggests that although the presence of a visual impairment seems to have a 'moderating' influence on the development of communicative competence,[1] the child with a visual impairment may well follow the same path to communicative competence as his or her sighted peers, and the range of competence the child eventually achieves is often 'well within the range of reaction we accept as normality'.

The presence of additional disabilities however strongly increases the possibility of communication difficulties and Warren (1994) suggests that, 'If the child with a visual impairment must find alternative/adaptive routes to the acquisition of language and other communicative behaviours then the child with an additional handicap is even more challenged.'

Language and communication development

Language and communication can be viewed as opposite sides of the same coin (Sperber and Wilson 1986) since 'the essential feature of language is that it is used for communication, and the essential feature of communication is that it involves the use of language as a code'.

For children with multiple disabilities, communication may not essentially involve the comprehension and production of spoken or written language. Instead, 'non-verbal' skills may be used to encode and decode messages. These skills may involve the use of a formal gestural 'code', such as the use of a signing system in which units of information are encoded into gestures with the possibility of re-combination. The 'de-codeability' of the signals will depend on the knowledge and skills of both communication partners regarding the system in use.

'Informal' non-verbal signals may also be used to communicate but their individual nature often makes them more difficult to decode. For example a child may make a particular vocalisation and facial expression to indicate pleasure. If the child has a physical disability, the execution of movements and sounds may not be accurate or consistent, and their meaning may be unclear to those who do not know the child well. A shared code of signals which are mutually understandable may be built up over time through shared communicative experience in a variety of settings.

The signals themselves may not be discrete, and may not lend themselves to use in combination, in the manner of a formal linguistic code. However with shared knowledge and experience, it is possible to identify signals that can be used to share non-verbal messages.

Non-verbal communication skills can also be used to support or augment a child's understanding of spoken language. Key word signing, such as 'Makaton', may be used to provide gestural support to enhance a child's understanding of spoken language.

When considering early language development, a distinction can be made between the development of understanding of language or **comprehension**, and the development of forms of expression or **production**. Bloom and Lahey (1978) point out that although comprehension usually precedes production in the developmental sequence, children will often learn the meaning of a word through using it correctly and receiving feedback from the communication partner. This may be illustrated by reference to a child profile.

Jamie is a three year old boy who attends a pre-school assessment centre for children with a visual impairment and additional disabilities. At the centre, Jamie uses a few words to make his needs known, and is able to answer 'yes' or 'no' to closed questions. He uses a voice output communication aid operated by two manually operated switches. Each switch is identifiable by a tactile marker with a different texture and shape to represent each choice, for example a plastic bottle top to represent 'orange juice', and a piece of tin foil to represent 'blackcurrant juice'. When a switch is pressed, a pre-recorded phrase is 'spoken' via the voice output device, for instance 'orange juice please'.

When the aid was originally introduced, Jamie was given a physical and verbal prompt to assist him in locating and exploring the switches. When a switch was activated, Jamie received the requested item. Over a period of time Jamie made an association between the texture on the switch, and the resulting reward. He learned that the tactile marker on the switch resulted in a spoken message, and a desirable consequence – his preferred drink.

Jamie learned therefore to understand the arbitrary symbols presented to him, through feedback derived from their use.

Research evidence: visual impairment

Recent research studies in the field of early communication development offer clues as to why the establishment of a shared pre-language signal system may be more difficult for a child with a visual impairment.

Research which has focused on the early mother–child interaction, however, has not produced conclusive evidence. A number of studies, for instance, those of Rowland (1983) and Kekelis and Anderson (1984), have reported that communication patterns used by mothers of infants with a visual impairment are not unlike those used by mothers of sighted children, and would not be considered 'abnormal'. Other studies have suggested that mothers of children with a visual impairment:

- use a higher percentage of labelling of objects in their attempts to enrich language learning (Urwin 1983);
- tend to dominate the balance in turn taking interactions (Rowland 1983);
- use a lower level of 'interactive responsiveness' based on vocalisation (Rogers and Puchalski 1984).

In early communication exchanges between mothers and children who are fully sighted, non-verbal behaviours such as eye contact and facial expression are usually the first to be used and responded to in early communication exchanges. The adult working with a child with a visual impairment will need to be aware that non-visual responses, such as the adult's use of touch and voice, may be more important. Alternative cues will need to be identified as the basis of subsequent interactions and may include bodily expressions, attention to the use of sound, the use of touch or attention to other parts of the body as an indicator of interest (Fraiberg 1977).

In considering the differences in the environment in the early stages of communication development between the sighted and blind child, Warren (1994) suggests that one conclusion might be that the environment 'is not completely different but is significantly different', and can therefore significantly influence the communication exchange.

Symbolic communication

Although the means that the child uses to communicate may be 'non-symbolic', the child's communication partner may well have access to a wider range of communication methods including symbolic and non-symbolic behaviours. The main distinction between the symbolic and non symbolic behaviours is the degree of transparency or 'guessability' of the child's communicative behaviours. Behaviours that approximate the adult's use of formal/symbolic codes will require less 'guesswork', and will therefore be more discrete and efficient communication signals (Siegel-Causey and Guess 1989).

The nature of the signal will vary according to the methods available to the child, but may include some of the behaviours illustrated in Table 33.1. These behaviours are based on a model of communication interaction developed for children who are fully sighted and highlight the primary methods available to communication partners. For children with a visual impairment a number of these methods will need to be adapted so that they can be accessed through alternative modalities such as touch or hearing. Examples of these adaptations are italicised in Table 33.1.

Table 33.1 Symbolic and non-symbolic behaviours used in early communication interactions (adapted from Siegel-Causey and Guess 1989)

Non-symbolic behaviours	Symbolic behaviours
Voice	Verbal (e.g. words)
Affect (eg mood)	Sign language
Touch	Photos/pictures
Objects	Representational Graphic systems
Gesture (e.g. pointing/reaching)	*representational tactile symbols* (e.g. Moon braille, objects of reference)
	Body-referenced signs (e.g. adapted Makaton)
Physiological responses	
Body movement	
Vision (e.g. eye contact)	

Function of communication

Pre-verbal signals

Kiernan and Reid (1987) suggest that early pre-verbal communication signals fulfil one or more of the following purposes (examples provided by the author).

- Seeking attention: 'Look at me'
- Need satisfaction: 'I want'
- Simple negation: 'I don't want'
- Positive interaction: 'I enjoy being with you'
- Negative interaction: 'I don't want to be with you'
- Shared attention: 'We are both focusing on the same item/activity'.

Bates (1976) outlines two major functions of communication at the pre-verbal level, proto-imperatives and proto-declaratives.

Proto-imperatives

Proto-imperatives are the child's attempts to direct the actions of others. The child needs to be able to formulate goals relating to desired objects in the environment and to evoke and sustain the attention of adults. At a pre-verbal level both adult and child establish a cycle of 'action' and 'reaction' in which the first requests emerge. This is often established in a child who is sighted by the child's use of directed eye-gaze, which is interpreted by the adult. An example might be a child looking at his or her bottle and the adult subsequently offering it saying, 'Do you want some of this?' The child in this case is making use of informal/pre-symbolic behaviour to achieve a goal.

It will clearly be more difficult for a child with a visual impairment to fulfil this function of communication, with the absence of vision presenting a 'significant impediment to the development of this shared communication' (Warren 1994). The child with a visual impairment is therefore more reliant on less distinct and transient cues such as sound, and may be unaware of the presence of external objects, people or activities in his or her immediate environment. In addition, a child with limited motor skills may have difficulty in displaying the gestural signs which might usually be used by a child to demonstrate his or her attention to a signal.

Proto-declaratives

In using a proto-declarative, interaction with the adult is in itself the goal, rather than interaction being a means to an object-related goal. Bates (1976) has summarised this function of communication as 'communicating for the pleasure of communicating', and outlines three main stages of development of the proto-declarative children who are fully sighted :

1. exhibiting self
2. showing objects
3. giving or pointing to objects.

A child with a visual impairment may develop through a progression which starts with his or her own body behaviours, but the subsequent stages of 'showing' and 'giving/pointing to' objects might be more difficult to achieve. Warren (1994) suggests that at this stage the goal of the communication partner will be 'to increase the tactual and auditory experience and enlarge shared parental experience'.

The 'intuitive active listener'

It is clear from the literature relating to early child development, that the development of the proto-imperative and the proto-declarative functions in the development of children who are fully sighted relies heavily on the use of vision in establishing 'joint reference' with a communication partner. Mulford (1983) for instance, highlights the difficulties that the child with a visual impairment may have in establishing reference to external objects and emphasises the role of the 'intuitive active listener' who needs to be especially sensitive to the child's focus of attention. This sensitivity can be achieved through detailed knowledge of the child's responses to various experiences, in a variety of environments. It is important to note that patterns of response may be highly individualised and may not include the conventional use of the same facial expressions that a child who is fully sighted might display.

Intervention

Assessment of communication

Assessment should not be not regarded as an endpoint in itself, but rather as part of an ongoing process which arises from child-centred aims, goals, and objectives, and leads to programme planning, recording and evaluation (Coupe and Joliffe 1988). Aitkin and Buultjens (1992), suggest that it is only of interest 'if it offers practical information in order to help bring about beneficial change'.

Hogg and Sebba (1986) suggest that the use of structured observation and/or checklists may be more appropriate than formal assessments in reflecting the individual and complex nature of communication. Ware (1994) stresses the need to exercise caution in using checklists based on linear developmental sequences, and suggests that progress should be defined in terms of the needs of the individual rather than in terms of the individual's progress along a linear sequence, to a predefined endpoint.

Assessment of communication should involve observation of the child in a variety of settings, and extensive liaison with relevant carers and professionals in the environment. Although the majority of formal pre-verbal assessment procedures assume that the child is fully sighted and depend on the use of vision for successful attainment of the stages, the procedures summarised below have been found to be appropriate for use with children with multiple disabilities and a visual impairment, at an early level of communication.

The *Affective Communication Assessment* (ACA) (Coupe *et al.* 1985) provides a format for structured observation of behavioural responses to a range of stimuli at a pre-symbolic level. It offers a focus for determining possible communicative interpretations of behaviour which can aid the development of consistent and appropriate communication strategies by all communication partners.

The *Reynell–Zinkin Scales* (Reynell 1979) provide a guide to developmental stages and subsequent progression for young children with a visual impairment, many of whom are likely to have additional disabilities. The first three sub-scales are concerned with the assessment of, 'sensori-motor understanding', 'social adaptation' and 'exploration of environment'. Four further sub-scales cover various aspects of language development including comprehension and production. However, they provide limited information at a pre-verbal level, and a number of items rely on use of motor responses which may be problematic for the child with physical disabilities.

The *Callier-Azuza Scale* (Stillman 1978), is a developmental scale covering many aspects of development in children with dual sensory impairments (deaf-blind). The sections on cognitive development and receptive/expressive communication development define useful stages around which to structure early intervention, although the scales lack the detail required for comprehensive programme planning.

The *Oregon Project for Visually Impaired and Blind Pre-school Children* (Anderson *et al.* 1991) is an assessment and skills teaching pack, covering all aspects of development. The sections on cognitive, language, socialisation, and compensatory skills provide a helpful framework around which to build a communication curriculum. The Oregon Project was not designed for use with children with additional/multiple disabilities, and the authors advise that only the earlier stages of some skill areas may be applicable to children in this population. An additional assessment from a speech and language therapist to supplement the information gained from the profile is therefore recommended.

Assessing Communication Together (ACT) (Bradley 1991) offers a summary of the communication techniques that may be used between an individual with sensory impairments and his or her communication partner, across a range of early communication functions. The procedure provides a format for standardising the communication methods adopted by the child's various communication partners. The use of augmentative communication methods such as hand-over-hand signing and objects of reference, are covered in detail, and detailed case examples are provided.

Any assessment of a child should be viewed in the context of the child's environment, which will need to be 'audited' to ensure that both appropriate stimulation and suitable communication strategies are available. A combination of various assessment procedures may well be required to obtain accurate information to meet the child's communication needs.

The role of the communication partner

Communication is a two-way process that relies on at least one of the communication partners recognising the communication attempts of the other, assigning meaning to them, and responding to behaviours as if they had communicative value (Dunst and Lowe 1986). Bates (1976) proposes that the concept of **presupposition** underlies early communication exchanges. This is defined as the knowledge shared between speaker and listener which forms the basis of the decision regarding what aspects of a situation to encode into a communication act (formal or informal). The establishment of a shared basis of experience provides the foundation for subsequent communicative development and intervention.

At a pre-verbal level, the role of the child's communication partner is of paramount importance. A skilled partner has the flexibility to adapt and switch between modes and techniques of communication in order to meet the needs of the listener in a given context. The child with multiple disabilities may not be able to access 'formal' communication systems such as speech or manual signing. The onus therefore is on the skilled communication partner to accurately receive and interpret meaning and map that meaning onto non-intentional or unconventional communication signals. A useful protocol for the collation and sharing of such information is provided by the *Affective Communication Assessment* (ACA) (Coupe *et al.* 1985), which was referred to earlier in this chapter.

In considering the role of the communication partner, Bell (1985) makes a clear distinction between teaching and intervention. Intervention is defined as the 'process of manipulating the environment in order to accelerate the acquisition of communication and language'. It is emphasised that the role of the child's communication partner is one of intervention, as opposed to teaching which serves to confine the child to a more passive role.

Siegel-Causey and Downing (1987) recommend that the child's communication partner:

- develops nurturance by becoming aware of the child's needs and preferences;
- enhances sensitivity through recognising and responding to non-symbolic behaviours;
- sequences experience by establishing routines and providing turn taking opportunities;
- increases opportunities by creating needs and choices;
- utilises movement by responding to body movement and using movement as a form of communication.

In addition Porter and Kirkland (1995) define a number of characteristics that are desirable in a child's 'appropriately responding communication partner'. These characteristics are summarised in Table 33.2.

Table 33.2 Characteristics that are desirable in a child's communication partner (adapted from Porter and Kirkland 1995)

Expecting communication
Providing opportunities for the child to communicate
Encouraging attention to communication and sharing attention on what the communication is about
Actively looking for the communication meaning of a child's behaviour and responding to the message
Selectively responding to shape more specific communication behaviours
Modelling the use of language in context, talking about what the child is seeing, hearing, doing, feeling
Providing the child with natural feedback as to understanding of their message
Expanding the child's message to model the next step
Providing strategies to repair communication breakdown

Greenfield and Smith (1976), suggest that a child will encode the aspects of a situation which are undergoing greatest change or uncertainty. They call this 'theory of informativeness'. Each interaction involves a dynamic interplay with communication partners, who can recognise and adapt to changes in the focus of attention. The child with multiple disabilities and a visual impairment will have difficulty in influencing the environment and so will be more reliant on others to provide changes in activity and stimulation. The overall aim of the child's communication partner will therefore be to ensure that appropriate and structured stimulation is provided within an interactive context.

A range of activities designed to promote the development of early communication skills for individuals within the early stages of sensory and communication development can be found in the work of the following authors; Longhorn (1988), Bunning (1996), Nielsen (1990), and McInnes and Treffry (1982).

Augmentative and alternative communication

In considering the child with a visual impairment, strategies will need to be adopted to aid the child in understanding a world based mainly on the frame of reference of sighted communication partners. The child's communication partners may need to use augmentative/alternative communication (AAC)[2] strategies to aid the child's comprehension of verbal forms. These may include the use of manual signing systems such as Makaton, objects of reference, and tactile symbols. If the child does not then go on to effectively use spoken language, the same forms may later provide a means of expression, or can be used to support unclear attempts at communication.

Adaptations of signing may be necessary for children with a visual impairment. These may include adaptations such as the wearing of brightly coloured gloves when signing to children who are partially sighted. Signs may be adapted to become more tactile by using hand-over-hand ('co-active') signing. Further details of adapted signing are provided in Bradley (1991) and Lee and McWilliam (1995).

More 'concrete' tactile representations such as objects of reference may also be used to support and develop communication skills. Objects of reference are objects which intrinsically represent an object or event, for example a towel may be used to represent 'swimming'. If an object is consistently used in the context of a particular event, an association may be made between the object and the event. The object may subsequently be presented in order that a topic of conversation be clarified via a tactile cue. The object may also be presented with other objects of reference, for the purpose of making choices and requests. A more detailed discussion of tactile representation is provided in Bloom (1990), Ockleford (1994b), Park (1995), Hendrickson and McLinden (1996).

Conclusion

The development of communicative competence for children with multiple disabilities is intrinsically linked with the experiences and adaptive communication techniques offered by their communication partners.

Warren (1994), highlights three potential problems for children with a visual impairment in acquiring experience:

- a restriction in the extent of the environment with which the infant can engage;
- lesser stimulus value in the part of the environment that the infant encounters;
- lack of appreciation of the infant's impact on the objects manipulated.

The role of the child's communication partner is to ensure that these effects are minimised by providing structured, motivating experiences centred on tactile and auditory information.

The communication signals of the child may not be readily 'de-coded' due to their unique and informal nature. It is therefore the responsibility of those in the child's environment to:

- recognise and respond to any behaviour as being communicative;
- gradually expect more of the child by providing opportunities for the child to join in with shared experiences and routines.

The combination of appropriate experience and responsive interaction enables the child with multiple disabilities and a visual impairment to meet the complex challenge of communication development.

Summary

- The incidence of communication difficulty in children with a visual impairment and additional disabilities is higher than the incidence in children with a visual impairment and no additional disabilities.
- The incidence of language disorder in children with a visual impairment is higher than that found in the population of sighted children.
- The development of communication skills is of paramount importance in enabling children to access other curriculum areas.
- Parallels can be drawn between theoretical and functional aspects of language and communication development.
- Communication should be viewed as a two-way process. There are various strategies involving the use of augmentative communication which may be used to aid a child's understanding.
- Significant differences have been reported in the interactions of communication partners with children with a visual impairment. It is the responsibility of skilled communication partners to examine and re-structure the dynamics of the difference.

- A thorough evaluation of a child's informal communication strategies and the subsequent sharing of that knowledge will enable consistent and appropriate responses to be made by the child's communication partner(s).
- Intervention strategies will vary depending on the child's needs. The provision of individualised, motivating, structured activity, directed through appropriate sensory modalities, will help to provide the foundations of two-way communication.

Notes

1. Communicative competence refers to the 'quality or state of being *functionally* adequate in daily communication, or of having *sufficient knowledge, judgement* and *skill* to communicate' (Light 1989).
2. Definitions of augmentative and alternative communication are given by Lloyd and Blischak (1992). Augmentative communication is defined as 'an approach which is clearly an addition to speech or writing'. Alternative communication is used to refer to 'an approach that is clearly a substitute for (or alternative to) natural speech and/or handwriting'.

Chapter 34
Educational Technology

Nick Bozic

Introduction

This chapter explores some of the issues involved in the use of educational technology with children who have a range of multiple disabilities and visual impairment (MDVI). (For a review of educational technology for learners without additional/multiple disabilities, see Chapter 20.) The term 'educational technology' can refer to a wide range of equipment, from microcomputers and multi-sensory rooms to closed circuit televisions and communication aids. However rather than describing in detail what every form of educational technology can provide (an endless task with quickly outdated results), this chapter will instead consider some of the processes that determine the successful use of technology with this group of children.

The needs of children with multiple disabilities and a visual impairment are complex and will vary from individual to individual. A cyclical process is therefore proposed which should enable educational technology to be deployed in a way which is sensitive to the individual needs of each child. Cyclical approaches are evident in many areas of special education (see for example, Evans 1993, Fisher and Thursfield 1996, Nisbet 1996). They allow educational programmes to be flexibly adapted at the start of each fresh cycle to take account of the way a learner has coped with previous activities and experiences.

The approach, which is summarised in Figure 34.1, allows the use of technology with children with multiple disabilities and a visual impairment to be conceptualised as a four stage process.

Each of the four phases within this process will be discussed and case study material used to illustrate some of the main ideas.

Aims

Some forms of educational technology, for instance a multi-sensory room,[1] seem to offer a limitless range of potential uses, serving a variety of teaching aims. A recent study (Bozic, 1997) investigated how staff described the way they used multi-sensory rooms in four different schools where children with multiple disabilities and a visual impairment were being educated. Looking more closely at the way teachers defined their educational aims,

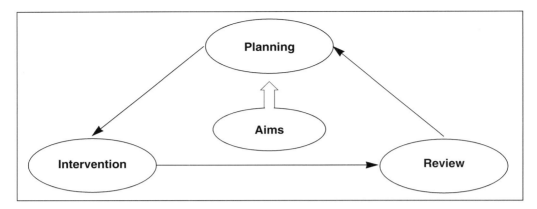

Figure 34.1   A cyclical approach to the use of educational technology

it became clear that staff drew from two discrete sets of terminology or 'repertoires'.

1. A developmental repertoire: describing multi-sensory rooms as tools teachers could use to help children move gradually through progressive levels of development.
2. A child-led repertoire: describing multi-sensory rooms as areas in which children could choose to do things without the teachers' direction. They were seen as relaxing places which offered physical and emotional comfort.

Teachers interviewed in two of the schools were more influenced by the 'developmental' approach. They saw their role as essentially presenting children with specific experiences that would encourage them to use their remaining vision. Although it was technically possible for children to change the environment by operating switches harnessed to the room's lighting effects, the teacher generally controlled the environment for them.

> ... for the two in my class I use it for, visual stimulation. I haven't yet used it for the other uses that the equipment has got, which is the interactive switches – they're not at the point yet where I want to begin that.

In schools which favoured the 'developmental' approach, terminology from the 'child-led' repertoire tended to be reserved for describing marginal activities. For example the room might be depicted as an ideal place for children to relax after they had worked hard:

> So we really use the light room as enjoyment, visual enjoyment and relaxation. We tend to use it at the end of the day and the end of the week, actually it's a wind-down, they've worked hard.

A third school in the study illustrated another way in which the aims for multi-sensory rooms were organised. In this school, teachers had consciously developed ideas from the 'child-led' repertoire to form a distinctive approach that emphasised the value of child-choice and communication. Here the multi-sensory room was seen as a place that contrasted with the rest of the school in that it provided a supportive context in which learners were able to express themselves and make real decisions. One teacher described a pupil she worked with:

> [He] responded badly to noisy atmospheres and that sort of thing [but] became the dominant person when I took him into the white room. He was the dominant person, he chose where to sit, he chose to arrange me how he wanted me, so he could be comfortable – because he was in charge. And in fact it was the only time he was in charge. When it comes to decision making that was quite an important part of his week.

The way teachers talk about teaching can reveal underlying assumptions of which they are sometimes unaware but which nevertheless determine their teaching aims and practice. A way of making these assumptions explicit is for staff at each establishment to negotiate and write down policy aims – a practice that was carried out at some of the schools in the study.

Planning

Once general aims have been agreed more specific objectives can be considered. Educators will need to make some kind of assessment of the individual needs of each child they work with, and know something about the extent to which various pieces of equipment and software can help to realise these objectives.

Assessment

Assessment of a child's abilities does not have to be a daunting task involving the administration of a range of time-consuming procedures. It is important however, to have some idea of the range of abilities that a child has in the area targeted by the educational aims, so that appropriate work can lead on from this point. If we are considering developing a child's use of his or her visual skills in a multi-sensory room for instance, we might ask: what is the child's current repertoire of visual abilities? Similarly, if we are considering developing a child's communication skills we might ask: how much can they express and comprehend at the moment?

In this context it may be useful to consider Vygotsky's (1978) concept of the 'zone of proximal development' (ZPD). Vygotsky claimed that there are two levels that one should be interested in when assessing a learner's abilities in any domain:

1. the learner's actual level of development, that is, what the learner can achieve alone;
2. the learner's potential level of development, that is, what the learner can currently achieve with the help of others.

It is the space between a learner's actual and potential level of development which Vygotsky called the ZPD (see Figure 34.2). Instruction should aim to place the child into situations just beyond what they can already achieve alone, but no higher than what they can reasonably achieve with the support of others. With successful learning the level of actual development will then shift into what is currently defined as the ZPD, and the level of potential development will rise into new uncharted territory.

Figure 34.2   Before and after successful instruction. (ZPD, zone of proximal development.)

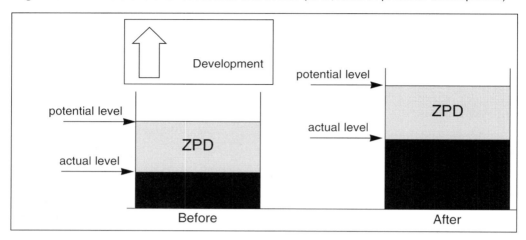

What then is the effect of educational technology on learners with multiple disabilities and a visual impairment? Although computers and multi-sensory rooms did not exist in Vygotsky's day (the 1920s and early 1930s), he certainly believed that any kind of tool has the power to extend human potential. It can be assumed that Vygotsky would have agreed that with the help of technology, as well as a teacher, a child may be able to achieve more than he or she would with only the teacher for support.

Children's actual level of development can be assessed much more easily than we can assess their potential level. In using microcomputers[2] as a focus for joint activities to develop the functional communication skills of children with multiple disabilities, including those with a visual impairment (Bozic and Sherlock 1996), the *Pre-Verbal Communication Schedule* (PVCS) (Kiernan and Reid 1987) was used to assess children's actual levels of expressive communication development. Given the conducive social and physical environment created by computer-based joint activities it was possible only to estimate what the potential levels of the children might be in this study.

Indeed Detheridge (1996) suggests that microcomputers might have a role to play in the assessment of a child's potential level of development, because they can offer such optimised conditions for performance. However it should be stressed that optimal levels of performance are only possible if appropriate equipment has been selected.

Affordance

It should be clear that we need to consider the possibilities afforded by a particular child's use of specific forms of technology (Bozic and Murdoch 1996). For any area (such as communication, visual abilities, relaxation, and so on), we need to think about the kind of equipment that can be selected to place a learner within his or her ZPD, while simultaneously extending the zone's upper boundary.

Sometimes technology is designed to specifically do this job for a particular domain. Communication aids are a good example of this as they have been expressly developed to increase the range of communications that a person with disabilities can make.

At other times educational technology may be used for a different purpose from the one which tends to be associated with it. In the study referred to earlier (Bozic and Sherlock 1996) simple image-based computer programs, which are often used in visual stimulation work with children (for instance Spencer and Ross 1989) instead afforded a focus for shared activity between educator and child. Here is an example of such a program being used with Charlotte, a young girl aged 1 year and 8 months who has nystagmus and moderate learning difficulties.

> The speech and language therapist cued up Charlotte with 'Ready Steady' and then paused before saying 'Go', hoping that Charlotte would say it herself (or make an equivalent kind of gesture/vocalisation), to demand the triggering of an exciting screen-based pattern. On one of the first times, Charlotte said 'Oh' when the therapist said 'Go' and reached out with her hand to touch the therapist's head. Later when the therapist paused after saying 'Ready Steady', Charlotte would pat the screen with both hands, while still looking at the therapist from time to time, and this was interpreted as a signal to trigger the pattern.

Wertsch (1995) warns us that any tool that affords certain possibilities, will also deny others. It is wise to maintain a critical stance towards the use of educational technology and always be willing to ask the question: in what ways does this equipment fail to meet my requirements? (See also Chapter 20.) When we considered the suitability of much commonly available switch software for the kind of intervention outlined above, we discovered its affordance was limited in important ways (Bozic 1995). For example, software failed to offer totally predictable sequences of events with teacher-controlled options for variation. Sometimes software was too slow or unable to offer the right kind of choices.

With astute assessment of a child's actual and potential development and careful selection of technology to afford appropriate possibilities, we might now consider what happens within the context of intervention.

Intervention

Newman *et al.* (1989) consider the child, the piece of technology and the educator as together forming what is termed, a 'functional system': a system that functions to attain specific goals. This type of arrangement can move a child with multiple disabilities into a position where they are able to control events, make choices and generally become a more active participant in their own learning (Daniels 1996). However, such a scenario is heavily dependent on the educator intervening to support activities step by step in a sensitive and flexible way. One approach which seeks to achieve this goal is called 'contingent teaching'.

Contingent teaching

Contingent teaching is defined by Wood (1988) as a style of instruction in which the amount of intervention is manipulated to suit the individual needs of a given child, more assistance, or 'scaffolding', being given when a child is struggling, but less when he or she is coping. When educational technology is added into this equation we see that a child's progress can be scaffolded in a number of ways, by both the educator and the technology. Three functions of scaffolding (cf. Wood *et al.* 1976) are illustrated below using examples from work with a closed-circuit television[3] (CCTV) (Bozic *et al.* 1996).

1. Scaffolding that reduces the demands of an activity

By taking responsibility for some elements of a task, the educator/technology makes it possible for a child to complete the remaining actions successfully.

> Peter (aged 10 years) has a severe visual impairment due to retinopathy of prematurity (ROP). He has a severe hearing loss and severe learning difficulties. Luke (aged 8 years 7 months) is diagnosed as having CHARGE association [Coloboma, Heart defect, Cloacal Atresia, Retardation, Genitourinary defects, Ear anomalies]. He has a severe visual impairment, a profound hearing loss and severe learning difficulties.
>
> Peter and Luke used a CCTV to explore objects. The CCTV reduced the visual demands of the activity: when Peter examined an object its image was magnified, and the magnification could be adjusted from moment to moment to allow optimal viewing. Similarly the teacher held a tray of objects nearby to facilitate Peter's selections and retrieved objects which accidentally slipped off the viewing platform. However, the teacher's interventions increased in scope if, for example, it appeared that the CCTV camera needed to be re-focused.

2. Maintaining direction

Scaffolding actions may be used to ensure that a learner's attention does not wander too far from the task in question.

> At one point Luke stopped manipulating objects under the CCTV camera. His head dropped forward, he pushed his hands up so that they touched the underside of the CCTV monitor and he began to vocalise. His teacher responded by gently massaging his back and saying softly 'Getting yourself excited aren't you?' She then held his hand and with her other hand slowly brought a new object to his grasp. Luke's vocalising diminished and he continued exploring.

3. Highlighting critical features

An educator may highlight significant features of a task. This type of scaffolding serves to draw attention to some aspects rather than others.

> Prior to the CCTV work the teacher had selected a range of objects that would highlight particular visual features. Objects varied in texture, colour and shape; some were moving, some spinning, others static. During the session she drew attention to other features. For example, on handing Luke a rubber ball she first squeezed it and, placing it under the CCTV camera, directed Luke's attention to the way the ball and its image swelled back up to full size.

Appropriation

There is a danger that contingent teaching and scaffolding may be understood as an excessively educator-directed form of instruction (Cole and Griffin 1984). The concept of appropriation (Leont'ev 1981, Newman *et al.* 1989) helps us to see how this is not necessarily the case.

A child appropriates (or develops ownership over) the concepts and technologies with which he or she is presented in instructional interactions. However, '[the] appropriation process is always a two-way one. The tool may also be transformed, as it is used by a new member of the culture' (Newman *et al.* 1989). A child therefore has some room to develop his or her own ways of relating to and ways of using the technologies that are introduced.

Returning to the case studies of Luke and Peter, it emerged that over time, each child had developed his own approach and way of using the CCTV. In discussing this aspect of the work the teacher described each child differently. In considering Luke the teacher commented:

> I don't think I have had anybody who's so intent on using the controls as Luke has been. That has been a new area. He just seemed to discover it himself.

When the teacher reflected on Peter's use of the CCTV she concentrated more on his selection of objects for viewing:

> It has taken him quite a long time to get the confidence. It is confidence, because he often looks 'shall I, shan't I?' but now he just gets up and sorts out what he wants.

It is clear from these comments that each child had appropriated the CCTV in a slightly different way.

Appropriation can also work the other way around. Often, at an early stage of instruction, educators react to, and appropriate, a child's actions *as if* they have a specific meaning (Newman *et al.* 1989, Stone and Wertsch 1984). The idea is that through time and repeated interactions, children will recognise that their behaviour is interpreted by adults in a consistent and meaningful way, and they will come to learn the significance of their own actions. This kind of approach is often advocated in communication interventions with children who have disabilities (for instance, Coupe and Jolliffe 1988, Nind and Hewitt 1994) and can also be seen in some aspects of the CCTV work.

> Towards the end of the CCTV session Peter put his finger near to the on/off switch (which was housed at the front of the monitor). The teacher interpreted this action as meaning that Peter wished to end the activity and return to his classroom.

As mentioned above contingent teaching and appropriation are very dependent on the sensitivity and skill of the educator (Stone and Wertsch 1984, Newman *et al.* 1989), particularly in recognising the upper limits of how far a child's actions can be scaffolded or appropriated.

Review

In the hurly-burly of daily school life it is not always easy to find the time to review systematically the work that is being carried out. However, a child's use of educational technology should be periodically reviewed to ensure some kind of progress is being made. An important aspect of the review stage involves comparing achievements with the objectives set during the planning stage. For this purpose it is useful to maintain detailed written records during each intervention phase.

Obstacles to progress

There are many possible reasons why the use of educational technology may fail to result in progress for a learner. A review phase allows careful analysis of each of the previous stages in order to remedy the situation.

1. Aiming too high or too low

One potential problem is that initial objectives might simply have been too ambitious, attempting to make the child work in the area above his or her ZPD (see Figure 34.2). This might be happening if an educator finds it impossible to reduce the amount of scaffolding that they are contributing towards a task.

The opposite problem occurs when the activities being devised for a child are found to be not demanding enough. In such a case, a child may only be required to practise skills which he or she can already perform independently.

A major advantage of educational technology is the flexibility it affords in such a learning situation. If a child is unable to participate in a microcomputer-based joint activity with one type of switch, he or she may be able to do so with another different type of switch. If the computer software requires too many high-level visual skills, there may be ways of choosing software with simpler images or alternative auditory output. In these examples the possibilities *afforded* by the educational technology are manipulated by alterations to the equipment.

2. Difficulties in interpretation

Problems can also occur in the moment-to-moment performance of a task when an educator fails to correctly interpret the signals that a child is displaying. For example, educators may over-scaffold (in other words, be too directive) because they wrongly interpret a child to be struggling. Alternatively they may under-scaffold and consequently fail to pick up signals that a child is unable to cope.

A related problem occurs when an educator misappropriates a child's response: imposing a meaning on the child's action which is so foreign to the child's intention that the child is unable to appreciate how the educator is interpreting the situation.

These problems are particularly acute in children with multiple disabilities and a visual impairment whose perception of the world is so different from that of the educator. However, the choice of educational technology can have an ameliorating effect here.

Suitable technology can offer children a better chance of communicating without misunderstanding, for example, by providing switches that can be reliably activated, or environments in which perceptual events are clear and easy to understand.

Progress

In Vygotskian terms, if a child has progressed it means that his or her zone of proximal development will have shifted upwards (see Figure 34.2). The educator is likely to find that as a result there is less need to scaffold the child's actions: more and more of the work with the educational technology can be undertaken independently by the child.

> In the work with the CCTVs the teacher found that over time the children took over more and more of the functions that she initially had responsibility for. For example, ultimately some of the children started to take responsibility for focusing the CCTV camera – a task requiring a fair degree of fine motor control.

It may well be that progress is not in exactly the direction that was initially anticipated. But, to some extent, this is to be expected: learners are likely to appropriate their experiences with educational technology in personal ways. For example, when talking about children's experiences in multi-sensory rooms, staff often mention personal ways in which particular children learn to interact with the equipment.

> I think that what happens in there varies with each child, and what they discover from exposure to it. I mean with my two new arrivals at school, one is totally dependent for almost everything, and so he's just discovering the pleasure of the optic fibres. The other girl ... is becoming interested in looking.

The educator might now consider what happens once progress has been demonstrated. What, for instance, might be an appropriate next step for the boy once he has discovered the pleasure of the optic fibres, or the girl, once she is interested in looking?

For a child who has developed new skills, new slightly more demanding activities need to be devised; once again stretching the child to work within his or her now more developed ZPD. It may be necessary first to reflect on the aims that are being worked towards before considering carefully how a further cycle of intervention could be organised.

Summary

Below are some guiding questions that may help to orientate educators to the issues raised in this chapter.

Think about a particular child, whom you know fairly well and who is using some form of educational technology. Now consider your responses to the following questions:

- Do you have a firm understanding of the aims that motivate the use of educational technology with this child?

- How has the child's actual level of ability been assessed?
- In what ways do you expect the child's potential ability to be raised by the use of educational technology?
- What are the possibilities and limitations that educational technology affords this child?
- How do educators scaffold the child's use of educational technology?
- Has the child appropriated the educational technology?
- How is the child's progress to be monitored?
- How will the child's progress be reviewed?

Notes

1. Multi-sensory rooms are specially adapted rooms often furnished with soft flooring and cushioned areas for sitting and lying, with switch-controlled visual and auditory effects. For their origins see Hulsegge and Verheul (1986). Hutchinson and Kewin (1994) offer an interesting collection of ideas on how multi-sensory rooms can be used.
2. Microcomputers can be used with a variety of software and connected to all sorts of equipment (switches, concept keyboards and touchscreens, etc.) to make them more useful for children with multiple disabilities. See Aitken and McDevitt (1995) for an overview.
3. CCTVs are usually used to magnify text for print-reading purposes but, as with other equipment, do not have to be used for the purpose for which they were designed. See Jose (1983) for a more traditional treatment of their role.

Chapter 35

Functional Vision Assessment and Development in Children and Young People with Multiple Disabilities and Visual Impairment

Marianna Buultjens

Introduction

Functional vision may be defined as:

> any remaining sight, no matter how little, by means of which the learner can add to his experience, enjoyment and learning about the world. This includes sight which is so poor as to enable the person to tell only light from darkness.' (Aitken and Buultjens 1992).

The importance of functional vision is now widely accepted and it is rare to hear the once common saying about young people with multiple disability and visual impairment: 'Vision is the least of their problems!'

Assessing functional vision in these young people remains a complex and daunting task. However, approaching it in a systematic and structured way and accepting it as an ongoing process in which a range of participants – parents, professionals and the young person – are involved, yields valuable results.

A chapter such as this will provide guidelines but not the whole story. For the reader who is embarking on the process for the first time, activities are suggested which accompany the reading so that it does not remain abstract but can be applied to the reader's situation.

As well as the process of information gathering, the application of that information in an instructional programme will be considered. Three short case studies will illustrate how it all comes together to ensure an appropriate and enjoyable learning experience for the young person and more satisfaction for parents, carers and educators.

Starting point: know the young person!

There could be several answers to the question 'Where do I start?' but for the purposes of this chapter, start thinking about a real situation. If you are a parent, think of your child.

If you are a class teacher, think of the pupil or student whose functional vision you most want to find out more about. If you are an advisory teacher, lecturer, carer or other professional, choose a young person you are often asked to help or advise on.

Activity 1

Now write down information about this young person, such as: first name; age; stage in the educational process; past educational experience; likes and dislikes; abilities; cause of visual impairment, and any other disabilities. Then give one answer to the question: 'What do I want to know about this young person's vision?'

You will discover that you already know a great deal but that there are some gaps. We all rely sometimes on assumptions, vague recollections and intuition, and you will find that you will have to look up some information and ask parents or other professionals about other aspects. One of the things that may strike you, if you go to the files, is how little information there is about your student's vision. Unless you are pleasantly surprised by the background information in school or college files, or unless you have very good first-hand links with medical personnel, you may have to use the appropriate procedures in your own situation to get information from the ophthalmologist, paediatrician and orthoptist, or to arrange for a vision test if this has not been done recently. Some paediatric ophthalmologists and paediatricians now send to parents, and to those recommended by parents such as class teachers, reports on their findings written in lay person's language, with the educational implications spelt out. These reports are worth their weight in gold but unfortunately, at the moment, they are the exception rather than the rule.

When beginning the assessment, start with the background information you have already or utilise what you already know about the young person's visual functioning. If you know for example, that he or she can see a medium sized object across a room, there will be no need to begin by assessing whether the student has light perception!

The young person's likes and dislikes, abilities, present and previous experience are important as they will inform you about the person and how he or she interacts with other people and relates to objects within a range of environments. It is important to know what might motivate the young person so that the assessment process can be a pleasant one for all concerned.

What vision assessment has been done?

Chapter 7, Assessment of Vision, provides a description of the different types of vision tests currently available. Some of these, such as preferential looking or electrophysiological tests such as VER (visual evoked response) or ERG (electroretinogram), may already have been carried out with the young person you are assessing. This information will be helpful in deciding at which point of the visual continuum – from light perception through to the presence of visual activity – to start assessing functional vision.

The young person in question may have spectacles to correct refractive errors of long sight, short sight or astigmatism. Corrective lenses can be provided without his or her active cooperation but standard tests for visual acuity rely on cooperation and a certain level of conceptual development. This developmental level is equivalent to an 18-month old child for a simple picture assessment and 3-years plus for those tests using letters. As a result, 'off the peg' assessments for many young people with multiple disabilities will not be suitable.

Developmental level

In planning for both curriculum and assessment it is important to be aware of the level at which a young person is functioning. Fifteen to twenty years ago intelligence quotients (IQ) were commonly given as a measure. Although some professionals now use developmental as opposed to chronological ages to record an assessment, this can be less than helpful if a 20-year-old is reported as having a developmental age of 3 months.

Aitken and Buultjens (1992) propose the use of organising themes which describe increasingly complex stages of responding to visual and other sensory stimuli.

Awareness represents the most basic stage where the young person shows signs of becoming or being aware that something has 'happened' or 'changed' in the environment but with no appreciation of 'what' or 'why'.

Attending is a more 'specialised' response in that the person is beginning to be able to distinguish or differentiate between people, objects, places, events.

Localising describes more consistent differentiation in relation to specific events in the surroundings and being able to 'locate' an event.

Recognising means the young person can isolate particular features of an object or event and has some capacity to construct a mental representation of that object and event.

Understanding means that the young person not only recognises the features of an object but also understands the relevance, significance and use of that object or the meaning of an event.

Activity 2
Write down the following information:
> What vision testing has been done on the young person under consideration and what information did it provide?
> Describe the developmental level of the young person in question.

Causes of visual impairment

It is helpful to consider the causes of visual impairment under two headings:
- ocular visual impairment
- central or cortical visual impairment.

Ocular visual impairment

In young people with multiple disabilities, ocular visual impairment may be caused by a range of conditions including: retinopathy of prematurity, cataract, optic atrophy, optic nerve hypoplasia, and so on. A summary of common eye defects is provided in Chapter 5. As mentioned previously, refractive errors may be present and correction by appropriate lenses should therefore be provided.

Central or cortical visual impairment (CVI)

Central or cortical visual impairment (in former years known as Cortical Blindness) has been used in the past as a global term describing the visual impairment common to many children and young people with physical disabilities and complex learning difficulties. Cortical visual impairment (CVI) is caused by brain damage which may occur before, during or after birth or as a result of injury or disease. The eyes may 'look' normal but visual messages to the brain are not properly interpreted or acted upon.

However, we know that the majority of these children and young people have some functional vision and gradual improvement may, in some cases, continue into the teens.

Anomalies of cognitive vision may also result from blindness at an early age as we cannot 'know things' we have not experienced. Thus, the education of blind children and those with brain damage associated with visual problems is a major challenge (Dutton 1994).

Common problems for those with CVI include:

- distinguishing objects in cluttered environments
- dealing with more than one object at a time
- recognising shape and size of objects
- slowness in understanding what is required of them in a situation, and in carrying out tasks.

Recent developments in neurology have made it possible to diagnose and describe more precisely certain processing difficulties in the brain. These are sometimes called 'cerebral visual dysfunctions'. This indicates that damage may be to areas of the brain other than the visual cortex. Individuals with these conditions may experience one or more of the following dysfunctions (Dutton 1994).

Akinetopsia. An inability to see moving objects.

Blindsight. People who are blind because of damage to the occipital lobes are able to see to navigate by using another part of the brain which is responsible for reflex vision. They, therefore, have limited conscious awareness of their visual function. The person may also be able to see moving objects. This vision is primarily to the side and usually does not involve central vision.

Simultanagnosia. Most commonly occurs in young people who have quadriplegia. It means that items in complex pictures cannot be simultaneously processed and the picture needs to be broken down into its constituent parts.

Topographic agnosia. A disability in route finding. It affects finding one's way around in the environment as well as finding objects in a room or on a table. It is often accompanied by an inability to recognise faces (prosopagnosia).

Hyvärinen (1995b) also describes a functional loss in some children and young people of recognition of shape and size through vision, though they are able to do so through touch. In some cases the child may be able to grasp objects based on visual information but does not look at objects or people and uses hands for exploration of detail. Hyvärinen points out that because of their manipulation of objects and lack of eye contact these children are often thought to be autistic or to have severe learning difficulties, especially if there is simultaneous disturbance of the auditory pathways so that the child hears but does not decode language (Hyvärinen 1995–6).

Assessing functional vision

The visual continuum has already been mentioned. Table 35.1 provides a summary of the functions and abilities along this continuum which can be used in assessing vision.

Table 35.1   Visual functions and abilities

Responses to light
Responses to reflected light
Responses to approaching objects
Responses to moving objects: horizontal, vertical, clockwise and anti-clockwise
Responses in visual fields: upper, lower, field preference, and visual attention
Responses to contrast: high, medium and low
Responses to large, medium and small objects
Responses to faces
Vision for mobility
Ability to: fixate, track, shift gaze (saccade), accommodate to light and dark

Activity 3
Using Table 35.1 as a guide, describe any use of vision by the young person you have been considering in the earlier activities.

Presentation of visual stimuli
When presenting a visual stimulus it is important to make sure that no other sensory stimulus interferes. Obvious examples are the click of a light switch, the rustle of tinsel or even the sound of voices in the background.

If you are assessing for the most basic levels of vision, it helps to do this in a dimly lit or darkened room so that the light or illuminated objects will stand out. Contrast and appropriate levels of lighting are important factors to bear in mind for all assessment situations.

A visual stimulus will need to be presented within the young person's 'visual sphere'

(Lindstedt 1986). This term refers to the area and distance within which the child will pay attention to a visual stimulus. You may have to experiment to find out the exact visual sphere of each young person.

A related phenomenon is visual inattention. It is often difficult to differentiate between a visual field loss resulting from changes in the anterior visual pathways and a loss of awareness, for instance, of one body half. A field loss cannot be restored but can be compensated for by the young person learning to scan to the side of the field loss, if they are able to, or by adults taking care to present objects to them or communicate with them within their existing field of vision. Rehabilitation or training can help the young person become aware of the lesser functioning half of space by, for example, pairing an object with other sensory information, or passively moving a hand to touch the object (Aitken and Buultjens 1992, Hyvärinen 1995b).

It is always important to structure the assessment carefully. The sequence of presentation of material and appropriate methods of recording responses need to be carefully thought out beforehand. A checklist on its own, without documentation, is potentially problematic unless you have someone experienced who can guide you in its use. Texts referred to in this chapter, for instance Aitken and Buultjens (1992), and Hyvärinen (1995–6), have an internal consistency, grew out of research and development and deal specifically with assessing functional vision in learners who are at an early developmental level.

What is meant by 'response'?

It is sometimes very difficult to determine whether a learner at the most basic developmental level of awareness is responding to a stimulus. The following range of reactions to a visual stimulus are described by Hyvärinen (1995b).

- Eyes turn only a little toward the light source.
- Head turns toward the light source.
- The child seems to get dazzled.
- Eye aperture becomes larger.
- Breathing, heart rate or motor activity may change.
- There is a change in the facial expression.

It can be helpful to establish a 'baseline' of behavioural responses which may include the following stages.

1. Observe and record the young person's behaviour when the teacher/carer is absent (baseline).
2. Observe and record the behaviour when the teacher/carer is present.
1. Observe and record the behaviour when a specific event is introduced. (Aitken and Buultjens 1992).

While carrying out research for *Vision for Doing* (Aitken and Buultjens 1992) the two authors found that ascertaining responses to non-visual information gave a wider knowledge of the learner's abilities and a means of comparing visual responses with those responses made to information detected through the other senses. Four sections in *Vision for Doing* are devoted to observing and considering the learner's: responses to sound; sense of touch; sense of smell; sense of taste.

A simple (and true) example might help. While trying to assess whether a child could see reflected light, the authors were shining torch light on to a shiny tin lid, with absolutely no signs of any response from the child. One of the authors, by mistake, let the tin lid fall, which it did with a clatter. The child startled and then began to chuckle, his face wreathed in smiles. Quite a different animated little boy from the one who couldn't see the light reflected on the lid but enjoyed its noisy fall.

Using and developing functional vision

Research and long-term studies have provided us with important information regarding the use and development of functional vision, and suggest that early intervention and visual stimulation are vital to avoid further neurological defects. The majority of children with CVI have some functional vision and continued and gradual improvement, in some cases, continues into early adulthood. However, intensive visual stimulation on its own is ineffective. The term 'stimulation' implies passivity, whereas active participation is necessary for learning to take place. A visual environment and visual experiences from daily life, adapted to the individual visual and cognitive needs of the young person, may result in gradual improvement in visual response (Jan 1993).

Any programme to encourage use of vision has to be constantly monitored and evaluated in order to:
- avoid over-learning or boredom;
- ensure transference of the skill to other situations;
- identify progress or deterioration (if a progressive disease is present);
- take into account maturation or transition, for instance, moving from school to college or work situation.

The programme needs to be based on a clearly outlined structure of progression, so that those designing it know where it should be leading, and those implementing it understand why certain things are being done. The following section offers one example of a structured programme and is based on the levels of visual response described by Aitken and Buultjens (1992) and the levels of instruction as described in *Management of Low Vision in Children* (World Health Organization 1993). The examples given are not intended as a comprehensive menu; rather they are used to illustrate a progression towards increasing independence and control by the young person.

Stage one: awareness level
Use of variety of light stimuli: different colours, patterns, intensities. Linking cause and effect, such as movement and vocalisation, can be linked to light or to illuminated objects.

Stage two: attending/localising level

Use of form, shape, size, colours of objects reinforced by tactual exploration (everyday objects); eye–hand, eye–body coordination if possible; encouraging use of vision for communication for instance talking to someone; shared attention; for instance talking about a held object; indicating or asking for something which is seen. Use of vision to encourage exploration of objects or environment. Introduction of pictures, illustrations along with real objects; use of vision for anticipating and identifying activities.

Stage three: recognising/understanding level

Use of vision for choice by means of objects, pictures or symbols; encouraging independence by awareness and use of environmental cues; developing compensatory eye, head or body movements; strategies for self-help activities which take into account when and where not to use vision.

Case studies

The following case studies attempt to illustrate the ideas contained in this chapter, bringing together background information, results of functional vision assessment and its integration within an instructional programme to encourage use of vision within the daily environment.

Case study 1

Paula is 3 years old. She has cerebral palsy, and corrected long sight. She displays a general lack of visual interest in objects or people but loves to be held and cuddled. She communicates her dislikes and distress by crying and thrashing movements of her limbs.

Functional vision assessment

Paula was assessed in a darkened room to determine her response to light source, and reflected light source (coloured streamers). She responded showing 'awareness', that is, she was aware that something had 'happened' or 'changed', but had no appreciation of 'what' or 'why'.

Programme

Paula's programme is based on Stage one, awareness level. In one-to-one interaction an adult's face, puppet or highly contrasted toy is used to encourage use of vision in communication. High contrast objects and patterns are presented in the dark room for short periods during the week. Only when lying over a wedge does Paula have voluntary movement in her arms and hands, so in that position, brightly coloured toys are placed so she can see and touch. Vision stimulation videos or software with sound effects, to help develop attention and perception of pattern, are used as part of her programme.

At other times use of vision is not specifically addressed unless a situation arises spontaneously. The programme is constantly monitored for change in Paula's response or time of response, so that it can be evaluated and further developed.

Case study 2

Gerry is 8 years old. He has suspected toxoplasmosis, cataracts, right hemiplegia and unspecified damage to his eyes. He enjoys independent movement around the floor by rolling. Gerry has no language or structured communication system, although he is able to vocalise pleasure and displeasure.

Functional vision assessment

Gerry is able to see medium sized objects, although he has difficulty tracking horizontally and is visually inattentive to his right field. He does not respond to faces and his general level of response is one of 'localising', that is, he is able to locate objects and events.

Programme

Stage two: attending/localising. In particular this will focus on coordinating visual information with other senses and actions and encouraging awareness of his right side. It will include table-top activities of between 5 to 10 minutes. Gerry has a longer attention span for independent exploration on the floor. He is visually able to locate objects then explore them by mouthing and banging them. Further assessment will be needed to determine if he has the visual functions for shape and colour recognition. Development in the use of vision may depend on his general level of development.

Case study 3

Janey is 14 years old and has cerebral palsy. She can recognise pictures if brought very close to her left eye, but has only light perception in her right eye. Janey communicates through spoken language which is mostly meaningful but which displays occasional echolalic characteristics. She operates at the Stage three: 'understanding' level, that is, she is able to recognise the features of an object, understand its relevance and use, and can interpret the meaning of an event. Although she can only distinguish detail when an object is held very close to her left eye, she makes use of form, outline and colour to let her know what is happening in her wider surroundings.

Programme

Janey's programme involves utilisation of vision at Stage three, Recognising/understanding. This involves Janey :

- altering her body position (within the limits of her voluntary movements) to take part in activities with a visual component, such as social games involving objects or cards;

- being an active participant in enhancing her use of low vision by perceiving and interpreting environmental clues when moving in her powered wheelchair;
- knowing when use of vision is inappropriate and another medium needs to be used and asking for help; for instance too small, detailed or complex illustrations which need either to be explained verbally or for the information conveyed through a simplified visual representation or tactile/3-D symbols.

At this level Janey's 'programme' functions mainly as a useful reminder for all concerned of her optimal use of vision in daily activities.

Summary

This chapter deals with the process of assessing and developing functional vision. It considers:

- the background information which must be available about a young person before embarking on assessment
- the implications of different causes of visual impairment in young people, and how the general developmental level of the young person must be taken into account in designing and interpreting the assessment
- visual functions and abilities within a visual continuum
- guidelines for presenting material and information about how to recognise a response to visual stimuli
- a structure for designing a programme to encourage the use of and to enhance functional vision.

Chapter 36
Multi-sensory Impairment

Heather Murdoch

Introduction

What do learners with multi-sensory impairment (deafblindness) have in common? Impaired vision and hearing, certainly, but as case studies 1 and 2 below illustrate, they may share little else. Given this diversity, a chapter of this length cannot hope to offer a thorough overview. Instead, the aim is to present some aspects of current thinking on multi-sensory impairment in children. Sources offering more comprehensive accounts of this topic may be found in the References section at the end of this book.

The population of learners with multi-sensory impairment

Case study 1

Zaheed is eight years old and attends a specialist deafblind unit where the staffing ratio is 1:1.5. His vision (currently 6/36 corrected) is deteriorating, and he has a hearing loss of 70–80 dB, so that with his hearing aids he hears many environmental sounds and some speech. He tends to use hearing rather than sight to gain information, but relies heavily on adults to confirm and explain what is happening around him. He is generally outgoing and quick to respond to environmental cues; as a result, adults often assume that his vision and hearing are considerably better than they are. He uses both speech and signing to communicate, although his communication through both channels is very delayed and his speech is unclear. He loves picture books and reads familiar names and 'timetable' words. His signing and mobility are slightly affected by hemiplegic cerebral palsy, and he has a number of medical problems, caused by the same rare syndrome as his sensory impairments.

Case study 2

Yvonne is a young adult whose epilepsy and frequent chest infections affect her ability to respond to her environment. She has profound and multiple learning difficulties including spastic quadriplegia. She seems to enjoy watching bright mobiles move and gazes intently at people's faces as they talk to her, but she pays no attention to anything more than arm's length away. She startles if her peers shout or scream in her ear, but shows no response to other sounds unless they are loud and low enough to cause vibration, which she loves. She enjoys the jacuzzi and being tickled. It seems that her sight and hearing were both tested when she was young, but the results are recorded as 'poor' and 'untestable' respectively.

Definitions and prevalence

Multi-sensory impairment has probably the lowest incidence of any recognised disability. Current estimates suggest a figure of around 0.018% in the UK, and this accords with other European countries and the USA (Best 1994). Exact figures are not available, partly because there is no universally agreed definition of multi-sensory impairment or deafblindness. Definitions involving visual acuity scores and decibel levels of hearing loss have generally been abandoned, recognising that the interactive effects of the sensory impairments are more important than their levels *per se*. Medical models of definition, which focused on the nature and degree of the impairment have largely been superseded by functional definitions or descriptions which emphasise the ways in which the disability affects daily living. Some recent descriptions have suggested lists of criteria, with individuals showing a certain number of characteristics identified as having multi-sensory impairment (for example, Fowler 1991). A number of authors have sought to differentiate the terms 'deafblindness' and 'multi-sensory impairment', arguing for example that multi-sensory impairment is associated with the field of learning disabilities, and that the term may be used synonymously with 'multiple disabilities and a visual impairment' (MDVI) or 'multiple disabilities and a hearing impairment' (MDHI) (Etheridge 1995). In this chapter, the terms 'multi-sensory impairment' and 'deafblindness' are both used to cover the continuum of individuals with congenital or early onset hearing *and* visual impairment.

The absence of a universally agreed definition relates less to a divided and irresolute band of professionals than to a rapidly changing and developing field and population. Best (1994) refers to a 'grey zone with adjacent diagnoses on all sides – PMLD [profound and multiple learning difficulties], adventitious disabilities, blind with additional difficulties, autism and so on'. The high prevalence of disabilities additional to multi-sensory impairment, and the difficulties inherent in accurate assessment of this population, together with a scarcity of skilled assessors, have contributed to rather patchy identification. Yvonne in Case study 2, for example, might be identified as having multi-sensory impairment in one area of the country, as profoundly physically disabled in another and as having PMLD in a third. In fact she has all three impairments, but services tend to require identification of a 'lead disability' before assessing the full range of needs from that perspective.

Causes of multi-sensory impairment

Until the 1980s, most learners of school age and above identified as having multi-sensory impairment were disabled by congenital rubella syndrome. Although they were not a homogeneous group, there was some common ground within the population. Many of the learners shared similar multiple disabilities (notably visual impairment, hearing impairment and cardiac problems), and similar patterns of hearing loss and types of visual impairment (notably congenital cataracts). Common behaviour patterns such as light-gazing, feeding problems, unusual sleep patterns and tactile defensiveness have also been identified, although some writers relate these to poor early intervention, rather than seeing them as a direct result of rubella damage (McInnes and Treffry 1982, Wyman 1986).

Vaccination and medical advances increasing the survival rates of very small and very frail babies, have served to change the nature of the population to one in which no aetiology is now dominant. SENSE (the National Deafblind and Rubella Association) lists more than 70 causes of multi-sensory impairment in the UK in what is a very small population. This picture is mirrored in other developed countries, including the United States (Collins *et al.* 1991). Compared to the earlier, rubella-dominated perspective, the current spectrum of aetiologies leads us further into Best's 'grey zone'.

Additional disabilities

Aetiologies that cause damage to both the eyes and the ears, or to the neurological systems supporting both sight and hearing, tend to be severe enough in their effects to damage other systems as well. Many of the 'new' population i.e. the non-rubella population, have profound disabilities which severely limit their potential achievements. Linked to this, however, is the potential misidentification of additional disabilities by assessors inexperienced with this group. For example, to someone unfamiliar with the effects of multi-sensory impairment an individual may appear to have 'learning difficulties' (because they learn slowly, and cannot learn incidentally); or 'autism' (because they show extreme difficulties with communication and social interaction) or 'motor impairment' (because mobility is hesitant or delayed).

If the learner has spent time in inappropriate provision, the situation is likely to be still more complex. If he or she needs an augmentative communication system, such as objects of reference, for example, and either none has been provided or a system is being used ineffectively, communication development will be deviant or further delayed. This will in turn influence development in other domains dependent on communication.

A failure to accept that learners with multi-sensory impairment are bound by their sensory disabilities alone to learn slowly and to require intensive support leads inexorably to the assumption of additional learning disabilities. A survey by the Department of Education and Science in 1986 found nearly two-thirds of learners with multi-sensory impairment were recorded as having 'severe learning difficulties' (Department of Education and Science (DES) 1989a). The term is unfortunate, in that while multi-sensory impairment undoubtedly causes severe difficulties in learning, the equation with cognitive impairment may be unwarranted. A number of writers, from medical as well as from educational backgrounds, have warned against the easy attribution of learning difficulties to learners with multi-sensory impairment (Blake *et al.* 1990, Fox, 1983).

The implications of multi-sensory impairment for development

'Distant' and 'close' senses

Sight and hearing provide the 'distant' information which allows us to anticipate events and act to control them, as well as to monitor the effects of our own actions and those of other people. Touch, taste, smell and the movement and balance senses provide good quality 'close' information (about what is happening here and now), but scant, poor quality data about distant events. Individuals with multi-sensory impairment cannot use information from one 'distance' sense fully to compensate for the impairment of the other, and they cannot use either sense to maintain effective contact with the wider social or physical environment. Those children with multiple disabilities but without impaired hearing may have difficulty *interpreting* the distance sensory information they receive through hearing, but its use is potentially open to them, and may, for example, provide reassurance that they are not alone.

People with multi-sensory impairment are 'unable to utilise their distance senses of vision and hearing to receive non-distorted information' (McInnes and Treffry 1982). At best they receive limited, distorted information about the people, places, objects and events which make up their environment; at worst, they receive no information at all. Fox (1983) compares the sensory input of a child with multi-sensory impairment to that of a newborn infant, describing it as 'imprecise, unpredictable and unfiltered', and suggests that the net effect is one of 'isolation in the midst of confusion'. This description may sound overstated when children like Zaheed in Case study 1 are considered, but it should be remembered that Zaheed's achievements rest on intensive teaching and support. Without focused input from an adult, he is unable to order or anticipate the happenings around him.

Hearing differs from vision in a number of ways. We hear round corners, through thin walls and when we are asleep, so that hearing is the primary sense used to warn us of changes in the environment, such as people approaching. Sight deals largely with spatial information, and hearing with temporal: we hear someone speaking whether they stand in front of or behind us, but once they have finished speaking the sound is gone for ever. Normally our use of sight and hearing is so well integrated that we are not aware of the ways in which we use each sense to complement the other. When hearing is impaired, visual information is used to compensate where possible (peripheral vision to scan the environment; central vision to lip-read or interpret signing) and to supplement residual hearing. The disruption of communication and language development is a major risk with hearing impairment, but when visual impairment is also present the effects can be far greater than the sum of the single disabilities alone.

Developmental implications of multi-sensory impairment

Siegel-Causey and Downing (1987) stress that multi-sensory impairment 'alters the way in which the individual (i) receives and sends information, and (ii) interacts with the social and physical environment'. Few, if any, of the bases for motivation and learning are left unaffected, and multi-sensory impairment (with or without additional disabilities) usually affects development globally. A number of functional definitions stress the impact of the disability on communication, information and mobility (Deaf-Blind Services Liaison Group 1988, for example), and the effects appear to begin at birth, with the process of mother–child bonding and attachment (Nafstad 1989). McInnes and Treffry (1982) suggest that children with multi-sensory impairment may:

- lack the ability to communicate with their environment in a meaningful way;
- have a distorted perception of their world;
- lack the ability to anticipate future events or the results of their actions;
- be deprived of many of the most basic extrinsic motivations;
- have medical problems which lead to serious developmental lags;
- be mislabelled as retarded or emotionally disturbed;
- be forced to develop unique learning styles to compensate for their multiple handicaps;
- have extreme difficulty in establishing and maintaining interpersonal relationships.

In the past few decades, practitioners and researchers from a variety of countries have proposed models of development in the context of multi-sensory impairment. These models (invariably developed from direct work with the multi-sensory impaired population) originate from different philosophies and priorities, but show remarkable similarities in their estimates of developmental need (Brown 1994). The concept of deprivation is common to many, although the emphasis varies between emotional deprivation (Van Dijk 1991), social deprivation (Chulkov 1989) and environmental deprivation (McInnes and Treffry 1982).

Mediation/intervention

All the writers mentioned above stress the need for mediation; for another person to present those aspects of the environment which the person with multi-sensory impairment cannot access independently. This process, of course, is necessary for any young child's learning, and the idea that children must use concepts and skills with a more competent adult before they can use them independently (Vygotsky 1978) is now increasingly accepted in mainstream psychology. For those with multi-sensory impairment, however, the need for mediation to access any aspects at all of the wider environment is so critical that the term 'intervention' has been coined, to describe one-to-one working in which the sighted hearing partner provides the information not delivered through sight and hearing. The importance of the mediator's role is supported by the findings of case study research (Murdoch 1994), as well as by the theorists mentioned above.

Successful mediation or intervention must, however, be based on shared understanding. The perceptual differences between a learner with multi-sensory impairment and a sighted, hearing mediator may be so great that breakdowns in communication are not easily repaired. Santin and Nesker Simmons (1977), writing about blind children, use mislabelling as an example: when a sighted two-year-old says 'cat' for dog, the mediator understands why the child has confused the two, and can help to further the child's understanding. A blind child, on the other hand, may smell that the cat has recently been sitting on a chair, although the chair is now empty. If the mediator does not realise why the child says 'cat' in this situation, she or he is unlikely to be able to help the child's development and may in fact increase confusion by an inappropriate explanation.

Functionally equivalent behaviours

Mismatches of expectation or understanding are more likely with learners with multi-sensory impairment. Their sensory perceptions differ more radically from those of sighted hearing individuals and their communication is less likely to be at a formal symbolic stage where they are able to use words, signs or symbols to express specific meanings.

Best (1994) discusses the concept of functionally equivalent behaviours: 'in the presence of sensory impairments, different behaviours can have identical meaning and identical behaviour can have different meaning'. The blind child who stills to listen, for example, is demonstrating functional equivalence: using available sensory information to try to identify the meaning of the sound, when a sighted child would look around with the same aim. The child with hearing impairment using peripheral vision to scan the environment for changes because they cannot use hearing for this purpose is likewise behaving in a functionally equivalent way. Similarly the child described by Santin and Nesker Simmons in the example above is doing the same using smell instead of sight.

A further example of a child demonstrating functionally equivalent behaviours is illustrated by Xavier, a young child with multi-sensory impairment. Xavier hates swimming, but cries brokenheartedly if he has an ear infection and cannot go with the rest of the group. It is not that he 'likes swimming really', or that he 'enjoys making a fuss'; but that he demonstrates understanding of the routine, and the significance of swimming as an activity that happens at a particular time, after some events and before others. His distress may be a functionally equivalent way of demonstrating both his understanding of the routine and his need for the security it provides.

Functional equivalence is an essential concept for those working with learners with multi-sensory impairment, but acceptance of the idea does not ensure understanding of the learner's meaning. Xavier, for example, has no formal communication and adults working with him cannot know for certain that the explanation given above is correct. Working with learners with multi-sensory impairment frequently entails a process of hypothesis formation and testing. This may involve trying to work out the learner's meaning, responding as though the interpretation is correct, watching the learner's reactions for clues, and beginning again if the interpretation is 'wrong'. This process, although painstaking and sometimes frustrating for all parties, has the potential to allow each learner to contribute to his or her own development (Daelman *et al.* 1993), affecting the quality of the learning environment including the quality of interactions with caregivers. For individuals with multi-sensory impairment to be active participants in their own development however, certain conditions must be met.

- Each learner must be considered as an individual, with a unique repertoire of behaviour.
- The patterns of interaction observed may be those seen at a much earlier age with sighted hearing children, and must be responded to appropriately whatever the learner's chronological age.

There must, above all, be sensitivity to the effects of multi-sensory impairment, not only on the learner's behaviour, but on the adult-learner interaction.

Assessment and intervention

Assessment

Multi-sensory impairment is associated with complex educational, social and medical needs, and hence individuals with the disability require expert, inter-disciplinary, clinical and functional assessment. Unfortunately, due to the very low incidence of multi-sensory impairment, this requirement may not be met. Inadequate or inappropriate assessment may hamper the identification of multi-sensory impairment, any additional disabilities, the educational, social or medical needs of the learner, and consideration of how the needs of the learner may best be met.

Case study 3

Wendy was diagnosed at 18 months as having a profound hearing loss and given powerful hearing aids which appeared to cause her great distress. The audiologist had little experience of children with a visual impairment, and had not taken Wendy's blindness into account when evaluating her reactions. Wendy's parents recognised that she stilled to listen, but they were not encouraged to contribute during the hearing test. The advisory teacher for visual impairment attempted to contact the audiologist to explain, but without success. Re-assessment at a different clinic six months later suggested that Wendy's hearing loss was moderate, and that she had recruitment, that is, loud sounds, including any sounds transmitted through the powerful hearing aids, caused her discomfort or pain. Issued with more appropriate hearing aids, Wendy had to overcome her fear of the aids, relearn that sound could be pleasurable and informative, and set about making up six months' loss of learning through her one accessible distance sense.

Case study 4

Vincent, at 14 years, had not developed any formal communication, although he was encouraged to use Makaton signing. He would copy signs, but did not use them spontaneously. Regular multi-disciplinary assessment had repeatedly confirmed that he had severe learning difficulties, emotional problems and challenging behaviour, and suggested that his constant rejection of his spectacles and hearing aids meant that he was better off without them. When the family moved house, Vincent was reassessed yet again. This assessment suggested that he was not realising his potential, and that communication should be a priority. Staff at his new school identified a range of idiosyncratic gestures which he used consistently, and to which they responded. Objects of reference were introduced to signal the activities in his day. Vincent became interested in these, and began to tolerate first his glasses and then his hearing aids, developing interests in pictures and music as his sight and hearing were aided. Picture symbols and musical cues were introduced, and Vincent's idiosyncratic gestures were augmented by signs. As his vocabulary spiralled, his challenging behaviour diminished and learning difficulties were no longer identified as his primary disability.

Requirements for assessment

Aitken (1995) suggests that assessment of learners with multi-sensory impairment should follow a 'systems led' or 'environment sensitive' approach, considering 'the learning setting, attitudes of staff, training and information needs, and not just reflect[ing] a narrow focus on the individual learner'. With this approach, assessment cannot be seen as an entirely objective procedure, placed somehow 'outside' the learner, the learning environment and the assessor, and results should not be interpreted solely in terms of the learner's abilities and disabilities. The contribution of the learning environment, including staff attitudes and skills, must be evaluated as an integral part of the process, and with a view to change where appropriate.

Without knowledge and experience of multi-sensory impairment, even a systems-led approach is likely to prove insufficient. Training for those working in the multi-sensory impairment field is more widely available now than at any point in the past (for educators at least), but this brings its own dangers. Awareness-level training, which may include simulation work using blindfolds and earplugs, can significantly increase awareness of multi-sensory impairment but cannot fulfil further expectations. Such training cannot, for example, provide a grounding in how to teach children with multi-sensory impairment, how to act as an aide to an individual child, or how to accurately assess such pupils. Only long-term, specialised training, or specific training tied to appropriate experience in the field, can do these things.

In the UK, the Department for Education and Employment (DfEE) recognises the importance of appropriate training for teachers working in this field. There is a legal requirement for teachers of children with multi-sensory impairment (as for those with hearing or visual impairment) to complete a recognised training course. The University of Birmingham runs a two-year distance education course in multi-sensory impairment which is recognised by the DfEE, and this is currently the only such course running in the UK. For other professionals, such as intervenors, nurses, educational psychologists, residential social workers and classroom support staff, training is not regulated in a comparable way. Overall, the move towards generic special needs training is unlikely to work for the good of learners with multi-sensory impairment.

Intervention

Intervention, like assessment, demands expertise, knowledge and inter-disciplinary working over time. Teaching pupils with multi-sensory impairment has been compared by Van Dijk (cited by Best 1994) to teaching reading: symbols must be recognised, decoded and combined to make meaning. Learners with multi-sensory impairment, however, may need to be taught to decode their whole environment, rather than written words.

Recent research has suggested that normal child development provides the most appropriate basis for models of intervention. It is likely that educators will need to interpret the functionally equivalent behaviours of learners in this context, and they will also need to consider how to make the conditions in which sighted hearing children learn accessible to those with multi-sensory impairment. How can pupils with multi-sensory impairment learn to recognise, for example, the significant people around them? How can they identify an activity about to happen? The whole of the learning environment (people, places, objects and events) needs to be analysed in this way. How would a sighted hearing child learn? What obstacles will confront the child with multi-sensory impairment, trying to learn in the same situation? How can these obstacles be overcome?

Some solutions, tested and found successful over time, may be hard to implement in settings catering for learners with a range of needs. Visser (1988), for example, stresses that one-to-one work, over time, in a consistent adult–learner partnership, is essential for the development of communication and attachment. The development of routines to aid anticipation, and the use of objects of reference or other systems signalling aspects of the environment, must be inexorably consistent for the learner to benefit. It would be unreasonable, for instance, to expect learners with multi-sensory impairment to predict which events in the day have been planned to be predictable by those working with them.

Most learners with multi-sensory impairment have some useful residual hearing and/or vision, and optimising the use of residual senses should be a priority. Qualified teachers of children with hearing impairment, visual impairment or multi-sensory impairment will be able to advise on the best approach for an individual child. Again, however, the needs of other children may conflict with the interests of the learner with multi-sensory impairment. A child with limited vision, for example, may benefit from an uncluttered visual environment, without bold wall displays, hanging mobiles, equipment scattered around the room or people walking to and fro. A child wearing hearing aids is likely to find shouting peers uncomfortable or painful to be near, and background music or chatter distracting and confusing. Busy classrooms may be among the least desirable environments for learners with multi-sensory impairments.

A model of intervention

One model of intervention is shown in Table 36.1. Although simplistic, it stresses the need for attention to detail when working with learners with multi-sensory impairment. Sighted hearing children learn many things incidentally, but those with multi-sensory impairment cannot do so because they cannot access incidental information. It follows that none of their learning can be left to chance. Every aspect of every learning situation, whether the pupil is interacting with others or exploring alone, needs to be carefully assessed and optimised.

Currently accepted principles

The education of learners with multi-sensory impairment (in terms of both the identification and the meeting of needs) has been influenced by theories and approaches from a number of sources. Brown (1994) draws together the influences of 'American behaviourism, Russian social learning theory, Van Dijk's deprivation theory, Nordic humanism, McInnes and Treffry's ecological theory and British family orientation' in his summary of currently accepted principles.

Table 36.1   A model of intervention for learners with multi-sensory impairment

Aspect	Questions to ask regarding intervention	Optimising the learning situation
Context	Who? When? Where?	*Ordering the environment:* Reducing the number of people working with the learner Clearly identifying each person (e.g. by tactile cue and greeting routine) Signalling activities and places by tactile, visual, auditory and/or olfactory cues Developing and maintaining consistent routines within activities Maintaining consistency in the physical environment (not moving furniture; using the same objects in activities) Breaking or delaying routines only when the learner is able to anticipate the next step
Content	What?	Based on 'normal' development, especially 'normal' interaction patterns Priorities decided from assessment, especially of the learner's interests Dependent on preferred curricular model (e.g: developmental; ecological) (In the UK for school-age learners:) with regard to the National Curriculum
Process	How?	*Recognising the implications of multi-sensory impairment:* Developing attachment between learner and educator Acceptance and interpretation of functionally equivalent behaviours Recognising the learner's communication and using augmentative communication Encouraging the learner to control situations rather than to respond passively Allowing increased time for learners to receive, interpret and respond to stimuli Working co-actively (hand-over-hand) through activities the learner cannot perform independently, to give access to all stages of the activity Recognising the stress created by multi-sensory impairment, and giving opportunities for relaxation
Purpose	Why?	To increase the learner's autonomy and sense of self-worth Short-term goals will depend on assessment findings and the preferred curriculum model

- The child is an active participant if the signs are understood.
- Personal interaction is the great motivator and educator.
- Behaviour has meaning.
- Communication precedes language and is multi-modal.
- Natural surroundings and activities are the best environments and have their own effect.
- Structure and routine establish the security and knowledge base from which to explore.
- Experience must be given and is used for learning.
- There is development over time.
- Consistency and attention to detail is vital.
- Maximum use must be made of available sensory perception.
- Gradual transfer of control to the child is essential.
- Emotional security is a crucial factor.

Summary

- Multi-sensory impairment is a complex, low incidence disability creating a wide range of special needs.
- The high prevalence of additional disabilities and changing patterns of causation have contributed to the complexity of the field.
- The developmental implications of multi-sensory impairment incorporate those of hearing and of visual impairment, together with emotional, social and environmental deprivation due to the loss of distance sensory information.
- Learners with multi-sensory impairment require mediation to access and control their wider environment.
- Successful mediation demands the acceptance and interpretation of functionally equivalent behaviours.
- Expert, inter-disciplinary assessment is needed, but is not always available.
- Assessment must evaluate the learning environment as well as the learner.
- Specialised training and experience are vital for both assessment and intervention with learners with multi-sensory impairment.
- Normal child development provides the most appropriate basis for models of intervention.
- Currently accepted principles of intervention have been developed from a variety of theoretical approaches.

Acknowledgements

I would like to thank Norman Brown and Liz Hodges for commenting on earlier drafts of this chapter.

Chapter 37
Curriculum Issues

David Hussey

Introduction

Professionals face difficult decisions when selecting the most appropriate curriculum for children and young people with multiple disabilities and a visual impairment. They need to strike a careful balance between meeting each child's entitlement to a broad curriculum base and serving the unique needs of the individual. The structure of the curriculum depends upon the decisions that professionals make about priorities for the child's education. Careful judgement is required to accommodate the educational requirements of the National Curriculum with the range of complementary therapies and approaches that are vital to the child's welfare. A range of stimulating experiences and carefully structured learning approaches is a fundamental requirement if two of the major goals of education are to be achieved; quality of life and maximum independence for every child.

Curriculum models

Current educational philosophy suggests that the curriculum framework for children and young people with multiple disabilities and a visual impairment will consist of three elements, the National Curriculum, a developmental curriculum and the complementary curriculum.

Based upon the three principles of breadth, balance and relevance, the content of this framework needs to be planned, delivered and evaluated through a multi-disciplinary approach. While accepting that breadth across the curriculum is an entitlement for every pupil it is important to recognise the need for flexibility in the balance within the curriculum. Some children require high levels of additional therapies for extended periods; for example, children with low vision who are ambulant will benefit from a curriculum that includes learning designed to enhance their use of vision combined with daily opportunities to practise their orientation and mobility skills. Conversely children with no vision and severe physical disabilities will need a programme that emphasises physiotherapy to maximise their physical ability to access learning and the environment around them. Identifying needs is central to the planning process and involves, target setting, reviewing and reporting as specified in the Code of Practice (Department for Education (DfE) 1994).

The balance between the elements of the curriculum will vary according to the child's individual needs.

The National Curriculum

All children are legally entitled to the broadly based and differentiated curriculum specified under the Education Reform Act (Department of Education and Sciene (DES) 1988a). Perhaps for the first time in the history of special education, the impulse of the legislation was to promote a curriculum to be shared by all schools, rather than a discrete one for children with special needs. One of the key principles of the National Curriculum is differentiation within a common framework. Children in special schools share in the common curriculum but it is acknowledged that the methods of supporting their access to the curriculum may be different.

The transition to an educational framework based on the National Curriculum has not been a smooth one. Attempts to achieve the balance between the National, developmental and complementary curricula have highlighted the differences in philosophies and practices among professionals. For a time many educationalists working with children and young people with multiple disabilities and a visual impairment regarded the National Curriculum as irrelevant and an intrusion on the precious time allocated to the developmental and complementary curricula. Much of this anxiety was justified, because originally it was clear that the National Curriculum had not been designed with much thought for pupils with special needs. However, the National Curriculum has evolved and recent amendments seek to ensure that it is both relevant and realistic in its approach to children with disabilities.

An examination of the area of communication skills will demonstrate how the National Curriculum provides a context for the learning of children and young people who have multiple disabilities and a visual impairment. The document *English in the National Curriculum* (Department for Education (DfE) 1995) sets out clearly the aim of allowing all pupils to access English in a relevant way and states 'The programme of study for each key stage should be taught in ways appropriate to their abilities.' It continues, 'For the small number of pupils who may need the provision, material may be selected from earlier or later key stages where this is necessary to enable individual pupils to progress and demonstrate achievement. Such material should be presented in contexts suitable to the pupil's age.' The document specifies that appropriate provision should be made for pupils who need to use:

- means of communication other than speech
- non-sighted methods of reading
- technological aids in practical and written work
- aids or adapted equipment to allow access to practical activities.

As well as being an important subject its own right, English underpins all areas of the curriculum and the elements of English, that is, speaking and listening, reading and writing, can be accessed in a form compatible with the methods used to educate children with multiple disabilities to allow them to be given credit for their achievements. For example the Level 1 description for speaking and listening requires that 'pupils talk about matters of immediate interest'. Interpreting the word 'talk' as 'communicate' allows recognition to be given to children who use non-verbal methods such as signing. Similarly the Level 1 description for reading states that, pupils are required to 'recognise familiar words in simple texts'. Again, for some children the substitutes for 'words' might include objects of reference, Moon letters or tactile symbols. The Level 1 description for writing suggests that: 'Pupils' writing communicates meaning through simple words and phrases.' Alternatives for writing might include signing and gesture. This inclusive approach allows children to demonstrate their abilities within the national educational context and acknowledges the validity of methods of access such as tactile symbols, communication aids and signing.

The route into the National Curriculum that is most appropriate for children with multiple disabilities and a visual impairment is through the programmes of study. These define the processes of learning in terms of knowledge and understanding as well as skills and competencies. Their context is an investigative, problem solving view of education, well suited to the experiential approach that underlies much of the methodology suited to children with multiple disabilities and a visual impairment. They allow experience as well as achievement to be acknowledged and credited, and provide a framework for approaches such as 'topic work' which will be examined later.

The developmental curriculum

As stated earlier the National Curriculum provides the context in which learning takes place and ensures a breadth of experience and a recognition of achievement. However, it is also clear that, for children and young people with multiple disabilities and a visual impairment, curriculum planning has also to take account of the aspects of early development which are an important element of their educational need. The developmental curriculum is concerned with four fundamental (but not exclusive) areas of development:

- physical development (including the development of body awareness and control of movement);
- social development (including promotion of the emergent personality and the development of acceptable behaviour);
- intellectual development (the promotion of awareness, understanding and knowledge);
- communicative development (the promotion of the expressive and receptive skills needed in human relationships and for learning).

For children with low vision there is additionally the area of the development of visual skills for the optimal use of sight. The weighting between these areas will be reflected in the child's individual educational programme with the balance changing during the child's school career.

Defining the developmental curriculum can ensure continuity across periods of transition and prevent the loss of momentum between classes or teachers. In addition, it can secure achievements within the National Curriculum. For example the element of 'physical development' within the developmental curriculum provides children and young people with multiple disabilities and a visual impairment with the opportunity to gain from a largely experiential approach in which increasingly complex learning tasks can be undertaken. Confidence and self-worth are products of physical skill acquisition, and situations where the child takes control during the physical dimension are a vital part of the learning process.

Opportunities to develop control and understanding of the body can be carried out on journeys within school, during formal movement sessions, physiotherapy sessions, horse riding, country dancing, gymnastics, bike riding, swimming, and also during leisure activities. Objectives for achievement can be set within each area of development, so for example, the objectives for 'skills in personal space' might include: knowledge of parts of the body, body awareness, sound location, following movements on request and taking account of their body in restricted space. Clearly much of this work dovetails directly into the PE National Curriculum and provides an overlap with the complementary curriculum, particularly in the physiotherapy and mobility programmes.

The complementary curriculum

The National Curriculum and the developmental curriculum are two important components of the education of children and young people who have multiple disabilities and a visual impairment. The third significant strand is the complementary curriculum. Access to education is often dependent on the ability of the child to explore his or her environment and to develop a communication system. Programmes like MOVE (Mobility Opportunities Via Education) use specialist physiotherapy equipment to allow children with a physical disability to move through their environment independently and significantly improve their ability to explore the environment, develop spatial understandings and to make choices.

The complementary curriculum may be delivered by a variety of professionals including speech and language therapists, mobility officers, physiotherapists and nurses. Fortunately the interventionist model, where the work of therapists was regarded as separate from the 'mainstream' purpose of education seems to have been replaced by a recognition that the education of children with complex needs requires the efforts of a multi-disciplinary team. A cross-curricular approach allows each professional to advise how their aims can be incorporated into a child's individual educational plan. Their role needs to be valued within the whole approach of the school. Bringing together professionals as an effective team can be a challenging task, but it provides the opportunity to apply a relevant holistic approach to each child's education. For professionals to collaborate successfully they need to be able to share problems and responsibilities in order to support the child in achieving skills and knowledge.

... effective multi-professional work is not easy to achieve. It requires co-operation, collaboration and mutual support. Each professional adviser needs to be aware of the role of his colleagues and should seek to reach agreement with them on their several roles and functions (DES 1983).

One approach that facilitates multi-disciplinary working is for those involved with the child to set objectives and targets each term for the children with whom they work. These are then shared and shaped at regular planning meetings about individual pupils. The staff present at the meeting might include the class teacher, the physiotherapist, speech and language therapist, social care worker, a nurse and the mobility teacher. The aim of the meeting is to share information about the child's achievements and to plan realistic targets for the future. Members of the team can collaborate to ensure they are consistent in their expectations and approach at each step. For example the speech and language therapist's target may be to encourage a child to use the Big Mac communication aid (a simple switch device allowing a child to give a short message). All the staff working with the child need to know how the Big Mac works, its specific purpose for the child and how to respond when the child uses the aid to ensure that the child is given the best opportunity to be successful (Figure 37.1).

Advice may have already been given by the physiotherapist or the occupational therapist on the best way to position the aid to allow the child to activate it. This is an ideal situation which may not be achievable in all settings due to constraints of time but the principle of a team approach is fundamental to successful teaching and learning. The recording and sharing of objectives by each professional, though time consuming, is important to ensure communication, consistency and continuity.

Figure 37.1

The role of pupils and parents

An essential element of the multi-disciplinary approach is the involvement of the children and their families. A trend in the curriculum framework over the past ten years has been to advocate greater pupil autonomy, encouraging children to become more effective in assisting and evaluating their own learning. The clearest example of this has been the development of records of achievement where children are assisted in collating information about their achievements such as examples of their work, photographs and certificates, which reflect their experiences and learning. Realistic measures need to be taken to ensure that pupil preferences are considered in the development of the curriculum. If the child is unable to communicate, careful assessments of their preferences using a procedure such as 'Assessing Communication Together' or ACT (Bradley 1991) can guide professionals in making decisions. Further details about ACT are provided in Chapter 33.

As stated earlier, individual educational plans enable educators to respect the individual nature of pupils' learning, making the children's needs and preferences the starting point rather than requiring children to fit into the framework provided by the school. This may present problems for educators, for instance a child who has some low vision, but for years has refused to use it in any effective way is making a choice, and the educator needs to think about the most appropriate way of presenting material in the light of that choice.

The most significant advocates on behalf of the children are their families, and their involvement in the curriculum process is essential. Parents hold important information and insights into the management of their children which can provide a short cut for professionals when deciding the most effective methods of providing access to learning. This can be particularly useful in areas such as the assessment of functional vision where the view of the parents does not always correspond with the results of clinical tests. The parents need to be given an environment that makes them confident about sharing their views, even when they are in conflict with the opinions of others. Their experience of the child is most likely to have produced the greatest insights and their practice in managing the child is a crucial consideration in designing a suitable educational approach.

The notion of 'parent partnerships' relies on effective two-way communication. The dialogue should be continuous with parents provided with relevant information which can be passed on through a range of routes including home books, telephone calls, newsletters, annual reviews and social meetings. It is not enough to acknowledge the entitlement of the child and the family to participate in curriculum development, the curriculum framework and the educational environment must be designed to ensure that it takes place.

The learning environment and teaching approaches

For children and young people with multiple disabilities and a visual impairment the classroom learning environment is a particularly important factor in their learning.

Stimulating environments present some children with exciting challenges and opportunities to explore, but other children will benefit from conditions where there are no distractions and which allow them to give all their concentration to a specific task. The environment has to be designed to ensure that the child can receive information about what is happening in the room and to ensure that the child can orientate himself or herself within it.

Attention to sound is an important factor, and spaces can be created within rooms to isolate the work taking place there. Separate rooms are often used for individual work, but unless they are close to the classroom the movement to the space can be time-consuming and disorienting for the child. Sounds such as chimes near doors can be useful as reference points, helping the orientation of the children within the classroom, but they need to be used with care as they can be too intrusive. Floor coverings can also provide orientation clues, hard resonating surfaces and contrasting carpeted areas providing both tactile and sound clues. Children can use surfaces to aid anticipation, for example work on the carpet may indicate a more passive activity, whereas work at a table brings expectations of individual work.

The tactile environment is also significant, and needs to be clear and predictable. Clear routes need to be defined around the learning area by using tactile clues to encourage those children who are able to explore or move independently around their environment. There are natural tactile cues in every classroom but important points of reference within the room may need to be signified with a specific clue. In corridors routes can be marked by 'foot clues' such as changes in the flooring materials or 'wall clues' like tactile pictures. A certain amount of consistency is required and changes in the layout of rooms need to be thought through carefully and then demonstrated to the children. Hazards in the environment such as half-open doors and wheelchairs left on routes not only carry the risk of physical injury for the child but can limit the child's confidence in moving unaided. Tactile 'objects of reference' can also be used to aid anticipation of a task, or to reinforce understanding, for example, a cup can indicate drink time (Figure 37.2), or part of a seat belt can be used to indicate a journey in the school minibus.

Figure 37.2

These aids can be used to encourage the child to make choices with the child or young person presenting the preferred object of reference chosen from a selection. Once the link between a tactile object and an activity or choice has been established, some children may move on to understand more formal tactile symbols and may use Moon to recognise letters or words as a step on the path to literacy (Figure 37.3).

For children with low vision, the visual environment is also important. Optimum lighting can be achieved by controlling natural and artificial lighting. Some children will require additional task lighting from adjustable desktop lamps. It cannot be assumed that all children benefit from the same level of lighting and professionals need to seek advice from an ophthalmologist or peripatetic teacher of the visually impaired to understand each child's lighting requirements. Contrasts in edges to furniture and surrounds to doors are also important aids to visual understanding and together with brightly coloured furniture and contrasting displays help create an appropriate visual context.

Figure 37.3

The design of the learning environment represents a compromise between the different needs of the children or young people in the group. Similarly the decisions about the approach to teaching (whether to use individual or group work, topics or behavioural methods) will involve balancing different methods to suit a variety of learning aims. Clearly there is an important role for individual work in a distraction-free environment, particularly for assessment purposes and for work aimed at developing specific skills, for example helping a child to understand the function of a communication aid. Immediate feedback from the supporting adult is guaranteed in a way that might not be possible in a group setting. However, individual work is often neither practical nor desirable in terms of the development of other social skills. Learning is a social activity and groups provide opportunities for the development of, for example, language or for reinforcing appropriate behaviour. For children and young people with multiple disabilities and visual impairment, attention to group work and groupings is essential. Flexible organisation can perhaps allow an individual to join another group for a particular purpose if the benefits are clear. For instance, a child with profound and multiple learning difficulties, dependent on staff for all but very limited movements, joined an ambulant group for a number of periods a week because it had been noted that he was visually tracking other pupils during break times and was clearly stimulated by their boisterous nature. In contrast an ambulant child who is easily distracted might benefit from working with a more passive group for some of her time, to improve her attention to sounds in the environment.

Differentiation is the key to successful group work and this is achieved by well developed individual educational plans. The educator needs to have in mind the potential learning opportunities presented by each teaching activity for each child. A broad and balanced curriculum entitles each learner to participate in a range of activities and situations, but understanding may only come after many experiences of the same situation. For example, Natalie, a five-year-old girl with no vision and severe learning disabilities was reported to hate pony riding an activity it had been assumed she would enjoy. Natalie had no experience or understanding of a pony and had made a sensible choice that sitting on a pony felt unsafe. Steps were planned to introduce Natalie to a pony over a number of weeks, with no expectation that she would need to sit on it or go for a ride. She touched the pony, fed the pony, heard other children go for a ride and finally sat on the pony. Only when she had a reasonable understanding of a pony and what a pony ride represented did she have the confidence to go for a ride, escorted by two members of staff. The approach was slow, but necessary to achieve successful understanding and the motivation to participate.

Evaluation of the curriculum

The purpose of the assessment of children and young people is sometimes misunderstood and it is often unfairly regarded solely as a means of judging individual performance. However assessment can indicate the most appropriate methods of teaching and help to define teaching objectives. The DES TAT Report (Department of Education and Science National Curriculum Task Group on Assessment and Testing; DES 1988b) recognised four purposes for assessment:

- formative – recognising the achievements of the pupils to facilitate planning;
- diagnostic – allowing the diagnosis of learning difficulties to aid remedial help;
- summative – allowing the recording of overall achievements in a systematic way;
- evaluative – facilitating aspects of the work of the school local education authority (LEA) or a service to be assessed and reported upon.

Assessment of children with a visual impairment and multiple disabilities needs to be detailed and comprehensive concentrating on all areas of development. It is only with this evidence that the educator will be able to plan with confidence the next steps of learning for each individual. Individual educational plans presuppose that all children learn in different ways and that a range of teaching methods will be used. If a strategy that has worked for three children is judged to be failing a fourth, teachers will rely on the evidence of the assessment to select another route.

Observation remains an important element of assessment. The class teacher or the visiting peripatetic teacher of the visually impaired, can often gain insights by standing back and observing what is happening in the learning process. Videos have been used successfully by teachers to evaluate teaching sessions and when shared with colleagues they can provide a useful tool for staff development. Clearly assessment must be regarded as an ongoing process, rather than a one off or staggered occurrence. Functional assessments offer a better route to reliable evidence than norm-tested or criterion-referenced assessment for children with multiple disabilities and visual impairment. One example of a functional assessment is *Vision for Doing* (Aitken and Buultjens 1992), which not only provides useful evidence but includes suggested educational approaches to meet identified needs (see Chapter 35).

Finally the importance of the curriculum audit cannot be understated. This may focus on a particular subject, cross-curricular area, or on the whole timetable, but the information acquired provides an overview of what the child is actually receiving. An audit conducted over two full days examined one boy and focused on the time that was given to the range of activities that he experienced. Because of his need for significant additional physiotherapy, the time it took to meet self-help needs such as feeding and toileting, plus the travelling around the school, the actual time given to class-based activities was minimal. Such evidence provides an opportunity to examine the organisation of the timetable to see if there are other ways to meet a child's needs without sacrificing the focus of his or her programme.

Conclusion

Children and young people with multiple disabilities and a visual impairment need specialist approaches and environments, but share the need for a broadly based curriculum that provides an entitlement to a full range of experiences. It is the job of educationalists and therapists to work in partnership with the individual and their families to provide a realistic educational programme suited to each child's needs. Every learning experience offers opportunities to practise skills and gain knowledge. So much has to be achieved that the management of the child's precious time is vital, and no opportunity should be lost to enhance learning opportunities while preserving the individual's quality of life as a central focus.

Summary

The curriculum framework for children and young people with multiple disabilities and a visual impairment consists of three elements: the National Curriculum, a developmental curriculum and the complementary curriculum.

All children are legally entitled to the National Curriculum and a key principle is differentiation through a common framework. One route into the National Curriculum for the children considered here is through appropriate programmes of study which define the processes of learning in terms of knowledge and understanding as well as skills and competencies.

The developmental curriculum is concerned with four fundamental areas of development physical, social, intellectual and communicative. For children with low vision there is the additional area of visual skills development.

The complementary curriculum includes providing children in this population with the ability to explore the environment and the development of an appropriate communication system.

An essential element of curricular development for children and young people with multiple disabilities and visual impairment is the active involvement of the pupil and their families. The curriculum framework and educational environment must be designed to ensure that this can take place.

Consideration of the learning environment is an important factor in delivery of the curriculum. Particular attention needs to be given to design of the auditory, tactile and visual environment.

Assessment can serve a number of purposes. Evaluation of the curriculum relies on accurate and ongoing assessment and should include a detailed curriculum audit.

Chapter 38

Management Issues in Multiple Disabilities

Anthony Best

Introduction

Pupils with multiple disabilities and visual impairment (MDVI) sometimes seem to belong to sub-groups that consist of just one child! The wide range and variety of combinations of disabilities are a characteristic of the population and a needs-led service must be organised to take this vast range into account. This chapter discusses how staff can be organised and managed by identifying clear roles and using effective work groups.

The need for teams

One consequence of the range of needs within the population is interdependency. Each professional involved with a child must think of themselves as part of the team supporting that child. No one person will have all the answers to all the challenges presented by a child; they should feel dependent on colleagues. If they do not, then it is possible that they are seriously misjudging the contribution that each person is able to make and, perhaps, misjudging their own role as more central than it probably is.

The degree of cohesion within a team is partly a result of the interactions between individual personalities within the team. However, the concept of the team and its culture is also influential and, perhaps, more significant as it can be planned rather than being dependent on individuals.

The concept of a transdisciplinary team is one in which each member can take on some part of the role of the others, and where each member gives up some of their professional expertise to allow another member to carry out part of their job. This requires considerable professional security and confidence, as well as trust in colleagues.

It is a long way further down the road of team working than the traditional multi-disciplinary team where each person has a distinct role, passes on information to others, and receives information from colleagues. This *cooperation* is essential, but often not sufficient to meet the complex challenges of a child with MDVI. A *coordinated* service is better, in that members of the team agree on their separate responsibilities and so ensure all aspects of the child's needs are met. A *collaborative* approach implies a degree of working together on targets and joint evaluation of what happens. This produces the highly desirable result of more than one discipline working together on a problem.

Transdisciplinary teams go even further, with a blurring of roles as each person shares the delivery of their specialist area of expertise with colleagues. Rather than being called 'teams', McGrath (1991) suggests they may be more accurately described as 'workgroups' or 'networks'.

To operate effectively, there needs to be an understanding of each person's expertise. One way to achieve this is through service statements. These list the knowledge and skills of the team member and indicate what they are able to contribute to the team's work.

Another concept that may be helpful is the 'learning team'. Each professional is considered an equal member of the team that decides on the child's education: the learning targets, teaching strategies, environmental needs. The learning team can be easily organised within a special school if the professionals are on the school staff. When, as is often the case, visiting colleagues have a key input, then finding a time for these meetings can be problematic. However, for children with complex problems, it is doubtful whether this practical problem can really be a good enough reason for not providing a service that is, at the least, coordinated. To deny a child such a service seems to seriously disadvantage that person; while this may not be so essential if children have a single disability, the production of an adequate education plan for a child with MDVI requires such a transdisciplinary approach and, probably, learning team meetings.

Timetabling within schools does not always allow sufficient non-contact time for such regular meetings. As this need becomes recognised, it may have a major impact on conditions of work, particularly for teachers. This has happened, for example, in the further education (FE) sector where lecturers often have up to six weeks non-contact time in a 42-week year. Although not designed to plan for special educational needs, this model recognises the need for adequate planning to deliver an educational programme.

The role of the class teacher

The classroom teacher has the central role. It involves:
- managing class staff;
- organising the content and delivery of learning programmes;
- supervising the delivery of the programmes.

It also involves some teaching but, with many pupils who have multiple disabilities, teachers often spend as much time organising and supervising as they do in direct teaching.

Managing staff

Managing class staff requires classroom organisation and room management. The teacher needs to be clear about the role of the assistants and will need to talk this through with staff so they are clear about expectations. Teachers can identify appropriate roles only when they have established how they will organise their classes and will need to consider whether:

- pupils will work as a group;
- there should be 'holding' activities and intensive one-to-one work going on together;
- pupils should rotate through a series of activities.

When these decisions have been made, then teachers can decide how to assign their staff.

Well established principles of room management usually identify three roles – individual helper, group activity management and 'mover' (Lacey 1991, Thomas 1992). The individual helper works with one child at a time usually, providing an intensive work session. This may be only for a few minutes, if that is what the child needs, although a much longer session is probable. The group activity role involves ensuring that other children have something to occupy them, perhaps providing an experience rather than skills teaching. The mover attends to all those activities that would impede the smooth running of the class: preparing materials, clearing up a mess, dealing with telephone interruptions or visitors. These roles may change round every hour or so, depending on the needs of the pupils. A management system such as this should result in much more of the pupils' time being spent on purposeful activities than occurs with a less structured use of staff. Ware and Evans (1987), however, have suggested that while this system is good at increasing levels of adult attention for each pupil, it does not necessarily result in more engagement in the tasks. It should certainly increase the 'flow' of the activities so that interruptions are minimised and the maximum time is spent in productive activity.

For such a system to work, it is essential that each person understands exactly what is expected of them. One approach to achieving this is for the teacher to describe and discuss the roles, probably writing down what is expected, that is, a mini job description, so everybody in the team knows what is to happen. This can apply not only to principles, but also to the detail of key activities; for example, not just 'make sure they put their coats on' but writing down and explaining the target skills for each pupil and asking the assistant to record performance at appropriate intervals.

In many cases, assistants can take responsibility for important activities (given appropriate training and supervision) and may prefer to be involved in significant work rather than always being assigned trivial tasks on an unplanned and *ad hoc* basis. Certainly common complaints from assistants are that teachers interfere when a difficulty arises instead of letting them see the problem through; that they have to find jobs to do because the teacher seems wrapped up in what he or she is doing; and, perhaps worst of all, that teachers simply shout orders from time to time without fully explaining what is required nor giving the opportunity for the work to be properly planned and carried out. Steel (1991) provides a useful discussion on collaboration or conflict in teams, with suggestions for good working practice.

However the class may be organised, discussion between members of the team or workgroup is essential. One characteristic of this communication is that it must be frequent. Although most of it may be informal and simply for the *exchange of information*, the effective teacher will try to ensure there are times for the group to *plan future work*, *report back* on what has been achieved, *review* what has happened, and to *solve problems* that individuals have experienced. Discussions on these five issues can be key elements in creating, building and developing an effective team.

While each team member needs to communicate effectively, the ethos, or culture of the team is often set by the team leader (Lacey and Lomas, 1993). Their attitude and skill will create the atmosphere, perhaps authoritarian, mutually supportive, democratic or creative. For pupils who are taught by a team which is not cohesive, the result is an educational programme that is inconsistent in what is delivered, unpredictable in how it is delivered, confusing in what is expected, and lacking purpose in structure and progression.

Designing educational programmes

A second role for the teacher is to plan activities. For pupils with multiple disabilities this is likely to involve writing precise objectives for each child. This is a skill that needs to be mastered by all class teachers. Visiting teachers who provide support within a school also need to be able to think and plan in this way, as do the classroom assistants who work in the school. The approach, using task analysis and behavioural objectives, is not specific to pupils with visual impairment and can be learnt from a range of books, training videos, courses and from colleagues (see for example, Solity and Bull 1987). Although a very accessible concept and an easily acquired skill, its expert use can transform an educational programme from a 'wish list' to a precise set of targets that can be used to measure progress. It enables staff to observe and teach with attention to detail and should ensure pupils receive a consistent daily programme.

Supervising staff

The role of supervisor is an essential element in team working. All staff need feedback on their work and this may be particularly important to clarify roles and remove some of the uncertainties and ambiguities that are often present in a classroom. Supervision through self-evaluation, probably through watching and discussing videotapes of staff at work, are almost always found to be very helpful, but most staff have difficulty finding time to use this approach. Teachers more usually provide supervision through commenting on incidents as they happen. While this can be helpful, a compromise in which there is regular observation, discussion and reflection can be much more effective. Staff will often see such supervision as essential management support, rather than criticism, and there is abundant evidence from education and industry that it is one of the most effective forms of staff development.

Supervision is a skill, and not all teachers feel comfortable taking on this role. The skill involves asking questions and responding to the replies as well as giving out information and opinions. Hanko (1995) has described the art of asking 'insight-generating questions' and 'of supplementing, not supplanting staff strengths'. Supervision is easier if there is a joint understanding of objectives for the pupils and of the role of the member of staff. Discussion can then be based on specific incidents, or on aspects of the job description. Staff must be told what their strengths are, not just their weaknesses, although it is often more difficult for the supervisor to identify those strengths.

Classroom assistants

Whatever their title – learning support assistant, social pedagogue, teacher's aide – the work of these support staff is usually a critical element in successful classroom practice. With pupils with multiple disabilities an element of this work is likely to be teaching. In mainstream education, there is sometimes a clear distinction between the work of the teacher and that of the classroom assistant. The latter provides practical support in preparing, clearing up or taking responsibility for non-teaching tasks. Within the field of multiple disabilities this distinction is less likely to exist. Teaching often requires careful and consistent work, perhaps with frequent repetition over a period of time. It may involve physical assistance particularly for pupils with severe physical impairments; it may focus on teaching practical rather than academic skills, often under the heading of PSE (Personal and Social Education) and much of the work may be carried out on a one-to-one basis. For all these reasons the classroom assistant will need to be centrally involved in delivering the curriculum.

In some services, there is a distinction between these teaching-related activities, and self-care routines such as toileting. Different staff are employed for each of the two types of activities. However, far more often the full range of activities is considered educational, and will be planned, delivered, recorded and evaluated as integral parts of the school curriculum.

To carry out this role, staff need training in the 'technical' skills associated with teaching. In the UK, the majority of staff in these posts do not receive training, although a number of initiatives have taken place during the 1990s. A review of the courses show a number of common elements:

- implications of sensory loss on development;
- the nature of vision and sensory loss ;
- the extended curriculum, that is communication, mobility, social and independence skills, visual and tactile skills;
- approaches to teaching, that is how children learn, task analysis, setting targets, observing and recording;
- challenging behaviour and behaviour management.

In addition a number of elements are usually part of any induction training with pupils with MDVI. Examples are:

- epilepsy and medication;
- handling and lifting;
- managing enuresis;
- the Children Act.

In addition to these technical skills and knowledge, classroom assistants will need to have the skills and attitudes that enable them to function effectively as members of a team. These have been discussed above in the section on teams.

Other team members

Other members of the school staff may be involved in work within the classroom and will certainly be involved in work with the pupils. What is their contribution likely to be?

Physiotherapy is commonly needed by pupils with MDVI as at least a third of the population has significant physical impairments. The contribution of the physiotherapists may be confined to:

- developing good posture when sitting and standing;
- maintaining flexibility and movement in limbs;
- provision of appropriate aids and equipment.

However, they may also use approaches based on 'educational physiotherapy', such as are embodied in the MOVE (Mobility Opportunities Via Education) curriculum or in conductive education. With these approaches, skills are learnt through educational activities, rather than being acquired through exercises and repetition. Some practitioners and parents have enthusiastically endorsed these approaches as compared with traditional work, as they seem to provide relevant purposeful activities combined with high but realistic expectations of the child's progress.

Whatever the approach, the work can be carried out either in the classroom or in a physiotherapy centre, and by qualified physiotherapists or by classroom staff working under the supervision of the physiotherapist. Choice between these options will be determined by the needs of the child, and the preferences of all the staff involved. A clear policy on this is needed, so that time, training and equipment can be organised to ensure a programme can be delivered. The Society of Physiotherapist's code of practice defines what an unqualified assistant can be asked to undertake, and what training should be provided.

Speech, or speech and language therapy may also be offered. The training for this group of professionals varies and so they may be primarily concerned with:

- articulation and the production of clear speech;
- the development of communication and use of language through an appropriate symbol system;
- early motor skills such as those used for chewing, swallowing and the production of sounds.

The work, as with the physiotherapist, is likely to involve assessment of skills using a procedure that will draw on the expertise of the classroom staff in observing and understanding a pupil's behaviour.

A number of other therapists and support staff may be involved. This may include an occupational therapist, an educational psychologist, a psychiatrist (perhaps with a remit of responsibility for management of epilepsy), a music and drama therapist, as well as massage and aromatherapy specialists. Mobility teachers may also be included both for totally blind children and for those with low vision. Each will have to define their own contribution to the children and the individual education plan (IEP), and ensure that their contribution is understood by colleagues and, wherever possible, supported in all the pupils' activities.

A communication system must also be built into working practices, so that information on targets, activities and progress can be exchanged. This may be, for example, through weekly meetings, written targets, forecasts or programme sheets, debriefing time after each session, or half-termly Learning Team target review meetings. Whatever the method, the purpose should be to ensure all staff understand the aims of the physiotherapy programme, are clear about their own role within the programme delivery, and understand how this fits into the pupil's overall IEP.

Target setting and the programme delivery, again, may be carried out solely by the therapist or in conjunction with classroom staff and work. The latter procedure may well be more useful, particularly where it involves staff in gaining complementary skills, for example teachers understanding more about feeding and therapists acquiring knowledge of behaviour management (Kersner and Wright 1996).

The specialist teacher

The visiting teacher of the visually impaired should have an important role for children placed in a special school which is not designated specifically for children with a visual impairment, for example a school for children with severe learning difficulties. General skills in approaching the role, such as consultancy skills, are dealt with elsewhere in this volume. A recent survey (Griffiths and Best, 1996) identified some of the specific tasks that schools had found the visiting teacher could usefully undertake. These include:
- advice on the physical environment including lighting and contrast;
- help with delivering the sensory curriculum;
- suggestions for modifying classroom materials so they could be used by pupils with low vision or who were totally blind;
- advice on the presentation of activities and on specialised teaching strategies.

In addition to these areas identified by the schools, teachers will probably want to contribute to:
- the assessment and development of the pupil's vision;
- the development of movement and mobility skills;
- providing staff with an understanding of the nature of the visual impairment and its effect on learning.

Although these tasks may be similar to those provided to pupils and staff in mainstream settings, the content will need to reflect the severity of the pupil's disability and the advice will need to be given with an understanding of the team teaching context and the precision teaching approaches that have been outlined above.

Providing staff development

If the visiting teacher is familiar with children with MDVI, he or she may well want to work directly with the child. For other teachers, the role may be more one of staff development and training the staff to observe significant behaviours and to deliver appropriate specialist learning experiences. This staff development need not be just through talks and courses, although there will need to be time for group presentations, away from the pupils. These sessions can cover both general principles and discussion on specific cases so that staff come away with more than a list of good ideas. They can develop new skills that will enable them to apply principles, for example in presenting visual material, to pupils with a variety of eye conditions.

However, there may be limited opportunities for such training sessions and much of the staff development will have to use other formats. There are many possibilities. Wall displays of material, advice sheets, photographs and articles can help staff learn incidentally. Active displays will add questions and requests for ideas so that staff can contribute comments to the display. The availability of key articles in a staffroom can result in some staff choosing to acquire knowledge. Information sheets and ideas lists are often well received, but can be enhanced with a quiz for the reader to self-check if the points have been fully understood. If the school ethos allows it, a video can be made of pupil and of staff teaching, then written comments provided by the specialist teacher, who returns the video for the teacher to watch in their own time. Material development projects, in which staff are guided in producing assessment or curriculum documentation can be an excellent way of learning. Some staff find that listening to audiotaped information, perhaps on the journey to school, is a successful way to acquire new knowledge. Of course, visiting other centres, where finances permit, can be really useful, and particularly so in this low incidence field where most staff are working in professional isolation.

Residential schooling

Most children with MDVI attend LEA day schools. However, about 5% of this population are placed in special schools for pupils with visual impairments, and the majority of these children attend on a residential basis. This raises a different, but important set of management issues.

Few of the placements are made because the school is simply too far away for daily travel. Pupils attend because the school's curriculum, equipment and staffing are necessary for them to receive an appropriate education. Many of the pupils need an extended curriculum in which self-care skills, social skills (such as developing friendships, sharing possessions, making choices of leisure preferences) are important parts. Some children do not sleep overnight and need to develop this routine. Other children require a consistent 24-hour delivery of the curriculum if they are to make progress, often in both developing appropriate behaviour as well as in acquiring practical skills. Some children have regressive conditions which require considerable medical intervention, as well as 24-hour care. Other children benefit in self-confidence from living with children with whom they can compete equally. As adults, the job many people with MDVI will do could be said to be 'employing carers'. Knowing how to do this – what options they prefer, what they can do for themselves, how to receive help – will be an important part of preparation for adulthood. For any of these reasons, a residential education may be appropriate.

The delivery of educational programmes in a residential school will involve, equally, class-based staff and staff from the residential units. The pupils' programmes should be developed by the whole team of staff and each department will deliver some of the activities. For example, a child beginning to make sets of two objects can do so in the classroom through maths activities. Equally they can practise the skill while setting the table in the residential unit. A child developing communication through signing would have opportunities to experience a signing environment in both the classroom and in the residential unit. This consistency of expectations, and the continuity in programme delivery, can make learning possible for some pupils with severe disabilities.

A residential school may have a large team of staff, including therapists, mobility officers and nurses, as well as class and residential unit staff. This provides a need, and opportunity for staff development, through necessary facilities such as in-house training courses, the library, training events, staff arranging presentations on their work to visitors, and so on. These events also enable staff to exchange information about their work and should facilitate the development of effective staff teams. It has been advocated in this chapter that these teams are an essential component in the delivery of an effective service, it follows that the residential special school, should be able to provide a particularly appropriate and high quality service.

Summary

This chapter has described some of the management issues surrounding education of children with MDVI. The roles of the key staff involved in designing and delivering educational programmes have been described, and ways in which professional colleagues can form, and perform as working groups have been discussed.

The teacher needs to identify roles for each of the classroom staff, and supervise their work. There needs to be communication within the class team, so that there are common understandings on purpose, approaches and progress. The visiting teachers must understand the teaching strategies used within the school so that they can provide relevant advice. Part of their role will be to offer staff development opportunities, using a range of approaches.

Some children within this population will receive their education in residential schools. These provide an extended curriculum which should include practical life skills essential for this population. The curriculum is delivered over 24 hours, and can offer continuity and consistency of approach in the delivery of an intensive educational programme. It is suggested that this is the most appropriate placement for a small proportion of children with multiple disabilities and a visual impairment.

THE ROLE OF THE SPECIALIST TEACHER

The range of educational provision now available to children and young people with visual impairments is very diverse and consequently the roles of teachers of the visually impaired have become wide ranging. Specialist teachers of children and young people with visual impairments now work in a variety of settings including special schools for children with moderate or severe learning difficulties; schools for children with physical disabilities; units and resource centres in mainstream provision and advisory and learning support services. This section considers the responsibilities of teachers in these different arenas of work.

Chapter 39 addresses the issues which face teachers who are working with the families of a child with a visual impairment. This is a particularly sensitive area and if the collaboration between parents and professionals is to be successful, teachers need to be clear about what the needs of parents and families might be.

Chapter 40 discusses the skills required by the advisory teacher who acts as an external visitor to schools. It is important that the role of these teachers is clarified and that mainstream schools and advisory services have clear perceptions about the extent of each other's responsibility to the pupil with a visual impairment, and realistic expectations of what each can contribute to the child's education.

Chapters 41 describes the role of specialist teachers who are based in a resource centre or unit for children with a visual impairment within a mainstream school and considers their relationship to colleagues who are class or subject teachers. Tensions may develop when the role and responsibility of the specialist teacher is unclear and this chapter explores the principles of successful in-class support.

As the role of the special schools has changed, so have the demands on the professional skills of the teachers working within them. Chapter 42 considers the generic and the specific skills required by teachers in special schools for children with visual impairments and the positive and innovative contribution that special schools continue to make to the development of expertise and within the field.

Finally, Chapter 43 examines the interpersonal and organisational skills which are required by the large number of teachers of the visually impaired who are required to act as a consultants. The personal and professional qualities of the successful consultant are defined, and recent theories regarding the consultative process in education are reviewed and applied to the field of visual impairment.

Chapter 39
Working with Families

Juliet Stone

Introduction

It has long been realised that many families need support if they are not only to cope with a child with a disability, but help the child to reach his or her potential in adulthood. The literature abounds with references to the challenges which families of children with visual impairments may face. In the earliest stage these include adjusting to the birth of a baby with an impairment or facing a dearth of information on diagnosis and prognosis (Fraiberg 1977, Sommers 1944, Wills 1978). Normal life events, such as the first entry into school, transfer at secondary stage, leaving school and finding employment may bring unique anxieties for the children with a visual impairment and their families. In this chapter, some of the needs of families will be described and the ways in which professionals can help to meet these needs will be addressed.

Services for families

Research on families of children with visual impairments by Langdon (1970) found that parents were often given little information at the time of diagnosis and that few were referred to other agencies where advice on development, management and education was available. Parents often received their information through friends and neighbours. The Vernon Report (Departmenrt of Education and Science (DES) 1972) said that one of the most pressing requirements was to provide a comprehensive service to parents and families from the time of diagnosis. A pilot scheme to support families begun by the Birmingham Royal Institute for the Blind confirmed this need and the service was later taken over by the Royal National Institute for the Blind. A few local education authority advisory services to schools and families were established in the early 1970s and one of their main aims to offer parents information and support (see Chapter 1).

The importance of parent involvement was again raised in the Warnock Report (DES 1978) which had as one of its main themes, 'parents as partners'. This supported the change in the attitudes of professionals in education to the involvement of parents and set the basis for future legislation. The Committee argued that the successful education of children with special educational needs is dependent on the full involvement of their parents: indeed, unless the parents are seen as equal partners in the educational process, the purpose of our report will be frustrated.

They also stressed that the relationship between parents and the school has a crucial bearing on the child's educational progress. On the one hand if parents are to work collaboratively with teachers, they need information and advice from the school about the provision being made for their child; on the other hand a child's special needs cannot be assessed and met fully in school without the insights of the parents, who know the child better than anyone.

The Warnock Report was the impetus for the widespread development of advisory services by local education authorities. These advisory services worked with the parents and families of pre-school children and supported children and young people in schools and colleges. The 1981 Education Act (DES 1981) formalised links with parents, involving them fully in the statementing process and establishing procedures by which parents could appeal against decisions of the local education authority. The Code of Practice (DfE 1994) has extended the formal collaboration with parents and says that provision should be 'taking account of the wishes, feelings and knowledge of parents at all stages'. It also states that 'children's progress will be diminished if their parents are not seen as partners in the educational process with unique knowledge and information to impart'.

In many areas of the United Kingdom schools and services have worked hard to make this collaboration and cooperation a practical reality, but there are still gaps in the provision, for example, many parents from ethnic minorities feel that they do not have equal access to information and advice (Priestley, 1995). In addition, teachers of children with visual impairment fear that services to pre-school children and their families are currently under threat as a result of the re-organisation of local government and the financial restraints placed on local education authority services.

The needs of families

Hornby (1994) identifies a continuum of reactions which parents may experience before they are able to come to terms with their child's impairment: shock, denial, anger, sadness, detachment, reorganisation and adaptation. This description is, however, a generalisation. Some parents may reach acceptance and adaptation very quickly, whereas in other cases, the impact of the impairment on the family may not become apparent for some considerable time. When the babies are lying in the pram, there may be no apparent difference between a baby with a visual impairment and one without. It may not be until babies who are fully sighted start reaching for toys and later, crawling and walking, that the difference in development becomes apparent. Some parents of children with visual impairments say that the differences only really show when the child reaches school and other parents say they do not feel the real impact of their child's impairment until the latter end of the school years, when the transition to adulthood does not take a normal course.

Parents will have high expectations of professionals. Their needs, which probably cannot be met by one professional, may include a desire for:

- full information on their child's eye defect and its implications;
- information on educational provision and advice on the appropriate placement for their child;
- information on their child's progress;
- support through the various transitional stages of the child's education.

A further need, which is often an urgent one for parents of a child with multiple disabilities, may be for respite care. Several schemes exist to provide this, such as short-term fostering or temporary placements in residential homes or schools.

Not only parents are affected if their baby has a visual impairment; this will have an impact on the rest of the family too. In reality, many siblings do not appreciate any difference in their brother or sister for some years. This is a very positive characteristic for all the family, as the siblings will develop natural relationships and the child with the visual impairment will not come to expect any special treatment and will learn to cope with the rough and tumble of family life. However, some parents become very absorbed and concerned with the implications of their special baby's life, and this concern may be passed to the siblings who may either become worried themselves or perhaps resentful of the attention which is paid to their brother or sister. Parents must try to ensure that their attention is equally divided between all the children. The siblings of a child with a visual impairment have their own rights in the family situation and must not be seen as extra teachers or carers.

The extended family, particularly the grandparents, also need consideration. There can be tensions between the parents and grandparents about the care and education of the child and the grandparents may well feel the very natural over-protective instinct which is not in the best long-term interests of the child. However the grandparents, as in any family, can have an enormously positive input and often have the patience and the time to give the child the practical experiences which are so essential to the child's development.

In some areas of the country not enough attention has been paid to the needs of families of ethnic minorities. The language problem is usually overcome through providing interpreters during home visits or at school meetings, although this is not always the case. Sufficient regard and respect for the culture and customs of families of a child with a visual impairment must be given.

Families of a child who has additional or multiple disabilities have all the difficulties and many of the joys of families whose child's visual impairment is the only disability. The needs of the child with additional disabilities are much more complex and meeting the needs of the child or young person is likely to be a very demanding task, physically, mentally and emotionally. Caring for such a child will need enormous patience and require many varied skills. Parents who do not feel that they have these skills feel very vulnerable. A long list of professionals may be involved with the child and parents may be required to make many visits to hospitals and clinics and welcome many visitors to the home. This in itself can be a very heavy burden and professionals need to collaborate with each other so that hospital and home visits can be rationalised.

Stages of transition

There are stages of transition in a child's life where professional help may be particularly welcomed.

The early years

In some areas of the country, hospitals, social services and education authorities work together and parents are offered all the support they require at the diagnosis of their child's visual impairment. Unfortunately this is still not true of all areas and it may be many months after parents are told of their child's visual impairment before they are offered information on, for example, educational provision and benefits which may be available.

If the baby is born with a severe visual impairment, the mother–baby bonding may be affected through the lack of or diminished eye contact. The difficulties in bonding can be exacerbated if the baby has to stay in hospital because of prematurity or illness. Parents may need advice as to how to interpret the baby's behaviours and thus establish the special relationship between parents and child. For example, one blind baby curled up her fingers and toes when she heard mother or father approaching, an action she did not perform for anyone else. Once the parents had seen this and were comfortable that their baby knew them, it made a great difference to how they felt about their baby and interacted with her.

As the child grows, parents may find it helpful to be in contact with professionals who can help them with the day-to-day management of their child, for example on how to encourage feeding, dressing and toilet training, or on how to persuade their child to wear his or her glasses. Professionals can also help by advising on appropriate toys and play materials and on activities that will keep the child constructively occupied. In some areas there may be a local toy library where parents can see a selection of toys and borrow them for their child to use.

When the child reaches the age of two or three, the possibility of a pre-school placement will arise and parents may require advice on nurseries and play schools. The person most likely to be involved with the family at this time is a specialist teacher of visually impaired children and it will be the teacher's responsibility to ensure that an appropriate placement is found and that the child has the necessary access to other professionals, such as a mobility officer.

The school years

Parents will need full and accurate information about their child's schooling and the Code of Practice (DfE 1994) has confirmed the right of parents to this information and to their involvement in the decision making process. Once the child is at school, there will be communication from the school in the form of reports and home–school diaries and opportunities to talk to the teachers at the end of the school day or at parents' evenings.

Home–school contact will vary according to the type of placement. Some children will attend day special schools or resource bases which are several miles away from their home and their parents will be unable to visit their child's school regularly. This will call for different responses from schools, perhaps in the form of more telephone contact or correspondence. It may also call for a teacher to take responsibility for visiting homes and being the school–home link person. Hopefully, all schools now take seriously their responsibility to involve parents. Most do so in very positive ways and parents speak warmly of their relationships with their child's school.

Adolescence

Parents and families may find a particular need for guidance and support when the children reach puberty and adolescence. At this time, young people are striving to assert their individuality and are moving to increasing independence. This may be impeded for the young person with a visual impairment, in ways which are discussed in Chapter 11. Parents and the young person will be wondering about what will happen when the school years are finished. Parents also recognise that they themselves are growing older and the responsibility of caring for their child may become an increasing worry, particularly if the young person has additional disabilities and requires physical support. Currently, many services which provide for these young people are under threat and parents may face, for the first time in the life of their child, a feeling of isolation and a fear for the future.

The concern of parents over the future may transfer to the young people themselves. The Code of Practice (DfE 1994) underlines the need for the involvement of parents in the transition from school to either further education, training or employment (see Chapter 12). Where there are tensions between the young person and the rest of the family about which route to follow, professional mediation can be helpful.

The siblings, too, may have concerns at this stage as they see their parents becoming older and wonder about their future responsibility for their brother or sister who has a visual impairment, at a stage when they are looking for increasing independence. Siblings may feel restricted by their responsibility to the rest of their family. Opportunities for all the family to explore their own feelings and to understand the views of the other members can be very helpful.

Models of interaction

Cunningham and Davis (1985) described three models of relationships between parents and professionals; the 'expert', 'transplant' and 'consumer' models. These are useful in that they help to focus on the interaction between parents and professionals and highlight the effects of the forms of support which are offered to parents.

In the 'expert' model, the authors suggest that 'professionals select the information that they think is relevant to the parent and likewise elicit only that information that they feel is required'. As Cunningham and Davis point out, this model fosters a dependency on the professional and prevents real interaction taking place. Professionals, however, may employ this model to promote their own self-confidence and status, and there is a great danger for any professional who is involved in the sensitive area of working with families that they work to meet their own needs, rather than those of the family. Hopefully, few professionals fall into this trap.

The 'transplant' model is one which is far more likely to typify the interactions between professionals and parents. Professionals recognise the usefulness of involving parents and pass on their teaching skills and involve parents in carrying out assessments and educational and therapy programmes. This approach certainly involves the parents, but it can assume that all parents share the aims and beliefs of the professional and have the time and motivation to carry out the suggested programme and, in some circumstances, it can take little account of the individual family culture.

Cunningham and Davis (1985) suggest that the most appropriate model is the 'consumer' model, where negotiation within the context of a mutually respecting relationship is the foundation and where decision making is within the parents' control. In these circumstances, parents may choose to reject support and professionals may have difficulties in accepting this fact. The roles of the professional and the parents need to be specified so that neither party has incorrect expectations of the other.

Aspects of collaboration

Parents have a great deal to offer in the partnership with professionals. They can give an invaluable input to the assessment process through collecting information on the child's response in a variety of situations and through recording the child's progress. They can also share in the planning and implementation of the educational programme for the child. Professionals must, as has been indicated, be open to the information, advice and criticism they will receive from parents who know their child so intimately. However, this should be a two-way process. If parents can also receive, with an open mind, the comments from professionals who work with their child, they may be able to stand back and see how their own involvement could improve. Parents can easily become too protective concerning the independent movement of their children, or they may know them so well that they anticipate their every need or request and unwittingly prevent the development of language or of independence skills. Listening to comments or criticisms about your own parenting can be very difficult, but it can be constructive for the long-term benefit of the child.

The skills required of the professional

Supporting parents and families in an appropriate way calls for very specific qualities on the part of professionals. These include genuineness, personal warmth and an empathy for others. Professionals, however, need to understand family dynamics and recognise that within a family there are many pressures and changes in circumstance. The child with the visual impairment may not be the main focus of their attention. Unemployment, elderly parents or concerns over other children may be uppermost in their minds.

It is perhaps surprising that many professionals are expected to take on the additional role of working with families without receiving any additional training. Frequently, visiting homes and talking to parents is seen as a simple extension of their main role, but unfortunately, a record as an excellent therapist or teacher is no guarantee that the person possesses the particular qualities and skills which are required for helping families appropriately. Any provider of services should ensure that the selection of personnel is made carefully and that thorough training is provided.

Professionals need to know the limitations of where they can help and just as importantly, where they cannot. All professionals who are working with families will have limits to their expertise and should set clear objectives for their involvement. Clearly, any professional who has the privilege of visiting homes to offer support will make efforts to build up a good relationship with the family. This relationship may include encouraging the family to discuss any problems which are uppermost in their minds, but it may be that professionals will be tempted to involve themselves more closely with the family's problems than this role requires. Teachers should not make themselves counsellors and therapists should not become teachers, beyond what their expertise or what their role allows. This may lead at best to confusing messages being given to the families and at worst, to real harm being done to the family relationships. Any professional working with a family must keep in close and open collaboration with colleagues from other disciplines which are involved. There is no room for any possessiveness of expertise or role with regard to the family. The role of counsellor is a distinct one which is not encompassed in the roles of the professionals discussed above. However, some knowledge of the skills involved in counselling can be very useful for the professional who is interacting with parents.

A crucial skill of professionals is to be able to evaluate their own input; for example it is easy to become so involved in a conversation that the effect of what one is saying is not appreciated. Real harm can be done if the professional does not keep an objective view of their own intervention.

Organising effective intervention

It has already been noted that cooperating with professionals can pose difficulties for families; for example having to be involved with a number of different people can in itself prove onerous. Meetings which take place in the home can also become a cause for concern because of uncertainty about timings and objectives of visits, the feelings that professionals will be judgemental about the family, the home and so on. Professionals can do much to prevent these anxieties.

Professionals frequently make visits to families at a time that suits them rather than at times which suit the family. Nine-thirty in the morning may fit in very well with the professional's working timetable, but may be a very chaotic time for families of young children. In addition it is not safe to assume that parents will object to the timing if it is inconvenient. They may be very grateful for any help and support being offered and worry that any objections will not further their child's cause. If the visitor wants to have a really productive session with the parents and child, a mutually convenient time will have to be negotiated.

The frequency of visits also needs consideration. Visiting teachers and therapists will often make a number of helpful suggestions for educational or therapeutic intervention. It is sensible to then allow the family enough time to implement these. In a busy family, there may not be much time available for trying new activities with the child and it may only add to the negative feelings of the family if too much is expected of them too quickly.

The sensitive visitor to the home knows that there is no place for judgements of the family's lifestyle. All families have their own individual culture and traditions, such as mealtimes, bedtimes and so on. One way of doing things is not necessarily better than another, just different. However sensitive to this aspect professionals are, families often feel that judgements are being made about them, their homes and the way they handle their child and even worse, that these judgements are being recorded somewhere in a filing system. This fear will often be masked by the hospitality that most families will offer all visitors to their homes, professionals or otherwise.

Provided both parties are aware of these potential pitfalls, parents and professionals can establish a thoroughly worthwhile relationship which brings benefits to all.

Some families may find meeting other families in the same situation helpful and there are parent groups in most major towns. 'Look', the national federation of parent and family groups has literature and a regular bulletin which contain useful information about local parent groups. Many parents will welcome the opportunity to be put in touch with these, although some will not. It is the parents' right to reject such contact. One very useful experience for parents of young children is to meet young people with visual impairments who have been through the education system and experienced several types of provision. The young people will probably be very honest about their experiences, and their accounts will balance any information given to the parents by the local authority who may have political or financial reasons for suggesting one type of provision over another.

These local groups often provide opportunities for siblings of children who are visually impaired to meet and this can also be helpful.

Conclusion

If as Mittler (1979) said, 'the relationship between home and learning, reported so widely in the literature for normal children, is likely to be stronger in the case of handicapped children', it is crucial that efforts are made to develop and maintain high standards of support to parents and families. This calls for a recognition by parents that professionals with a wide experience of children and young people with visual impairments have something to offer. It also calls for very high standards of professionalism from those who try to offer support to the families.

Chapter 40

The Peripatetic/Advisory Teacher

Dorothy Spragg and Juliet Stone

Introduction

The role of the advisory teacher for children and young people with visual impairments has changed and developed significantly in the past 20 years. This chapter provides the reader with an overview of the advisory teacher's role in supporting the child or young person with a visual impairment. This support extends to the parents and family and also to the staff of the schools and colleges which these children and young people attend. The types of support which can be offered are discussed and the need to work in close cooperation with other professionals is emphasised.

Structure of services

Although this chapter refers to the 'advisory teacher' there are many other terms which are used to describe this role, including the 'peripatetic teacher' or the 'visiting teacher'. These titles seem to be interchangeable and appear to have no significance in defining the role of the teacher. There are, however, distinct differences in the ways in which services to children and young people are organised. The majority of advisory teachers are employed by local education authorities and are part of the provision for special educational needs. An increasingly favoured practice within authorities is to establish a sensory support service where both advisory teachers of children with visual impairments and those of children with hearing impairments work under a single head of service or manager.

The factors which affect the way in which services operate include:
- the length of time that a service has been established;
- the number of teachers in the service;
- the number of pupils on an individual teacher's caseload;
- the geography of the area, for instance rural or urban;
- how teachers are employed.

In some services teachers are assigned to a particular district and are responsible for all children and young people with visual impairments across the age and ability range. In other services teachers have responsibility for a particular group of pupils, for example those of secondary age or those with multiple disabilities.

Criteria for involvement

In recent years, services have defined criteria for their involvement and these are usually related to the degree of the child's visual impairment. Other factors which are also taken into account include the child's age, ability, background, level of achievement and the type of school the child attends. The advisory teacher is required to make decisions, based on sound evidence, about which children to support and the degree of support that those children need. The organisation of the service needs to be flexible enough so that support can be increased or reduced as children's needs change. Decisions about the level of support needed cannot be based solely on the degree of vision. For example it is not always the case that a blind child working through non-sighted methods will have a greater need for support than a child who is severely partially sighted. A child who is congenitally blind who can read and write competently and travel independently may well require a lower level of support than a child who is struggling with deteriorating vision and has not yet acquired alternative learning strategies.

The roles of the advisory teacher

Spungin and Taylor (1986) discussed the development of the roles and functions of the advisory teacher in the USA. They concluded 'It is necessary, therefore to realise the continual evolution of the roles of teachers of visually handicapped pupils in the context of the ever-changing population of children to be served.'

Although the need for a sound core of specialist knowledge in visual impairment remains, the increasing proportion of children with additional disabilities, the changes to the curriculum and teaching styles, and improvements in information technology have all influenced the range of skills required in the teacher of the child who is visually impaired.

Benton (1984) felt that the role of the advisory teacher covered four main areas of responsibility:

- assessment and evaluation;
- support for children;
- consultation with class teacher;
- involvement with parents.

The work of Spungin and Taylor, and Benton, suggest that the key elements of the role of advisory teacher are likely to include:

- assessing pupils' needs;
- assessing the learning environment;
- teaching pupils/students in the special skill areas such as the use of functional vision, communication skills, and so on;
- advising class and subject teachers;
- advising families;
- providing in-service training to staff;

- facilitating access to the curriculum;
- adapting materials;
- advising on technology;
- linking with special schools.

Some of these elements will now be considered in more detail.

Assessing pupils' needs

In assessing the needs of individuals, the advisory teacher will require information from a variety of sources including the medical and social services, the parents and the school. The advisory teacher's contribution to an assessment of a school-aged child might include an evaluation of the child's functional vision, the child's reading medium, the child's listening skills, mobility skills, and self-help and social skills. The information may be required in order to:

- prepare a statement of special educational need;
- help decide appropriate educational placement, or transfer;
- formulate individual education plans as part of Stage 3 of the Code of Practice.

The assessments will also be important in helping advisory teachers to determine their input for each pupil and set priorities for their caseload.

Assessment of the learning environment

In addition to assessing the individual, it will be necessary for the advisory teachers to evaluate the learning environment of the school in which the pupils are placed (see Chapter 21 for detailed information). This will include an assessment of:

- the quality and quantity of lighting and the practicality of making adaptations such as the provision of blinds, additional task lighting;
- access to, and within buildings, for instance a consideration of steps and stairways;
- teaching methods;
- quality of audiovisual resources such as chalkboards.

Information obtained from this observation can be used to advise schools on the ways in which the pupils' access to the learning environment can be facilitated.

Direct teaching

The structure, organisation and philosophy of the advisory service will dictate whether their staff are involved in direct teaching to individual pupils or whether they solely advise the class teachers who work with the pupils. There are many advantages of being directly involved with the pupil. It can:

- extend and expand the teacher's knowledge of the pupil;
- ensure time for the specialist curriculum ;
- help close monitoring of progress;
- allow time for the discussion of pastoral concerns.

The content of any such teaching sessions needs to be planned in full cooperation with the class or subject teachers, particularly if the teaching is supporting the school curriculum. Two areas of the special curriculum where direct teaching will be particularly important are communication through braille and the development of mobility and self-help skills. These are both areas which will be outside the mainstream teacher's expertise. It may be the advisory teacher's task to teach braille and to arrange for the provision of brailled material, perhaps organising volunteer transcribers. The area of mobility and self-help skills may be one in which, after the initial assessment, the advisory teacher links up with a mobility teacher or rehabilitation officer. In addition to teaching on a one-to-one basis, the pupil may need in-class support in particular subjects such as science.

Advising the staff in school

If pupils with visual impairments are to succeed within the mainstream school, the staff of the school will require information in order to develop expertise in adapting their teaching. It is the role of the advisory teacher to help staff access this information. All the staff will need an awareness of the general needs of these children, but more specific information will be required by those teachers who are in direct contact with them. Such information might include the principles of adapting learning materials, making effective use of technology and making appropriate arrangements for examinations.

Mainstream teachers will also need to understand why the pupil with a visual impairment is likely to process work at a slower pace. Once this is clearly understood, teachers can ensure that though the quantity of work processed by the pupil may be less than that of sighted peers, there need not (and should not) be a lowering of the quality of work expected.

Providing in-service training

One approach to preparing the staff of the school to meet the needs of pupils is through in-service training (INSET), and advisory teachers are frequently required to provide this kind of support to schools. They are also often asked to provide awareness training sessions for other professionals such as health visitors and educational psychologists. Addressing an unfamiliar group of professionals may be a daunting task for the advisory teacher, particularly one new to the post. There is not space in this chapter to discuss this in detail, but preparation is the key to success and practical advice can be obtained from more experienced colleagues on how to organise these sessions. As experience grows, delivering in-service training can be an enjoyable part of the role, providing opportunities to pass on one's own enthusiasm and interest in the fascinating area of visual impairment.

Facilitating access to the curriculum

It is not the role of the advisory teacher to take over the responsibility for the child's learning, though sometimes class teachers seem to believe that it is. The specialist teacher's role is to offer advice as to how access to the curriculum can be facilitated. This may mean advising teachers on the most appropriate print size, font, spacing and layout for visual materials. Teachers who have pupils who use non-sighted methods of learning may require support in developing and using taped materials, as well as guidance and instruction in the preparation of tactile diagrams, three-dimensional models, braille and Moon text. In many services, the advisory teachers do the actual adaptation and preparation of materials themselves. This is not an effective use of their time. Access to technical help and a working knowledge of the local and national facilities for the production of large print, tape and tactile materials offers a more efficient solution.

Where a multi-media approach is employed, both mainstream and specialist teachers should do everything possible to ensure that the pupil is not separated from the rest of the class in the learning experience. Much important learning, both academically and socially, comes from interacting with peers. There are instances where pupils with visual impairments have so much equipment and brailled or large print material that they are placed at a table completely apart from the rest of the class. If this occurs too frequently, the integration is not truly functional and the education is not inclusive.

Specialist technology

One aspect of the advisory teacher's role which has become increasingly important is the responsibility for ensuring that the pupils have access to the appropriate technology. The range of specialist technology for pupils with visual impairments has expanded dramatically. Closed circuit televisions (CCTVs), word processors and braille input and output devices have become more widely used and increasingly sophisticated. Advisory teachers need to keep abreast of developments and be able to make sensible decisions as to which piece of equipment will be useful and appropriate in each individual situation. It will probably also be their responsibility to train both the pupils and the mainstream staff in the use of this technology and to arrange for its installation and maintenance. All of this will require a major time commitment from them.

Linking with special schools

In some areas of the country there are no special schools nearby for pupils with visual impairments, and children who need this form of education will receive it some distance away from their homes in a residential setting. In this case the advisory teacher in the home area becomes the link person between the home and school, visiting the child at home during school holidays and visiting the school on the behalf of the local education authority (LEA) to check the child's progress in meetings such as the statutory annual review.

Working with pupils with additional and multiple disabilities

As has been pointed out in other chapters of this book, the majority of children with a visual impairment have additional disabilities, and in some cases these disabilities are profound. Only something like 2% of these children are in special schools for children with visual impairments and additional disabilities, the majority are in LEA schools for pupils with severe learning disabilities. In some areas, there will be an advisory teacher of the visually impaired with specific responsibility for supporting the pupils and staff in these local schools. However, the major aspect of the advisory teacher's work with these pupils will be an inter-disciplinary one, which calls for a high level of professional and personal skills. Specific guidance on working with these children whose needs are so complex is given in the section of this book which deals with multiple disabilities and visual impairment.

Support for the child and family

Advisory services provide support for children with visual impairment during the school years and most also provide support in the early pre-school years.

The early years

The earlier a child's visual impairment is identified, the earlier the professional services can assess the child's needs and make appropriate provision. Education, social services and area health authorities are required to appoint officers who have responsibility to liaise with parents and with each other in support of the child. The LEA is not obliged to provide educational services for children under the age of two years. Many sensory support services however, recognise the importance and long-term benefits of working with parents and very young children. The teacher's role here is primarily to support the needs of the developing child. The expectations of professionals and parents for the support of the child are fairly well defined, but in practice, the level and extent of the support afforded varies. This is further discussed in the previous chapters on the young child and the support of families.

Home liaison is often complicated, and a flexible approach is required to coordinate visits to suit the family's daily routine in order to maximise their effectiveness. The role within the home will vary according to the needs of the child, but will usually involve all or some of the following activities:

- liaising with other professionals and services involved with the family;
- continuous assessment of the child's functional vision;
- monitoring and recording the child's progress;
- providing advice to parents on visual and developmental programmes;
- providing support and information on educational services available at each stage of development.

It must be recognised that for families where English is not the first language it may be necessary to work closely with a language specialist skilled in the language used at home.

Due to time restrictions, many advisory teachers are unable to offer the commitment that is required to meet the young child's needs fully. One of the important aspects of the teacher's role is to develop the parent's confidence to work with their child and to pass on to them some of the essential skills and knowledge.

The advisory teacher will often be asked to make recommendations to both the parents and the LEA on the appropriate pre-school educational placement for individual children. Many children with visual impairments attend their local nursery or playgroup. For children with complex needs, local mainstream provision may be unable to offer appropriate support and placement might be sought in a specialist environment. Few nursery schools for children with special needs have a resident qualified teacher of the visually impaired and will rely heavily on the advice and support of the advisory teacher of the visually impaired.

It is at this stage that the role of the advisory teacher may change. He or she will continue to advise parents when necessary but the emphasis of the support will transfer to the teachers and educational assistants working with the child. It is preferable if the support for the family by the advisory teacher is reduced gradually. The child, in most cases, will continue to receive direct support from the advisory teacher at a level determined through assessment and by the resources of the local authority.

The advisory teacher will, no doubt, be involved in the decision as to which type of schooling will meet the child's needs best, and may be the liaison person between authority, school and family. Transition to school will change the role of the advisory teacher yet again.

Support for the child at school

The role of supporting children in a number of mainstream schools demands a high degree of professionalism and organisational ability on the part of the visiting teacher. The initial preparation for visits is a key element of success. The lines of communication required to support a child within a primary school are relatively short, involving only a small number of professionals usually comprising the head teacher, the special educational needs coordinator, the class teacher, the educational support assistant and the school psychologist. In the secondary school the picture is somewhat different and includes subject specialists, year heads and pastoral tutors. Most schools have their own system of communicating pupil information on a regular basis to the staff concerned and have an equally effective system for teachers to report any problems or concerns. Linking in to such a system saves time and is less disruptive for the school staff. The special needs coordinator is usually the 'key person' in the school who provides the link with other staff on support for pupils with special needs.

Advisory teachers who are visiting many different schools must make themselves aware of the differences in organisational arrangements within schools. These include differences in:

- the management structures and hierarchies;
- class groupings, such as streaming (vertically or horizontally) or mixed ability;
- the pastoral arrangements;
- the social environment;
- the ethos of schools and individual teachers;
- discipline procedures;
- the deployment of ancillary staff.

Only by understanding these differences, can they operate diplomatically within the schools and observe the professional etiquette for visits which is expected by each school.

Confidentiality is a matter about which visiting staff should have complete integrity.

Working on a regular basis, teachers will get to know the school and the staff well and will become party to sensitive issues and information. Advisory teachers need to remain discreet and maintain the trust that is placed in them.

There are no hard and fast rules regarding the way in which support is delivered in the mainstream school. Dawkins (1991), in her research, found that 'Different services hold sharply opposing views about what a peripatetic teacher should do'. The time and resources available are usually the factors which determine whether the advisory teacher works directly with the child or provides the skills and expertise through training teachers and support staff. Realistically, there needs to be a compromise. In schools where staff have well developed skills and alternative strategies for working with a child who is visually impaired, it will not be necessary to work alongside the child on a regular basis. However, staff in a school which is receiving a child with a visual impairment for the first time may derive confidence and skills more rapidly if they are able to observe the advisory teacher working in the classroom. Supporting the child in the classroom as opposed to withdrawing the child for teaching sessions is a matter for careful consideration. In many primary schools, additional support in the classroom is a daily event and the children accept this as routine. The older pupil may find support in the classroom unacceptable, as it makes them appear 'different' and they will prefer to take a more independent approach to their studies.

The skills of the advisory teacher

It is clear that if all the functions described above are to be fulfilled effectively, the advisory teacher needs a number of skills over and above expertise in visual impairment. What is surprising, perhaps, is that few teachers are given any additional training to enable them to develop these skills, some of which are discussed below.

Consultancy and negotiation

As so much of the role is concerned with interacting with other people, it is critical that the advisory teacher has interpersonal skills of a high standard. The main emphasis of the role is to cooperate with other people in working towards the best provision possible for the child or young person with a visual impairment. In most situations this will be straightforward with all parties following the same philosophy and policy, working together towards the same objective. However, there will always be occasions where one person's idea conflicts with that of another. A mainstream teacher may, for example, feel that the child with a visual impairment in the class needs full-time support. It may be felt by the advisory teacher that this would obstruct the child's full integration into the class, or it may be an inefficient use of a scarce resource. This situation calls for sensitive negotiation where the differences of opinion can be resolved, and this is further discussed in Chapter 43.

Communication with other professionals

It is also important that advisory teachers have the skills to communicate with other colleagues. This communication will take place in meetings and case conferences, over the telephone or through written communication in the form of letters and reports. Information must be passed to colleagues accurately, clearly and efficiently. Spoken communication comes naturally to most teachers, but report writing is a skill which many need time and practice to master.

Time management

Few advisory teachers would deny that there is not enough time in the day. The time available needs to be allocated to include work with:

- the child;
- class or subject teachers;
- classroom assistants;
- parents;
- other agencies involved with the child and family;
- colleagues in the team.

Time must also be allocated to travelling and administration. The advisory teacher in a rural area, for example, is expected to travel long distances to service the caseload and will spend a greater proportion of time travelling than one who works within a small geographical area. A consideration of the time and cost of travelling may need to be balanced against the needs of the child and the demands of the child's timetable.

Administration can be an onerous burden on advisory teachers if time for it is not built in to the weekly schedule. On average, a visit to a child entails one hour of additional time which may be taken up arranging the visit, writing reports, attending case conferences and reviews and liaising with colleagues. There can be a temptation to feel that administration is not productive work and not to be overly careful about completing it, but it is an essential part of the role and can save time in the long term.

Coping with stress

One skill that is essential for all teachers is to manage their own stress levels, and this is particularly true for the advisory teacher. The job is an exciting and challenging one which carries a large amount of responsibility. It can also be a rather solitary and frustrating one. If teachers are working as part of a team, this can be helpful. Regular meetings with colleagues provide a 'sounding board' and help to reduce the feeling of isolation that the advisory teacher often feels, especially when newly qualified. However, a sense of perspective, a realistic view of one's own limitations and above all a sense of humour are also important.

Professional development and training

As was said at the beginning of this chapter, the role of the advisory teacher continues to evolve. It is essential, therefore, that teachers keep abreast of changes, take steps to keep their professional standards high and ensure that their knowledge and skills are up to date. Many advisory teachers meet regularly with colleagues from other authorities and schools and arrange their own training informally, and there are now excellent opportunities for studying for higher education awards in the additional skills they need. Employers do have the responsibility of allowing and supporting the professional development of their advisory teachers.

One of the major concerns of those working as teachers in support services for the visually impaired is the lack of opportunities for promotion. Young teachers entering this particular section of provision need to be aware of this. Special education itself is a minority field, visual impairment is a small element in the field and the advisory services constitute yet another sub-section. With more services being incorporated with those for children with hearing impairments, the openings for promotion or for career development have been further reduced.

Future developments

As in all areas of educational provision, the future holds some uncertainties. The rise of new unitary authorities, and the possible decentralisation of services present new challenges for advisory services and their staff. Services which market their expertise and remain accountable for their costs will have the best chances of success. However, while the philosophy of inclusiveness prevails it appears that there will be a continuing role for the advisory teacher for children and young people with visual impairments.

Chapter 41

Support for Pupils within Mainstream Provision

Jeanette Lomas

Introduction

The 1981 Education Act, strengthened by the Education Reform Act (Department for Education (DfE) 1988a), advocated that pupils with special educational needs should be provided for within mainstream education wherever possible. This chapter will consider the types of support given to pupils with a visual impairment who attend a mainstream school. The skills and characteristics required of the specialist staff who support these children will be discussed, as will the school systems required to ensure appropriate and inclusive education for these children.

Most children with visual impairments who are placed in a mainstream school will require support from a specialist service. This support may be provided by either an external advisory service for pupils with visual impairments or by a resource base within the school and can take three different forms:

- advisory support which is aimed at enhancing the skills of the pupils' teachers;
- support for the pupils within the classroom;
- support for pupils in withdrawal sessions.

Advisory support

In this type of support, the specialist teacher acts primarily as an advising 'consultant' and does not teach the child directly. Some advisory teachers claim very successful results from this approach, although others feel that for their own credibility they need to be seen to making some contribution to teaching the child.

The initial point of contact within a mainstream school will usually be the Special Educational Needs Coordinator (SENCO). The advisory teacher will liaise with the SENCO and agree upon the type of support the school requires to ensure that the pupil with a visual impairment has access to the whole curriculum and is fully integrated into the life of the school. The SENCO acts as the filter for all information and advice with regard to the day-to-day provision for the pupil. The specialist teacher will occasionally meet with the pupil to explore any difficulties the pupil is having which have not been brought to the notice of the SENCO, but most of the support will be given through contact with the class and subject teachers.

Support within the classroom

The aim of this approach is to facilitate curriculum access for pupils by intervention within the classroom. In-class support can address the pupil's needs as soon as they become evident and avoid the stigma which can sometimes be associated with withdrawal. Appropriate support given by a well trained person can ensure that class teachers recognise their responsibilities towards the child with a visual impairment and become familiar with the child's needs and how they can be addressed.

Frequently the person appointed to provide in-class support for a pupil with a severe visual impairment is a 'non-teaching assistant' or a 'special support assistant'. Specialist teachers of the visually impaired are rarely employed to support a single child permanently as this is considered to be an inefficient use of resources. However, in schools where there is a resource base which provides for several children with visual impairments, the specialist teacher of the visually impaired will regularly support children in the classroom for part of their timetable.

Working within a classroom with another teacher can either be a very rewarding experience for all involved or a source of friction. Garnett (1988) states that the sum of two qualified professionals can be greater than one plus one if the working relationship is correct. Thomas (1992) carried out extensive research into classroom support and entitled his resulting book *Classroom Teamwork: Support or Intrusion?*. He thought that unless the situation was carefully organised, an additional adult in the classroom could create more difficulties than no support at all.

While the majority of teachers involved in providing in-class support would acknowledge the importance of joint planning with the class teacher, the time available for liaison is often restricted. Methods for reaching agreement about the aims of the support and how it can be provided, the way the classroom is managed and the style of discipline are described by Garnett (1988). The class or subject teacher and the specialist worker will need to work together and identify:

* when they can meet to plan and prepare adaptations to lessons;
* what resources are needed ;
* record keeping procedures;
* the ethos of class management and discipline.

The latter is a particularly sensitive issue and those who are working with either individuals or small groups of pupils must be careful not to interfere with the class or subject teacher's style of class management.

A recent report from the Office of Her Majesty's Chief Inspector of Schools (HMI 1996) stated that

> ...in the nursery, and at Key Stages 1 and 2, all pupils gain from extra in-class support, but pupils with SEN gain most. In Key Stages 3 and 4 with few exceptions, the same effect was only apparent where the support was provided by a teacher.

The report concludes that

...where support is not available, or where it is insufficiently well-informed, both the standards of achievement and the quality of education suffer...at all key stages the most influential factor on the effectiveness of in-class support is the quality of joint planning of the work between class/subject teacher and the support teacher or special support assistant (SSA)...SSAs are effective in helping to raise standards at primary phase, but markedly less so at secondary phase.

Support provided in withdrawal sessions

Withdrawing pupils from the classroom was a common practice in the 1970s and is still preferred by a few teachers today. However, it is now widely believed that regular use of this approach to support may do harm to a child's self-esteem and leave the class teacher feeling undervalued and deskilled. Removing the child from the class may be seen to imply that only the specialist teacher of the visually impaired has the skills required to provide access to the curriculum. It is argued that class and subject teachers need to maintain a feeling of ownership of the education of the pupil and to feel that their views are valued.

Richmond and Smith (1990) stated that withdrawal of groups of children experiencing difficulties in the primary setting was a popular method of intervention and many teachers argued that provided the programme for the withdrawal session was jointly planned, then it was an effective method for meeting the diverse needs of the pupils. Planning time appears to be the factor which has the major influence upon the success of any kind of support. The recent report from Her Majesty's Chief Inspector *Promoting High Achievement for Pupils with Special Educational Needs* HMI 1996) confirms that time is the essential element in ensuring quality planning.

A combination of approaches

The three methods of support identified above are not mutually exclusive. Learning support strategies for pupils with a visual impairment often consist of a combination of all three approaches. It is recognised that at critical stages during a child's school life, for example when a child is starting or transferring to school, increased levels of support will be needed. The type of support will vary according to the needs of the child and the needs of the school. Whatever the nature of the support systems, the class teacher remains the key person and continues to have the major influence on the child's programme and the prime responsibility for the child's learning.

Issues associated with provision of support

Within the field of special education there is currently an extensive debate about who should offer support to children with special needs. As has been seen, specialist teachers may not be the most appropriate people to provide day-to-day support and many pupils are supported by non-teaching assistants. The Ofsted survey (1996) suggests that less than half the local education authorities (LEAs) provide appropriate training for these staff. However, many advisory services for pupils with visual impairments have non-teaching assistants attached to the service who receive training from the specialist teachers of the visually impaired.

The support provided for individual pupils needs to be targeted carefully and too much individual help can be as damaging as too little. The continual presence of an adult working alongside the child may inhibit the independence of the child and prevent the social interaction which can help scaffold a pupil's learning (Wood 1988). Another danger is that class teachers may abdicate their responsibilities to the non-teaching assistant and fail to develop their own skills in working with the child with the visual impairment.

The status of support teachers who work in-class is frequently confusing to both pupils and mainstream staff. How these staff are introduced is of vital importance, and many specialist teachers take the opportunity of teaching mainstream classes for part of the week to demonstrate their class teaching skills and to establish their credibility with children and teachers. It is good practice for visiting support staff to offer to take the lead during a lesson and free the class teacher to work with the child with a visual impairment.

An issue in delivering in-class support in secondary schools is the extent of the expertise of the specialist teacher in the subject that the child is studying. When the writer was working with support teachers the following comment was heard: 'The experiences I felt supporting in a subject which I had not studied to examination level gave me some understanding of how the child with learning difficulties would feel.' Such experiences can give insights into what adaptations are required and discussion with the subject teacher may lead to appropriately differentiated materials and more appropriate teaching strategies. However, some support staff honestly admit that it can be very difficult to explain a concept or make relevant adaptations to materials without in-depth knowledge of the subject matter.

Non-teaching assistants who provide support within the mainstream setting may feel extremely isolated if they are not attached to the specialist service for the visually impaired or if they do not have regular contact with the specialist teacher. Opportunities for accredited training are limited but several establishments are developing courses which will meet the identified needs of classroom assistants and care staff who work with children with a visual imparment. Recognition within the pay structure for additional qualifications can be an incentive for classroom assistants to develop their skills.

Skills and characteristics of staff working in a mainstream support setting

Teachers and non-teaching assistants who support children with a visual impairment need to be flexible and adaptable. They will be required to be a member of a team, sometimes taking the lead and at other times being led. The most successful staff display the interpersonal skills and the enthusiasm and commitment to make inclusion work and are prepared to put in additional hours of work to adapt materials, ensuring that their planning and preparation is of the highest quality. The skills and characteristics of advisory teachers and consultants are also discussed in Chapters 42 and 43.

The support member of staff needs to be able to identify and point out to the class teacher any elements of the planned activity which are unsuitable for the child with a visual impairment or any aspects of the classroom organisation which are likely to cause difficulties for the pupil. They also need to be sensitive to the demands made upon classroom teachers.

School systems

Thomas (1992) is very clear about the steps to be taken to ensure effective support. He states that the whole school community should be involved in developing a policy on the organisation of support in the classroom. The Code of Practice (DfE 1994) calls for all schools to have a Special Educational Needs Policy which outlines at each stage agreed ways of working to meet the needs of pupils. Within the policy there should also be clarification of how concerns about children will be monitored.

The whole-school policy should clearly state the tasks and roles of those involved in offering support and the senior management team (SMT) of the school should provide administration time for the SENCO and designate time for staff to meet to plan provision. The individual strengths of members of the support team should be identified at the beginning of the support process so that each member understands how they can complement each other. Regular meetings to evaluate the effectiveness and appropriateness of the support should be attended by a member of the SMT. This information can then be fed into the termly/annual review meeting with parents and external agencies and will provide the basis for setting new targets within the child's individual education plan (IEP).

It may be necessary for the specialist teacher of the visually impaired to undertake in-service training with staff and governors to ensure that they are fully aware of the needs of the pupil(s) and how the school can meet those needs.

The needs of the family who have opted for their visually impaired child to be integrated into mainstream schooling will also need consideration. The specialist teacher will want to maintain regular contact with the family and enable the parents to participate fully in the annual review process.

Training for inclusive education

Since the Code of Practice was instituted there has been extensive training for SENCOs on the implications of the Code itself and on the stages of assessment and identification of special educational needs (SEN). Less training has been given about how to teach pupils with special educational needs more effectively and on issues regarding effective collaboration between professionals.

In the report to the Department for Education and Employment by the Special Educational Needs Training Consortium (SENTC 1996), it was recommended that the mandatory qualification for teachers working with pupils who have impairments of hearing and vision should be extended to specialist teachers working with hearing and visually impaired pupils in mainstream settings and in support services, including those working with pre-school children and their families. The recommendations also state that there should be an element of SEN training in all initial teacher training and that there should be the opportunity for teachers to update their knowledge, skills and understanding of SEN at regular intervals.

While the training needs of teachers are generally well recognised, the training of classroom support assistants has received less attention. This is surprising in the light of figures from the RNIB which suggest that there are now three times more support assistants working with children with visual impairment than specialist teachers.

Conclusion

The success of children and young people with a visual impairment in mainstream schools is heavily dependent upon the quality of support that is available to them. As children with more complex needs enter local schools, the demands on the professional skills of those supporting them can only increase.

Chapter 42
The Special School Teacher

Jeanette Lomas

Introduction

In the first chapter of this book it was seen that special schools have long had a central role in the education of children with visual impairments. There are conflicting views about the role of special schools. Dessent (1987) wrote that 'Special Schools do not have a right to exist. They exist because of the limitations of ordinary schools providing for the full range of abilities and disabilities among children.' Conversely, others argue that special schools will continue to play an important role in the range of provision to meet special educational needs. This chapter will explore some of the issues facing special schools and will consider both the general and the specific skills demanded of teachers who work in special schools for children with visual impairments.

Special schools for pupils with visual impairments

At the present time there are an estimated 20,000 children with visual impairments in the UK (see Chapter 2). Only 7% of these children attend special schools for children with visual impairments; nevertheless special schools continue to be a major influence in the field and are continuously evolving to adjust to a changing educational climate.

As has been seen in Chapters 1 and 2, the distribution of special schools and the location of these schools owes more to historical accident than regional requirements. Special school provision takes two main forms:
- local educational authority (LEA) day special schools serving local areas;
- non-maintained and LEA residential special schools with a regional or national intake.

The LEA day special schools are generally found in the major conurbations such as London and Birmingham. The non-maintained residential special schools are found throughout the country and are supported by voluntary agencies such as the Royal National Institute for the Blind, the Royal London Society for the Blind and the Catholic Blind Institute.

All the special schools tend to cater for the whole range of visual impairment from partial sight to total blindness. There are some schools which cater only for the primary (Key Stages 1 and 2) age range or only for secondary (Key Stages 3 and 4) pupils, but most are all-age schools and include pre-school and post-16 provision.

One of the advantages of the specialist setting is that pupils are generally taught in very small groups and there is a high staffing level. All staff teaching the pupils must gain a specialist qualification, which is recognised by the DfEE within three years of taking up their position and any special educational assistants employed at the school will have the advantage of having experienced colleagues to learn with and from.

With the growth of specialist support services and inclusive education the numbers of pupils attending the special schools has decreased and the ability range has become more diverse.

The changing role of special schools

Teachers in special schools for pupils with visual impairments have had to adjust to teaching classes of children with diverse and often complex educational needs. A few special schools for pupils with a visual impairment follow a mainstream curriculum and teach the full academic range; however, the majority of pupils who have a visual impairment as their only disability, and who are within the average ability range are now supported in their nearby mainstream school or in a resource base within a school in the locality. It is fair to say that pupils who attend special schools demonstrate a range of needs which require high levels of specialist staffing and equipment.

The special school teacher

Teachers working in special schools for children with visual impairments need to be able to demonstrate both the general skills of an effective class teacher and the specific skills appropriate to the specialist setting.

General requirements

Knowledge of the curriculum

All teachers in special schools obviously require a sound working knowledge of the National Curriculum. Within the primary phase, the ten subjects which make up the National Curriculum must be delivered together with the components that make up the additional or 'special' curriculum of any school. Secondary subject specialists need to be aware of the National Curriculum demands for their subject within Key Stages 3 and 4 and of the progression of skills and knowledge which the child brings with them from Key Stages 1 and 2. The specialist teacher will have to be able to make relevant adaptations in order to ensure equality of access to the curriculum for children with a visual impairment.

Planning

Sound planning and preparation is clearly essential to ensure contact hours spent with the pupils are as fruitful as possible. The specialist teacher's planning has also to take into account the total learning processes of the child with a visual impairment and where necessary, the child's individual education plan (IEP). The daily planning for lessons will include a consideration of the ways in which work will be differentiated and how activities will be assessed and evaluated. Frequently one hears the comment that special school teachers only have small groups to teach but each pupil within that small group may require an individual programme with material adapted to a specialised medium.

Commitment

The demands of teaching are such that teachers should not enter the profession unless they have a commitment to high quality education for all pupils. As in all schools, teachers in special schools will be required to devote additional time and to work well beyond the contractual contact time. Teachers throughout the profession must also show a commitment to equality of opportunity for all their pupils regardless of ability, gender, religion or race. This commitment needs to underpin a teacher's philosophy of education when working with pupils with special educational needs. The special school teacher should be one who believes in providing equality of opportunity for his or her pupils in order for them to achieve in a society where there is high unemployment among adults with a visual impairment and an increasing demand for sophisticated skills in the workforce.

Reflective teaching

The reflective teacher is one who is considered to be skilled in critical enquiry and who is adaptable and self-motivating. Ashcroft (1992) states that the teacher for the twenty-first century will need to be equipped with a variety of higher order management and interpersonal skills. No longer can teachers regard classrooms as their private domain; they are required to work collaboratively in the classroom and to keep abreast of new developments and assess their relevance for the pupils with whom they work. For example, special school teachers must keep in touch with developments in specialist equipment and be able to assess its relevance and value for their pupils.

Organisational skills

The best teachers in special schools demonstrate the ability to plan and organise lessons or contact time effectively, so that other teachers and any special educational assistants involved in the lesson know exactly what is to be undertaken and achieved. Materials which require adapting or enlarging are prepared before the lesson and not during it and specialist equipment is checked and serviced regularly.

In order to encourage independence and resourcefulness in young pupils, the classroom and learning areas are organised for easy access. The equipment is stored so that it can be easily reached and collected by the pupils and clear labelling is provided to enable the pupil with a visual impairment to locate the materials required easily.

Training skills

Special schools have increasingly become centres where there is a constant flow of visitors and observers. The call upon special schools for children with visual impairments to provide placements for those in training is increasing, and this demand has intensified partly because of the reduction in the numbers of specialist establishments and partly because of the increase in the number of teachers requiring training to support children in mainstream schools.

Special schools have a long tradition as training establishments. This role is likely to continue, and teachers working in special schools must expect to have visitors looking round their classrooms on a regular basis. Most schools organise 'visitors' days which channel callers to certain days in an attempt to reduce the amount of disruption to lessons. In order to minimise disruption, the class teacher needs to know in advance who will be visiting and what information they will require.

Team working

Within the secondary department of a special school the specialist teacher may have to work with several special assistants at different times of the day and will need to provide clear instructions so that each assistant in turn can move the lessons forward and support the pupil(s) in an appropriate and meaningful manner. Thomas (1992) has undertaken extensive research into the dynamics of teams of adults working together within the classroom setting and calls for joint training to ensure the effectiveness of support.

The role of non-teaching staff is crucial. In order to ensure that these staff are able to support the children in an appropriate and meaningful manner the teacher needs to delegate work appropriately. The City and Guilds Course 'Support for Learning' is one way in which formal training for classroom assistants can be provided.

Specific requirements for teachers in special schools

The Special Educational Needs Training Consortium (SENTC) Working Party Report (SENTC 1996) states that 'teachers who receive specialist training in the field of visual impairment require competence in both the generic areas in special educational needs and the specialist area of visual impairment'. The report goes on to point out that this generic component should relate directly to visual impairment and provide a broad context in which it can be studied.

A knowledge and understanding of the implications of visual impairment for the physical, cognitive, emotional, social and language development of the child is a basic requirement for the special school teacher. In addition, teachers should also be confident in their ability to deliver the specialist curriculum, such as the teaching of braille, techniques to enhance residual vision, the production of tactile diagrams and the orientation and mobility techniques which can foster independent travel in their pupils. Special schools for children with visual impairments are generally very well resourced with specialised information technology. The special school teacher is required to become skilled and knowledgeable in the use of specialist equipment and to make judgements on its appropriateness for individual pupils.

As stated earlier, teachers in special schools will be expected to interact and work collaboratively with a range of professionals. As members of a team they will have to find the time to liaise with colleagues outside class time and to share information about the progress of children in the relevant areas of their programmes.

As a member of a multi-professional team, the special school teacher will require the personal and professional skills to make that team effective. Although children may be supported by a number of professionals because of their diverse needs, it is the class teacher who is ultimately responsible for coordinating and in some cases delivering the programmes. The teacher will be expected to organise the adults who work within their classroom to ensure the minimum disruption to the class routine. Special educational assistants working within special schools are often well trained and experienced, and the special school teacher needs a clear idea of how the skills of the assistant can be used to the maximum benefit of the children.

The special school class may consist of between four and 12 pupils. As each pupil may be working at a very different level the teacher needs skills in differentiating work, ensuring that it is broken down into small achievable steps. They need to be able to adapt the learning programmes for each child, having regard to the child's age, pace and style of learning and cultural background.

As the number of pupils with diverse needs in addition to their visual impairment is increasing, teachers in special schools require a working knowledge of a range of special needs. For example they will be expected to understand the implications of learning difficulties or emotional and behavioural difficulties and to be able to initiate and sustain appropriate intervention.

Teachers who work in special schools require sophisticated assessment skills and the ability to record and interpret data accurately and they should be willing to share their findings with others in the field. There is no room for guarding professional discoveries about how the needs of a child can be met.

Other issues concerning special school teaching

Unless the senior management of the school are architects of change and continually forge links with mainstream establishments, then the special school teacher may feel isolated. Aubrey (1990) states that isolationism may occur when access to critical dialogue about standards is restricted. The moderation of work with local mainstream schools should be common practice in all special schools so that work is not assessed in isolation and expectations are appropriate. Opportunities to attend in-service training about the curriculum with mainstream teachers can help the special school staff keep in close contact with the developments and the challenges within mainstream schools.

The question of low expectations is another issue which has to be continually addressed within the special school setting. Pupils within the special school for the visually impaired will frequently have additional difficulties, and the dangers of early labelling and the self-fulfilling prophecy of under-achievement in educational contexts are well established (Harris and Rosenthal 1989, Rogers 1989, Rosenthal 1985). By ensuring that children can access the curriculum and are continually challenged, the low expectations which can damage children's achievements will be minimised. Monitoring performance should be a normal part of curriculum development.

It has been stated that pupils attending special schools will have very diverse needs and will undoubtedly require individual programmes. However, the importance of group working so that pupils 'scaffold' each other's learning, must not be overlooked. The social context plays an important part in the development of children. Teachers with small groups who are teaching within the constraints of an examination syllabus may lose sight of the advantages of this aspect of learning. Within the mainstream setting, class numbers require the incorporation of group work and informal peer tutoring occurs naturally. Where group sizes are small, visits to mainstream schools can provide opportunities for collaborative learning.

Special schools need strong links with mainstream schools and mainstream schools can benefit from the facilities that specialist schools can offer to them. Special schools have traditionally offered the reflective teacher the opportunity to carry out research and to develop new ways of working.

Conclusion

Baker and Bovair (1989) point out that much of the good practice which is commonplace in mainstream schools with regard to pupils with SEN was first developed in special schools. It is certainly true to state that many special schools have continued to be innovative in their teaching approach and remain challenging and stimulating environments for the dedicated teacher.

Chapter 43

Consultancy Skills

Jeanette Lomas

Introduction

Many specialist teachers for the visually impaired have an advisory role working with headteachers, teachers and professionals from other disciplines. The skills relevant to this work are varied and the term that encompasses them is 'consultancy skills'. Specialist teachers can be described as 'consultants' who are trying to bring about change in order to ensure success for pupils with a visual impairment. This change can be at classroom, school or local authority level. This chapter covers the skills required to be a successful agent of change and examines some of the factors to be considered in this complicated process.

Consultancy within schools and services

Consultants can either be internal or external/visiting agents. Internal consultants are those within a school or service who have the task of identifying areas of change in order to provide more efficient and effective provision. Development within any organisation relies upon continual monitoring and evaluation in order to ensure that those practices which enhance provision are retained and those which hinder progress are changed. Schools and services are not merely subject to change; their very nature makes them the agents of change. They are required to respond positively to the changing demands of society by adjusting their aims, objectives and practice accordingly.

There will always be some resistance to change because it is human nature to feel secure with familiar routines. However, effective managers ensure that all those who are involved in change are fully informed and take an active part in the process. An effective leader is one who has the ability to influence colleagues to accomplish tasks while maintaining positive interpersonal relationships.

Within a school the 'consultancy' role may be taken on by a member of the senior management team. It is essential that the person taking on this role has the authority to bring about change. Members of senior management have the knowledge of the systems which can trigger change in their establishment. However it must be acknowledged that the processes involved in changing the school's or service's current position from within may be complex, and it is frequently more difficult to change procedures when working on a day-to-day basis with familiar colleagues. It has been known for LEAs to appoint external heads on a temporary, fixed-term contract in order to instigate change which is well overdue.

The internal consultant should not only be thought of as a manager but a leader with a vision. True leadership requires the courage to recreate the organisation and challenge the existing systems. This approach to leadership is one that specialist teachers/members of a senior management team are required to adopt if schools and services are to meet the increasing demands for accountability and radical change which are imposed from external sources (such as the publication of league tables for school performance, curriculum changes and Ofsted inspections).

The instigators of change must concentrate on disseminating their 'vision', taking each member of the organisation through each step until there is acceptance and adoption of the plan. Personal contact, effective communication and discussion are of paramount importance. Many schools and services now have systems in place whereby a project team or working party is appointed and trained in the new alternative methods of working before they are taken to the whole staff and implemented within the institution.

From her research into training internal consultants, Aubrey (1990) concludes that unless the change agent is in a position of formal leadership or authority, it may be difficult to effect change beyond the sub-group and thus influence organisational change. This might be taken to imply that the specialist teacher of the visually impaired needs the full backing of the senior management team to develop practice throughout the school which improves access to the curriculum for children with a visual impairment.

Classroom teachers themselves are in a strong position to ensure improved access on a daily basis for the pupil with a visual impairment. Teachers who devise successful teaching strategies to meet the special needs of children often share their findings and knowledge with colleagues informally in the staff room. These teachers should be encouraged to record their findings and to discuss them with senior colleagues. Action research of this kind is an excellent way of identifying the areas for change and devising strategies to bring it about, and records of this type of research can become important sources of information for colleagues and governors.

The origin of change, be it at micro or macro level, is immaterial if it ultimately brings about an improvement in educational access for pupils with a visual impairment. All teachers should regard themselves as change agents and should aim to develop the consultancy skills required to bring change about in an effective manner, and to present their arguments clearly, rationally and calmly.

External or visiting consultants

One advantage of being a visiting specialist teacher of the visually impaired is being emotionally, but not professionally, removed from the situation under consideration. As an external consultant it is easier to be objective and, relying on a base of specialist knowledge/expertise in visual impairment, to identify pockets of good practice and to point out areas which need improvement. For visiting 'consultants', a knowledge of the way schools function, their power structure, and the locus of control within schools, may ultimately determine how effectively a specialist teacher can influence working practices. As an agent of change, it may be necessary to decide whether to start by working with individuals or with the whole staff. Whichever approach is adopted, an understanding of the needs of the institution/organisation and the roles that individuals play within the system is essential.

When working with schools, it may be useful for the consultant to seek answers to the following questions.

- Is there agreement on the aims and purposes of the school/establishment?
- Are people clear as to their duties and responsibilities?
- Is there a reasonably efficient communication system?
- What is the general ethos of the school/establishment?
- Is power in the establishment fairly distributed and how is the management structure viewed?
- Are staff skills under used?
- Is morale generally good?

Aubrey (1990) states that the consultant may adopt two basic roles: the resource consultant and the process consultant. The resource consultant, drawing on expert knowledge, recommends a particular course of action to improve the performance of the organisation. The process consultant will attempt to pass on methods, approaches and values to enable the organisation to diagnose and remedy its own difficulties through a process of problem identification, goal setting and evaluation. Specialist teachers of the visually impaired may be required to be able to adopt both these basic roles.

Central to successful change is the quality of the collaborative relationship developed between consultant and 'the client(s)'. This requires interpersonal skills from the consultant which will facilitate cooperation and communication (Lacey and Lomas 1993).

Collaborative working

Reports from Her Majesty's Inspectorate (HMI 1989, 1991), which looked at the support of pupils with special educational needs in schools, stated that good practice was associated with inter-disciplinary working and that the services which were best received in schools had carefully negotiated the exact nature of the support they were giving. These reports called for support services to develop a clear definition of their roles and structure. The need for continuous evaluation of the support that was given and the provision of training for personnel from the supported establishments were also highlighted as key factors.

Effective collaboration during the consultancy process relies upon the development of team work. Methods of creating an environment for effective team working are discussed in detail in Rowntree (1989), and Lacey and Lomas (1993). Within special education the needs of the children are so diverse that one professional could not be expected to have all the answers. The needs of the child or young person will best be met where people from different disciplines work together and there is an exchange of information, knowledge and skills. Specialist teachers will come into contact with professionals from the four main elements involved in provision for children with a visual impairment: health, education, social services and voluntary organisations. An ability to work effectively with others is essential to the consultant's success.

The professionalism of the consultant is constantly under scrutiny and according to Davies and Davies (1988) credibility can be achieved by the following means.

- Demonstrating relevant practical skills. It is essential that the teacher of the visually impaired makes recommendations which are practical and can demonstrate how to implement them. Activities for the parent or class teacher which are too time consuming or impossible to undertake undermine the consultant's credibility. The specialist teacher must demonstrate competence and experience in their field of expertise.

- Communicating openly. The key to being an effective consultant within any team is effective communication. Teachers communicate with others through meetings, report writing and face-to-face discussions where sophisticated negotiating skills and interpersonal skills are often demanded. Communication is a two-way process and clear and articulate speakers are only considered good communicators if they are also active listeners. In order to communicate effectively, it is necessary to know not only what needs to be said but when to say it. Effective consultants will ask for clarification if they do not fully understand something that has been stated or written.

- Demonstrating respect for others and acknowledging the skills already possessed by others. Communicating with people in a respectful manner will demonstrate a willingness to work as a member of a team. A team becomes all the stronger for a recognition that skills, knowledge and experiences are complementary. The inexperienced consultant will tend to be slower to recognise the skills of others whereas the more experienced person will actively seek out the expertise of colleagues.

The competencies of the consultant

Negotiating skills

There may be occasions when there are differences of opinion, for example about the level of support given to a pupil or the funding or provision of specialised equipment. A successful negotiation is one in which all the relevant facts are collated and the advantages and disadvantages of each option are examined. The skilled consultant ensures that everyone is fully aware that they have looked at other avenues before deciding upon a particular path. The negotiation itself should be conducted without acrimony and should be concerned only with material relevant to the topic under discussion.

Meetings

Meetings are time-consuming and costly and consultants should be certain that they are necessary before calling or attending them. Meetings should be carefully prepared and materials/papers for discussion should be circulated beforehand. An effective chairperson will ensure that there is careful time control and clear outcomes and that everyone at the meeting has had the opportunity of expressing an opinion. Rowntree (1989) states that if members come out of a meeting describing it as a waste of time then they have only themselves to blame. Minutes with decisions and action points should be followed up by the chairperson.

Written communication

Any document which will have a wide readership should be carefully written and presented. Local authorities will often have an agreed format for reports. Jargon should be avoided, especially when working in a multi-disciplinary team and sources of information should be acknowledged and confidentiality respected. It is always a good test when writing a report about a pupil to ask oneself the question 'if I was the parent of the child what would I think on reading it?'

Personal qualities

Having reviewed the skills required to be an effective consultant, it is appropriate to examine the intellectual and personal qualities of successful consultants.

Kubr (1983, quoted in Aubrey 1990) suggested that effective consultants display the following characteristics:

- intellectual ability;
- ability to understand people and work with them;
- ability to communicate, persuade and motivate;
- intellectual and emotional maturity;
- personal drive and initiative;
- ethics and integrity;
- physical and mental health.

People with a consultancy role are often referred to as 'experts', but every situation should be viewed as a learning experience. The 'know it all syndrome', as Bowers (1984) calls it, must be avoided if professionals are to work productively together. Baker and Bovair (1989) state that self-confidence is critical and that making mistakes is not only inevitable but is an essential part of learning. Given the diverse nature of the role of consultant it is inevitable that mistakes will be made, but the able consultant will learn from the situation.

The consultancy process

Whenever consultants are appointed to carry out a task there should be a clear description of what is required of them. In planning a consultancy it is useful to consider the following process:

- a definition of the problem;
- an analysis which breaks down the problem into its component parts;
- a plan to address each element of the problem;
- implementation and evaluation of the plan;
- a review of the outcomes.

This process can help to organise the effective intervention which will improve the quality of access for the child with a visual impairment.

Conclusion

In order to increase opportunities for children and young people with visual impairments, consultants will need the skills required to liaise effectively across the various disciplines in the field of visual impairment. The key to success is a willingness to acknowledge and draw out the skills of others through collaborative working.

TEACHER EDUCATION

Chapter 44

Competencies of Teachers of Children and Young People with a Visual Impairment

Heather Mason

Introduction

This chapter examines, very briefly, some of the changes taking place in teacher training in the United Kingdom and their effects upon the professional development of special educators working with children and young people with a visual impairment.

Trends in professional development

Those wishing to work with children and young people with a visual impairment must first obtain qualified teacher status through the various routes of initial teacher training. Normally, teachers come into work with pupils with a visual impairment after a minimum of three years of successful practice in mainstream classrooms.

Teachers in England and Wales working in the special schools for pupils with disabilities of sight have to undertake an additional mandatory course of training (a one-year full-time equivalent programme) and successfully complete it within three years of their appointment to the school (Department of Education and Science (DES) 1993). The regulations as they apply to those teachers working in other schools are less clear. The teacher who is working with a class of children with visual impairments is certainly required to undertake mandatory training but the regulations do not apply to:

- peripatetic/advisory teachers;
- support teachers in mainstream schools;
- teachers working in resource centres for children with visual impairments in mainstream schools;
- teachers working in schools for pupils with profound and multiple disabilities (PMLD), physical disabilities (PD), moderate or severe learning difficulties (M/SLD), even though there may be significant numbers of children in these schools who have a visual impairment.

In spite of the fact that there is no legal compulsion for these teachers to undergo this additional training, the trend during the last ten years has been for many of them to do so. This has been the result of many factors, such as support from enlightened employers and pressure from professional organisations and charitable bodies, and increasingly, from parents of the children, who believe that teachers in this specialist area should be specially trained. In practice, most teachers working in peripatetic services and resource bases have the additional specialist qualification. But few teachers in schools for pupils with PMLD, PD or M/SLD are qualified to teach pupils with a visual impairment.

The role of a specialist teacher of children and young people with a visual impairment has changed dramatically and continues to change. Twenty-five years ago the training of specialist teachers prepared them exclusively for work in the designated special schools for children with visual impairments, where they would generally teach classes of children of comparable age and ability (see Chapter 2). Teachers now need preparation for work in a variety of settings with a wide range of ages and abilities. They can no longer assume that they will have one type of job for life: special schools for the visually impaired are decreasing in number; the integration/inclusion debate continues, and there are observable changes in the defined population, for instance a greater proportion of children with a visual impairment have additional disabilities (see Chapter 32).

Recruitment rates of young male and female teachers to all areas of special education, including visual impairment, are low; the gender and age profile suggests that the teacher of the visually impaired is most likely to be a female, in the 35+ age range who has perhaps returned to teaching after raising a family. This could be seen as an advantage, since many of these teachers will have received their initial training at a time when the study of aspects of child psychology was a compulsory element of teacher preparation. Teachers who have qualified recently do not necessarily have any formal knowledge of child development – important background for any person working with children with special educational needs.

Funding for professional development in the area of special education has mainly been devolved to schools. Some money can be retained by local education authorities in order to fund teachers to attend training courses in the mandatory areas such as visual impairment and hearing impairment. Funding teachers to attend a one year full-time university-based course is expensive, and employers are turning to cheaper alternatives such as school-based 'twilight' (evening/weekend) courses. University departments find it increasingly difficult to sustain full-time specialist courses and this option for training has all but disappeared.

Over eight years ago the universities involved in training teachers of the visually impaired formed an association (Visually Impaired Trainers Consultative Group, VITCG) to ensure that they would have 'one voice' when dealing with the Department for Education and Employment (DfEE) on training issues. The trainers were concerned to preserve the quality of specialist courses and defined core elements of training required and the competencies that all specialist teachers should be able to demonstrate.

Over the last four years the members of the VITCG have been involved in drawing up and refining a list of competencies which all teachers of the visually impaired should be able to demonstrate after a period of mandatory training. These have now been incorporated into a national report to the DfEE, prepared by the Special Education Needs Training Consortium (SENTC 1996), which represents all the disability training groups.

It is clearly important to be precise about what is required of teachers and Jordan and Powell (1995) make a distinction between competencies and skills. They believe that teachers employ a range of skills in their professional practice which are often equated with 'competencies'. They argue that the teachers' effectiveness does not depend upon so much upon the discrete skills that they possess but rather on the way in which they go about making decisions concerning:

- which of those skills to apply;
- in which situations;
- the way in which they monitor pupil responses and adjust their approach accordingly.

They argue that the acquisition of skills does not guarantee competency. Instead, to be competent is to have a set of skills and be able to employ them using a flexible, responsive set of higher order strategies.

A major impetus for identifying particular skills in teachers of children with special educational needs has come from the legislation regarding the monitoring of standards in education. All schools are now required to be externally inspected on a four year cycle (Ofsted 1993). However, there is concern that inspectors, in spite of having undergone a rigorous period of training, are not always fully aware of the needs of pupils with low incidence disabilities such as visual impairment nor of the specialist skills needed by the teachers to meet these needs (Jordan and Powell 1995, Mason 1994).

Parents who are not satisfied with the quality of education their child is receiving may resort to appeal through a special needs tribunal.

Training for new roles

The courses which offer the mandatory training for teachers of children and young people with visual impairments must take account of the fact that the teachers they train will be expected to be able to cover the whole age range (from pre-school to adult) in a variety of educational settings which will include:

- special schools/classes
- units in mainstream schools or colleges
- resource centres in mainstream schools or colleges

They may also be required to work as part of a peripatetic/itinerant service and visit children and parents/carers in their homes. These teachers will also be required to work with a range of intellectual ability, spanning children and young people with:

- profound and multiple disability (PMLD)
- multiple disability and visual impairment (MDVI)
- deafblindness
- visual impairment and moderate learning difficulties
- visual impairment and intellectual giftedness.

In carrying out their roles, they will be called upon to meet the needs of those for whom the effect of their visual impairment ranges from total blindness to limited but useful vision.

These teachers will be:

* working directly with individuals and groups;
* supporting class teachers or institutions in assessment, curriculum planning, the preparation of materials and the planning of a learning environment;
* working alongside parents and professionals from other disciplines, such as doctors and social workers;
* providing professional support and advice to learners, parents and teachers.

During the last 11 years, there have been many changes in the profile of teachers coming forward for training. As we have seen, initially most teachers who received training were based in the specialist schools for the visually impaired. Today an increasing number come from the advisory services and from schools for children with multiple disabilities. (There are at least 6000 such children of school age in the UK.) The 1993 (Department for Education (DfE) 1993) Education Act and the ensuing Code of Practice (DfE 1994) have served to accelerate the placement of children with visual impairment in mainstream schools and many more staff from these schools are undertaking training.

These changes in educational provision, and a greater awareness of the incidence of visual impairment among pupils with multiple disabilities, has meant that the specialist training has to reflect an enormous range of skills and competencies. It could be argued that during the equivalent of one year of study, teachers cannot be expected to master all the skills they are likely to require. Perhaps like the progression of medieval workers, from apprentice to journeyman and finally craftsman, the skills they acquire in training will need to be honed through practice and experience and perhaps further specialisation.

The competencies

This final section lists the competencies required by a teacher of the visually impaired as suggested by the VITCG. It is hoped that they will form a basis for discussion by teachers, and will provide parents with the information with which to assess the skills and understanding of those responsible for delivering the National Curriculum and the special curriculum to their child. It cannot be a definitive list because competencies develop to reflect the changing nature of a disability and the educational processes.

Assessment of the competencies must take into account two elements.

* The demonstration of knowledge and understanding. This would be assessed through written assignments, seminars, workshops, teaching files, and a teaching practicum.
* The demonstration of practical ability. This would be assessed mainly through observation during their practicum and also through practical workshops. Personal evaluation would take place in written assignments.

A   *The teacher should be able to demonstrate a knowledge and understanding of:*
- current national developments in curriculum and assessment and their implications for learners with a visual impairment;
- the anatomy and physiology of visual functions in normal development;
- the implications of visual impairment on physical, cognitive, emotional, social and language development;
- the educational implications of the pathology and treatment of eye diseases and conditions;
- the significance of visual impairment for those with severe learning difficulties or multiple impairments;
- the principles of assessment of functional vision;
- an awareness of the importance of mobility training;
- appropriate strategies to enhance functional vision;
- appropriate equipment and techniques in the area of communication technology for those with a visual impairment;
- the different roles of a teacher in a special school, a peripatetic teacher or a resource teacher in a mainstream school or college;
- the range and functions of support services available to those with a visual impairment.

B   *The teacher should be able to demonstrate an ability to:*
- carry out an appropriate assessment of the needs of pupils with a visual impairment and to present a report of that assessment, taking note of any potential audience (such an assessment should include the use of developmental scales and/or orientation and mobility checklists);
- evaluate competing demands in the planning of the curriculum for a student who is visually impaired, for instance the impact upon other areas of the curriculum including time for mobility training;
- design and implement appropriate curricula, taking into account the individual learner's needs, age, culture and stage in education;
- design, produce, present and evaluate material in the appropriate medium, for instance skills in producing braille, large print, tactile diagrams, using both traditional methods and new technology;
- choose and employ appropriate methods of teaching and appropriate methods of communication for each student with a visual impairment, including those with multiple or dual sensory impairment;
- monitor and evaluate the implementation of individual student programmes;
- use materials designed to evaluate and train residual vision;
- cooperate with a qualified mobility specialist in the design and delivery of mobility programmes;
- employ appropriate strategies for teaching literacy and numeracy to the young print user and the young braille user;
- use techniques for teaching braille to all students who need it;

- read and write braille to acceptable standards;
- assess and plan for the application of microtechnology in meeting the needs of students with a visual impairment;
- use a range of hardware and software and employ criteria for evaluating its usefulness and appropriateness;
- locate and employ network resources, both learning material in schools and other centres; advise and help colleagues in the choice and implementation of appropriate curricula (this should include the use of appropriate technology to promote communication, the production of materials in a range of media, concept learning and access to information);
- lead training sessions for teachers, non-teaching assistants, parents and relevant others in the field of visual impairment;
- assist parents and learners (where appropriate) to participate in the decision making process;
- support the integration of a visually impaired student into the community;
- demonstrate the above competencies in relation to special and mainstream schools and in a peripatetic advisory role.

References

Abbs, P. (1989) *Aa is for Aesthetic*. Lewes: Falmer Press.

Abbs, P. (ed.) (1995) *Living Powers: The Arts in Education*. Basingstoke: Falmer Press.

Adair, J. (1984) *The Skills of Leadership*. Aldershot: Gower Press.

AEB-WJEC (1996, 1997, 1998) *Coursework Guidelines and Assessment Criteria*. Bristol: AEB (Associated Examing Board).

AEWVH (Association for the Education and Welfare of the Visually Handicapped) (1986) *Braille for Infants*. London: RNIB.

AEWVH (1987) *Braille for Infants: Teachers' Handbook*. London: RNIB.

AEWVH (1990) *Take Off*. London: RNIB.

AEWVH and RNIB (1991) *Response to the Select Committee on Sport in Schools*. London: House of Commons.

Aherne, P. and Thornber, A. (1990) *Communication For All*. London: David Fulton.

Ainscow, M. (1995) 'Education for all: making it happen', *Support for Learning*, **10** (4), 147–155.

Aitken, S. (1995) 'Educational assessment of deafblind learners'. In: D. Etheridge (ed.) *The Education of Dual Sensory Impaired Children*. London: David Fulton.

Aitken, S. and Buultjens, M. (1992) *Vision for Doing. Assessing Functional Vision of Learners who are Multiply Disabled*. Edinburgh: Moray House.

Aitken, S. and McDevitt, A. (1995) *Using IT to Support Visually Impaired Learners: Books 1, 2 and 3*. Birmingham: School of Education, University of Birmingham.

Aldrich, F. K. and Parkin, A. J. (1989) 'Listening at speed', *British Journal of Visual Impairment*, **7**(1), 16–18.

Anderson, E. M. and Clarke L. (1982) *Disability in Adolescence*. London: Methuen.

Anderson, N. (1995) 'Comment: an advocate's notebook', *Visability*, **14**, 29–30.

Anderson, S., Boigon, S. and Davis, K. (1991) *The Oregon Project For Visually Impaired and Blind Preschool Children*, 5th edition. Medford, Oregon: Jackson Education Service District.

APH (1995) *Psychological Assessment of Visually Impaired Persons*, [Video]. New York: American Printing House.

Armitage, T. R. (1886), *Education and Employment of the Blind: What it Has Been, Is, and Ought To Be*, 2nd edn. London: Harrison and Sons.

Armstrong, B. and Davies, P. (1995) 'The transition from school to adulthood: aspirations and careers advice for young adults with learning and adjustment difficulties', *British Journal of Special Education*, **22**(2), 70–75.

Arter, C. and Mason, H. L. (1994) 'Spelling for the visually impaired child', *British Journal of Visual Impairment*, **12**(2), 18–21.

Arter, C., McCall, S. and Bowyer, T. (1996) 'Handwriting and children with visual impairments', *British Journal of Special Education,* **23**(1), 25–29.

Ashcroft, K. (1992) 'Working together: developing reflective student teachers'. In: C. Biott and J. Nias (eds), *Working and Learning Together for Change.* Milton Keynes: Open University Press.

Ashcroft S. C. and Henderson F. (1963) *Programmed Instruction in Braille.* Pittsburgh: Stanwick House.

Asher, C. (1993) 'Using the target language as the medium of instruction in the communicative classroom: the influence of practice on principle', *Studies in Modern Languages Education,* **1**, 53–71.

Asher, C., Heys, S. and West, M. (1995) 'MFL for pupils with emotional and behavioural difficulties: exploring the possible', *Language Learning Journal,* **11**, 14–16.

Ashman, A. and Conway, R. (1989) *Cognitive Strategies for Special Education.* Routledge: London.

Aubrey, C. (1990) *Consultancy in the United Kingdom, its Role and Contribution to Educational Change.* London: Falmer Press.

BAALPE (1995) (The British Association of Advisers and Lecturers in Physical Education) *Safe Practice in Physical Education.* Leeds: White Lion Press/BAALPE.

Backhouse, J. (1987) 'Changing teaching method through INSET', *British Journal of In-Service Education,* **14**(1), 25–28.

Bagley, M. (1983) *Career Development of Blind and Visually Impaired Persons.* Mississippi: Mississippi State University.

Baird, G. and Moore, G. T. (1993) 'Epidemiology of childhood blindness'. In: A. Fielder, A. Best and M. C. O. Bax (eds), *The Management of Visual Impairment in Childhood.* London: Mackeith Press.

Baker, D. and Bovair, K. (1989) *Making the Special Schools Ordinary? Volume 1.* London: Falmer Press.

Banting, P. (1971) *The Design of Clapham Park School for the Partially Sighted.* London: GLC. 16–19.

Barker, P., Barrick, J. and Wilson, R. (1995) *Building Sight: A Handbook of Building and Interior Design Solutions to Include the Needs of Visually Impaired People.* London: HMSO and RNIB.

Barnhill, A. (1875) *A New Era in the Education of Blind Children or Teaching the Blind in Ordinary Schools.* Glasgow: Charles Glass.

Barraga, N. C. (1976) *Visual Handicaps and Learning: A Developmental Approach.* Belmont, California: Wadsworth.

Barraga, N. C. (1983) *Visual Handicaps and Learning.* Austin, Texas: Exceptional Resources.

Barraga, N. C. (1986) 'Sensory perceptual development'. In: G. T. Scholl (ed), *Foundations of Education for Blind and Visually Handicapped Children and Youth.* New York: American Foundation for the Blind.

Bates, E. (1976) *Language In Context.* New York: Academic Press.

Bauman, M. K. (1971) 'Foundations for vocational choice in grades 1–9', *Education for the Visually Handicapped,* **3**, 40–45.

Bee, H. (1985) *The Developing Child.* New York: Harper and Row.

Bell, I. (1985) 'Communication and language in mental handicap: 5: Don't teach – intervene', *Mental Handicap,* **13**, 17–19.

Bell, J. (1993) 'Educating the Multiply Disabled Blind Child'. In: A. Fielder, A. Best and M. C. O. Bax (eds), *The Management of Visual Impairment in Childhood.* London: Mackeith Press.

Bennett, D. and Mason, H. L. (1997) *Low Vision Aids – Effective Management of Children with a Visual Impairment*. [video notes] Birmingham: University of Birmingham.

Benton, S. (1984) 'Supporting visually impaired children in ordinary schools', *British Journal of Visual Impairment*, **2**(1), 3–7.

Berger, P. and Luckman, T. (1979) *The Social Construction of Reality*. Harmondsworth: Penguin.

Berry, N. (1992) *Fingerprints*. London: RNIB.

Best, A. (1986) 'Implications of visual impairments'. In: D. Ellis (ed.) *Sensory Impairments in Mentally Handicapped People*. London: Croom Helm.

Best A. B. (1996) 'Are special schools here to stay?' *British Journal of Visual Impairment*, **14** (2), 73–74.

Best, A. B. (1992) *Teaching Children with Visual Impairments*. Milton Keynes: Open University Press.

Best, A. B. (1994) 'Developing and sustaining appropriate provision'. In: J. Summerscale and E. Boothroyd (eds). *Deafblind Education: Developing and Sustaining Appropriate Provision: Proceedings of the UK Conference, Birmingham, 23 March*. London: SENSE.

Best, A. B. (1994) 'Ultra violet lighting', *Information Exchange.*, **41**(9).

Best, C. and Brown, N. (1994) *Introduction to Multi-Sensory Impairment*. Birmingham: Distance Education Unit 2, School of Education, University of Birmingham.

Beveridge, S. (1989) 'Parents as teachers of children with special educational needs'. In: D. Sugden (ed.), *Cognitive Approaches to Special Education*. London: Falmer Press.

Bischoff, R.W. (1979) 'Listening – a Teachable Skill', *Journal of Visual Impairment and Blindness*, **73**(2), 59–65.

Bishop, V. E. (1971) *Teaching the Visually Limited Child*. Springfield, Illinois: Charles C Thomas.

Blagden, S. and Everett, J. (1992) *What Colour is the Wind?* Corsham: National Society for Art Education (NSEAD).

Blake, K. D., Russell-Eggitt, I. M., Morgan, D. W., Ratcliffe, J. M. and Wyse, R. K. H. (1990) 'Who's in CHARGE? Multidisciplinary management of patients with CHARGE Association', *Archives of Disease in Childhood*, **65**, 217–223.

Blenkhorn, P. (1986) 'The RCEVH project on micro-computer systems and computer assisted learning', *British Journal of Visual Impairment*, **4**(3), 101–103.

Blessing, D. L., McCrimmon, J., Storall, J. and Williford, H. N. (1993) 'The effects of regular exercise programs for visually impaired and sighted school children', *Journal of Visual Impairment and Blindness*, **87**(2), 50–52.

Bloom, L. (1990) *Objects Symbols: A Communication Option*. North Rocks, Australia: The Royal New South Wales Institute for Deaf and Blind Children and North Rocks Press.

Bloom, L. and Lahey, M. (1978) *Language Development and Language Disorders*. New York: Wiley.

Board of Education (1934) *Report of the Committee on Partially Sighted Children*. London: HMSO.

Bone, M. and Meltzer, H. (1989) *OPCS Survey of Disabilities in Great Britain, Report 3: The Prevalence of Disability Among Children*. London: HMSO.

Booth, T., Swann, W., Masterton, M. and Potts, P. (1992) *Policies for Diversity in Education*. Milton Keynes: Open University Press.

Boucher, J. (1996) Editorial. *British Journal of Special Education*, **23**(3), 98–99.

Bovair, M. (1995) 'Only the top sets did French. Teaching modern languages to SEN pupils', *Special*, **4**(1), 31–32.

Bovair, M. and Bovair, K. (1992) *Modern Languages for All*. London: Kogan Page.

Bowe, F. (1987) 'Making computers accessible to disabled people', *Technology Review*, **90**(1), 52–59.

Bowers, T. (1984) *Management and the Special School*. London: Croom Helm.

Bozic, N. (1995) 'Simple switch software (and the concept of affordance)' [mimeo], *RCEVH Centre Software Newsletter*, **38**, 9–12. Birmingham: School of Education, University of Birmingham.

Bozic, N. (1997) 'Constructing the room: multi-sensory rooms in educational contexts', *European Journal of Special Needs Education*, **12**(1), 54–70.

Bozic, N. and Murdoch, H. (1996) 'Introduction'. In: N. Bozic and H. Murdoch (eds), *Learning Through Interaction*. London: David Fulton.

Bozic, N. and Sherlock, C. (1996) 'Joint activities and early functional communication'. In: N. Bozic and H. Murdoch (eds), *Learning Through Interaction*. London: David Fulton.

Bozic, N., Lambert, J. and Fletcher, N. (1996) 'Creative use of CCTVs', *Eye Contact*, **15**, 25–27.

Bradley, H. (1991) *Assessing Communication Together*. Penarth: MHNA (Mental Health Nurses Association).

Braille Mathematics Notation (1987) Braille Authority of the United Kingdom. London: RNIB.

Braille Mathematics Notation – A Simplified Version (1995) Dorton House School, Sevenoaks, Kent: RLSB (Royal London Society for the Blind).

Brennan, W. K. (1985) *Curriculum for Special Needs*. Milton Keynes: Open University Press.

Britten, P. (1984) *Master Maths 1*. Oxford: Oxford University Press.

British Association for Community Child Health (1994) *Disability in Childhood, Towards Nationally Useful Definitions* [discussion document]. London: British Paediatric Association.

British Journal of Visual Impairment (1981) *Arts Pack*. Coventry: VIEW.

Brookes, C. (1992) 'Relationships of theories and practice in art and design teaching', *Journal of Art and Design Education*, **11**, 2.

Brothers, R. (1972) 'Arithmetic computation by the blind: a look at current achievement', *Education of the Visually Impaired*, **4**(1), 1–8.

Brown, D., Simmons, V. and Methvin, J. (1986) *The Oregon Project for Visually Impaired and Blind Pre-school Children, 3rd edn*. Medford, Oregon: Jackson County Education Service Department.

Brown, M., Hart, K. and Kuchemann, D. (1985) *Chelsea Diagnostic Mathematics Tests: Teachers Guide*. Windsor: NFER-Nelson.

Brown, N. (1994) 'The developmental theory underlying the education of deafblind children'. In: J. Summerscale and E. Boothroyd (eds), *Deafblind Education: Developing and Sustaining Appropriate Provision: Proceedings of the UK Conference, Birmingham, 23 March*. London: SENSE.

Buckle, C. F. (1986) Lecture at Birmingham University, 2 (unpublished.) November 1986.

Budoff, M., Thorman, J. and Gras, A. (1984) *Microcomputers in Special Education*. Cambridge, Massachusetts: Brookline Books.

Bunning, K. (1996) *Development of an Individualised Sensory Environment for Adults with Learning Disabilities and an Evaluation of its Effects on their Interactive Behaviours*. Unpublished PhD Thesis. London: City University.

Burchard, S. N. Haszi, J. S., Gordon, L. R. and Yo, E. (1991) 'An examination of lifestyle and adjustment in three community residential experiences', *Research in Disabilities*, **12**(2), 127–144.

Burgin, V. (1986) *The End of Art Theory*. London: Macmillan.

Butterfield, N. (1991) 'Assessment of preverbal communicative abilities in students with severe intellectual disabilities', *Australia and New Zealand Journal of Developmental Disabilities,* **17**(4), 347–364.

Camaioni, L. (1992) 'Mind knowledge in infancy: the development of intentional communication', *Early Development and Parenting,* **1**, 1.

Campbell, R. (1995) *Reading in the Early Years Handbook.* Buckingham: Open University Press.

Careers Service (1995) *The Careers Service Requirement and Guidance for Providers.* London: HMSO.

Carr, W. and Kemmis, S. (1986) *Becoming Critical: Education, Knowledge and Action Research.* London: Falmer Press.

Carroll, T. J. (1961) *Blindness: What It Does and How to Live With It.* Boston: Little, Brown.

Cartier, F. (1952) 'An experimental study of the effect of human intent on listenability', *Speech Monographs,* March.

Carty, M. and Crow, B. (1991) 'Developing creativity in modern languages through music and IT', *CILT Languages and Special Educational Needs Project Bulletin,* **1**, 6–7.

CEC (1988) *Education and Vocational Guidance Services for the 14 to 25 Age Group.* Brussels: EEC Official Publications.

Centre for Information on Language Teaching and Research (1991) *Languages and Special Educational Needs Project Bulletin.* London.

Chalmers, F. G. (1996) *Celebrating Pluralism, Art Education and Cultural Diversity.* California: J. Paul Getty Trust.

Chapman, E. K. (1978) *Visually Handicapped Children and Young People.* London: Routledge and Kegan Paul.

Chapman E. K. and Stone, J. M. (1988) *The Visually Handicapped Child in Your Classroom.* London: Cassell.

Chapman, E. K., Tobin, M. J., Tooze, F. H., Moss, S. (1989) *Look and Think: A Handbook for Teachers' Visual Perception Training for Visually Impaired Children (5–11 years)* 2nd rev. edn. London: RNIB.

Child, D. (1973) *Psychology and the Teacher.* New York: Holt, Rinehart and Winston.

Chulkov, V. N. (1989) 'Principles of education of the deaf-blind in the USSR'. In: A.B. Best (ed.) *Papers on the Education of the Deaf-Blind, Volume 1: Proceedings of a European Conference, Warwick, UK, 6–11 August.* London: International Association for the Education of the Deaf-Blind.

CILT (Centre for Information on Language Teaching) (1996) *Comenius News* Issue 5, Spring.

Clamp, S. A. (1978) *The Adaptation of the NFER Junior Maths Test C.1 for Use with Low Vision Children, and Subsequent Findings.* Unpublished BPhil (ed.) dissertation. Birmingham: University of Birmingham.

Clamp, S. A. (1988) *An Investigation into the Mathematical Understanding of Number Operations, Fractions, Measurement and Algebra by Visually Handicapped Children Aged 11–15 Years.* Unpublished MEd Thesis. Birmingham: University of Birmingham.

Clare, M. (1990) *Developing Self-Advocacy Skills with People with Disabilities and Learning Difficulties.* London: FEU (Further Education Unit).

Clark, S. (1991) *Children with Profound/Complex Physical and Learning Difficulties.* Coventry: NCSE (National Council for Special Education).

Clayton, I. P. (1977) 'The work experience program at the Maryland School for the Blind', *Education for the Visually Handicapped* **9**(3), 91–94.

Clement, R. (1993) *The Art Teacher's Handbook.* London: Hutchinson.

Clement, C. and Tarr, E. (1992) *A Year in the Art of a Primary School.* Corsham: NSEAD (National Society for Education in Art and Design).

Clough, P. and Lindsay, G. (1991) *Integration and the Support Service: Changing Roles in Special Education.* Windsor: NFER-Nelson.

Clunies-Ross, L. and Franklin, A. (1997) *Where Have All the Children Gone? An Analysis of the New Statistical Data on Visual Impairment amongst Children in England, Scotland and Wales.* British Journal of Visual Impairment, **15**(2), 48–53.

Clunies-Ross, L. and Franklin, A. (1996a) *Number of Visually Impaired Children in England, Wales and Scotland.* London: RNIB.

Clunies-Ross, L. and Franklin, A. (1996b) *RNIB survey of LEAs: Educational Placements of Children who are VI and MDVI in England, Wales and Scotland.* London: RNIB.

Cockburn, C. (1987) *Two Track Training: Sex Inequalities and the Youth Training Scheme.* Basingstoke: Macmillan Education.

Cole, M. and Griffin, P. (1984) 'Current activity for the future: the zo-ped'. In: B. Rogoff and J.V. Wertsch (eds), *Children's Learning in the 'Zone of Proximal Development'.* San Francisco: Jossey-Bass.

College of Teachers of the Blind and the National Institute for the Blind (1936) *The Education of the Blind.* London: Arnold.

Collins, E. and Borgwart, S. (1996) *Deutsch? Kein Problem! German Songs for Special Educational Needs.* London: John Murray.

Collins, M., Majors, M. and Riggio, M. (1991) 'New deaf-blind population: etiological factors and implications for the future'. *Quality of Life: Proceedings of the 10th IAEDB Conference, Örebro, Sweden, 4–9 August.* London: International Association for the Education of the Deaf-Blind.

Conway, D., Green, M. and Zaluchi, M. (1982) 'Physical education, recreation and extra curricular activities with the visually impaired'. In: K.A. Hanninen (ed.), *The Horizons of Blindness.* Michigan: Blindness Publications.

Conway, J. (1989) 'Local and regional variations in support'. In: J. D. Davies and P. A. Davies, (eds), *A Teacher's Guide to Support Services.* Windsor: NFER-Nelson.

Corbett, J. and Barton, L. (1992) 'The rhetoric and reality of transition to adult life'. In: T. Booth, W. Swann, M. Masterton and P. Potts (eds), *Learning for All.* Milton Keynes: Open University Press.

Corder, P. (1966) *The Visual Element in Language Teaching.* London: Longmans.

Corn, A. and Ryser, G. (1989) 'Access to print for students with low vision', *Journal of Visual Impairment and Blindness,* **83**, 340–349.

COTIS (Confederation of Tape Information Services) (1992) *Guidance Notes.* London: COTIS.

Coupe, J. and Joliffe, J. (1988) 'An early communication curriculum: implications for practice'. In: J. Coupe and J. Goldbart (eds), *Communication Before Speech.* Kent: Croom Helm.

Coupe, J., Barton, L., Barber, M., Collins, L., Levy, D. and Murphy, A. (1985) *The Affective Communication Assessment.* Manchester: Manchester Education Committee.

Couper, H. (1996) 'Teaching visually impaired children', *Language Learning Journal,* **3**, 6–9.

Cox, M. (1992) *Children's Drawings.* Harmondsworth: Penguin.

Cratty, B. J. (1971) *Movement and Spatial Awareness in Blind Youth.* Springfield, Illinois: Charles C Thomas.

Cratty, B. J. and Sams, T. A. (1968) *The Body Image of Blind Children.* New York: American Foundation for the Blind.

Cronin, P. (1986) *Facing the Crowd.* Melbourne: Royal Victoria Institute for the Blind.

CTB/NIB (1936) *The Education of the Blind.* London: Edward Arnold.

Cunningham, B. (1993) *Child Development.* New York: Harper and Collins.

Cunningham, C. and Davis, H. (1985) *Working with Parents: Framework for Collaboration.* Milton Keynes: Open University Press.

Cutsforth, T. D. (1932) *The Blind in School and Society: A Psychological Study.* New York: American Foundation for the Blind.

Daelman, M., Nafstad, A. and Rodbroe, I. (1993) 'The deafblind person as an active participant in his own development'. *Equal and Exceptional: Proceedings of the 3rd European Conference of the International Association of Deafblind People, Potsdam, Germany, July 31–August 5.* Potsdam, Germany: IAEDB (International Association for the Education of the Deaf-Blind)/Oberlinhaus.

Daniels, H. (1996) Foreword. In: N. Bozic and H. Murdoch (eds), *Learning Through Interaction.* London: David Fulton.

Davies, J. (1989) 'Reading schemes for partially sighted beginning readers', *British Journal of Visual Impairment*, 7(1), 19–21.

Davies, J. D. and Davies, P. (1988) 'Developing credibility as a support and advisory teacher', *Support for Learning,* **3**, 1.

Davies, J. D. and Davies, P. (eds), (1989) *A Teacher's guide to Support Services.* Windsor: NFER-Nelson.

Dawkins, J. (1990) *Bright Horizons.* London: RNIB.

Day, C., Whittaker, P. and Johnston, D. (1990) *Managing Primary Schools in the 1990s.* London: Paul Chapman.

Deaf-Blind Services Liaison Group (1988) *Breaking Through: Developing Services for Deaf-Blind People.* London: SENSE (National Deaf-Blind and Rubella Association).

Deane, M. (1992) 'Teaching modern languages to pupils with special educational needs? With pleasure!', *Language Learning Journal,* **9**, 43–47.

Dearing, R. (1994) *The National Curriculum and its Assessment: Final Report.* London: SCAA (Schools Curriculum and Assessment Authority).

Dearing, R. (1996) *Review of Qualifications for 16–19 year olds.* London: SCAA.

Dench, S., Meager, N. and Morris, S. (1996) *The Recruitment and Retention of People with Disabilities.* Brighton: Institute of Employment Studies.

Department for Education (1992) *Further and Higher Education Act.* London: HMSO.

Department for Education (1993) *The Education Act 1993.* London: HMSO.

Department for Education (1994) *Code of Practice on the Identification and Assessment of Special Educational Needs.* London: Central Office of Information.

Department for Education (1994a) *The Parent's Charter.* London: HMSO.

Department for Education (1995) *English in the National Curriculum.* London: HMSO.

Department for Education (1995a) *The National Curriculum (1995).* London: HMSO.

Department for Education (1995b) *Art in the National Curriculum.* London: HMSO.

Department for Education (1995c) *Modern Foreign Languages in the National Curriculum.* London: HMSO/WO.

Department for Education (1995d) *Science in the National Curriculum.* London: HMSO.

Department for Education and Employment (1994) *Better Choices: Working Together to Improve Careers Education and Guidance – the Principles.* London: DfEE.

Department of Education and Science (1944) *Education Act.* London: HMSO.

Department of Education and Science (1970) *The Education (Handicapped Children) Act.* London: HMSO.

Department of Education and Science (1972) *Report of the Committee on the Education of the Visually Handicapped.* (The Vernon Report.) London: HMSO.

Department of Education and Science (1975) *A Language for Life (Bullock Report).* London: HMSO.

Department of Education and Science (1978) *Special Educational Needs – Report of the Committee of Enquiry into the Education of Handicapped Children and Young People.* (The Warnock Report.) London: HMSO.

Department of Education and Science (1981) *The Education Act 1981.* London: HMSO.

Department of Education and Science (1981a) Design Note 25 *Lighting and acoustic criteria for the visually handicapped and hearing impaired in schools.* London: DES/Architects and Building Branch.

Department of Education and Science (1982) *'Mathematics Counts' (Cockroft Report).* London: HMSO.

Department of Education and Science (1983) *DES Circular 1/83: Assessments and Statements of Special Educational Needs.* London: HMSO.

Department of Education and Science (1985) *The Curriculum from 5 to 16.* London: HMSO.

Department of Education and Science (1987) *Modern Foreign Languages to 16 (Curriculum Matters 8).* London: HMSO.

Department of Education and Science (1988a) *The Education Reform Act.* London: HMSO.

Department of Education and Science (1988b) *National Curriculum: Task Group on Assessment and Testing Report, a Digest for schools.* London: Department of Education and Science: Welsh Office.

Department of Education and Science (1989a) *Educational Provision for Deaf-Blind Children.* London: DES.

Department of Education and Science (1989b) *English for Ages 5 to 16.* London: HMSO.

Department of Education and Science (1989c) *The Children Act.* London: HMSO.

Department of Education and Science (1989d) *Circular 18/89 The Education (Teachers) Regulations 1989.* London: DES.

Department of Education and Science (1990) *Circular 11/90 Staffing for Pupils with Special Educational Needs.* London: DES.

Department of Education and Science (1991) *National Curriculum. Physical Education Working Group. Interim Report.* London: HMSO.

Department of Education and Science (1992) *Building Bulletin 77.* London: DES/HMSO.

Department of Education and Science (1993) *The Education (Teachers') Regulations 1993.* London: DES.

Department of Education and Science/Welsh Office (1988) *Modern Languages in the School Curriculum: A Statement of Policy.* London: HMSO/WO.

Department for Employment (1993) *Trade Union Reform and Employment Rights Act.* London: HMSO.

Department of National Heritage (1995) *Sport. Raising the Game.* London: Department of National Heritage.

Dessent, T. (1987) *Making the Ordinary School Special.* London: Falmer Press.

Detheridge, T. (1996) 'Developing information technology competencies'. In: N. Bozic and H. Murdoch (eds), *Learning Through Interaction.* London: David Fulton.

Dickie, G. (1974) *Art and the Aesthetic: An Institutional Analysis.* London: Cornell University Press.

Disability Discrimination Act (1995) *DL60 Definition of Disability.* London: HMSO.

Dobree, J. H. and Boulter, E. (1982) *Blindness and Visual Handicap: The Facts.* Oxford: Oxford University Press.

Dubowski, J. K. (1986) 'Art therapy with the visually impaired'. *Journal of Visual Impairment and Blindness,* **4**(3), 109–110.

Dunn, L., Whetton, C. and Pintilie, D. (1982) *British Picture Vocabulary Scale.* Windsor: NFER-Nelson.

Dunst, C. and Lowe, L. (1986) 'From reflex to symbol: describing, explaining and fostering communicative competence', *Augmentative and Alternative Communication*, **2**, 11–18.

Dutton, G N. (1994) 'Cognitive visual dysfunction', *British Journal of Ophthalmology*, **78**, 723–726.

Dykema, D. (1986) *They Shall Have Music: a Manual for the Instruction of Visually Handicapped Students in the Playing of Keyboard Instruments.* Carbondale, Illnois: Author.

Dyson, A. (1990) 'Effective learning consultancy: a future role for special needs co-ordinators', *Support for Learning*, **5**, 116–127.

Easen, P. (1985) *Making School-Centred INSET Work.* Milton Keynes: Open University Press.

Edman, P. (1992) *Tactile Graphics.* New York: American Foundation for the Blind.

Edwards, A. D. N. (1991) *Speech Synthesis Technology for Disabled People.* London: Chapman.

Eisner, W. E. (1972) *Educating Artistic Vision.* London: Collier Macmillan.

Elementary Education (Blind and Deaf Children) Act, 1893. London: HMSO.

Elliott, C.D., Murray, D.J. and Pearson, L.S. (1983) *British Ability Scales.* Windsor: NFER-Nelson.

Ellis, D. (ed.) (1986) *Sensory Impairments in Mentally Handicapped People.* London: Croom Helm.

Elstner, W. (1983) 'The abnormalities in the verbal communication of visually impaired children'. In: A. E. Mills (ed.) *Language Acquisition in the Blind Child Normal and Deficient* London: Croom Helm.

Engelen, J. and Besson, R. (1995) 'Accessible formats and interpersonal communication'. In: P.W.R. Roe, (ed.) *Telecommunications for All.* Brussels: ECSC-EC-EAEC.

Erin, J. N., Corn, A. L. and Wolffe, K. (1993) 'Learning and study strategies for secondary school students with visual impairments', *Journal of Visual Impairment and Blindness*, **87**, (7), 263–267.

Etheridge, D. (1995) 'Recognising and developing ability'. In: D. Etheridge, (ed.) *The Education of Dual Sensory Impaired Children.* London: David Fulton.

Etheridge, D. T. and Mason, H. L. (1994) *The Visually Impaired: Curriculum Access and Entitlement in Further Education.* London: David Fulton.

Etheridge, E. G. (1978) 'An approach to career development for visually impaired students on the elementary level', *Education of the Visually Handicapped*, **10**, 87–91.

Evans, P. (1993) 'Some implications of Vygotsky's work for special education'. In: H. Daniels (ed.) *Charting the Agenda: Educational Activity after Vygotsky.* London: Routledge.

Evans, P. and Ware, J. (1987) *Special Care Provision in the Education of Children with Profound and Multiple Learning Difficulties.* Windsor: NFER-Nelson.

Everard, B. and Morris, G. (1990) *Effective School Management.* London: Paul Chapman.

Fantl, E. W. (1964) 'The eye in cerebral palsy', *Pediatrics*, **48**, 31.

Farley, F. H. and Neperud, R. W. (eds) (1988) *The Foundations of Aesthetics, Art and Education.* New York: Praeger.

Fawkes, S. (1995a) *With a Song in My Scheme of Work. Pathfinder 25.* London: CILT (Centre for Information on Language Teaching and Research).

Fawkes, S. (1995b) 'How does it fit? Matching experiences to needs', *Studies in Modern Languages Education*, **3**, 75–91.

FEFC (Further Education Funding Committee) (1996) *Report of the Learning Difficulties and/or Disabilities Committee (The Tomlinson Report).* Coventry: HMSO.

FEU (Further Education Unit) (1992) *Supporting Transition to Adulthood.* London: FEU.

Fichtner, D. (1979) *How to Raise a Blind Child.* Bensheim: CBM (Christofel Blinden Mission).

Field, G. (1974) 'Recorded and Braille textbooks: everything the blind student needs to know', *New Outlook for the Blind*, **68**, 4.

Finkelstein, V. (1991) 'Disability: an administrative challenge?' In: M. Oliver (ed.), *Social*

Work, Disabled People and Disabling Environments. Jessica Kingsley Publishers.

Fisher, D. and Thursfield, C. (1996) 'Augmentative communication'. In: N. Bozic and H. Murdoch (eds), *Learning Through Interaction.* London: David Fulton.

Fitzsimons, S. (1988) *Spot the Dot.* London: RNIB.

Forsyth, P. (1991) *How to Negotiate Successfully.* London: Sheldon Press.

Foulke, E. and Sticht, T. G. (1969) 'The intelligibility of compressed and accelerated speech', *Psychological Bulletin,* **72**, 50–62.

Fowler, C. (1991) *A Study to Identify Multi-Sensory Impaired Children in Birmingham.* Unpublished BPhil(Ed) dissertation. Birmingham: University of Birmingham.

Fowler, M. (1989) 'Modern languages and low achievers'. In: A. Ramasut, (ed.), *Whole School Approaches to Special Needs.* London: Falmer.

Fox, A.M. (1983) 'The effects of combined vision and hearing loss on the attainment of developmental milestones'. *Proceedings of the First Canadian Conference on the Education and Development of Deaf-Blind Infants and Children.* Ontario, Canada: Ontario Ministry of Education.

Fox, R. and Looney, A. (1993) 'Teaching modern foreign languages to pupils with special educational needs – a Berkshire project', *Studies in Modern Languages Education,* **1**, 43–52.

Fraiberg, S. (1974) 'Blind infants and their mothers: an examination of the sign system'. In: M. Lewis and A. Rosenblum (eds), *The Effects of the Infant on its Caregiver.* New York: Wiley.

Fraiberg, S. (1977) *Insights from the Blind: Comparative Studies of Blind and Sighted Infants.* London: Souvenir Press.

Freeman, A. and Gray, H. (1989) *Organising Special Educational Needs: a Critical Approach.* London: Paul Chapman.

Further Education Funding Council (1996) *Inclusive Learning – Principles and Recommendations.* FEFC: London.

Gall, M., Gall, J., Jacobsen, D. and Bullock, T. (1990) *Tools for Learning',* Alexandria, Virginia: Association for Supervision and Curriculum Development.

Gardner, H. and Perkins, D.N. (Eds) (1989) *Art, Mind, and Education.* Urbana and Chicago: University of Illinois Press.

Garnett, J. (1988) 'Support teaching: taking a closer look', *British Journal of Special Education* **15**(1), 15–18.

GCSE Examination Specifications (1995–6). London: VIEW/RNIB/GCSE Joint Council Guidelines.

Gibson, J. J. (1950) *The Perception of the Visual World.* Boston: Houghton Mifflin.

Gibson, J. J. (1966) *The Senses Considered as Perceptual Systems.* Westport, Connecticut: Greenwood Press.

Gill, J. M. (1993) *Access to Graphical User Interfaces by Blind People.* London: TIDE-GUIB Consortium/RNIB.

Gill, J.M. (ed.) (1996) *Smart Card Interfaces for People with Disabilities: The Saturn Project.* London: RNIB.

Goble, J. L. (1984) *Visual Disorders in the Handicapped Child.* New York: Marcel Dekker.

Goldsmith, S. (1976) *Designing for the Disabled Great Britain.* London: RIBA.

Good, W. V. (1993) 'Ophthalmology of visual impairment'. In: A. Fielder, A. Best and M. C. O. Bax (eds), *The Management of Visual Impairment in Childhood.* London: Mackeith Press.

Gould, E. and Sonsken, P. (1991) 'A low vision aid clinic for pre-school children', *The British Journal of Visual Impairment,* **9**(2), 44–46.

Gray, C. (1988) *Organizing an Exchange Trip Abroad for Visually Handicapped Pupils.* Unpublished dissertation for the Diploma in Special Education (Visually Handicapped).

Birmingham: University of Birmingham.

Gray, C. (1997) 'Coping with the National Curriculum in Modern Foreign Languages: an equal opportunities issue', *British Journal of Visual Impairment*, **15(1)**, 10–14.

Greaney, J. Arter, C., Hill, E., Mason, H., McCall, S., Stone, J. and Tobin, M. (1994) 'The development of a new test of children's braille-reading ability', *British Journal of Visual Impairment*, **12**(2), 54–56.

Greene, J. (1987) *Memory, Thinking and Language: Topics in Cognitive Psychology*. New Essential Psychology Series. London: Methuen.

Greenfield, P. and Smith, J. (1976) *The Structure of Communication in Early Language Development*. New York: Academic Press.

Greenwood, S. (1995) 'Involving the child: some thoughts on a code of good practice for the secondary school', *Support for Learning*, **10**(4), 177–180.

Griffiths, J. and Best, A. (1996) *Survey of Visually Impaired Children in Schools for Children with Severe Learning Difficulties*. Shropshire: RNIB Condover Hall School.

Griffiths, M. (1979) 'Associated disorders in children with severe visual handicap'. In: V. Smith and J. Keen (eds), *Visual Handicap in Children*. London: William Heinemann Medical Books.

Griffiths, M. (1994) *Transition to Adulthood: the Role of Education for Young People with Severe Learning Difficulties*. London: David Fulton.

Groenveld, M. (1993) Effects of visual disability on behaviour in the family. In: A. Fielder, A. Best and M. C. O. Bax (eds), *The Management of Visual Impairment in Childhood*. London: Mackeith.

Gulliford, R. (1987) 'Education'. In: A. D. B. Clarke and A. M. Clarke (eds), *Mental Deficiency*. London: Methuen.

Hall, A. (1982) 'Teaching specific concepts to visually handicapped students'. In: S. Mangold (ed.) *A Teacher's Guide to the SEN of Blind and Visually Handicapped Children*. New York: American Foundation for the Blind.

Hanfling, O. (ed.) (1992) *Philosophical Aesthetics: An Introduction*. Oxford: Blackwell.

Hanko, G. (1995) *Special Needs in Ordinary Classrooms*. London: David Fulton.

Hanninen, K. (1975) *Teaching the Visually Handicapped*. Michigan: Blindness Publications.

Harley, R.K., Henderson, F.M. and Truan, M.B. (1979) *The teaching of Braille Reading*. Springfield: Charles C Thomas.

Harley, R.K., Truan, M.B. and Sanford, L.D. (1987) *Communication Skills for Visually Impaired Learners*. Springfield: Charles C. Thomas.

Harris, M. J. and Rosenthal, R. (1985) 'Four factors in the mediation of teacher expectancy effects'. In: R. S. Feldman (ed.), *The Social Psychology of Education: Current Research and Theory*. Cambridge: Cambridge University Press.

Hartley, E. (no date) *Art and Touch Education for Visually Handicapped People*. Leicester: Leicester University.

Hartley, J. (1990) 'Author, printer, reader, listener: four sources of confusion when listening to tabular/diagrammatic information', *British Journal of Visual Impairment*, **8**(2), 51–53.

Harwood, R. (1968) 'The teaching of science to blind students'. In: R. C. Fletcher (ed.) *The Teaching of Science and Mathematics to the Blind*. London: RNIB.

Hathaway, W. (1964) *Education and Health of the Partially Seeing Child*. New York: Columbia University Press.

Havighurst, R. J. (1964) 'Youth in exploration and man emergent'. In: H. Borrow (ed.) *Man in a World of Work*. Boston: Houghton-Mifflin.

Hawkridge, D. and Vincent, T. (1992) *Learning Difficulties and Computers: Access to the Curriculum*. London: Jessica Kingsley.

Hayes, S. P. (1941) *Contributions to a Psychology of Blindness*. New York: American Foundation for the Blind.

Haynes, M. E. (1987) *Make Every Minute Count – How to Manage Your Time Effectively*. London: Kogan Page.

Heinrich, P. (1966) 'Getting set up – using I.T. Whole-School Policy', *Interactive*, 29–30.

Heinze, T. (1986) 'Communication skills'. In: G. T. Scholl (ed.), *Foundations of Education for Blind and Visually Handicapped Children and Youth*. New York: American Foundation for the Blind.

Henderson, F. (1974) 'Communication skills'. In: B. Lowenfeld (ed.), *The Visually Handicapped Child in School,* London: Constable.

Hendrickson, H. and McLinden, M. (1996) 'Using tactile symbols: a review of current issues', *eye contact*, 14. London: RNIB.

Higham, J. A. (1993) 'Cross-curricular prospect', *Studies in Modern Languages Education,* **1**, 73–90.

Hill, E. and Blasch, B. B. (1980) 'Concept development'. In: R. Welsh, and B. Blasch (eds), (1987) *Foundations of Orientation and Mobility.* New York: American Foundation for the Blind.

Hill, E.W. (1986) 'Orientation and mobility'. In: G. T. Scholl (ed.) *Foundations of Education for Blind and Visually Handicapped Children and Youth. Theory and Practice.* New York: American Foundation for the Blind.

Hinton, R. (1992) 'Free drawings' ("I want to paint")', *British Journal of Visual Impairment* **10**(2), 63–64.

HMI (Her Majesty's Inspectorate) (1989) *A Survey of Support Services for Special Educational Needs.* London: HMSO.

HMI (1990) *Information Technology and Special Educational Needs in Schools, A Review.* London: Department of Education and Science.

HMI (1991) *Interdisciplinary Support for Young Children.* London: HMSO.

HMI (1996) *Promoting High Achievement – for Pupils with Special Educational Needs in Mainstream Schools.* London: Department for Education and Employment.

Hodson, D. (1990) 'A critical look at practical work in school science', *School Science Review* **70**(256), 33–40.

Hodson, D. (1992) 'Redefining and reorienting practical work in school science', *School Science Review,* **73**(264), 65–78.

Hogg, J. (1991) 'Developments in further education for adults with profound intellectual and multiple disabilities'. In: J. Watson (ed.), *Innovatory Practice and Severe Learning Difficulties.* Edinburgh: Moray House.

Hogg, J. and Sebba, J. (1986a) *Profound Retardation and Multiple Impairment. Vol. 1: Development and Learning.* London: Croom Helm

Hogg, J. and Sebba, J. (1986b) *Profound Retardation and Multiple Impairment. Vol. 2: Education and Therapy.* London: Croom Helm.

Holmes, B. (1991) *Communication Revisited.* Pathfinder 6. CILT (Centre for Information on Language Teaching).

Home Office, Department of Health, Department of Education and Science, Welsh Office (1992) *Working Together Under the Children Act 1989.* London: HMSO.

Hopkinson, R.G. (1973) 'Lighting in schools for the visually handicapped', *Light, Lighting and Environmental Design.*

Hornby, G. (1994) *Counselling in Child Disability: Skills for Working with Parents.* London: Chapman and Hall.

Howard, I. and Templeton, W. (1966) 'Human spatial orientation'. In: R. Welsh, and B.

Blasch (eds) (1987) *Foundations of Orientation and Mobility*. New York: American Foundation for the Blind.

Huebner, K. M. (1986) 'Social skills'. In: G. T. Scholl (ed.) *Foundations of Education for Blind and Visually Handicapped Children and Youth. Theory and Practice*. New York: American Foundation for the Blind.

Hull, J. M. (1990) *Touching the Rock: An Experience of Blindness*. London: SPCK

Hull, T. and Mason, H. L. (1993) 'The speed of information processing test for the blind in a tactile version', *British Journal of Visual Impairment*, **11**(1), 21–23.

Hulsegge, J. and Verheul, A. (1986) *Snoezelen: Another World*. UK: ROMPA.

Hurt, J. S. (1988) *Outside the Mainstream*. London: Batsford.

Hutchinson, D. (1982) *Work Preparation for the Handicapped*. London: Croom Helm.

Hutchinson, R. and Kewin, J. (eds) (1994) *Sensations and Disabilities: Sensory environments for leisure, snoezelen, education and therapy*. UK: ROMPA.

Hutchison, T. (1995) 'The classification of disability', *Archives of Disease in Childhood*, **73**, 91–93.

Hyvärinen, L. (1995a) 'Considerations in evaluation and treatment of the child with low vision', *American Journal of Occupational Therapy*, **29**(9), 891–897.

Hyvärinen, L. (1995b) *Vision Testing Manual*. Villa Park, Illinois: Precision Vision.

Hyvärinen, L. (1995–96) *Observation and Tests for Assessment of Functional Vision in Children at an Early Developmental Level. Text to accompany Vision Testing Manual*. Villa Park, Illinois: Precision Vision.

Hyvärinen, L. and Lindstedt, E. (1981) *Assessment of Vision in Children*. Stockholm: the authors.

ICEVH (International Council for the Education of the Visually Handicapped) (1992) The Multi-Handicapped Working Group.

Illingworth, R. S. (1972) *The Development of the Infant and Young Child: Normal and Abnormal*. Edinburgh: Churchill Livingstone.

Jan, E. J., Freeman, R. D. and Scott, E. P. (1977) *Visual Impairment in Children and Adolescents*. New York: Grune and Stratton.

Jan, J. (1993) 'Neurological causes of visual impairment and investigations'. In: A. Fielder, A. Best, and M. C. O. Bax (eds), *The Management of Visual Impairment in Childhood*. London: Mackeith.

Jay, P. (1980) *Fundamentals, Light for Low Vision*. London: Chartered Institute of Building Services and the Partially Sighted Society.

Jordan, R and Powell, S. (1995) 'Skills without understanding: a critique of a competency-based model of teacher education in relation to special needs', *British Journal of Special Education*, **22**(3), 120–124.

Jose, R. T. (1983) *Understanding Low Vision*. New York: American Foundation for the Blind.

Keeffe, J. (1995) *Assessment of Low Vision in Developing Countries – Assessment of Functional Vision*. Geneva: World Health Organization (WHO).

Keeling, G. (1995) 'Making it real', *Interactive*, 27–29.

Kekelis, L. and Anderson, E. (1984) 'Family communication styles and language development', *Journal of Visual Impairment and Blindness*, **78**, 54–65.

Kelleher, A. and Mulcahy, M. (1986) 'Patterns of disability in the mentally handicapped'. In: J. Berg and J. De Jong (eds), *Science and Service in Mental Retardation*. London: Methuen.

Kelly, M. (1991) 'The role of learning support: a trefoil catalyst?', *Support for Learning*, **6**(4), 171–2.

Kendrick, D. (1993) *Jobs to be Proud of: Profiles of Workers who are Blind or Visually Impaired*. New York: American National Federation of the Blind.

Kenning, M. (1993) 'Diversification of MFL provision', *Studies in Modern Languages Education,* **1**, 1–17.

Kenning, M. (1994) 'Foreign languages and special needs: implications for teacher support', *British Journal of Special Education,* **21**(4), 152–155.

Kersner, M. and Wright, J. (1996) 'Collaboration between teachers and speech and language therapists working with children with severe learning disabilities (SLD): implications for professional development', *British Journal of Learning Disabilities,* **24**, 33–37.

Kiernan, C. and Reid, B. (1987) *The Pre-Verbal Communication Schedule (PVCS) Manual.* Windsor: NFER-Nelson.

Kiernan, C., Reid, B. D. and Jones, J. M. (1982) 'Signs and symptoms – a review of Literature and Survey of Visual Non-verbal Communication Systems', *Studies with Education,* **11**, 106. London: University of London, Institute of Education.

King's Fund Centre (1986) *An Ordinary Life.* London: King's Fund Centre.

Klein, M. (1976) 'Mourning and its relationship to manic depressive states'. In L. Pincus (ed.), *Death and the Family.* London: Faber.

Kluckhohn, C. Murray, H. A. and Schneider, D.M. (1953) 'Personality in nature, society and culture'. In: V. Shackleton and C. Fletcher (eds) (1984), *Individual Differences, Theories and Applications.* London: Methuen.

Koestler, K. (1976) *The Unseen Minority: A Social History of Blindness in the United States.* New York: David McKay.

Kolk, C. J. V. (1977) 'Intelligence testing for visually impaired persons', *Journal of Visual Impairment and Blindness,* **71**, 158–63.

Krischer, C., Meissen, R. and Ing, D. R. (1983) 'Simulated reading speed under real and simulated visual impairments', *Journal of Visual Impairment and Blindness,* **77**, 386–388.

Lacey, P. (1991) 'Managing the classroom environment'. In: C. Tilstone (ed.) *Teaching Pupils with Severe Learning Difficulties.* London: David Fulton.

Lacey, P. and Lomas, J. (1993) *Support Services and the Curriculum.* London: David Fulton.

Langdon, J. N. (1970) 'Parents talking', *The New Beacon,* **54**, 643.

Lawrence, D. (1988) *Enhancing Self-Esteem in the Classroom.* London: Paul Chapman.

Lawrence, M. (1973) 'The self-reliance institute: filling the gap in work experience', *New Outlook for the Blind,* **67**, 221–225.

Lee, B. (1991) *Extending Opportunities: Modern Foreign Languages for Pupils with Special Educational Needs.* Windsor: NFER (National Foundation for Education Research).

Lee, M. and McWilliam, L. (1995) *Movement, Gesture and Sign.* London: RNIB.

Leont'ev, A. N. (1981) *Problems of the Development of Mind.* Moscow: Progress Publishers.

Levi, A. W. and Smith, R. A. (1991) *Art Education: A Critical Necessity.* Urbana and Chicago: University of Illinois Press.

Lewis, M. (1970) 'Must visually handicapped students be low achievers in maths?', *Education of the Visually Handicapped,* **2**(2), 60–61.

Lewis, V. (1987) *Development and Handicap.* Oxford: Blackwell.

Light, J. (1989) 'Toward a definition of communicative competence for individuals using AAC systems', *Augmentive and Alternative Communication,* **5**, 137–144.

Lindqvist, B. and Trowald, N. (1971) *Report 4.* Teachers' College, Uppsala, Sweden.

Lindstedt, E. (1986) *How Well Does a Child See? A Guide for Parents, Attendants, Teachers.* Stockholm: Elisyn.

Lloyd, L. and Blischak, D. (1992) 'AAC terminology policy and issues update', *Augmentative and Alternative Communication,* **8**(2), 104–109.

Lock, R. (1988) 'A history of practical work in school science and its assessment, 1860–1986', *School Science Review,* 70, 250.

Lombana, J. H. (1980) 'Career planning with visually handicapped students', *Vocational Guidance Quarterly*, **28**, 219–224.

Longhorn, F. (1988) *A Sensory Curriculum for Very Special Children*. London: Souvenir Press.

Lorimer, J. (1962) *The Lorimer Braille Recognition Test*. Bristol: College of Teachers of the Blind. (Now available from VIEW, formerly the Association for the Education and Welfare of the Visually Handicapped, c/o Exhall Grange School, Coventry, Warwicks.

Lorimer, J. (1977) *Outlines of a Short Course to Improve the Braille Reading Efficiency of Children in Lower Senior Classes*. Birmingham: Research Centre for the Education of the Visually Handicapped, University of Birmingham.

Lorimer, J. (1988) *Braille in Easy Steps*. London: RNIB.

Lorimer, J. (1990) *Braille Teaching and Learning – A Unit of the Distance Education Course for Teachers of the Visually Impaired*. Birmingham: School of Education, University of Birmingham.

Loughran, F., Parker, P. and Gordon, D. (1995) *Children with Disabilities Living at Home: A Further Analyis and Interpretation of the Office of Population, Census and Surveys Investigation. Report to the Department of Health*. Department of Policy Studies, Woodland Road, Bristol BS8 1TN.

Lowenfeld, B. (1948) 'Effects of blindness on the cognitive functions of children', *Nervous Child*, **7**, 45–54.

Lowenfeld, B. (1974) *The Visually Handicapped Child in School*. London: Constable.

Lowenfeld, B. (1981) *Blindness and Blind People*. New York: American Foundation for the Blind.

Magee, B. and Milligan, M. (1995) *On Blindness*. Oxford: University Press.

Mangold, S. (1982) 'Art experience is fundamental to creative thinking'. In: S. Mangold (ed.) *A Teacher's Guide to the Special Educational Needs of Blind and Visually Handicapped Children*. New York: American Foundation for the Blind.

Marcuse, H. (1978) *The Aesthetic Dimension*. London: Macmillan.

Martin, J., Meltzer, H. and Elliot, D. (1988) *OPCS Surveys of Disability in Great Britain, Report 1: The Prevalence of Disability Among Adults*. London: HMSO.

Mason, H. L. (1994) 'OFSTED inspections and their challenge', *British Journal of Visual Impairment*, **12**(3), 90–92.

Mason, H. L. (1995) *Spotlight on SEN: Visual Impairment*. Tamworth: NASEN (National Association for Special Educational Needs).

Mason, H. L. and Gale, G. (1997) 'Advisory services for the visually impaired in the Northern Territory of Australia – a unique experience', *British Journal of Visual Impairment*, **15**(2), 55–58.

Mates, B.T. (1990) 'CD-ROM: A new light for the blind and visually impaired', *Computers in Libraries*, 19(3), 17–20.

Mathieson, K. (1993) *Children's Art and the Computer*. London: Hodder and Stoughton.

McCall, S. (1990) *Mobility and Orientation and Self Help Skills. Unit 16 Distance Education Course (VI)*. Birmingham: School of Education, University of Birmingham.

McCall, S. (1994) Communication – options and issues. In: D. Etheridge and H. L. Mason (eds), *The Visually Impaired: Curricular Access and Entitlement in Further Education*. London: David Fulton.

McCall, S. and Stone, J. (1992) 'Literacy for blind children through Moon: a possibility?', *British Journal of Visual Impairment*, **10**(2), 53–54.

McCall, S., and McLinden, M. (1996) 'Literacy: a foot in the door', *eye contact*, **16**, Autumn (Supplement).

McCall, S., McLinden, M. and Stone, J. (1996) *Moon Cats Reading Scheme*. London: RNIB.

McGinty, J. and Fish, J. (1992) *Learning Support for Young People in Transition: Leaving School for FE and Work*. Milton Keynes: Open University Press.

McGrath, M. (1991) *Multi-disciplinary teamwork*. Wales: Gower Publishing.

McGurk, H. (1983) 'Effectance motivation and the development of communication-competence in blind and sighted children'. In: A. Mills (ed.), *Language Acquisition in the Blind Child: Normal and Deficient*. London: Croom Helm.

McInnes, J. and Treffry, J. (1982) *Deaf-Blind Infants and Children*. Toronto: University of Toronto Press.

McKendrick, O. (1991) *Assessment of Multi-Handicapped Visually Impaired Children*. London: RNIB.

McLaughlin, C. (1989) 'Working face to face: aspects of interpersonal work', *Support for Learning* **4**(2), 96–101.

Meltzer, H., Smyth, M. and Robus, N. (1989) *OPCS Surveys of Disability in Great Britain, Report 6: Disabled Children: Services, Transport and Education*. London: HMSO.

Mescheryakov, A. (1979) *Awakening To life: Forming Behaviour and the Mind in Deaf-Blind Children*. Moscow: Progress Publishers.

Millar, S. and Wilson, A. (eds) (1994) *Augmentative Communication in Practice: An Introduction*. CALL (Communication Aids for Language and Learning) Centre. Edinburgh: University of Edinburgh.

Mills, A. (ed.) (1983) *Language Acquisition in the Blind Child: Normal and Deficient*. Kent: Croom Helm.

Mittler, P. (1979) *Parents as Partners in the Education of their Handicapped Children*. Paris: UNESCO.

Morley, S. (1995) *Window Concepts: An Introductory Guide for Visually Disabled Users*. London: RNIB.

Muldoon, J. and Pickwell, D. (1993) 'Optometric needs of multiply handicapped children'. In: T. Buckingham (ed.), *Visual Problems in Childhood*. Oxford: Butterworth-Heinemann.

Mulford, R. (1983) 'Referential development in blind children'. In: A. Mills (ed.), *Language Acquisition in the Blind Child: Normal and Deficient*. London: Croom Helm.

Murdoch, H. (1994) 'The development of infants who are deaf-blind: a case study', *Journal of Visual Impairment and Blindness*, **88**(4), 357–367.

Myers, S. O. (1975) *Where Are They Now?* London: Royal National Institute for the Blind.

Myrberg, M. (1978) 'Towards an ergonomic theory of text design and composition', Uppsala Studies in Education 5, *Acta Universitatis Upsaliensis*. Upppsala: Uppsala University.

NACETT (1996) *Skills for 2000: Report on Progress Towards the National Targets for Education and Training*. London: National Advisory Council for Education and Training Targets.

Nafstad, A. (1989) *Space of Interaction: An Attempt to Understand how Congenital Deaf-Blindness Affects Psychological Development*. Dronninglund, Denmark: Nordic Staff Training Centre for Deaf-Blind Services.

National Association for the Education of the Partially Sighted (1992) *Partially Sighted Children* (1972): *A Summary of Their Needs and Existing Provisions*. Doncaster: National Association for the Education of the Partially Sighted.

National Council for Educational Technology (1990) *Careers Software Review*. Coventry: NCCET.

National Council for Educational Technology (1996) *Using Information Technology in Careers Education and Guidance: Getting Started*. Coventry: NCET.

National Curriculum Council (1990)) *Careers Education and Guidance*. York: NCC.

National Curriculum Council (1993) *Modern Foreign Languages and Special Educational Needs: A New Commitment*. York: NCC.

Neil, P. S. (1996) 'German in the classroom: what the pupils think', *Language Learning Journal,* **3**, 10–15.

Newman, D., Griffin, P. and Cole, M. (1989) *The Construction Zone: Working for Cognitive Change in School.* Cambridge: Cambridge University Press.

Nielsen, L. (1990) *Are you Blind?* Copenhagen: Sikon.

Nielsen, L. (1992) *Educational Approaches.* Copenhagen: Sikon.

Nikolić, T. (1986) 'Teaching a foreign language to visually impaired children in school', *Language Teaching,* 218–231.

Nind, M. and Hewitt, D. (1994) *Access to Communication: Developing the Basics of Communication with People with Severe Learning Difficulties through Intensive Interaction.* London: David Fulton.

Nisbet, P. (1996) 'The experience of mobility'. In: N. Bozic and H. Murdoch (eds), *Learning Through Interaction.* London: David Fulton.

Nisbet, P. and Kerr, J. (1996) *Testing with Special Technology.* Edinburgh: CALL Centre, University of Edinburgh.

Nixon, H. L. (1991) *Mainstreaming the American Dream: Sociological Perspectives on Parental Coping with Blind and Visually Impaired Children.* New York: American Foundation for the Blind.

Nolan, C. Y. (1964) 'Research in teaching mathematics to blind children', *International Journal for the Education of the Blind,* **13**(4), 97–100.

Nolan, C.Y. and Kederis, C. (1969) *Perceptual Factors in Braille Word Recognition.* New York: American Foundation for the Blind.

Norris, M., Spaulding, P. J. and Brodie, F. H. (1957) *Blindness in Children.* Chicago, Illinois: University of Chicago Press.

Norris, N. (1972) *Aims and Methods in the Teaching of English to the Visually Handicapped.* Birmingham: Research Centre for the Education of the Visually Handicapped, and the Oracy Research Unit, School of Education, University of Birmingham.

North West Support Services for the Visually Impaired (1994) *Guidelines for Maintaining the Educational Entitlement of Pupils who are Visually Impaired.* Manchester: Shawgrove School.

Ockelford, A. (1994a) *Music in Large Print.* London: RNIB.

Ockelford, A. (1994b) *Objects of Reference: Promoting Communication Skills and Concept Development for Visually Impaired Children who have other Disabilities.* London: RNIB.

Ockelford, A. (1996a) *Music Matters.* London: RNIB.

Ockelford, A. (1996b) *Points of Contact: a Braille Approach to Alphabetic Music Notation.* London: Braille Authority of the United Kingdom.

Ockelford, A. (1996c) *All Join In.* London: RNIB.

Odor, J. P., Sutherland, E. and Johnstone, A. (1988) *CALL Resource: Microtechnology for Disabled Learners.* Edinburgh: CALL Centre, University of Edinburgh.

Office for Economic Cooperation and Development/Centre for Education and Research Innovation (1986) *Young People with Handicaps: the Road to Adulthood.* Paris: OECD/CERI.

Office for Economic Cooperation and Development/Centre for Education and Research Innovation (1988) *Disabled Youth: the Right to Adult Status.* Paris: OECD/CERI

Office for Economic Cooperation and Development/Centre for Education and Research Innovation (1991) *Disabled Youth: From School to Work.* OECD/CERI: Paris.

Office of Population, Censuses and Surveys (1989) See Bone and Metzler (1989) London: HMSO.

OFSTED (Office for Standards In Education) (1993) *Framework for the Inspection of Schools.* London: OFSTED.

OFSTED (1995) *Guidance on the Inspection of Special Schools*. London: HMSO.

Olson, M. R. (1981) *Guidelines and Games for Teaching Efficient Braille Reading*. New York: American Foundation for the Blind.

Orelove, F. P. and Sobsy, D. (1991) *Educating Children with Multiple Disabilities: A Transdisciplinary Approach*. Baltimore: Paul H. Brookes.

Osborn, H. (1978) 'Aesthetic perception', *British Journal of Aesthetics*, **18**(4).

Page, G. (1995) *MIDI: Music Technology Access for Visually Impaired People*. eicester: Ulverscroft.

Park, K. (1995) 'Using objects of reference: a review of the literature', *European Journal of Special Needs Education,* **10**(1), 40–46.

Parkin, A. and Aldrich, F.K. (1989) 'Improving learning from audiotapes: a technique that works!' *British Journal of Visual Impairment* 7(2), 58–60.

Parsons, M. J. (1987) *How We Understand Art*. New York: Cambridge University Press.

Parsons, M. J. and Blocker, H. G. (1993) *Aesthetics and Education*. Urbana and Chicago: University Illinois Press.

Peters, M. L. (1967) *Spelling Caught or Taught?* London: Routledge and Kegan Paul.

Phillips, D. (ed.) (1989) *Which Language? Diversification and the National Curriculum*. Sevenoaks: Hodder and Stoughton.

Phillips, D. and Filmer-Sankey, C. (1993) *Diversification in Modern Language Teaching; Choice and the National Curriculum*. London: Routledge.

Porter, G. and Kirkland, J. (1995) *Integrating Augmentative and Alternative Communication into Group Programmes – Utilizing the Principles of Conductive Education*. Australia: Spastics Society of Victoria.

Postlethwaite, K. and Hackney, A. (1988) *Organising the School's Response*. Basingstoke: Macmillan Education.

Prentice, R. (ed.) (1995) *Teaching Art and Design: Addressing Issues and Identifying Problems*. London: Cassell.

Price, V. (1993) 'The teaching of modern languages to visually impaired children', *British Journal of Visual Impairment*, **11**(3), 119–120.

Price, V. (1994a) 'Languages for the visually impaired'. In: P. McLagan (ed.), *Steps to Learning. CILT 7*, 52–54.

Price, V. (1994b) 'Modern Language Dictionaries', *Visability*, Spring, **10**, 23.

Priestley, L. (1995) *The Education of the South Asian Child with a Visual Impairment: from the View of the Parents*. Unpublished BPhil (Ed) dissertation. Birmingham: University of Birmingham.

Ramasut, A. (1989) *Whole School Approaches to Special Needs*. London: Falmer Press.

Report of the Royal Commission on the Blind, Deaf and Dumb of the United Kingdom (1889) London: HMSO.

Rex, E. J., Koenig A. J. Wormsley, D. P., Baker, R. L. (1994) *Foundations of Braille Literacy*. New York: American Foundation for the Blind.

Reynell, J. (1978) 'Developmental patterns of visually handicapped children', *Child Care, Health and Development,* **4**, 291–303.

Reynell, J. (1979) *Manual for the Reynell–Zinkin Scales for Young Visually Handicapped Children*. Windsor: NFER-Nelson.

Richmond, R. and Smith, C. (1990) 'Support for special needs: the class teacher's perspective', *Oxford Review of Education* 16(3), 295–310.

Ritchie J. M. (1930) *Concerning the Blind*. London: Oliver and Boyd.

RNIB *Guidelines for Teachers and Parents*. London: RNIB.

RNIB (1987) *Out of Isolation: A Plan for Growth of Services to Multi-Handicapped Visually Impaired People*. London: RNIB.

RNIB (1990) *New Directions – Towards a Better Future for Multihandicapped Visually Impaired Children and Young People.* London: RNIB.

RNIB (1992) *Blind and Partially Sighted Children in Britain: The RNIB Survey.* London: HMSO.

RNIB (1993) *Looking into PE: Guidelines for Teaching PE to Children with a Visual Impairment.* London: Sports Council and the RNIB.

RNIB (1995a) *Research Survey on Visually Impaired Pupils in the United Kingdom: Preliminary Analysis.* London: RNIB.

RNIB (1995b) *Play it My Way: Learning Through Play with your Visually Impaired Child.* London: HMSO.

Robb, L. and Geoghegan, L. (1995) *Ten Songs for Young French Learners.* London: Language Centre Publications.

Rogers, C. (1989) 'Early admission: early labelling'. In: M. Woodhead, P. Light and R. Carr (eds) *Growing up in a Changing Society.* London: Routledge.

Rogers, S. and Puchalski, C. (1984) 'Social characteristics of visually impaired infants' play', *Topics in Early Childhood Special Education,* **3,** 52–56.

Rogow, S. M. (1972) 'Language acquisition and the blind retarded child: a study of impaired communication', *Education of the Visually Handicapped,* **4**(2), 36–40.

Rogow, S. M. (1988) *Helping the Visually Impaired Child with Developmental Problems.* New York: Teachers College Press.

Rosenthal, R. (1985) 'From unconscious experimenter bias to teacher expectancy effects'. In: J. Dusek (ed.) *Teacher Expectancies.* London: Erlbaum.

Rowland, C. (1983) 'Patterns of interaction between three blind infants and their mothers'. In: A. Mills, (ed.) *Language Acquisition in the Blind Child: Normal and Deficient.* Kent: Croom Helm.

Rowntree, D. (1989) *The Manager's Book of Checklists – A Practical Guide to Improving Managerial Skills.* Aldershot: Gower.

Salt, A.T., Sonksen, P.M., Wade, A. and Rayatunga, R. (1995) 'The maturation of linear acuity and compliance with the Sonksen-Silver Acuity System in young children', *Developmental Medicine and Child Neurology.* **3,** 505–514.

Salt, J. P. (1986) 'The development of listening skills in visually handicapped children', *New Beacon* 70(825), 1–3.

Santin, S. and Nesker Simmons, J. (1977) 'Problems in the construction of reality in congenitally blind children', *Journal of Visual Impairment and Blindness,* **71**(10), 425–429.

SCAA (Schools Curriculum and Assessment Authority) (1994) *The Review of the National Curriculum – a Report on the 1994 Consultation.* London: SCAA Publications.

SCAA (1995a) *Consistency in Teacher Assessment Key Stages 1–3.* London: SCAA Publications.

SCAA (1995b) *Looking Forward: Careers Education and Guidance with the National Curriculum.* London: SCAA Publications.

SCAA (1996) *Planning the Curriculum for Pupils with Profound and Multiple Learning Difficulties.* London: SCAA Publications.

SCAA (1997a) *Key Stage 1 and 2 Assessment Arrangements.* London: SCAA Publications.

SCAA (1997b) *Key Stage 1 and 2 Mathematics Tasks.* London: SCAA Publications.

SCAA (1997c) *Key Stage 3 Assessment Arrangements.* London: SCAA Publications.

SCAA (1997d) *Key Stage 3 Mathematics Tasks.* London: SCAA Publications.

Scholl, G. T. (ed.) (1986) *Foundations of Education for Blind and Visually Handicapped Children and Youth. Theory and Practice.* New York: American Foundation for the Blind.

Scott, E. P. (1982a) *The Visually Impaired Student.* Baltimore: University Park Press.

Scott, E. P. (1982b) *Your Visually Impaired Child.* Baltimore: University Press.

SCPR (1996) *Student Voices: the Views of Further Education Students with Learning Difficulties and/or Disabilities: Findings from a Series of Student Workshops.* Commissioned by the Learning Difficulties and/or Disabilities Committee. London: SKILL (National Bureau for Students with Disabilities).

SENTC (Special Educational Needs Training Consortium) (1996) *Professional Development to Meet Special Needs: Report to the Department for Education and Employment.* Stafford: Staffordshire County Council.

Sheppard, A. (1987) *Aesthetics: An Introduction to the Philosophy of Art.* Oxford: Oxford University Press.

Siegel-Causey, E. and Downing, J. (1987) 'Nonsymbolic communication development: theoretical concepts and educational strategies'. In: L. Goetz, D. Guess and K. Stremel-Campbell (eds), *Innovative Program Design for Individuals with Dual Sensory Impairments.* Baltimore: Paul H. Brookes.

Siegel-Causey, E. and Guess, D. (1989) *Enhancing Nonsymbolic Interactions among Learners with Severe Disabilities.* Baltimore: Paul H. Brookes.

Simon, G. B. (1986) *The Next Step on the Ladder: Assessment and Management of Children with Multiple Handicaps,* 5th edn. Kidderminster: British Institute of Mental Handicap.

SKILL (1993) *Setting up Parent Support Groups in Further Education Colleges.* London: SKILL (National Bureau for Students with Disabilities).

Smith, B., Povall, M. and Floyd, M. (1991) *Managing Diabetes at Work.* London: Jessica Kingsley.

Smith, R. A. (1968) 'Aesthetic criticism: the method of aesthetic education'. In: G. Pappas (ed.) (1970) *Concepts in Art and Education.* London: Macmillan.

Smyth, M. and Robus, N. (1989) *OPCS Surveys of Disability in Great Britain, Report 5: The Financial Circumstances of Families with Disabled Children Living in Private Households.* London: HMSO.

Solity, J. and Bull, S. (1987) *Special Needs: Bridging the Curriculum Gap.* Milton Keynes: Open University Press.

Solity, J. and Raybould, E. (1988) *A Teacher's Guide to Special Needs: A Positive Response to the 1981 Education Act.* Milton Keynes: Open University Press.

Sommers, V. S. (1944) *The Influence of Parental Attitudes and Social Environment on the Personality Development of the Adolescent Blind.* New York: American Foundation for the Blind.

Sowers, J. and Powers, L. (1991) *Vocational Preparation and Employment of Students with Physical and Mental Disabilities.* Baltimore: Paul Brookes.

Spain, J. B. (1981) 'Employment of handicapped people : an enigmatic future', *Journal of Visual Impairment and Blindness,* **75**, 122–125.

Spencer, S. and Ross, M. (1989) 'Assessing functional vision using micro-computers', *British Journal of Special Education,* **16**(2), 68–70.

Sperber, D. and Wilson, D. (1986) *Relevance.* London: Blackwell Scientific.

Spragg, J. (1984) 'Interfacing a Perkins brailler to a BBC micro', *Microprocessors and Microsystems,* **8**(10), 524–527.

Spungin, S. J. and Taylor, J. L. (1986) 'The Teacher'. In: G. T. Scholl (ed.) *Foundations of Education for Blind and Visually Handicapped Children and Youth.* New York: American Foundation for the Blind

Steel, F. (1991) 'Working collaboratively within a multi-disciplinary framework'. In: C. Tilstone (ed.) *Teaching Pupils with Severe Learning Difficulties – Practical Approaches.* London: David Fulton.

Stephenson, S. (1968) 'The teaching of science at Worcester College for the Blind'. In: R. C.

Fletcher (ed.) *The Teaching of Science and Mathematics to the Blind.* London: RNIB.

Stern, D. N. (1985) *The Interpersonal World of the Infant.* USA: Basic Books.

Stillman, R. (ed.) (1978) *The Callier Azusa Scale.* Texas: Callier Center for Communication Disorders.

Stocker, C. S. (1970) *Methods for Improvement of Listening Efficiency in Individuals with a Visual Impairment.* Project 83-RO 25.6.Kansas: Kansas State Department of Social Welfare, Division of Services for the Blind and Physically Handicapped.

Stockley, J. (1994) 'Teaching social skills to visually impaired students', *British Journal of Visual Impairment,* **12**(1), 11–14.

Stockley, J. and Richardson, P. (1991) *Profile of Adaptive Skills. A Rating Scale for Assessing Progressive Personal and Social Development in Young People with Visual Impairment in Association with Moderate to Severe Learning Difficulties.* London: RNIB.

Stone, C. A. and Wertsch, J. V. (1984) 'A social interactional analysis of learning disabilities remediation', *Journal of Learning Disabilities,* **17**(4), 194–9.

Stone, J. (1990) 'Educational advisory services – a national provision', *British Journal of Visual Impairment,* **8**(3), 92–94.

Stone, J. (1995a) 'Has Braille had its day?', *British Journal of Visual Impairment,* **13**(4), 80–81.

Stone, J. (1995b) *Mobility for Special Needs.* London: Cassell.

Sullivan, D. (1993) 'OCR's – Reading technology comes of age', *New Beacon,* **908**, 145–150.

Tamir, P. (1991) 'Practical work in school science: an analysis of current practice'. In: B. Woolnough (ed.) *Practical Science.* Milton Keynes: Open University Press.

Taylor, J. (1989) *As I See It.* London: Grafton Books.

Taylor, R. (1986) *Educating for Art: Critical Response and Development.* Harlow: Longman.

Thomas, G. (1992) *Effective Classroom Teamwork: Support or Intrusion?* London: Routledge.

Thomas, G. and Nichols, R. (1991) 'Foreign languages for all', *British Journal of Special Education,* **18**(1), 9–12.

Thomas, G. V. and Silk, A. M. J. (1990) *An Introduction to the Psychology of Children's Drawings.* London: Harvester Wheatsheaf.

Tillman, M. H. (1967) 'The performance of blind and sighted children on the Wechsler Intelligence Scale for Children: Study II', *International Journal for the Education of the Blind,* **16**, 65–74.

Tillman, M. H. (1973) 'Intelligence scales for the blind: a review with implications for research', *Journal of School Psychology,* II, 80–87.

Tobin, M. J. (1979) *A Longitudinal Study of Blind and Partially Sighted Children in Special Schools in England and Wales.* Birmingham: Research Centre for the Visually Handicapped, University of Birmingham.

Tobin, M. J. and Hill, E. (1984) 'A Moon-writer', *New Beacon,* **68**(807), 173–176.

Tobin, M. J., Tooze, F. H. G., Chapman, E. K. and Moss, S. (1979) *Look and Think: A Handbook on Visual Perceptual Training for Severely Visually Handicapped Children.* London: RNIB.

Tobin, M.J. (1990) 'Integrating visually impaired pupils: issues and needs. In P. Evans and V. Varma (eds), *Special Education: Past, Present and Future.* London: Falmer Press.

Tobin, M. J. (1992) *The Language of Blind Children: Communication, Words, and Meanings.* Birmingham: Research Centre for the Education of the Visually Handicapped, The University of Birmingham.

Tobin, M. J. (1994) *Assessing Visually Handicapped People: An Introduction to Test Procedures.* London: David Fulton.

Tooze, D. (1981) *Independence Training for Children and Young People.* London: Croom Helm.

Tooze, F. H. G. (1962) *The Tooze Braille Speed Test.* Bristol: College of Teachers of the Blind. (Now available from VIEW, formerly the Association for the Education and Welfare of the Visually Handicapped.)

Toriyama, Y. (1985) *A Teacher's Guide to Experiments and Observations for the Visually Handicapped (Chemistry).* Tokyo: Unpublished Dissertation. National School for the Blind, University of Tsukaba.

Trafford, J. (ed.) (1994) *Primary Foreign Languages – A Fresh Impetus.* London: Association for Language Learning.

Travis, P. (1993) 'Employment officer for visually impaired students ... in a recession?', *The New Beacon,* **77,** 49–52.

Trevarthen, C. (1974) 'Conversation with a two month old', *New Scientist* **62**, 230.

Trowald, N. (1978) *Presentation of Research Work from Uppsala.* In Proceedings of the International Conference on the Education of the Visually Handicapped. Paris: 134–139. ICEVH.

Urwin, C. (1983) 'Dialogue and cognitive functioning in the early language development of three blind children'. In: A. Mills (ed.) *Language Acquisition in the Blind Child: Normal and Deficient.* London: Croom Helm.

Van Dijk, J. (1991) *Persons Handicapped by Rubella: Victors and Victims – A Follow-Up Study.* Amsterdam: Swets and Zeitlinger.

Vaughan Huxley, M. (1993) 'The FEFC for England – ensuring quality'. In: Hewitson-Ratcliffe (ed.), *Meeting the Needs of Students with Learning Difficulties and Disabilities in Specialist Colleges.* NATSPEC (National Association of Specialist Colleges)/SKILL.

VIEW. *Arts Pack.* Coventry: VIEW.

Vincent, T. A. (1994) 'Distance teaching and visually impaired students: an electronic environment for learning'. In: T. A. Vincent (ed.), *All Our Learning Futures: The Role of Technology in Education.* Glasgow: Scottish Council for Educational Technology.

Visser, T. (1988) 'Educational programming for deaf-blind children: Some important topics', *Deaf-Blind Education,* **2,** 4–7.

Vygotsky, L. S. (1978) *Mind in Society: The Development of Higher Psychological Processes.* Cambridge, Massachusetts: Harvard University Press.

Wahl, M. (1993) *Wer? Wie? Was? Lieder machen Spaß.* Bonn: Gilde.

Walker, E., Tobin, M. and McKennall, A. (1992) *Blind and Partially Sighted Children in Britain: the RNIB Survey. Volume 2.* London: HMSO.

Walker, S. (1992) *Getting off the Ground.* London: RNIB.

Warburg, M. (1986) 'Medical and ophthalmological aspects of visual impairment in mentally handicapped people'. In: D. Ellis (ed.), *Sensory Impairments in Mentally Handicapped People.* London: Croom Helm.

Ware, J. (1994) *Educating Children with Profound and Multiple Learning Difficulties.* London: David Fulton.

Ware, J. and Evans, P. (1987) 'Room management is not enough?', *British Journal of Special Education* **14**(2), 78–80.

Warren, D.H. (1977) *Blindness and Early Childhood Development.* New York: American Foundation for the Blind.

Warren, D. H. (1984) *Blindness and Early Childhood Development* 2nd edn. New York: American Foundation for the Blind.

Warren, D. H. (1994) *Blindness and Children: An Individual Approach.* Cambridge: Cambridge University Press.

Watkins, M. (1995) 'Excuse me Miss, are you the Bonjour lady? Some observations on teaching French to special needs pupils', *Studies in Modern Languages Education,* **3**, 47–62.

Watson, A., Stuart, N. and Lucas, D. (1995) *Impact of New Management Arrangements in Pathfinder Career Services*. London: DfEE Careers Service Branch/HMSO.

Watson, E. (1994) *A Guide to Braille Music Notation*. Peterborough: RNIB.

Weddell, K. (1981) 'Concepts of special educational need', *Education Today,* **31**, 3–9.

Weitz, M. (1966) 'The nature of art'. In: W. E. Eisner and D. W. Ecker (eds), *Readings in Art Education* London: Blaisdell.

Welsh, R. L. and Blasch, B. B. (1980) *Foundations of Orientation and Mobility*. New York: Amercian Foundation for the Blind.

Wertheimer, A. (1988) *Self Advocacy and Parents*. London: FEU.

Wertsch, J. V. (1995) 'Sociocultural research in the copyright age', *Culture and Psychology,* **1**(1), 81–102.

Wexler, A. (1961) *Experimental Science for the Blind – An Instruction Manual*. Oxford: Pergamon Press.

White, R. T. (1988) *Learning Science*. Oxford: Basil Blackwell.

Williams, M. (1956) *Williams Intelligence Test for Children with Defective Vision*. Windsor: NFER-Nelson.

Williams, M. (1971) 'Braille reading', *Teacher of the Blind,* **59**(3), 103–116.

Wills, D. M. (1978) 'Early speech development in blind children', *The Psychoanalytic Study of the Child,* 32, 85–117.

Wilson, E. L. (1974) 'Assessing the readiness of blind persons for vocational placement', *New Outlook for the Blind,* **68**, 57–80.

Wilson, H. J. (1907) *Information with Regard to Institutions, Societies and Classes for the Blind in England and Wales*, 4th edn. London: Farmer and Sons.

Woal, S. T. (1974) 'A career education program for visually handicapped students', *Vocational Guidance Quarterly,* **23**(2), 172–173.

Wood, D. (1979) 'Some considerations for teaching physical education to children with impaired sight'. In: L. Groves, *Physical Education for Special Needs*. Cambridge: Cambridge University Press.

Wood, D. (1985) *Some Considerations for Teaching Physical Education to Children with Impaired Sight*. London: RNIB.

Wood, D. (1988) *How Children Think and Learn*. Oxford: Blackwell.

Wood, D. and Trickey, S. (1996) 'Transition planning: process or procedure?' *British Journal of Special Education,* **23**(3), 120–125.

Wood, D., Bruner, J. S. and Ross, G. (1976) 'The role of tutoring in problem solving', *Journal of Child Psychology and Psychiatry,* **17**(2), 89–100.

Woods, A. (1995) 'Modern foreign languages and special educational needs: an LEA perspective', *Studies in Modern Languages Education,* **3**, 17–37.

Woolnough, B. E. (1988) *Physics Teaching in Schools 1960–85*. Lewes: Falmer Press.

Woolnough, B. E. and Allsop, T. (1985) *Practical Work in School Science*. Cambridge: Cambridge University Press.

Workman, S.H. (1986) 'Teachers' verbalisations and the social interaction of blind preschoolers', *Journal of Visual Impairment and Blindness,* **80**, 532–534.

World Health Organization (1980) *International Classificiation of Impairments, Disabilities and Handicaps; A Manual of Classification Relating to the Consequences of Disease*. Geneva: WHO.

World Health Organization (1993) *Management of Low Vision in Children*. Geneva: WHO.

Wyman, R. (1986) *Multiply Handicapped Children*. London: Souvenir Press.

Zell Sacks, S., Keklis, L. S. and Gaylord-Ross, R. J. (1992) *The Development of Social Skills by Blind and Visually Impaired Students*. New York: American Federation for the Blind.

Index